From Séance to Science

THE CENTER FOR THE HISTORY OF PSYCHOLOGY SERIES

The Center for the History of Psychology Series

David B. Baker, Editor

David B. Baker and Ludy T. Benjamin Jr., *From Séance to Science: A History of the Profession of Psychology in America*

C. James Goodwin and Lizette Royer, Editors, *Walter Miles and His 1920 Grand Tour of European Physiology and Psychology Laboratories*

Ludy T. Benjamin Jr. and Lizette Royer Barton, Editors, *Roots in the Great Plains: The Applied Psychology of Harry Hollingworth, Volume 1*

Ludy T. Benjamin Jr. and Lizette Royer Barton, Editors, *From Coca-Cola to Chewing Gum: The Applied Psychology of Harry Hollingworth, Volume 2*

From Séance to Science
A History of the Profession of Psychology in America

SECOND EDITION

David B. Baker and Ludy T. Benjamin Jr.

The University of Akron Press
Akron, Ohio

First University of Akron Press edition, 2014

First published 2004 by Wadsworth, a division of Thomson Learning, Inc.
Copyright © 2004 by David B. Baker and Ludy T. Benjamin Jr.

All New Material Copyright © 2014 by The University of Akron Press

18   17   16   15   14   5   4   3   2   1

ISBN: 978-1-937378-42-4 (paperback)
ISBN: 978-1-937378-43-1 (ePDF)
ISBN: 978-1-937378-44-8 (ePUB)

LIBRARY OF CONGRESS CATALOGING-IN-PUBLICATION DATA
Benjamin, Ludy T., 1945–
From seance to science : a history of the profession of psychology in America. —
Second edition / David B. Baker and Ludy T. Benjamin Jr.
     pages cm. — (The Center for the History of Psychology series)
Revised edition of From seance to science : a history of the profession of psychology in America
[by] Ludy T. Benjamin Jr., David B. Baker.
Includes bibliographical references and index.
ISBN 978-1-937378-42-4 (paperback) — ISBN 978-1-937378-43-1 (epdf) —
ISBN 978-1-937378-44-8 (epub)
1. Psychology—Practice—United States—History. I. Baker, David B., author. II. Title.
BF75.B46 2014
150.973—dc23
                    2014020082

The paper used in this publication meets the minimum requirements of American National Standard for Information Sciences—Permanence of Paper for Printed Library Materials, ansi z39.48–1984. ∞

Cover images: Background: M. Kohl (1902) *Preisliste No. 12. Physikalische Apparate*. Chemnitz: Druck von Hugo Wilisch, o.J; Foreground (clockwise): Frontispiece from the journal *Human Nature*, 1875, Vol. 9; W. E. Robinson (1898). *Spirit slate writing and kindred phenomena*. New York City: Munn and Company; Photo courtesy of the CHP Still Images Collection, David Shakow papers.
Cover design: Amy Freels

All photographs, unless otherwise noted, are from the collection of the Center for the History of Psychology. For complete credit information, please see page 304.

From Séance to Science was designed and typeset by Amy Freels in Goudy Oldstyle, printed on 60# Natural, and bound by Bookmasters of Ashland, Ohio.

For
Sandi and Isabella
Priscilla

Contents

Preface to the Second Edition xiii

Preface to the First Edition xv

Chapter 1 | The Beginnings of Psychological Practice 1

Having Your Head Examined: Phrenology 4

It's All in the Face: Physiognomy 10

 Criminal Physiognomy 13

 Physiognomy in Vocational Guidance and the Workplace 14

Psychology's Other Occult Doubles 16

 Mesmerism 17

 Spiritualism 20

 Mental Healing 23

The New Psychology 25

Selling the New Psychology 29

 Child Study 31

 Counseling Psychology 32

 School and Clinical Psychology 33

 Psychology and Business 34

Conclusion 36

Chapter 2 | Clinical Psychology 38

Mental Asylums 38

Clinical Research by Psychologists in the 1890s 45

Lightner Witmer's Call for a Clinical Psychology 48

Intelligence Testing 50

The Early Clinical Psychologists 53

Influences on Clinical Psychology at the Turn of the Century 55

 Freud's Visit and Psychoanalysis in America 55

 Clifford Beers and the Mental Hygiene Movement 57

 Morton Prince and Clinical Psychology 58

 Elwood Worcester and the Emmanuel Movement 58

Clinical Psychology: Organization, Certification   61

An Outbreak of Psychology: The 1920s   64

An Organization for Professional Psychology   66

Between the Wars: The Rise of Clinical Assessment   69

    Shell Shock Cases   69

    Early Personality Testing   72

    Projective Personality Testing   73

    The Minnesota Multiphasic Personality Inventory (MMPI)   74

World War II and Clinical Psychology   76

    Clinical Psychology and the Scientist-Practitioner Model   78

Psychologists and Psychotherapy   80

Models of Psychotherapy   82

    Behavioral Therapies   84

    Cognitive Therapies   86

    Humanistic Therapies   86

Further Evidence of a Profession   87

    Licensure for Professional Psychologists   88

    Professional Ethics   88

    Professional Journals   89

    Professional Psychologists and the APA   89

    Professional Schools of Psychology   90

Clinical Psychology in the 1960s   92

    Community Mental Health Centers   93

    Independent Practice   93

Conclusion   95

Chapter 3 | School Psychology   96

Education and Democracy   96

Child Development and the Legacy of G. Stanley Hall   98

    Estimating IQs   100

    Arnold Gesell: The First School Psychologist   103

Individual Case Study and the Legacy of Lightner Witmer   105

    New Work in Applied Psychology   106

Special Education and School Psychology   110

    Psychology in the Schools   111

Organization and Identity 112

Recognition 115

School Psychology at Midcentury 118

    The National Institute of Mental Health and
School Psychology 119

    The Thayer Conference 120

    Expansion 125

Back to the Future 129

    The National Association of School Psychologists 129

    NASP and Division 16 130

Conclusion 132

Chapter 4 | Industrial/Organizational Psychology 134

The Salience of the Workplace 135

The New Psychology and the Business of Advertising 137

    Scott and the Power of Suggestion 138

    Harry Hollingworth and the Effectiveness of Advertising 139

    Watson's Behavioristic Approach to Advertising 140

Hugo Münsterberg and the "Founding" of
Industrial Psychology 142

Carnegie Tech's Division of Applied Psychology 143

    The Bureau of Salesmanship Research 146

    The End of the Division of Applied Psychology 147

The One Right Way: Scientific Management 147

    Problems with Scientific Management 150

    Workers Are Not Machines 151

World War I and Its Aftermath 151

Personnel Psychology in the 1920s 154

    Journal of Applied Psychology 154

    Psychological Consulting Firms 155

    Establishing Scientific Legitimacy 157

    Industrial Psychology Monthly 158

    Steady Growth 158

The Great Depression and the Beginnings of
Organizational Psychology 160

The Hawthorne Studies 162
Attitudes, Leadership, and Worker Satisfaction 164
Organizing Industrial Psychologists 166
World War II and Its Aftermath 168
Human Factors Psychology 169
Personnel Psychology After the War 172
The Evolution of Graduate Training 172
Organizational Psychology Comes of Age 173
Lewin's Continuing Influence 173
Industrial Strife 174
Contemporary I/O Psychology 175
Contemporary Personnel Issues 177
Training 177
Organizational Psychology 178
Organizational Development 178
Organizational Climate 179
Conclusion 180

Chapter 5 | Counseling Psychology 182
A Context for Counseling Psychology 183
A More Perfect Union 184
Seeking Guidance 185
The Work of Frank Parsons 187
The Expansion of Guidance 189
Education and Psychology 190
Vocational Psychology 194
Testing and the Times 195
Civilian Applications 196
Testing and the Great Depression 197
The Emergence of Counseling Psychology 198
Preludes to Boulder 201
The Meaning of Boulder 202
Constructing Counseling Psychology 202
A Model of Training 203
Influences on Identity 206

The Question of Identity   212

Consolidation   215

Recent Developments   217

  Organizational Structure   218

  Social Action   219

Conclusion   220

Chapter 6 | The Psychological Profession in the 21st Century   222

Managed Care   223

  Cost and Service Containment   224

  Ethics   225

  Impacts   225

  Responses to Managed Care   226

Prescription Privileges for Psychologists   229

Opposition to Prescription Privileges   230

  Clinical Trials for Psychologists   232

  Proponents for Prescription Privileges   233

New Practice Specialties   234

  Forensic Psychology   234

    Münsterberg and the Psychology of the Courtroom   235

    Contemporary Forensic Psychology   237

    Clients for Forensic Psychology   237

    The Psychological Autopsy   238

    Growth of Forensic Psychology   239

  Sport Psychology   240

    Coleman Griffith: Pioneer in Sport Psychology   241

    Modern Practice of Sport Psychology   243

    The Work of Sport Psychologists   244

  Health Psychology   246

    The Practice of Health Psychologists   248

    Interventions   248

    Health Psychology in Hospitals   249

Science and the Practice of Psychology   250

  Contemporary Concerns About Professional Schools

  of Psychology   251

The "Myth" of Professional Psychology   253
Doing and Applying Research   254
Practice Guidelines   255
Conflict Over Guidelines   256
The Future of the Profession   257
Growth in Health Psychology   258
Growth in Psychological Services to Minorities   259
Changing Roles for Psychologists   260
A Final Comment   261

Notes   263
Image Credits   304
Index   307

Preface to the Second Edition

We are pleased to offer a second edition of *From Séance to Science: A History of the Profession of Psychology in America*. It is been a decade since the first edition was published and much has changed. Interest in the history of professional psychology has grown. A review of the table of contents of the journal *History of Psychology* over the last 10 years shows a steady presence of articles on topics related to the history of the profession of psychology both in the United States and abroad. Likewise, numerous reference works such as encyclopedias and handbooks have regularly included entries related to the history of professional psychology. As professional psychology grows and matures this trend will only continue. We have benefited from these new works and they have helped inform updates for this edition.

Changes in professional psychology over the last decade have been substantial and dramatic. The number of mental health providers in the United States continues to grow, as do training programs, models of training, accreditation, and licensure. The provisions of the Affordable Care Act, which are just now being implemented, will certainly create greater access to mental health services. Greater numbers of patients seeking services means more opportunity for professional psychologists, but it also means greater competition among mental health service providers. We have updated much of the final chapter of the book to reflect these developments.

The history of professional psychology has a foundation that is now more than a century old. The rapid social changes that are occurring today will influence the role and course of professional psychology in ways that we cannot anticipate. We can be certain that things are likely to look much different by 2024.

We appreciate the encouragement and support of the University of Akron Press. Our thanks to Thomas Bacher, director; Amy Freels, editorial and design coordinator; and Carol Slatter, print manufacturing and digital production coordinator. A special thanks to Lizette Royer Barton, reference archivist at the Center for the History of Psychology for her work in locating and scanning many of the images used in the book.

Preface to the First Edition

This is a book about the professionalization of American psychology, that is, the birth and development of modern psychological practice in the United States from the 19th century to the present. Professional psychology is not a wholly American phenomenon; American psychology has certainly been influenced from abroad. We have chosen, however, to focus on the history of professional psychology in the United States because this geographic boundary makes the task a feasible one. Further, nowhere in the world has the profession been better received.

Too often much of the history of professional psychology is omitted from history of psychology textbooks that focus instead on the history of prescientific (philosophical) psychology and scientific (experimental) psychology. This book is intended to round out the picture of American psychology's past, adding the history of psychological practice to the story of psychological science.

This book tells the story of psychologists who sought and seek to apply the knowledge of their science to the practical problems of the world, whether those problems lie in businesses, schools, families, or in the thoughts, emotions, and behaviors of individuals. Their stories are told in the context of their times, emphasizing the social, political, and disciplinary factors that have shaped the profession. When the science was inadequate or was missing, these practitioners drew on their own observations and experiences, and on the "art" that is part of the practice of professional psychology, to solve those problems. This is the story of individuals, trained in psychology, who function as school psychologists, counseling psychologists, clinical psychologists, industrial psychologists, and numerous other specialty labels. These are psychology's *practitioners*, meaning that they take the knowledge base of psychology and use it for practical purposes outside of the classroom and outside of the laboratory. These are psychology's professionals, the individuals who comprise the *profession* of psychology.

What is a profession? Most people would reply to that question, not with a definition but by giving examples of one of several fields such as medicine or law or engineering or, maybe, teaching. Thus doctors, lawyers, engineers, and others are often labeled professionals, not in the sense of professional as contrasted with amateur, but professional connoting some special occupational expertise. The word "profession" emerged in the 12th century, meaning "a business ... that one publicly avows."[1] Thus a person professed, or publicly avowed, an interest in a particular business, a profession. Centuries later profession was a word limited to what were called the three "learned professions," namely theology, law, and medicine. In the 19th century the use of the word broadened to include other vocations, many of which clearly were not professions.

Do all occupations qualify as professions? Is accounting a profession? What about welding? Or hair styling? Consulting a dictionary does not help very much. One dictionary, whose definition is representative, identifies profession as "1. An occupation requiring considerable training and specialized study: the professions of law, medicine, and engineering. 2. The body of qualified persons in an occupation or field: members of the teaching profession."[2] Does accounting require considerable training and specialized study? What about hair styling? It seems that almost any job requires specialized study, so maybe the defining feature is the "considerable training." So just how much is "considerable?" And is that a defining issue? Most contemporary definitions of professions would consider welding and hair styling to be trades, not professions. There is still more that a profession entails that is not touched upon in the definitions given above. We prefer a more modern definition of profession such as the following:

> a calling requiring specialized knowledge and often long and intensive
> preparation including instruction in skills and methods as well as in the
> scientific, historical, or scholarly principles underlying such skills and

methods, maintaining by force of organization or concerted opinion high standards of achievement and conduct, and committing its members to continued study and to a kind of work which has for its prime purpose the rendering of a public service.[3]

This definition embodies those components that we see as central to the description of a profession: advanced and prolonged preparatory study; high standards for conduct, often defined as a code of ethics; continuing education so that professionals stay current in the latest theories, skills, and treatments; and provision of a service to the public.

So, is psychology a profession?[4] Psychology meets all of those criteria. The field certainly requires considerable training and specialized study. The doctoral degree is considered the minimal level of education and training for the practice of psychology by the American Psychological Association (APA) and by almost all of the 50 states that license the practice of psychology. That degree requires four to six years of graduate study, that is, education beyond the baccalaureate level, and for many professional psychologists includes a full-year internship in a professional setting, such as a hospital or counseling center. For professional psychologists to be licensed there are additional requirements beyond the doctoral degree, which usually include passing an examination administered by the state licensing board and undergoing one or more years of supervised practice, that is, guidance by an already licensed psychologist or psychologists. Most programs that train professional psychologists in the mental health-related fields seek APA accreditation, a stamp of approval that certifies that the doctoral programs meet a minimum standard of quality in education and training. Professional psychologists may seek additional credentials indicating special expertise by meeting the standards of the American Board of Examiners in Professional Psychology (ABPP), which awards diplomas in 12 different specialty areas, such as clinical psychology, industrial/organizational psychology, counseling psychology, school psychology, health psychology, and forensic psychology.

Psychologists subscribe to a code of ethics, in some cases as prescribed by the states in which they practice or, if they are APA members, by the *Ethical Principles of Psychologists and Code of Conduct*, published by the APA and updated most recently in 2010. Many states require, as a condition of relicensure, that psychologists complete a certain number of hours of continuing education, generally by completing workshops on specialized techniques. The APA, through its Education Directorate, coordinates a national program of continuing education for psychologists, reviewing and approving agencies that offer such training.

Finally, psychological practice exists to serve the public by, among other things, providing psychological evaluations and psychotherapy to individuals, families, and groups. Accreditation of doctoral training programs in clinical, counseling, and school psychology, as well as state licensure of practicing psychologists, exists to ensure an acceptable level of training of these professionals for the consuming public.

In summary, practicing psychologists have considerable advanced study and training, they are licensed in all 50 states, they abide by a published code of professional ethics, they keep abreast of new developments in the field through continuing education, and they exist to serve the public. Thus we would state unequivocally that psychology is a profession.

In discussions of the profession of psychology today, its origins are generally assumed to be in the science of psychology that reached American universities in the 1880s. And that is the profession that is the focus of this book. However, there was a profession of psychology that predated the modern one, a profession of the 19th century whose practitioners sought to provide individuals and businesses with many of the same services supplied by professional psychologists today. We will discuss these early American "psychologists" in the opening chapter, where you will learn why 'getting your head examined' was big business in the 19th century.

We devote the next four chapters to the four principal professional specialties recognized by the APA in 1981: clinical psychology (chapter 2), school psychology (chapter 3), industrial/organizational psychology (chapter 4), and counseling psychology (chapter 5).[5] As you might imagine, the histories of these fields are interconnected; thus, the specialties are not as clearly differentiated as the labels might make them sound. Some of the history of professional development is common to all four fields. Much of that history is discussed in chapter 2, because it is the first of the specialty chapters to be considered, yet some common material also appears in the other chapters when it seems more appropriate, or when repetition seems important for clarity.

In 1917, 25 years after the founding of APA, the membership of the association numbered 307. Of that total, only 16 members (about 5%) were engaged primarily in the application of psychology outside of universities.[6] For the first half century of American psychology, those psychologists engaged in college teaching and research outnumbered their colleagues in practice. That picture, however, changed dramatically after World War II. Today it is estimated that there are 174,000 psychologists in the United States. Among that number, approximately 93,000 are employed principally as psychological practitioners.[7]

This story of the development of the psychological profession is both a remarkable and a fascinating one. We follow it to its 21st century present in the concluding chapter, where we describe the development of additional practice specialties and several related professional issues, such as managed care, prescription privileges for psychologists, and practice guidelines.

Professional psychologists today play many roles, working in corporations, hospitals, military services, schools, courtrooms, clinics, counseling centers, prisons, and in independent, also called private, practice. We begin our history in the first chapter with several case studies typical of this work.

Chapter 1
The Beginnings of Psychological Practice

Consider the following three case studies. First, a boy in Patterson, New York, was taken by juvenile court authorities to a psychologist for assessment. The psychologist examined him and told the authorities that his test results indicated that the boy had a strong disposition to steal. That information proved crucial to the juvenile justice system because the boy had been caught stealing on several occasions.

Second, there was the case of Harriet Martineau, who suffered from depression. She was socially withdrawn, lacked energy, and often didn't eat. She had seen several physicians who had prescribed drugs for her treatment, but the depression continued. After five years of unsuccessful treatments, her physician expressed hopelessness that she could ever be cured. On the advice and recommendations of some friends, Martineau went to a psychologist, Spencer Hall. After four months in treatment with Hall, Martineau pronounced herself cured, her energy and zest for life restored.

Finally, there was the case of Charles, whose childhood was an unhappy one. Because of family debts he began work in a factory at the age of 12. Deprived of a formal education, he sought to teach himself. Eventually he obtained a job as a reporter for a small newspaper. Like many young men he was uncertain what he wanted to do in life. A psychologist who examined him said that he had a reflective intellect, had great powers of observation, was a shrewd reasoner, had a considerable mastery of language, and displayed great wit and humor. The psychologist noted that his temperament and talents were well suited to success as a writer.

Each of these vignettes describes actual cases in which psychological services were being used. In the first case, examination of the boy determined that he was a thief. In the second case, Ms. Martineau was cured of her depression. And finally, a vocational assessment of Charles indicated that he might have success as a writer. Yet, in fact, no psychologists were involved in any of these cases, at least no psychologists as we would define them today, because each of the cases just described took place in the mid-1800s, long before the science of psychology arrived in America.

The "psychologist" in the first case was a phrenologist who measured the bumps on the skull of the young boy to discover that the brain area said to be responsible for "acquisitiveness" was quite large, thus indicating his propensity to steal. In the second case, Ms. Martineau was treated by a mesmerist who used techniques similar to hypnosis to eliminate her depression. Finally, in the third case, Charles's face was examined by a physiognomist, someone who judged an individual's personality and intellect based on the person's facial features, a pseudoscience known as physiognomy. Actually Charles's face was not examined in person when he was a young man. Instead, the physiognomist studied it from a photograph when Charles was in his 50s and had already written *Oliver Twist, David Copperfield*, and *Great Expectations*. Thus armed with such knowledge, it was perhaps easy for the individual to predict that Charles Dickens had the temperament and talents to be a successful writer.[1] In the pages that follow, we discuss these pseudoscientific approaches that are part of the history of psychological practice.

This book is a historical account of the development of psychological practice in America, that is, the history of psychology's evolution as a profession. America is not the only place where a profession of psychology developed, but it is the focused locale of this history, selected in part to make this history a manageable one. It is estimated that there are more than 174,000 psychologists in the United States today and that the great majority of those work in some kind of applied setting, including many in independent practice. There are clinical psychologists, counseling psychologists, school psychologists, industrial/organizational psychologists, forensic psychologists, health psychologists, sport psychologists, educational psychologists, consumer psychologists, engineering psychologists, media psychologists, geropsychologists, community psychologists, and environmental psychologists, to name most of the applied psychology specialties.

The 21st-century psychological specialties owe their origins, in large part, to the emergence of scientific psychology in the late 19th century. Yet it is clear that many of these practice activities existed in the 19th century, before there were psychological laboratories and scientific psychologists. These early practitioners sometimes used the label "psychologist"; more commonly, however, they were known as phrenologists, physiognomists, characterologists, psychics, mesmerists, mediums, spiritualists, mental healers, seers, graphologists, and advisers. There were no licensing and certification laws at the time, so all who wanted to offer "psychological" services did so and could call themselves anything they wanted.

It is important to grasp the significance of these precursors to modern psychology. Too often the current understanding of psychology's history is that "there was a science of psychology and it spawned the practice of psychology." But clearly there was a practice of psychology, if not a profession, long before there was a science. Indeed one can find evidence of psychological interventions dating to the beginnings of recorded history. That there have been individuals throughout human history who sought to treat psychological problems or advise about psychological questions should not be surprising. When there have been human needs, there have been individuals willing to meet those needs. Today we expect professions like medicine, nursing, and psychology to be based on the sciences that underlie those professions. Yet all of those professions existed before there was science. Such services were needed and so individuals offered their potions, their rituals, their laying on of hands, and their advice to bring aid to their clients. Thus the story of the profession of psychology is one that is thousands of years old. For our purposes here, however, we will begin the story in the 19th century.

As we have noted, in the 1800s in America, individuals were engaged in exactly the kinds of psychological activities in which professional psychologists are engaged today. The theories are different and the methods are different, the education and training are different, and there are contemporary laws that regulate psychological practice for protection of the consumer. Yet the practitioners of the 1800s were engaged in the same "helping" activities, trying to assist people to enjoy success, health, and happiness in school, in the workplace, and in everyday life. This chapter

3

tells the story of some of these early practitioners and shows how their work relates to contemporary psychological practice.

Although the Civil War would tear the nation apart in the middle of the century, the 19th century was largely one of optimism, if not prosperity, for many Americans, at least those of European origins. Many had come to the New World in search of a better life and many had found it in the abundant opportunities of agriculture, commerce, and the trades. Land was still cheap for those adventurous enough to push westward, and dreams of great fortunes to be made were reinforced by tales from the great cities of the East and from the goldfields of the West. Of course there was much poverty and human misery as well, particularly in the cities, but this was America, the land where dreams of riches and success sometimes did come true. In pursuit of their dreams, Americans put their faith in education and religion as a means for personal and financial betterment. Yet other institutions offered hope as well, including a host of practitioners of varying pseudosciences that offered personal counseling that promised health, happiness, and success.

Having Your Head Examined: Phrenology

In 19th-century America, "having your head examined" was big business, largely due to the enterprising efforts of two brothers whom we discuss later. Having your head examined meant phrenology, certainly the best known of the applied psychologies of the 19th century. Phrenology originated with a German physician and anatomist, Franz Josef Gall (1758–1828), who argued that different parts of the brain were responsible for different emotional, intellectual, and behavioral functions. He believed that talents and defects of an individual could be assessed by measuring the bumps and indentations of the skull caused by overdevelopment or underdevelopment of certain brain areas. Phrenology was popularized by Johann Spurzheim (1776–1832), who collaborated with Gall on anatomical research on the brain and later promoted his own brand of phrenology consisting of 21 emotional faculties and 14 intellectual ones. Spurzheim died in Boston in 1832 on a lecture trip popularizing phrenology. His work was continued by a Scottish lawyer turned phrenologist, George Combe (1788–1858), whose 1828 book, *The Constitution of Man*, established him

4

as the leading voice of phrenology. Combe continued Spurzheim's American lecture trip, selling his books and establishing phrenological societies in the major cities of his travels. Although by 1832 there were critics of the scientific legitimacy of phrenology, Americans, by and large, accepted it, and its proponents, particularly Combe, were praised for the practical benefits to individuals and society that phrenology offered.

Combe adhered to the categorization of 35 faculties as described by Spurzheim. In describing the basis in 1835 for his practical phrenology he wrote:

> Observation proves that each of these faculties is connected with a particular portion of the brain, and that the power of manifesting each bears a relation to the size and activity of the organ. The organs differ in relative size in different individuals, and hence their differences of talents and dispositions. This fact is of the greatest importance in the philosophy of man...These faculties are not all equal in excellence and authority...Human happiness and misery are resolvable into the gratification, or denial of gratification, of one or more of our faculties...Every faculty is good in itself, but all are liable to abuse. Their manifestations are right only when directed by enlightened intellect and moral sentiment.[2]

What phrenology offered was not only the cranial measurement that identified the talents and dispositions but, more important, a course of action designed to strengthen the faculties and bring the overall complex of emotional and intellectual faculties into a harmony that would ensure happiness and success. This was practical phrenology, that is, phrenology applied.

In the United States, no one was more strongly identified with applying phrenological "science" than the Fowler brothers, Orson (1809–1887) and Lorenzo (1811–1896), who opened clinics in New York, Boston, and Philadelphia in the late 1830s. They franchised their business to other cities, principally through the training of phrenological examiners, and provided phrenological supplies to the examiners, such as phrenology busts for display and teaching, calipers of varying sizes for measurements, display charts for the wall, manuals to sell to the customers, and, for the itinerant phrenologists, carrying cases for tools and supplies (see Figure 1-1). They began publication of the *American Phrenological Journal* in 1838, a magazine

Figure 1-1. *A 19th century phrenology bust. Phrenologists often kept these in their offices for clients to see. Today, original phrenology busts sell for thousands of dollars.*

for phrenologists and people interested in phrenology, which enjoyed an existence of more than 70 years. For years its masthead carried the phrase "Home truths for home consumption."

Some historical accounts have stated that the Fowlers were unconcerned with the arguments over the scientific validity of phrenology, and instead simply accepted it as valid. Their magazine, however, was filled with articles and testimonials intended to attest to the scientific basis of their subject. The Fowlers and others dedicated to phrenology recognized that it was not an accepted science, and there were some efforts aimed in increasing its respectability. For example, several of the phrenological societies, with the support of the Fowlers, sought to have phrenology taught as one of the sciences in the public schools and offered as a subject in colleges. Such efforts were not successful. The rejection of the scientific community notwithstanding, the Fowlers never doubted the validity of phrenology, at least not in public, and they promoted the subject as divine truth, selling its applications. They "did a thriving business advising employers about employees, fiancés about fiancées, and everyone about himself."[3] Their business also included public lectures; classes in phrenology for those wishing to take up the profession, but also classes for ordinary curious citizens, including children; and countless publications including books, pamphlets, and magazines.

Giving examinations or "readings," as they were often called, was the business of the phrenologist. Some operated from clinics where clients could make appointments for their examinations. A phrenologist might test a potential suitor at the request of an anxious father. Parents also sought out help for raising children, especially children who presented behavioral problems. Couples contemplating marriage might be tested for compatibility. Individuals could be tested for vocational suitability. Businesses might use the phrenological clinics as a kind of personnel department, matching individuals to jobs or selecting workers with managerial skills or sales skills. In areas where clinics did not exist, there were traveling phrenologists who advertised their arrival in advance and rented space for the duration of their stay.[4]

One of the creations of the Fowler brothers, as part of their "franchising," was the "self-instructor" manual, first published in 1859. These cloth-bound books of approximately 175 pages were to be sold to the clients for 50 cents. By 1890 it was estimated that more than 250,000 copies of that manual had been sold. The title page of the book had a space for the name of the examiner and the name of the person being examined. The next two pages were tables of faculties that were to be marked by the examiner on a scale of 2 (small) to 7 (very large). In addition, beside each of the faculties were two boxes, one marked "cultivate" and the other "restrain" (see Figure 1-2). The examiner would mark the appropriate box for those faculties requiring self-adjustment. The examinee would leave with the book, including the marked exam pages (the tables), and thus be able to

BUSINESS ADAPTATIONS

IN A SCALE FROM 1 TO 7.

Artistical.
Architect.
Designer.
Engraver.
Musician.
Music Teacher.
Painter, Ornamental.
do., Portrait.
Photographer.

Commercial.
Accountant.
Agent.
Appraiser.
Auctioneer.
Banker.
Bookseller.
Broker.
Business Correspondent.
Cashier.
Collector.
Commis. Mer.
Conductor.
Druggist.
Expressman.
Importer.
Insurance.
Landlord.
Merchant.
Principal.
Publisher.
Salesman.
Shipping Clerk.
Speculator.
do., Real Estate.
Superintendent.
Trader.

Retail Dealer.
Wholesale do.
Dealer in —
Boots, shoes.
Leather.
Cattle, horses.
Coal, lumber.
Dry-goods.
Fancy Articles.
Grain, groceries.
Hardware.
Implements.
Jewelry.
Marketing.
Useful Articles.

Professional.
Actor.
Author.
Bishop.
Clergyman.
Conveyancer.
Correspondent.
Editor.
Elocutionist.
Governor.
Governess.
Historian.
Judge.
Lawyer.
Lecturer.
Literature.
Linguist.
Officer.
Poet.
Politician.
Professor.
Proof-reader.

Reporter.
Teacher.
Writer.

Mechanical.
Baker.
Blacksmith.
Boss Workman.
Builder.
Carpenter.
Chandler.
Compositor.
Contractor.
Cooper.
Dairyman.
Dentist.
Dressmaker.
Farmer.
Finisher.
Gardener.
Gunsmith.
Gas Fitter.
Inventor.
Laborer.
Locksmith.
Machinist.
Mason.
Miller.
Milliner.
Paperer.
Plumber.
Printer.
Tailor.
Tanner.
Tinsmith.
Turner.
Seamstress.
Stonecutter.

Shipbuilder.
Upholsterer.
Manufacturer of —
Boots, shoes.
Fancy Articles.
Furniture.
Trunks, harness.
Useful Articles.

Scientific.
Anatomist.
Captain.
Chemist.
Commander.
Engineer.
Geologist.
Manager R. R.
do., of Workmen.
Miner.
Naturalist.
Phrenologist.
Physician.
Representative.
Secretary.
Surgeon.
Surveyor.
Statesman.

Miscellaneous
Fisherman.
Housekeeper.
Livery Keeper.
Matron.
Nurse.
Restaurant.
Teamster.
Waiter.
Watchman.

MARRY one   In Size   Height   Blonde   Brunette

Figure 1-2. *A page from O. S. Fowler's 1869 book,* The Practical Phrenologist, *showing some of the faculties that would have been assessed in a phrenological examination.*

use the data in the tables to refer to the relevant sections of the book where help would be offered in cultivating and restraining various faculties. For example, if the "destructiveness" faculty were shown to be too large, the manual advised:

> To Restrain—Kill nothing; and offset destructiveness by benevolence; never indulge a rough, harsh spirit, but cultivate instead a mild and forgiving spirit; never brood over injuries or indulge revengeful thoughts or desires, or aggravate yourself by brooding over wrongs; cultivate good manners; and when occasion requires you to reprove, do it in a bland, gentle manner rather than roughly; never tease, even children, or scourge animals, but be kind to both, and offset by benevolence and the higher faculties.[5]

Psychologist Robert Brown has been collecting these self-instructor manuals for many years and has a data set of approximately 60 scored manuals. In examining the scoring in these manuals, he has observed what he has named the "Lake Wobegon Effect." Lake Wobegon is the fictional Minnesota community described by Garrison Keillor on his radio program *A Prairie Home Companion*. In Lake Wobegon, "all the children are above average," and according to Brown, so are all the phrenology examinees. That is, few faculties were ever marked in the 2–3 range. Instead almost all of the marks were at 4 (average) or above.[6] Such scoring would no doubt leave customers feeling better about themselves and meant that they would be more likely to recommend a phrenological reading to their friends. It was surely good business practice not to find too much to criticize in your clients.

The comments above are not meant to portray phrenologists as frauds or charlatans whose sole motive was to extract money from their clients in exchange for worthless services. No doubt there were unsavory characters in the business, as one would find in any of the contemporary professions. But there were also many whose motives were about helping. And what they may not have been able to judge from their cranial measurements, they likely determined from their powers of observation, honed by the examination of many clients. In the best empirical tradition, they used the knowledge of their senses to inform their diagnoses and their counsel. Regarding their powers of observation, historian Michael Sokal has written:

> After all, they had great opportunities to practice these powers on the individuals they examined. They spent a fair amount of time with their subjects, often in close physical contact. They spoke with these clients— and, especially, listened to them—as they introduced themselves and took in their accents and use of words. They shook their hands and felt their calluses. They observed their dress, and noted its style, cleanliness, and usage. They observed their subjects' carriage as they entered and walked about the examining room and read their "body language." They stood over and behind them as they moved their hands about their heads. And in a less clean age, they especially noted their subjects' odor.[7]

Thus there was much that could be learned about a client from a discerning phrenologist. Such observations likely improved the quality of the phrenologist's counsel while at the same time raising the client's confidence in the skills of the phrenologist. That confidence was important in gaining greater client compliance with the recommendations of the examiner and, of course, in creating good word-of-mouth advertising for the examiner's services.

Although phrenology came under increasing attack from the scientific community, it remained popular in America throughout the 19th century as a kind of counseling, clinical, and industrial psychology. By the beginning of the 20th century its popularity had declined considerably, as it was being replaced by other methods, most of which were being drawn from the new science of psychology. Did phrenology fall out of favor because it was shown to be scientifically invalid? The answer is no. It had remained popular for decades after science had abandoned it. But the 20th century offered a new set of psychological professionals who argued that their techniques were better. Eventually they supplanted the phrenologists and other 19th-century psychological practitioners.[8]

It's All in the Face: Physiognomy

There are, no doubt, many people today who would profess to being able to judge a person's character by looking at the person's face. The origins of that belief surely date back thousands, perhaps tens of thousands, of years. The system of judging a person's character from facial features is called physiognomy (sometimes referred to as characterology), and its invention is attributed to a Swiss theologian, Johann Lavater (1741–1801). Lavater's book, *Essays on Physiognomy*, was published in 1775. It was thus a precursor to Gall's work, although there is no evidence that it influenced Gall. Lavater's system emphasized the eyes, nose, forehead, and chin as the chief indicators of intelligence, morality, and many other characteristics. For example, about the nose, Lavater wrote:

> Noses which are much turned downward are never truly good, truly cheerful, noble, or great. Their thoughts and inclinations always tend to earth. They are close, cold, heartless, incommunicative; often maliciously sarcastic, ill-humored, or extremely hypochondriac or melancholic. When arched in the upper part they are fearful and voluptuous.[9]

Lavater's book, which contained more than 800 illustrations, some of them taken from famous artists, was exceptionally popular. Originally published in German, the book was soon translated into virtually every European language. Physiognomy's popularity ranged from its use as a parlor game at fashionable gatherings to its claims as the science of determining character. It spread over Europe in the late 18th century and to America shortly thereafter. Its popularity continued into the first half of the 20th century as American businesses used physiognomy in hiring and promoting employees. More about that a little later.

The Fowler brothers were also marketers of physiognomy, giving lectures on the subject, including many articles about it in their phrenological magazines, and publishing books and pamphlets on the topic. One of the more successful books was authored by Samuel Wells (1820–1875), a partner with the Fowlers, who was also their brother-in-law, having married their sister Charlotte in 1844, the same year he came to work with them. Wells's book, which appeared in 1866, was entitled, *New Physiognomy or Signs of Character as Manifested Through Temperament and External Forms and Especially in the Human Face Divine*. Wells's "New Physiognomy" was an adaptation of a system proposed by James W. Redfield, a New York physician. The system identified 184 separate areas of the face, each corresponding to a different character or trait, for example, kindness (2), eloquence (32), sympathy (71), inquisitiveness (102), cheerfulness (121), patriotism (136), and perseverance (151). You can use the numbers to match the facial areas shown in Figure 1-3.

In addition to being the science of character, physiognomy, like phrenology, was used to "validate" and thus perpetuate ethnic and racial stereotypes. For example, in describing the "Jewish nose," Wells wrote, "it indicates worldly shrewdness, insight into character, and ability to turn that insight to a profitable account." Other facial features led Wells to the following summary of a Jew. "He is religious; he is fond of trade; he is thrifty; he is unconquerably true to his racial proclivities; he is persistent in everything he undertakes. He is the type of stability and permanence— the model of steadfastness; but at the same time he is prejudiced, bigoted, stern, stubborn, irascible, exacting, secretive, and unrelenting." The sub-Saharan African nose was described by Wells as a "snubnose," a nose of

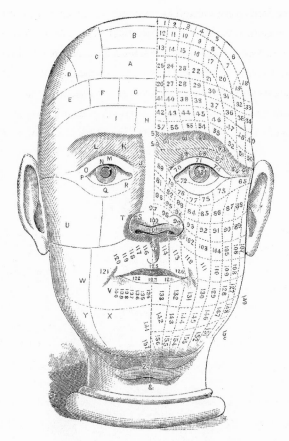

Figure 1-3. *A chart from Samuel Wells's 1866 book,* New Physiognomy, *showing locations of traits, characteristics, etc.*

"weakness and underdevelopment." He wrote, "Such a shortened and flattened proboscis can not...have made any legible mark on the records of the world's progress. Its wearers have never conquered realms and enslaved nations, like the owners of the royal Roman nose, or built magnificent temples and adorned them with works of high art, like the Greek-nosed children of genius."[10]

The eyes of devout Roman Catholics were said to indicate humility and penitence. Scots were characterized as economical, sensitive, and religious. The Irish were described as patriotic, fond of sport, witty, combative, and generous. The French were said to be vigorous and friendly, but low in moral standards. Spaniards were viewed as cunning, vindictive, and sullen, but also brave, noble, passionate, and courteous. All of those characteristics were, of course, supposedly observed from the features of the face, at least they were observable for anyone who believed in the "science" of physiognomy.[11]

Reading Wells and other similar treatises on physiognomy would allow you to learn that hazel-eyed women were more intelligent than romantic, that large mouths indicated more character than small ones, that coarse lips were a sign of strength and power, whereas fine lips were a sign of mental delicacy and susceptibility, and that murderers always had big necks. The last example ties physiognomy to criminology, a linkage that has a long history.

Criminal Physiognomy

Of the several systems that have proposed a criminal physiognomy, none is more famous than that of Cesare Lombroso (1835–1909), an Italian anthropologist/criminologist, nominated four times for the Nobel Prize in physiology and medicine, who proposed a physiognomy of innate criminal types. Lombroso published his physiognomic ideas in his book, *Criminal Man* and extended them in *The Female Offender*. He wrote that criminals were almost never tall, that their heads were large due to a large face, but that the brain was smaller in size. The ears were typically large and protruded more noticeably from the head; often they were pointed. The eyebrows were bushy and often were continuous over the nose. The nose was often twisted and for thieves it turned upward at the base. The upper jaws were exceptionally large, creating the oversized face. The chin was typically receding or flat. Lombroso's ideas about criminal types were controversial but nevertheless popular.[12] His influence was evidenced in a number of ways, including the physical description of Count Dracula in Bram Stoker's 1897 novel, *Dracula*. Asked to describe Dracula, one of the characters in the novel responded, "The Count is a criminal and of criminal type...and Lombroso would so classify him...."[13] The notion of criminal types defined by facial features gradually lost favor in 20th century science and criminology; it still, however, has not lost favor today with a public convinced that signs of evildoing are evident in the mug shots that stare out at them from the crime stories in their newspapers and on their televisions.

Physiognomy in Vocational Guidance and the Workplace

Another physiognomic system that enjoyed popularity in the early 20th century was that of Katherine Blackford, a physician, who marketed her system to businesses. Blackford wrote about a dozen books in the first quarter of the 20th century, almost all directed at personnel issues for business. This was a time in America in which there was great interest in vocational guidance. The urbanization of America, new waves of immigration, industrialization that created more factory jobs, changes in labor laws protecting children, and advertising and marketing strategies that were national in scope changed the nature of American business, creating a greater diversity of occupations. Thus occupational choice had a meaning that it had not possessed before. Frank Parsons' landmark book on vocational guidance, *Choosing a Vocation*, appeared in 1909; the National Vocational Guidance Association was established in 1913; and the National Vocational Education Act was passed in 1917, a law designed to ensure better guidance counseling in public schools.[14] Vocational aptitudes and vocational choice were not new issues; they had been a chief part of the phrenologists' business success in the 19th century. In the early 20th century, however, there was widespread public concern that young people had access to quality vocational guidance and widespread interest regarding career choices. Blackford wrote that her books were intended "to add our voice to those of many others in calling for more scientific vocational guidance of the young... [and] to arouse interest among all thoughtful people, and especially among parents, employers, teachers, and workers, in the possibilities of character analysis by the observational method."[15] Blackford's methods were very popular judging by the number of reprintings of her many books. She caused concern among psychologists, who noted her appeal to businesses and were dubious of her techniques. Yet for many American businesses in the early 20th century, the science of psychology didn't hold any more authority in solving the problems of business than did the "science" of characterology (Blackford's preferred label) or physiognomy. Blackford stressed the importance of the hiring decision. Businesses wasted too much time and money in hiring people who should never have been hired, or placed people in jobs for which they were ill-suited. Blackford's system began by looking at the shape of the face as a whole, viewed in profile. From these profiles she identified some faces as convex, some as concave, and some as plane (meaning a fl plane). She wrote that the possessor of a convex face has

> Superabundance of energy...[is] keen, alert, quick, eager, aggressive, impatient, positive, and penetrating...will express his energy in a practical manner....He will demand facts, and will act upon facts quickly and rapidly, being too impatient to wait for reasons and theories...[this type will] speak frankly and at times even sharply and fiercely, without much regard for tact or diplomacy. As indicated by his type of chin, the pure convex is impulsive, expends his energy too rapidly for his limited endurance, and, owing to his lack of self-control and disinclination to deliberate and reason, frequently blunders, and expends his energy uselessly or unprofitably or even harmfully.[16]

The concave face is, of course, the opposite. This individual would be characterized by mildness, slow thought, careful-thinking, reason-seeking, sometimes daydreaming, deliberateness, determination, and persistence. "What the convex wins or gains by his aggressiveness, keenness, and superabundance of energy, the concave wins or gains by his diplomacy and unwavering persistence and endurance."[17] The plane face was a balance of the other two and was the most common of the three types of faces.

For Blackford, these faces defined different types of people, and that information could be put to good use in hiring, or what Parsons had preached as the first law of vocational guidance, matching the person's talents with the job requirements. Thus a businessperson might want to hire an aggressive person for a sales job but not for a customer service job. So for Blackford, individuals with blond hair, because they were more likely to have convex faces, were to be preferred for sales jobs, where their qualities of aggressiveness, impulsiveness, persistence, and high energy would pay off. Blonds and brunettes also figured in Blackford's views on criminal physiognomy:

> Prison statistics show that the blond is most frequently guilty of crimes of passion and impulse, crimes arising from his gambling propensities and ill-considered promotion schemes; while the brunette is more likely to commit crimes of deliberation, specialization, detail, such as murder, counterfeiting, forgeries, conspiracy, etc. Because the blond is healthy,

> optimistic, and naturally good-humored, he eliminates anger, hatred, melancholy, discouragement, and all other negative feelings...easily...Because he is naturally slow, cautious, conservative, and inclined to be serious and thoughtful, the brunette is far more liable to harbour resentment, to cherish a grudge, to plan revenge, to see the dark side of life, and often to be melancholy and pessimistic.[18]

Such generalizations for blonds versus brunettes may seem ridiculous in the hindsight of the 21st century and you may find yourself wondering how people could have believed in the tenets of characterology. To understand that system and phrenology, you must understand them in the context of their times. Science was a relatively new enterprise in the 19th century and most people did not have a clear basis for distinguishing science from nonscience (surveys today show that many people still cannot make such a distinction). And even if they could, whether these systems were validated by scientific research was not a concern for the great majority of consumers. People had needs, whether it was to find a suitable marriage partner, choose an occupation, hire a worker, or raise a child. They looked to experts for help, and like today, it was not easy for people to make judgments about who was or was not an expert.[19]

Whereas phrenology was organized around the nucleus of the Fowlers' operations that controlled the *American Phrenological Journal* and had formal ties to phrenological clubs and societies around the country, there was no such nucleus for physiognomy, which instead operated as a number of independent systems. Likely that is why physiognomy, although in vogue for more than a 100 years in the United States, never attained the popularity and visibility enjoyed by phrenology. In addition, phrenology had greater status because it could at least lay claim to some neuroanatomical basis because mental and moral faculties were identified with specific brain areas. No such neural or anatomical claims were made for physiognomy.

Psychology's Other Occult Doubles

Thomas and Grace Leahey have written about psychology's pseudosciences of the 19th century, referring to them in the title of their book as "psychology's occult doubles." To this point we have discussed two of the most prominent of those occult doubles: phrenology and physiognomy. There are many others, and to cover them all in any depth is beyond the purposes of this chapter. Yet three of them deserve brief mention, either because they are important for understanding the nature of psychological practice in the 19th century or because they relate more directly to the 20th-century psychological profession. They are mesmerism, spiritualism, and mental healing.

Mesmerism

Franz Anton Mesmer (1734–1815) was an Austrian physician who discovered in 1774 that he could relieve a number of medical and psychological symptoms in his patients by treating them with magnets (see Figure 1-4). He named his procedure animal magnetism, although later it would be better known by the eponym mesmerism. In treating his first patient with the magnets, Mesmer described a kind of fainting spell, a crisis state, that lasted for a brief time, after which the symptoms abated for several hours. The spell was likely a hypnotic trance. In treating subsequent cases, Mesmer would tell his patients what they would experience, including this trance state, and many of them complied with his suggestions, thus going into a trance. Mesmer believed that the fluids in the human body were magnetized and that they could get out of alignment. The purpose of passing the magnets over the body was to move the fluids around and thus restore harmonious alignment to the body. Soon he abandoned the magnets altogether and just passed his hands over his patients' bodies, inducing trance states and affecting cures. He assumed that he was now serving as a powerful magnet and could produce the cures without need of the magnets.

Mesmer had become quite the sensation in Paris in the early 1780s, holding group sessions that allowed him to treat a dozen or more people at once (which allowed persons in the group to watch the behavior of others and thus see what they were "supposed" to do) and still charge outrageous fees. His treatments were for the wealthier citizens and Mesmer found himself ensconced in Parisian high society. Animal magnetism became very popular as other practitioners began to practice this healing art. And, of course, there were those who opposed mesmerism as fraudulent. These opponents, mostly from the medical community, brought pressure on King

Figure 1-4. *Franz Anton Mesmer.* Courtesy of the National Library of Medicine, Bethesda, Maryland

Louis XVI to appoint a group to investigate its validity. The blue ribbon commission appointed by the king in 1784 included, among others, Benjamin Franklin, as president of the commission; the famous chemist Antoine Lavoisier; and a French physician, Joseph Guillotin, whose invention of the guillotine would soon be used in France's Reign of Terror to remove the heads of many in the aristocracy, including the head of Lavoisier. The commission's report was quite damning. It argued that no animal magnetic fluids existed, nor was there any healing due to magnetic forces. The report did not result in any formal actions by the French government and so the fallout was mostly Mesmer's bruised ego.

Mesmer's work is generally viewed as the starting point for the history of modern hypnosis, although one can find written accounts of hypnotically induced states that precede Mesmer. It is not our purpose here to discuss the history of hypnosis. Instead we have presented this discussion of Mesmer because of the popularity of mesmerism in 19th-century America and because of related treatments that involved magnetism and suggestion. Many of these approaches were directed at medical ills, that is physical ailments, but psychological problems and needed behavioral changes figured prominently in the work of the mesmerists as well.

Mesmerism came to the United States in the 1830s. One of its practitioners was Charles Poyen, a French physician who traveled throughout the northeastern United States in 1836 giving demonstrations of its powers. The following year Poyen immigrated to the United States, settling in Providence, Rhode Island. He was a charismatic figure who drew a large number of converts to mesmerism. He began publication of *The Psychodinamist*, a magazine for mesmerists in the United States.

What did American mesmerists do? In general they were involved with healing and encouraging self-improvement. They relied on techniques that in some way attempted to create a trance state during which suggestions would be made by the mesmerist. Suggestion can be a powerful force. No doubt many clients went to mesmerists, not in a skeptical mood, but with expectations that they would be helped. After all, they often paid considerable fees for that help. Clients went to mesmerists for many different reasons: family problems, problems in the workplace, health problems. After the sessions the clients often confessed to feeling spiritually invigorated. They possessed a new energy and a will to solve the problems that had been plaguing them. Clients often reported that they had been set free by their treatments. Psychologist Philip Cushman described it this way: "Mesmerism was first and foremost an ideology of personal, *inner* liberation. It emphasized the inherent goodness of the inner self and led to the development of practices that were designed to expand, revitalize, and finally liberate the natural spirituality...."[20] Of course the Fowler brothers got into this act as well. Toward the end of the 19th century they began to promote lectures and courses in "personal magnetism" that promised a pleasing personality; the cultivation of success; how to succeed in love, courtship, and marriage; how to prevent disease; how to build character; and how to become a great power in the world.[21]

Mesmerism became quite popular in America in the last half of the 19th century and persisted as a lesser force into the early 20th century. Its impact on other 19th- and 20th-century occult doubles was considerable.[22] It has even been regarded as the beginning of psychotherapy in America. Cushman wrote, "In certain ways, mesmerism was the first secular psychotherapy in America, a way of ministering psychologically to the great America unchurched. It was an ambitious attempt to combine religion with psychotherapy, and it spawned ideologies such as mind-cure philosophy, the New Thought movement, Christian Science, and American spiritualism."[23] We turn now to a brief treatment of spiritualism and then to the mental healing that was part of the mind-cure movement.

Spiritualism

In the 1850s in a darkened room, people sat around a table, hands joined with each other and with the individual serving as the medium, who was the conduit to the other world, that is, to persons in the afterlife. There would be mysterious sounds—sometimes noises, sometimes voices—and ghostlike forms would appear, and the table would move on its own, and the windows would rattle, and the medium might have a seizure or at least would go into a trance state. These séances were the modus operandi of the practicing spiritualists, and they were part of the psychological scene in America during the last half of the 19th century. Among those interested in spiritualism was William James (1842–1910), arguably the most important figure in the history of American psychology. James wrote one of the most influential books in psychology's history, *Principles of Psychology* (1890), and he established the psychology program at Harvard University.[24] Although he was prominently identified with the new science of psychology, he had other intellectual interests that proved to be an embarrassment to many of his psychological colleagues.[25] For more than 25 years, James studied paranormal events in an attempt to provide scientific evidence for a number of psychical phenomena, including the actions of spiritualist mediums. In 1885 he met Mrs. Leonore Piper, a famous medium, and over the next 25 years he frequently attended séances she directed. In the initial séances Mrs. Piper is said to have told James and his wife intimate details about their lives, details that the Jameses felt sure no one could have known but them. Such revelations convinced James that Mrs. Piper had paranormal abilities but he was never able to satisfy himself about the origin of those abilities, that is, did her information come from the spirit world, from some kind of exceptional sensory skills, or from mental telepathy? James was apparently convinced that there was no trickery involved in the performances of Mrs. Piper, but that was not the opinion of several other scientists who visited her séances.[26]

Interestingly, the origin of spiritualism in America can be defined both in time and place—March 31, 1848 at a farm near Hydesville, New York— under what can only be called extraordinarily bizarre circumstances for the beginnings of a movement with such religious overtones. Two young sisters, Margaret (age 13) and Kate Fox (age 12), discovered that they could make weird noises by cracking the joints in their toes, and they used this ability to trick their superstitious mother into believing that a ghost was present.

> After several days of this mild poltergeisting, they tried questioning the "spirit" and ascertained that it was the ghost of a peddler who had been murdered in the vicinity of their cabin before they had moved in. Word of these amazing events soon spread. So many visitors came to their cabin that the older sister, Leah Fox Fish, noticed the financial possibilities of going into the ghost business.[27]

Leah took her two younger sisters to Rochester, New York, where they set up shop, holding séances, acting as mediums, bringing forth spirits of the deceased to communicate with the paying customers who were eager to make contact with lost loved ones. Initially the spirits were manifested by rapping noises on tables or by movements of the séance table. As those techniques lost their appeal, mediums added a board (the planchette, a forerunner of the Ouija board) that could be used to spell out the messages of the spirits, megaphones for spirit voices, and the spirit cabinet, a large piece of furniture from which sounds could be heard and from which visual apparitions would appear (and in which confederates could sometimes hide).

With so many Americans dead as a result of the Civil War, there were thousands of loved ones who longed to make contact once more. The demand for mediums rose and there were plenty of willing individuals, mostly women, ready to assume the role. In 1888, Margaret Fox confessed her chicanery and that of her sister, an action that diminished interest in spiritualism. Yet there would be another resurgence of interest in 1918 after World War I and the influenza epidemic had taken so many lives. Although the bread and butter of mediums was contact with the dead (see Figure 1-5) and the relief and joy that connection could bring to their

Figure 1-5. *In the 19th century, séances were popular with the public seeking to contact the deceased. From the frontispiece of William Robinson's 1898 book,* Spirit Slate Writing and Kindred Phenomena.

clients, they also provided other psychological services as counselor and adviser to their clients who might be suffering depression, anxiety disorders, difficulties in marriage, problems in the workplace, and troubles with their children.

Spiritualism was not connected with any specific religion although it may have seemed religious in nature because it was predicated on a belief in an afterlife. Yet organized religion opposed spiritualism and argued that belief in spirits was an act of heresy. "By claiming to produce empirical evidence of survival [after death], Spiritualism denied the need for faith. By claiming that there was no hell, and that a pleasant afterlife was in store for everyone, it denied the fear of God and of hellfire on which organized Christianity depends."[28] Spiritualism did not diminish in popularity because of the opposition of organized religion in America. Its demise in the 1920s was due, no doubt, to multiple causes, perhaps chief among them that many of the professional mediums were eventually exposed as frauds. Of course spiritualism did not disappear entirely. There are seers, mystics, and mediums working today who offer the promise of contact with the dearly departed. And there are many others—some trained in science—some not, who offer the other counseling psychological services.[29]

Mental Healing

The last of psychology's occult doubles that we cover are the mental healers, or what is also called the "mind-cure" movement, that began in New England in the 1850s. Its origins are attributed to a clockmaker, Phineas Parkhurst Quimby (1802–1866) who, after studying and practicing mesmerism for a decade, formulated his own theory and method of mental healing. Quimby believed that many diseases had causes that were wholly mental and that other diseases were exacerbated by mental conditions. His experiences with his own illnesses and his treatment by physicians left him convinced of the inadequacy of medical practice. Indeed, Quimby believed that physicians did as much good by what they said to patients and the way they said it as they did through medicines or surgeries.

Quimby was a keen observer and evidently had great powers of concentration. He listened intently as his clients told him about their problems. He established a close rapport with them from the beginning, something that he felt was crucial to effecting a cure. Quimby believed that many physical and psychological problems were caused by negative thinking and that those negative thoughts were often induced in individuals by physicians. Quimby's task was to help clients see the "truth," to achieve wisdom about their lives, to reach a spiritual healing. Quimby believed that disease was

> due to false reasoning in regard to sensations, which man unwittingly develops by impressing wrong thoughts and mental pictures upon the subconscious spiritual matter. As disease is due to false reasoning, so health is due to knowledge of the truth. To remove disease permanently, it is necessary to know the cause, the error which led to it. The explanation is the cure.[30]

In essence, Quimby believed that cure resided within the mental powers of the individual and not in the medical practices of physicians. Individuals could cure themselves if they could be shown the way to right thinking.

In 1859, Quimby moved to Portland, Maine, where he spent the last 6 years of his life dedicated to his mental healing practice. He is said to have treated more than 12,000 individuals.[31] Among those he cured was a woman who became one of his early disciples. Her name was Mary Baker Eddy (1821–1910), who in 1879 founded the Church of Christ, Scientist, better known today as Christian Science. Eddy was not only cured by Quimby but she was greatly influenced by his views on illness and healing. They maintained a frequent correspondence until Quimby's death in 1866.

The growth of mental healing spread throughout the United States in the 1860s. There were many different schools of the mind-cure movement, including Eddy's. "The movement enlisted the support of tens of thousands of American women and men. Literally hundreds of books and pamphlets in addition to scores of periodicals proclaimed the dawning of a New Age in which mind and spirit would achieve domain over matter and crude materialism."[32] Not surprisingly, given his interest in paranormal and spiritual events, William James, who had earned his medical degree from Harvard University, sought the services of a mental healer. In 1887 he wrote to his sister Alice:

> I have been paying ten or eleven visits to a mind-cure doctress, a sterling creature, resembling the "Venus of Medicine," Mrs. Lydia E. Pinkham; made solid and veracious looking. I sit down beside her and presently drop asleep, whilst she disentangles the snarls out of my mind. She says she never saw a mind with so many, so agitated, so restless, etc. She said my *eyes*, mentally speaking, kept revolving like wheels in front of each other and in front of my face, and it was four or five sittings ere she could get them *fixed*.[33]

Although Mrs. Pinkham pronounced James cured, he reported to his sister that after the "cure," he still lay awake nights. When the medical establishment in Massachusetts sought legislation that would have required mental healers to pass a medical exam and be licensed by the state, James vehemently opposed such a plan. In a 1894 letter to a Boston newspaper he wrote:

> And whatever one may think of the narrowness of the mind-curers, their logical position is impregnable. They are proving by the most brilliant new results that the therapeutic relation may be what we can at present

describe only as a relation of one person to another person; and they are consistent in resisting to the uttermost any legislation that would make 'examinable' information the root of medical virtue....[34]

By 1900 the craze of the mind-cure movement had largely ended, although mental healing continued, both in organized religion, such as Christian Science, and in home clinics where mental healers practiced. As mesmerism can be thought of as a precursor to contemporary psychotherapy, so too were the mind cures important in establishing belief in the importance of what today would be called the therapeutic relationship or therapeutic alliance. The importance of that construct in studies of the effectiveness of psychotherapy is highlighted by James in the previous quotation. We revisit this issue in our later chapters on clinical and counseling psychology.[35]

The New Psychology

To this point we have described the 19th-century practices of phrenology, physiognomy, mesmerism, spiritualism, and mental healing as prescientific applied psychologies. The practitioners in these disciplines used the knowledge and mythology of mind and body and fashioned it into a helping profession, thus offering, as noted earlier, many of the same services that are today provided by professional psychologists. Several of these "psychologies" were at their peak when a new psychology arrived from Europe in the 1880s. It was the experimental psychology of Wilhelm Wundt, and it would soon spawn a new psychological profession, one that would successfully battle the older medical establishment for rights to practice and one that would convince all 50 state legislatures to pass laws protecting the label "psychologist" and to establish licensure procedures controlling access to the profession.

The science of psychology emerged in the last quarter of the 19th century, an amalgam of sensory physiology, neurophysiology, psychophysics, and philosophy. This new psychology was called physiological psychology to emphasize its ties to physiology, or experimental psychology to stress its reliance on the scientific method, or the new psychology to distinguish it from the earlier philosophical variety, often known as mental philosophy. The founding of this new science is usually credited to Wilhelm Wundt

(1832–1920), trained in philosophy and medicine, who, in 1879, established a laboratory for research in psychology at the University of Leipzig, where he was a professor.

Wundt's psychology centered on understanding consciousness in terms of the elements—principally sensations and feelings—that made up consciousness and the ways in which the mind organized those elements into functioning processes. For Wundt, the mind was an active entity. That is, the mind acted on elements, analyzing, combining, and organizing them into psychic wholes that often bore little resemblance to their elemental structure. Thus a perception could be very different from the sensations that, in part, gave rise to it, and an emotion, such as anger, could be viewed as more than just an aggregate of simple feelings and perhaps a few sensations. Wundt's psychology went beyond mere mental chemistry. He was certainly interested in identifying the elements of consciousness, but he was more interested in understanding how the elements were organized into higher-order mental processes.

Research in Wundt's laboratory focused principally on three topics: sensation and perception, speed of mental operations, and perception of time. The bulk of the research was on sensation and perception, chiefly psychophysical studies on a large number of dimensions in vision, audition, and the other senses, for example, studies of auditory pitch, visual brightness, color saturation, and the detection of minimal differences between tones or lights or weights. The work on the speed of mental operations actually sought to measure the time required in making mental decisions, an area of cognitive psychology that is known today as mental chronometry. Using devices (chronoscopes) that measured time in thousandths of a second, Wundt and his students studied the time required in making simple decisions (is a light on or not?, a detection task) versus more complex mental decisions (is the light red or blue?, a discrimination task). In these experiments, subjects were told a response to make (for example, pressing a key) once they were able to answer the question. The timer would be started when the stimulus was presented and the time would stop when the subject made the appropriate response (see Figure 1-6).[36]

In his career at Leipzig, Wundt trained approximately 160 doctoral students in psychology, about 30 from the United States. Several of his

Figure 1-6. *Wilhelm Wundt performing a simulated reaction-time experiment in his Leipzig laboratory in 1912 on the occasion of his eightieth birthday. The others in the photo are German colleagues and former students.*

American students returned to establish early psychology laboratories as shown in Table 1-1.[37]

Other American laboratory founders also spent some time working in Wundt's laboratory, even though they did not take their degree with him. One such founder was G. Stanley Hall (1844–1924) who earned his degree with William James in 1878 and went to Leipzig the year Wundt's laboratory opened. Hall eventually founded what is usually considered the first psychology laboratory in America at Johns Hopkins University in 1883. In 1889 he became the founding president of Clark University and, with Edmund C. Sanford, established the psychology laboratory there as well. Other Hall doctoral students founded laboratories at Indiana University (1887), University of Wisconsin (1888), and University of Iowa (1890). By 1900, less than 20 years after the opening of the first American psychology laboratory at Johns Hopkins, there were more than 40 American

TABLE I-I. WUNDT'S AMERICAN STUDENTS WHO
FOUNDED PSYCHOLOGY LABORATORIES

Student	Laboratory	Year of Founding
James McKeen Cattell	University of Pennsylvania	1887
Harry Kirke Wolfe	University of Nebraska	1889
James McKeen Cattell	Columbia University	1890
Frank Angell	Cornell University	1891
Edward A. Pace	Catholic University	1891
Edward W. Scripture	Yale University	1892
Frank Angell	Stanford University	1893
George Stratton	University of California	1896
Charles Judd	New York University	1900
Walter Dill Scott	Northwestern University	1900

laboratories and they were turning out a ready supply of new doctorates in the new psychology.[38]

In the beginning of the 20th century the popularity of psychology was expanding in American universities, thus philosophy departments (where psychologists were trained in those days) increased in size. Most of the new psychology doctorates found jobs as professors in colleges or universities, but some found employment in other settings, particularly women doctorates; except for the jobs in women's colleges, most academic positions were closed to them because of their gender. Typically these women found ways to apply their psychology in education, child development, juvenile rehabilitation, and the world of business. We talk about their achievements in later chapters. They and their male colleagues who worked outside of the universities were among the pioneers of applied psychology, individuals who by choice or default found themselves testing the powers of the new science.

At the end of the 19th century, the new American psychologists pursued their study of consciousness, focusing principally on studies of perception and learning, both of which derived from the philosophies of the British empiricists, such as John Locke, David Hume, and John Stuart Mill, who argued that there were no innate ideas, that the mind was a blank slate to be written on by experience. Perception was crucial they believed, because all information came to the mind via the senses; learning was important because it was the mechanism by which permanent changes in the mind occurred, and because it was believed to be the way in which consciousness could be adaptive for the organism (a clear Darwinian influence on American psychology). In their laboratories, psychologists used methods of introspection, psychophysical techniques, psychological testing (mental tests), and experimental methods to study consciousness. Before long these same methods would be used to solve problems outside of the universities.

Selling the New Psychology

When American psychology laboratories began to appear, they were not the subject of front-page news. Remember that there was a psychology already in place, one that the public had been using for more than a hundred years. The new psychologists were aware of that and were eager to disabuse the public of its reliance on the extant pseudopsychologies. One of the first public relations campaigns by the new psychologists was the creation of an exhibit at the world's fair in Chicago, the World's Columbian Exposition that opened in 1893. Joseph Jastrow (1863–1944), who headed the psychology laboratory at the University of Wisconsin, and Hugo Münsterberg (1863–1916), who held the same position at Harvard University, organized the display of psychological apparatus, photographs, and mental tests. The photographs, many depicting psychological equipment and experiments with humans using this equipment (see Figure 1-7), and the displays of the psychological apparatus itself were selected to make clear psychology's existence as a laboratory science. In addition to the public exhibition, these early psychologists also wrote articles for the popular press—newspapers and magazines—that sought to inform the public about the new psychology and often warned against the dangers of embracing nonscientific psychologies. As the popularity of psychology grew in the first few decades of the 20th century there were even greater opportunities for such articles and also for speaking engagements before a variety of clubs and organizations whose members wanted to hear about the discoveries of the new psychology.[39]

Sciences are ultimately valued not only for the knowledge they produce but also for the application of that knowledge. If this new psychology was

Figure 1-7. *Hugo Münsterberg's psychology laboratory at Harvard University.*
Courtesy of Harvard University Archives

the one true science of the mind as its proponents maintained, then surely
it could be useful for matters related to the mind. Perhaps it could be used
to help students learn more efficiently, or to design product advertisements that were more effective, or to help parents raise their children, or
to assist people in choosing their careers more wisely, or to cure individuals
who suffered from disorders of the mind. These and many other potential
applications lay before the new psychologists, and they wasted little time
in offering their services.

The early psychologists did not differentiate themselves according to
specialty areas as they do today. Prior to 1920 it was rare to find individuals
who would have referred to themselves as clinical psychologists or business
psychologists. Those labels were used on occasion, but more commonly,
psychologists who worked outside academic settings referred to themselves
as consulting psychologists. That label would be used in the first national

effort to provide something akin to modern licensure of professional psychologists when in 1921 the American Psychological Association formed the Committee on the Certification of Consulting Psychologists, a largely unsuccessful certification effort that lasted only a few years. When the first national organization for professional psychologists was established in 1930 it was named the Association of Consulting Psychologists (ACP) and it had grown out of the New York State Association of Consulting Psychologists that began in 1921. The ACP founded the first journal for professional psychologists in 1937, the *Journal of Consulting Psychology*, which is still published today as the *Journal of Consulting and Clinical Psychology*.[40] But the origins of 20th-century consulting psychologists, the practitioners of psychology, go back to the science of psychology in the late 19th century.

Child Study

At the end of the 1800s, America was undergoing tremendous social changes. Industrialization, growth of cities, child labor laws, compulsory schooling laws, and thousands of new immigrants resulted in exploding school enrollments. There were national calls for school reforms that would educate the mixed citizenry for a productive life in a more mechanized world. There were renewed concerns about raising citizens of good moral character. The increased enrollments led parents to seek information about teaching children and improving parenting techniques. Psychology's answer to these problems was "child study," a scientific study of American children that enlisted parents and schoolteachers as data collectors to assist psychologists in developing a comprehensive picture of the child. Psychologists wanted to discover all there was to know about the ways in which children perceived, learned, remembered, solved problems, used language, played, and so forth. With this new knowledge, psychology would be able to train better teachers; educate students better, including designing educational programs that would reach children who had difficulty learning or did not learn in traditional ways; and improve parenting.

The Child Study Movement began in 1883 when G. Stanley Hall published an article in the *Princeton Review* entitled "The Contents of Children's Minds," an article based on a survey he conducted of Boston school children that seemed to demonstrate an appalling lack of knowledge among those children. There were serious flaws with the validity of the survey; for example, although the children being tested were urban children, they were asked a large number of questions about events that would have occurred on a farm. Nevertheless, the article added to the national concerns about the quality of education that American children were receiving.[41] Over the next several years psychologists and educators increased their attention toward matters of reform. Hall reentered the picture in 1891 with an important address on child study at the annual meeting of the National Education Association. Some historians date that address as the beginning of the Child Study Movement, as did Hall, because developments proceeded so rapidly after that. Hall made his own university, Clark University, a clearinghouse for information on child study, including hundreds of questionnaires on different subjects that individuals could order for research purposes. In 1891 he founded *Pedagogical Seminary*, a journal to publish the results of the child study research. Hall delivered another watershed lecture on child study two years later at the World's Columbian Exposition and followed that up with a popular magazine article entitled "The New Psychology as a Basis for Education." In his summary he wrote, "The one chief and immediate field of application for all this work [psychology] is its application to education, considered as the science of human nature and the art of developing it to its fullest nature."[42]

We discuss the Child Study Movement further in later chapters. For now we can say that it proved largely unsuccessful in meeting its diverse and ambitious goals, and by 1910 it had mostly disappeared as a force in psychology and education. But it had served as an important entry point for the new science of psychology in seeking to solve some of the problems facing education in a rapidly changing America. Further, there is no denying that child study proved especially important in informing the American public about the work of the new psychology and its potential applications.[43]

Counseling Psychology

Closely related to child study was the vocational guidance movement. As the 20th century began, the industrial cities of the Northeast and Midwest relied on a vast pool of labor to convert raw materials into finished products. Factory work was readily available, but the pay was meager. For a poor family, it was often necessary for every member to earn a wage. There were few rules protecting workers, including children who left school to work in the factories. Many believed it was inefficient and inhumane for children to drift aimlessly from one job to another never acquiring skills, and never receiving an adequate education. Social reformers were quick to take up the issue. Typical of such reformers was Frank Parsons (1854–1908), a Boston attorney and political progressive, who believed that the technology of efficiency could be applied to selecting an occupation just as it was applied to the mass production of the Ford Model T automobile. In 1908 Parsons opened the Vocational Bureau at the Civic Service House in Boston. In what we would think of today as a counseling session, Parsons met individually with young people and took them through a process of vocational guidance, a procedure that included information gathering, test taking, and advising. He reasoned that the well-planned choice of an occupation would lead to greater satisfaction for the worker and greater productivity for the economy. Parsons died unexpectedly in 1908. Details of his system of vocational guidance were published posthumously in 1909 in his book *Choosing a Vocation*. Because of his pioneering efforts, he is widely regarded as the founder of the American guidance and counseling movement.

Vocational guidance was an idea whose time had come and it was quickly adopted for use in public schools throughout America. The psychological study of individual differences led to advances in testing and selection that helped extend the reach of vocational guidance beyond education and into government and industry. Over time, the focus on adjustment to the world of work gave way to a focus on adjustment to everyday life. The story of this change in focus is the story of counseling psychology, and is the subject of chapter 5.

School and Clinical Psychology

In March of 1896 a schoolteacher visited Lightner Witmer (1867–1956) at the psychology department at the University of Pennsylvania. Witmer had taken over the psychology laboratory from James McKeen Cattell after finishing his doctorate with Wundt. The teacher brought with her a 14-year-old boy who had difficulty spelling. The teacher reasoned that the problem was a mental one and, if so, psychology, as the science of the mind, ought to be able to help him. Witmer treated the problem successfully and by the summer, when word of the success had spread, he began to see similar cases. That led to his founding, in that same year, the first psychology clinic in America, perhaps anywhere in the world. He was so enthusiastic about the results of his clinic that he gave an address at the annual meeting of the American Psychological Association that year, describing the cases that had been treated and encouraging his colleagues in the Association to use psychology "to throw light upon the problems that confront humanity."[44]

In the initial years of the clinic, Witmer handled most of the cases himself, principally children with learning and/or behavioral disorders. As the clinic grew he hired additional treatment staff and used some of his doctoral students to handle the new cases. A journal, *The Psychological Clinic*, was started in 1907 to publish the case studies, including the diagnoses made and the treatments rendered. In the first issue of that journal Witmer described a program of doctoral training in a field that he named "clinical psychology."[45] Because of his establishment of the psychological clinic, his work with learning and behavioral problems in children and adolescents, and his promotion of doctoral training in clinical psychology, Witmer is usually recognized as the founder of clinical psychology and school psychology (the subjects of chapters 2 and 3). There are other historical roots to these two fields as we will explore in later chapters. We mention Witmer here, however, because he is typical of many in the first generation of American psychologists who looked for ways to make their science useful in solving the problems of their world.[46] No doubt one of the motives for such application was to demonstrate the utility of the new science. But another motive, more salient for some than others, was clearly to make a living, or in the case of university professors, to supplement their often meager salaries.

Psychology and Business

In 1900, Walter Dill Scott (1869–1955), another of Wundt's American doctoral students, was in his first year of employment at Northwestern University. Shortly after his arrival there he was contacted by a local advertising executive and asked if he would be willing to give a lecture on the new psychology at a meeting of the Agate Club, Chicago's organization of advertising executives. After the lecture, Scott was approached by John Mahin, the head of a leading Chicago advertising agency. Mahin was interested in advertising campaigns that would be based on science, and he believed that psychology was the science that could help advertisers understand the principles of appeal, persuasion, and customer behavior. Mahin offered to begin publication of a magazine on advertising if Scott would agree to write a series of 12 articles on psychology. Scott agreed and the articles began to appear in *Mahin's Magazine* in 1902. A year later they were reprinted as Scott's first book, *The Theory of Advertising*. He would write another 21 articles for Mahin and those too would be collected in a second book, *The Psychology of Advertising*, published in 1908.[47]

A contemporary of Scott, Harry Hollingworth (1880–1956) was in his second year of teaching at Barnard College in New York City in 1911, having received his doctorate with Cattell at Columbia University. He was married and his salary barely covered the monthly bills. In the winter of 1911 he was contacted by attorneys for the Coca Cola Company, which was being taken to court by the federal government for violation of the Pure Food and Drug Act. The company was accused of manufacturing a beverage with a harmful ingredient. Coca-Cola asked Hollingworth if he would be interested in conducting research for them, research that they hoped would help them win their case. Hollingworth agreed to do the research but worried whether he could protect his reputation as a scientist while doing research that was being paid for by a company that clearly wanted results that supported its case. He decided to do the research which he eventually presented to the court in Chattanooga in April 1911 (see Figure 1-8). We describe that work in more detail in chapter 4.

Scott and Hollingworth were two of the many psychologists who pursued the application of psychology to business. They worked mostly from their university settings, although Scott did work for a few years for a consulting company he formed after World War I, the Scott Company. By the 1910s there were psychologists, both men and women, employed full-time in American business and industry. They called themselves consulting psychologists or business psychologists and later, industrial psychologists. They are the forerunners of today's industrial/organizational psychologists. The history of this professional specialty is covered in chapter 4.

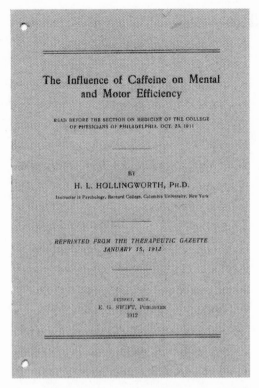

The Influence of Caffeine on Mental
and Motor Efficiency

READ BEFORE THE SECTION ON MEDICINE OF THE COLLEGE
OF PHYSICIANS OF PHILADELPHIA. OCT. 23, 1911

BY
H. L. HOLLINGWORTH, Ph.D.
Instructor in Psychology, Barnard College, Columbia University, New York

*REPRINTED FROM THE THERAPEUTIC GAZETTE
JANUARY 15, 1912*

DETROIT, MICH.
E. G. SWIFT, Publisher
1912

Figure 1-8. *Title page of Harry Hollingworth's 1912 monograph describing the caffeine studies he conducted for the Coca-Cola Company.*

Conclusion

The pioneer psychologists presented at the end of this chapter provide a glimpse of the professional specialties that developed in 20th-century American psychology. The next four chapters provide a history of each of the largest practice specialties: clinical psychology, school psychology, industrial/organizational psychology, and counseling psychology. There are other contemporary practice specialties as well, indicating the growth of the psychological profession in meeting the needs of a changing world. Several of those are discussed in the final chapter.

As we have shown in this chapter, the occupation of psychologist is an old one. As long as people have had psychological problems that needed solving or psychological questions that required answers, there have been individuals willing to deliver those services. In the 19th century, practitioners operating under many different names drew on myth, pseudoscience, intuition, observation, theology, superstition, trickery, and even a little science to provide their services. In the early 20th century, the new science of psychology, asserting its claim as the only valid psychology, began to send its graduates into the practice domains, offering services for the same centuries-old problems but under the flag of legitimate science. Thus was born the modern profession of psychology and its division into practice specialties. What follows in the next chapters is a history of that profession discussed in the context of the American history of which it is a part.

Chapter 2
Clinical Psychology

There are approximately 75,000 clinical psychologists[1] in the United States today, and, although the majority of those work in independent practice, you can find them employed in many venues, including hospitals, schools, clinics, business and industry, the military, the space program, universities, prisons, and the Federal Bureau of Investigation (FBI), the Central Intelligence Agency (CIA), and the Secret Service. Although the roots of modern clinical psychology can be found in the 19th century, the principal impetus for growth of the field is World War II. Evidence of that growth can be seen in the dramatic rise in membership of the American Psychological Association (APA) beginning in the 1940s (see Figure 2-1).[2] Most histories of clinical psychology in America begin with the opening of Lightner Witmer's clinic in 1896, as described in the previous chapter. Yet the history begins more than a century earlier when the first mental asylums in colonial America were opened in the mid-1700s. Those asylums marked the beginning of a new medical specialty aimed at treatment of the mentally ill, namely, psychiatry. Mental illness was thus part of the domain of medicine for more than one hundred years before the arrival of scientific psychology in America. The profession of clinical psychology would be carved out of medicine's territory in a series of turf disputes between psychiatry and psychology in the 20th century. We begin this story with the origins and evolution of America's mental asylums.

Mental Asylums

Historian Edward Shorter wrote that "the rise of the asylum is the story of good intentions gone bad."[3] Several factors converged in the 18th

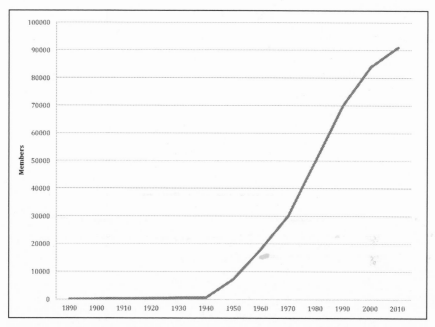

Figure 2-1. *This chart, showing the growth of APA membership since the founding of the association in 1892, dramatically illustrates the impact of World War II on American psychology.*

century to create a need for mental asylums. One was a change in general beliefs about the causes of mental illness, shifting from emphases on supernatural causes (including demonic possession) to a belief in physiological and psychological causes. Second, American cities were growing in population, which meant larger numbers of people who were labeled "distracted" or "lunatics." In the past, families had been able to care for these individuals within their homes. But as the numbers grew, there were more individuals whose families could not support their care, and more individuals whose freedom posed a danger to members of the community. The solution was to establish hospitals to care for these individuals. Historian Gerald Grob has described the changes in American society that led to the need for these hospitals.

> In preindustrialized society the family provided not only the basic necessities of life, but assumed responsibility as well for educating children, caring for the aged and infirm, and for supporting dependent members. The

39

separation of home from workplace—a characteristic of nineteenth-century industrialized society where labor was often centralized in factories and other industrial or commercial workplaces—led to the privatization of family life. This change in turn led to a diminution of the educational and welfare functions of the family, both of which were transferred to public or quasi-public institutions. The weakening of traditional means of socialization within the family and control by the family ultimately fostered the creation of public structures to take its place.[4]

Thus began America's insane asylums, also called lunatic asylums.

The first mental asylum in the colonies opened in the 1750s, in the city of Philadelphia. It is no surprise that Benjamin Franklin was one of the supporters of its establishment. The petition to the Pennsylvania Assembly began as follows:

> THAT with the Numbers of People the Number of Lunaticks, or Persons distemper'd in Mind, and deprived of their rational Faculties, hath greatly increased in this Province.
>
> THAT some of them going at large, are a Terror to their Neighbours, who are daily apprehensive of the Violences they may commit; and others are continually wasting their Substance, to the great injury of themselves and Families, ill disposed Persons wickedly taking Advantage of their unhappy Condition, and drawing them into unreasonable Bargains, etc.[5]

A second hospital for the insane opened in Williamsburg, Virginia, in 1773. Unlike the Philadelphia hospital that housed all kinds of patients, the Williamsburg hospital was exclusively for the mentally ill. A third hospital opened in New York City in 1791. Construction had begun in 1773 but a fire destroyed the building as it neared completion. The Revolutionary War postponed the opening still further. These three hospitals marked the beginnings of what would become known as the asylum movement in America, a movement marked by expansive growth of asylums in the 19th century, accompanied by controversies over treatments, the definition of cures, and the adequacy of funding. The good intentions at the beginning of the century would reap most undesirable consequences by the time of its close.

The asylum movement in America began with great benevolence in its care and optimism for its treatments. The asylums constructed in the first half of the 19th century tended to be small. The great majority were never expected to house more than 250 patients, a number considered to be the upper limit if effective treatments were to be maintained. The therapeutic strategies, quite similar across institutions, were collectively referred to as moral therapy or moral treatment. Such treatments were partly derived from the work and writings of Philippe Pinel (1745–1826), a French psychiatrist who was in charge first of the Bicêtre and later the Salpêtrière asylums in Paris shortly after the French Revolution. As superintendent of these mental asylums, Pinel had observed that the harsh punishments of the inmates (and they were more inmate than patient), which included beatings, isolation for long periods, and being kept in chains, were not producing improvements. In the late 18th century, most individuals believed that insanity was incurable, thus incarceration seemed the only alternative, especially for those patients who were dangerous, either to themselves or to others. Pinel, however, believed that insanity could be cured. He instituted a system of therapeutic changes that transformed hospital care. He initiated a training program for the hospital workers that instructed them in how to treat patients and forbade them ever to strike a patient, even in self-defense. Pinel's insights marked a significant turn of events in the treatment of mental illness. If you visit the Salpêtrière Hospital in Paris today, at the entrance to the hospital grounds you will see a large statue of Pinel ministering to the insane.[6]

In America's small asylums, moral therapy meant individualized care. The asylum superintendent (who usually was a physician) knew all the patients, knew something of their life histories, knew the problems they exhibited, and had designed a program of treatment to produce recovery, which meant restoring normal behavior to the patients so that they could return to society (see Figure 2-2). Moral therapy included occupational therapy, exercise and recreation, religious training, instruction in habits of good body hygiene, and participation in activities targeted at patients' specific interests, such as painting, gardening, writing, carpentry, and music. Yet moral therapy was not the only treatment mode; after all, the asylum superintendents were physicians. They supplemented the moral treatment

TABLE VIII. — *Showing the supposed causes of Insanity in* 592 *patients.*

	M.	F.	T.		M.	F.	T.
Ill health of various kinds	40	42	82	Celibacy	1	—	1
				Mortified pride	—	1	1
Intemperance	35	—	35	Anxiety for wealth	1	—	1
Loss of property, failures, &c.	30	10	40	Use of opium	—	2	2
				Use of tobacco	2	—	2
Dread of poverty	2	—	2	Puerperal state	—	22	22
Disappointed affections	6	6	12	Lactation too long continued	—	3	3
Intense study	9	1	10	Uncontrolled passion	1	1	2
Domestic difficulties	3	9	12	Tight lacing	—	1	1
Fright	3	7	10	Injuries of the head	7	2	9
Grief, loss of friends, &c.	8	22	30	Masturbation	4	—	4
Intense application to business	3	—	3	Mental anxiety	11	7	18
				Exposure to cold	1	—	1
Religious excitement	17	11	28	Exposure to direct rays of the sun	3	—	3
Political excitement	3	—	3	Exposure to intense heat	—	1	1
Metaphysical speculations	1	—	1	Disappointed expectations	3	3	6
Want of exercise	2	1	3	Unascertained	136	94	230
Engagement in a duel	1	—	1				
Want of employment	13	—	13		346	246	592

Figure 2-2. *A page from* T. S. *Kirkbride's* Report of the Pennsylvania Hospital for the Insane for the year 1844 *showing "supposed causes of insanity."*

with somatic and pharmaceutical treatments including bloodletting, cold baths, laxatives, opium, and morphine.

As American mental asylums grew in number, the superintendents banded together in their mutual cause to share ideas about hospital management, patient treatment, staff training, and strategies for securing the funding necessary to carry out their programs. In 1844 they formed the Association of Medical Superintendents of American Institutions for the Insane

(AMSAII). In that same year, they also founded a journal—the *American Journal of Insanity*—as a vehicle for publishing information important to the operation of mental hospitals. The journal also published information on psychiatric developments, but its focus was on those topics of management that were crucial to the fiscal and administrative duties of the superintendents. Toward the end of the 19th century as psychiatric interests developed outside of the asylums, the AMSAII considered broadening its membership and the scope of its organization. Reflecting the growth of medical science on questions of mental illness, the association changed its membership structure in 1892 to include hospital physicians other than superintendents. Its name changed as well that year to the American Medico-Psychological Association. It would undergo one more name change in 1921 when it became the American Psychiatric Association and changed the name of its journal to the *American Journal of Psychiatry*.

In the optimism of the first half of the 19th century, mental illness was seen as an acute condition, curable, especially if treatment began early. Chronic cases were thought to be rare; when chronic cases were encountered it was assumed that these patients could have been cured had they received treatment in the early stages of their illnesses. By the end of the century, however, moral treatment was an impossibility as the patients in mental hospitals sometimes numbered in the thousands instead of the low hundreds where such treatment had seemed feasible. The explosive growth of the asylums reflected substantial increases in admissions. Yet equally problematic, the percentage of patients released as cured or improved had declined steadily, creating a population of chronic cases. In 1869 the Willard State Hospital opened in New York, the first mental asylum in America designed exclusively for chronic cases. In other words, it was an institution from which there would be no return, where there were no treatments aimed at cures. It was a place for the hopeless, and assignment there assured patients of such a fate.

Numbers tell much of the story of decline. In 1820 the average number of annual admissions to a mental hospital had been 31. Fifty years later, in 1870, that number was 182. In the same time period the average number of patients per asylum had increased from a very manageable 57 to a totally unmanageable population of 473, an increase of 830%.[7] Several mental hospitals housed more than 1,000 patients, typically with only 3–4 physicians on staff. In the 1900s states added more and more wings to their mental asylums, allowing them to hold more and more patients. By the middle of the 20th century mental hospitals were warehouses for the hopeless cases, with at least one hospital housing more than 7,000 patients. Even with the expanded buildings, asylums could not keep up with the demands for space. By 1940 approximately one third of the states reported patient populations that exceeded capacity by more than 20%, and the average overcrowding for all mental hospitals in all states was more than 10%.

America's mental asylums, like all state institutions in which the constituency wields little power, were never well funded. Even at the beginning of the 19th century, superintendents struggled annually in budget fights with their state or private benefactors to secure the funding necessary to provide adequate housing and a staff of sufficient size and training to make therapy (and recovery) a reality. All of these institutions, whether public or private, had oversight boards. These boards focused on financial issues and cure rates. The only way to maintain financial feasibility was to keep the patient population relatively steady, and to do that meant that releases needed to match admissions. In an effort to reduce their patient populations, some hospitals released individuals who were known not to be cured, but who were assumed to present no problems to the community beyond, perhaps, odd behavior. But as admission pressures swelled it became impossible to provide individualized treatments and thus still fewer patients could be released as cured. Eventually these insane asylums (relabeled state hospitals in the 20th century) became institutions of patient management, not patient care. With a handful of professional staff to treat thousands of patients, therapy simply was not possible (see Figure 2-3).

After decades of largely warehousing people, often in most unsatisfactory settings; after decades of public dissatisfaction with the quality of institutional care and with the low rate of recovery of patients; after several media events (books and films) brought the deplorable conditions of state hospitals to greater public awareness;[8] and after the development of new drugs in the 1950s, particularly antidepressants and antipsychotics, which offered some success in treatment, it was decided that America could do without these large state edifices that appeared archaic in the social enlightenment

Columbus, Ohio, State Hospital for Insane.

Figure 2-3. *Postcards of mental asylums, such as this one, were common in the early part of the twentieth century. As can be seen in this illustration, many of these hospitals were enormous in size.*

of the mid-20th century. In 1963, President John F. Kennedy signed the Community Mental Health Centers Act that would remove hundreds of thousands of patients from the approximately 300 state hospitals and transfer their treatment to smaller community mental health centers that were to treat patients largely on an outpatient basis, relying on the cooperation of patients' families and the new miracle drugs. Sadly for the sufferers of mental illness, this change proved, once again, to be an example of good intentions gone bad. This radical shift in American mental health policy is often called "deinstitutionalization." We say more about its impact and its relationship to clinical psychology toward the end of this chapter.

Clinical Research by Psychologists in the 1890s

American psychiatry was undergoing significant changes at the end of the 19th century. Medical science was growing in importance, especially studies of the brain. Despite the lack of effective medical treatments of mental illness, somatic interpretations of mental illness were common, that is, that abnormalities of the brain were responsible for mental illness.

However, psychic interpretations of mental illness—the belief that mental illness could be due to psychological causes—were also gaining favor, in part because of the success of hypnotic and other suggestive treatments and later to the popularity of the ideas of Sigmund Freud (1856–1939). American psychologists thus found themselves involved in the search for causes and treatments of abnormal behavior as early as the 1890s.

Boris Sidis (1867–1923) was a student with William James. As a psychologist, Sidis established a laboratory in 1896 as part of the New York Pathological Institute, an institute whose functions included research that would benefit the mentally ill in New York's numerous state hospitals. Sidis's principal research area was hypnosis, resulting in his first book, *The Psychology of Suggestion*, in 1898. He continued his research while attending medical classes and earned his MD degree in 1905. In examining his many patients, Sidis argued that fear was the key component in producing psychopathology, the root cause of mental illness. He published an article in 1912 making that claim, but his ideas never had much influence.[9] Another research laboratory was established at the Eastern Hospital for the Insane in Kankakee, Illinois, in 1897 by psychologist William O. Krohn (1868–1927). Krohn was at the asylum for only a few years but did publish an article on psychological research as it related to insanity, indicating how the methods of experimental psychology could assist in improving the accuracy of psychiatric diagnoses.[10] Several other state hospitals followed suit in the early 20th century, founding research laboratories that included psychologists on their staffs. Some university doctoral programs in psychology (such as Clark University and Harvard University) established cooperative internship arrangements with state hospitals that allowed psychology graduate students to conduct research with patients as subjects.

Psychologists, who had developed research methods and apparatus to investigate the processes of the normal mind—processes of perception, learning, memory, feeling, and thinking—now used their methods to measure the processes of the abnormal mind. Chronoscopes that could measure time in thousandths of a second were used to measure reaction time to stimuli in a variety of sensory modes including vision, audition, and touch. Dynamometers measured strength of hand grip. Hot and cold cylinders were used to assess temperature sensitivity in different parts of the body.

Wundt's perimeter apparatus was used to measure color acuity. And there were several devices to assess memory.

Many of these assessments could have been labeled psychological tests or "mental tests." The latter term is said to have been coined in 1890 by psychologist James McKeen Cattell (1860–1944), who was mentioned in the last chapter as the first of Wundt's American doctoral students and the founder of psychological laboratories at the University of Pennsylvania and Columbia University. Cattell became interested in psychological tests when he was a graduate student at Johns Hopkins University before moving to the University of Leipzig for his doctorate. His Leipzig research continued in that vein. Stimulated a few years later by the testing program of Francis Galton[11] (1822–1911) in England, Cattell began a program of research using a battery of psychological tests that measured, among other abilities, grip strength, two-point threshold for tactile perception, discrimination abilities using weights, reaction time to a sound stimulus, memory task in repeating letters, time perception, color naming, pain sensitivity, and visual judgments of length.[12]

Cattell recognized the applied value of his tests that tapped an array of sensory, motor, and cognitive abilities. He wrote an article for the journal *Educational Review* in 1893 in which he described the potential value in the schools: "Tests of the senses and faculties...give a useful indication of the progress, condition, and aptitudes of the pupil....[S]uch tests would show whether the course of study is improving or blunting the fundamental processes of perception and mental life."[13] Arguing for similar potential educational benefits, Cattell convinced the administration at Columbia University to allow him to administer his psychological test battery to all incoming students, a practice begun in 1894 and continued each year for more than a decade.

Psychological testing also got a boost from the work of Joseph Jastrow as part of the psychology exhibit at the World's Columbian Exposition in 1893. Jastrow designed a battery of tests based on the work of Galton and Cattell. Over the course of the Chicago exhibition, thousands of visitors were measured by these tools of the new science of psychology (see Figure 2-4). These were the same psychological tests that found their way into the clinical laboratories in state hospitals in New York and Illinois and subse-

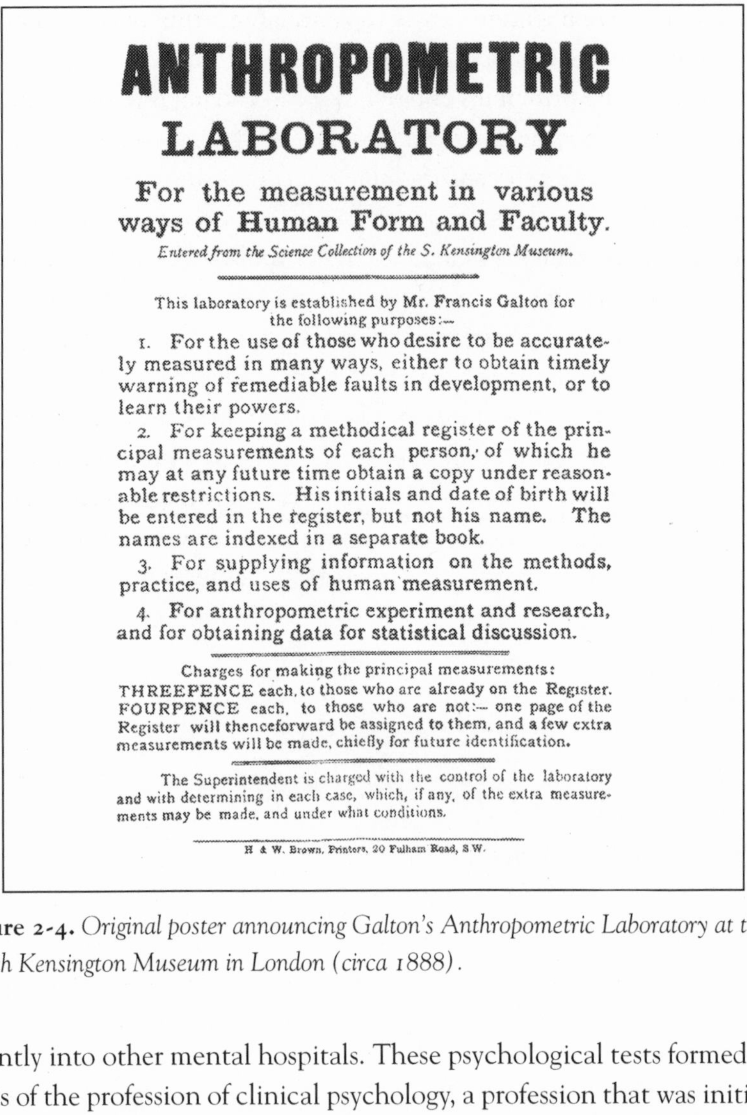

ANTHROPOMETRIC
LABORATORY
For the measurement in various ways of **Human Form and Faculty**.

Entered from the Science Collection of the S. Kensington Museum.

This laboratory is established by Mr. Francis Galton for the following purposes:—

1. For the use of those who desire to be accurately measured in many ways, either to obtain timely warning of remediable faults in development, or to learn their powers.

2. For keeping a methodical register of the principal measurements of each person, of which he may at any future time obtain a copy under reasonable restrictions. His initials and date of birth will be entered in the register, but not his name. The names are indexed in a separate book.

3. For supplying information on the methods, practice, and uses of human measurement.

4. For anthropometric experiment and research, and for obtaining data for statistical discussion.

Charges for making the principal measurements:
THREEPENCE each, to those who are already on the Register. FOURPENCE each, to those who are not:— one page of the Register will thenceforward be assigned to them, and a few extra measurements will be made, chiefly for future identification.

The Superintendent is charged with the control of the laboratory and with determining in each case, which, if any, of the extra measurements may be made, and under what conditions.

H & W. Brown, Printers, 20 Fulham Road, S W.

Figure 2-4. *Original poster announcing Galton's Anthropometric Laboratory at the South Kensington Museum in London (circa 1888).*

quently into other mental hospitals. These psychological tests formed the basis of the profession of clinical psychology, a profession that was initially grounded in clinical assessment. Before we describe that history we briefly revisit the contributions of Lightner Witmer because they are important for the development of clinical psychology as an identifiable field.

Lightner Witmer's Call for a Clinical Psychology

As mentioned earlier, Witmer founded the first psychology clinic in the United States in 1896 (perhaps the first anywhere in the world). In that same year he gave a lecture before the annual meeting of the American Psychological Association in which he called for "professional psychologists" to apply the principles of psychology to the fields of medicine and education.[14] In 1907 he began publication of a journal entitled *The Psychological Clinic*. The first article in the inaugural issue of that journal was written by Witmer and was entitled "Clinical psychology." That article is viewed as naming this new field, this professional specialty of psychology.[15]

By the time Witmer began publication of his journal, in part to chronicle the cases from his clinic, he had been seeing individuals, mostly children from the local Philadelphia schools, for a decade. He had developed what he called the clinical method for assessing these children and for planning a course of treatment. His clinical method included both a team approach to assessment, incorporating assessment tools from several disciplines, and a team approach to planning treatment. John O'Donnell has described how Witmer used this multidisciplinary method in his clinic:

> Children would be referred to the clinic through the school system. Following medical diagnosis, subjects would undergo an anthropometric,[16] optometric, and psychometric examination. . . . Witmer converted such experimental apparatus as the chronoscope, kymograph, ergograph, and plethysmograph into diagnostic devices merely by substituting the child for the trained introspectionist.[17] Similarly, the Seguin form board—formerly used as a pedagogical tool—was transformed into an instrument for testing a child's powers of memory, visual discrimination, and muscular coordination. Complementing psychologist and physician, the social worker would prepare a case study of the child's background. Clinical records were compiled with the threefold purpose of correlating case histories in order to produce generalizations, of standardizing tests, and of establishing new diagnostic techniques. Testing completed, a final diagnosis would be made, followed by attempts at remedial treatment.[18]

Some writers on the history of clinical psychology have criticized Witmer for failing to develop a clinical psychology that mirrored the modern version of the field. They note that Witmer stayed focused on the problems of school children and is thus more accurately the founder of school psychology and not clinical psychology. But such criticisms miss the point. As John

O'Donnell has written, it is too much to expect anyone in Witmer's time to foresee the contemporary professional specialties in psychology, and more specifically the several courses that clinical psychology would pursue. Clearly Witmer is a founder of school psychology as discussed in chapter 3. What Witmer did as a clinical psychologist was to recognize that there were cognitive and behavioral problems associated with children's poor performance in school and that the science of psychology could be used to remediate those problems. He adapted the research tools of psychology as diagnostic instruments, added other experts to his clinical team who could assess other aspects of his clients, and with their input developed treatments that alleviated the presenting problems. This was his clinical method that he advocated so forcefully. Arguably of greater importance for the modern profession of psychology was that more than any psychologist of his time Witmer called for a psychology that would "throw light upon the problems that confront humanity."[19] As O'Donnell has written, "while others called for an applied psychology, Witmer enacted one."[20] We examine his contributions in the next chapter on school psychology.[21]

Intelligence Testing

Witmer had shown how psychological measures could be used for the diagnosis of learning and behavioral problems. Similarly, Cattell believed in the utility of his mental tests and argued that they might be useful in identifying academic potential. When Galton invented the correlation coefficient, it allowed Cattell to measure the relationship between his mental tests and the academic performance of students. Sadly for Cattell those correlations were essentially zero. Although many of the students' grades in academic classes were found to correlate highly with their grades in other classes, there was no relationship between grades in any academic subject and any of Cattell's mental measures. Those data, published by one of Cattell's graduate students in 1901, effectively ended his career in anthropometric mental testing.[22] But the search for measures of intellectual functioning was an important one and others would take up the task.

Another of America's institutions in the late 19th and early 20th centuries was the home for the feebleminded, the label then used to describe individuals with intellectual disability.[23] American psychologists had conducted research on children with intellectual disability as early as 1894 and had been employed in institutions for them as early as 1896.[24] By far the most famous of the early psychologists to work in this field was Henry Herbert Goddard (1866–1957), who had received his doctorate in 1899 at Clark University under G. Stanley Hall. Goddard was a college professor in Pennsylvania when he met Edward Johnstone (1870–1955), the director of the New Jersey School for Feebleminded Boys and Girls, located in Vineland. Johnstone invited Goddard to visit the school, which he did in 1901. He made other regular visits over the next several years as he and Johnstone talked about the growth of institutions for the feebleminded and the general lack of information about the condition's causes and methods for remediation. In 1906, Johnstone invited Goddard to become director of psychological research at the Vineland school, and Goddard accepted.

Drawing on his training at Clark, Goddard assembled a laboratory of equipment to test sensory, motor, and mental functioning. He even designed some of the apparatus himself, such as an automatograph, a device that measured a child's ability to stand still. He read the extant literature on feeblemindedness to discover that little research on this condition had been done and thus little was known. He was in the potentially embarrassing position of being in charge of a research program and yet having few ideas about what he should be doing in the way of research. So he wrote to some of his colleagues in psychology and some of his former professors, hoping they could suggest some fruitful research approaches. All agreed that feeblemindedness was a topic worthy of study, but no one offered much advice about an appropriate program of research. Goddard used the psychological tests that had been used with children of normal intelligence but found that they did not work with the children at Vineland. Frustrated, he made a trip to Europe in 1908 because he had heard that there were schools there that were more advanced in their understanding of intellectual disability. He spent two months abroad, visiting 19 institutions for the feebleminded and several psychology laboratories. In Brussels, Goddard learned about a French psychologist who had developed a mental test in 1905 that was purported to measure performance in school children, especially those whose performance was poor. The test had been revised in 1908 and provided norms indicating at what ages children could typically perform particular tasks (essentially the concept of mental age). The French psychologist was, of course, Alfred Binet (1857–1911), and his test would initiate the modern approach to intelligence testing.[25]

Goddard was greatly intrigued by the Binet test which, unlike Cattell's tests that had emphasized sensory and motor abilities, stressed abilities more closely aligned to the abilities needed for success in school, for example, verbal fluency, comprehension, imagination, numerical skills, and reasoning. Goddard translated the Binet test into English and adapted it for use in the United States, publishing his version in 1908 as the Binet-Simon Measuring Scale for Intelligence. Whereas Cattell's anthropometric mental tests had failed to correlate with performance in school as measured by grades, Binet's test did. And, no doubt to Goddard's pleasure, the Binet test proved successful in use with feebleminded children and indicated differences in performance among those children. Goddard coined the term "moron" to label the highest group of feebleminded individuals (the terms "idiot" and "imbecile" already existed to describe lower-functioning individuals, with "idiot" being the lowest). The Binet test proved to be especially helpful in differentiating "morons" from persons of normal intelligence.[26]

There would be other versions of the Binet test in America, including the 1916 version by Lewis Terman (1877–1956) of Stanford University that, as the Stanford-Binet, became the dominant instrument for assessing intelligence in America over the next 40 years. This work by psychologists on intelligence testing in the years 1908 to 1916 would define for them their largest role, that of assessing the intellectual capacity of military recruits in World War I. Goddard and Terman and others met at Vineland in 1917 to develop what would be called the Army Alpha, an intelligence test that could be administered to large groups at once. By the end of the war, the test had been used to assess nearly 2 million military personnel and recruits (see Figure 2-5). Another version of the test, the Army Beta, was developed to be used with individuals who could not write or understand English. The validity of these tests and their effectiveness as screening devices had mixed reviews at the time and have fared more poorly in historical review.[27] Still, the publicity for psychologists surrounding this testing program was generally positive and would play a part in defining assessment as the key function for clinical psychologists in the years prior to World War II.

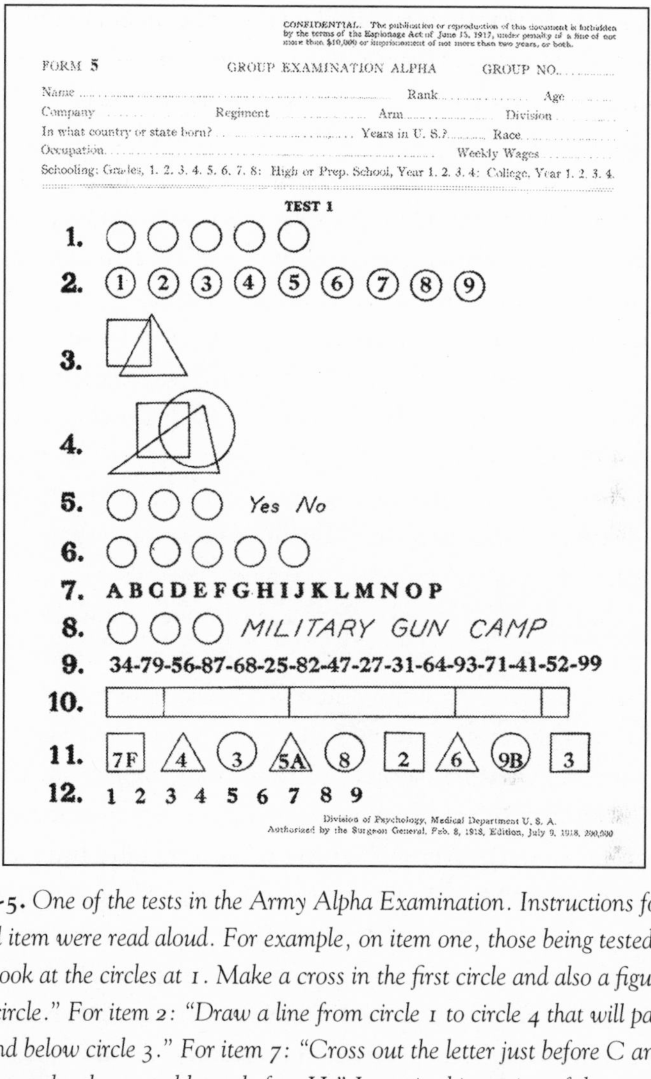

Figure 2-5. *One of the tests in the Army Alpha Examination. Instructions for each numbered item were read aloud. For example, on item one, those being tested were told to "Look at the circles at 1. Make a cross in the first circle and also a figure 1 in the third circle." For item 2: "Draw a line from circle 1 to circle 4 that will pass above circle 2 and below circle 3." For item 7: "Cross out the letter just before C and also draw a line under the second letter before H." Items in this section of the test assessed spatial abilities as well as the ability to follow verbal instructions.*

The Early Clinical Psychologists

Witmer's clinic was a decade old before other universities began to adopt his model of psychological services, but by 1914 there were psychology clinics at 19 universities in the United States. Some were more research oriented than Witmer's, for example the psychology clinic at the University of Iowa founded in 1908, but most followed his approach of assessment and treatment. Some universities, such as the universities of Minnesota and Washington, began to offer courses entitled "clinical psychology" at this time.

Clinical psychologists could also be found in the justice system. William Healy (1869–1963), a physician who was influenced both by William James and Henry Goddard, directed the Juvenile Psychopathic Institute in Chicago, a research, diagnostic, and treatment facility founded in 1909 to promote the welfare of juveniles within the Chicago juvenile court system. Healy was especially interested in the causes of juvenile delinquency at a time when there were heated debates arguing heredity versus environment. Healy hired a psychologist, Grace Fernald (1879–1950), to work with him, principally because of the assessment work she was expected to do. When she left, Healy replaced her with another psychologist, Augusta Bronner (1881–1966), whom he would later marry. Both Fernald and Bronner used the title "clinical psychologist" and both played important roles in research, assessment, diagnosis, and treatment design. The institute's goal was to assess individual children and make individualized treatment recommendations. The examination of each child was thorough and included "a family history; a developmental history; a history of the social environment; a history of moral and mental development, including school history, friends, interests, occupational history, and bad habits; and a history of the individual's contacts with law enforcement agencies or institutions.... [T]here was a complete medical examination, from psychiatric and neurological standpoints, as well as anthropometric and psychological studies." Healy, Fernald, and Bronner even designed many of their own psychological tests. It is obvious that the assessments and treatment prescriptions were incredibly labor-intensive.[28] (Note that women were disproportionately represented in professional psychology during this time because academic jobs were largely closed to them.)

Finally, prior to World War I, psychologists could be found working at mental hospitals and institutions for the feebleminded. Their work there was largely research and assessment. But they also contributed to the design of treatment programs and, in some cases, their actual delivery.

Influences on Clinical Psychology at the Turn of the Century

The first decade of the 20th century witnessed several events that would play important roles in shaping the future of clinical psychology. A Viennese physician made his only visit to the United States, during which he gave a series of lectures describing his psychological theories and his method of therapy. A former mental patient set in course a national movement with a goal of preventing mental illness. A physician began publication of what could be called the first journal of clinical psychology, one that predated Witmer's by a year and would prove much more important. And one of Wundt's American doctoral students serving as a minister in a Boston church began a program combining religion, psychology, and medicine that is regarded as the beginning of the practice of psychotherapy in America. Any one of these events could occupy a chapter by itself. For our purposes here however, we comment on each of them only briefly.

Freud's Visit and Psychoanalysis in America

Sigmund Freud (1856–1939) came to America in the fall of 1909 at the invitation of G. Stanley Hall, who was then president of Clark University. Hall was greatly interested in psychoanalysis and invited Freud to be a speaker at a conference to celebrate the 20th anniversary of the university. Carl Gustav Jung (1875–1961) accompanied Freud and also spoke at the Clark conference (see Figure 2-6). Freud gave his five lectures in German, beginning with the case of Anna O, describing her many symptoms and the treatment that led to her eventual cure. The five lectures would later be published in Hall's journal, the *American Journal of Psychology*, as "The Origin and Development of Psychoanalysis."[29] Prior to Freud's arrival, only a few individuals in America knew of his work (his most important book, on *The Interpretation of Dreams*, would not be translated into English until 1913). Yet in the decade following Freud's American visit, psychoanalysis gained a huge following in the medical community and with the public. Historian of psychology Gail Hornstein has written that by the 1920s, psychoanalysis had been accepted by the public as the one legitimate science of psychology, much to the consternation of psychologists.[30] Even though many academic psychologists regarded Freud's ideas as unscientific—they were derived from clinical cases rather than laboratory research; they stated

THE AMERICAN
JOURNAL OF PSYCHOLOGY

Founded by G. STANLEY HALL in 1887

VOL. XXI	APRIL, 1910	No. 2

THE ORIGIN AND DEVELOPMENT OF PSYCHOANALYSIS [1]

By PROF. SIGMUND FREUD (Vienna)

FIRST LECTURE

Ladies and Gentlemen: It is a new and somewhat embarrassing experience for me to appear as lecturer before students of the New World. I assume that I owe this honor to the association of my name with the theme of psychoanalysis, and consequently it is of psychoanalysis that I shall aim to speak. I shall attempt to give you in very brief form an historical survey of the origin and further development of this new method of research and cure.

Granted that it is a merit to have created psychoanalysis, it is not my merit. I was a student, busy with the passing of my last examinations, when another physician of Vienna, Dr. Joseph Breuer,[2] made the first application of this method to the case of an hysterical girl (1880-82). We must now examine the history of this case and its treatment, which can be found in detail in "Studien über Hysterie," later published by Dr. Breuer and myself.[3]

But first one word. I have noticed, with considerable satis-

[1] Lectures delivered at the Celebration of the Twentieth Anniversary of the opening of Clark University, Sept., 1909; translated from the German by Harry W. Chase, Fellow in Psychology, Clark University, and revised by Prof. Freud.

[2] Dr. Joseph Breuer, born 1842, corresponding member of the "Kaiserliche Akademie der Wissenschaften," is known by works on respiration and the physiology of the sense of equilibrium.

[3] "Studien über Hysterie," 1895, Deuticke, Vienna. Second edition, 1909. Parts of my contributions to this book have been translated into English by Dr. A. A. Brill, of New York. ("Selected Papers on Hysteria and other Psychoneuroses, by S. Freud.")

Figure 2-6. *Publication of Freud's lectures in the* American Journal of Psychology.

that human behavior was motivated by unconscious processes, which were by definition outside the realm of science—those involved in clinical psychology were more likely to find his ideas intriguing. Freud stressed psychic (rather than somatic or hereditarian) causes for mental illness, he offered explanations of etiology and prescriptions for treatment, and he argued that the practice of psychoanalysis should not be limited to physicians (even though the American medical community disagreed). Five years after his American visit there was a journal for psychoanalytic papers, an American Psychoanalytic Association, and programs to train psychoanalysts. Psychoanalysis would prove to be an important determinant in how psychologists would conceive of psychological disorders, and for many, how they would shape their work as psychotherapists.[31]

Clifford Beers and the Mental Hygiene Movement

At the age of 24, fearful that he would develop epilepsy as his brother had, Clifford W. Beers (1876–1943) attempted suicide. He subsequently spent nearly two years in two different mental asylums and was for a time confined to a straitjacket in a padded cell. Beers published a book in 1908, entitled *A Mind That Found Itself*, detailing his experiences as a mental patient, pointing out the cruelties he experienced and witnessed, noting the general lack of effective treatments, and calling for reform of mental institutions.[32] William James, who had read a draft manuscript of the book at Beers's request, sent Beers a favorable letter about the book that the author used as an introduction to the publication. Another person to take an interest in the book was Adolf Meyer (1866–1950), one of America's leading psychiatrists. Beers and Meyer met and found that they had mutual interests that involved reform not only of mental hospitals but also of American society, a social reform agenda that they believed would lessen the incidence of mental disturbances. Meyer gave the movement its name, the Mental Hygiene Movement, and in 1909 helped found the organization that would press its agenda nationally, the National Committee for Mental Hygiene (NCMH). Beers and Meyer were both involved in the leadership of NCMH, which was designed to "protect the public's mental health; promote research into and disseminate materials dealing with etiology, treatment, and prevention; seek federal funds and assistance; and promote the establishment of state societies for mental hygiene."[33] Although Meyer and Beers soon had disagreements that caused Meyer to leave the movement, Beers and others persisted, maintaining the movement by fits and starts until the beginning of the Great Depression when it effectively died out. Historians have judged the Mental Hygiene Movement to have had little impact. It certainly made no noticeable changes in American society, its prevention goals were never really tried, and there were no reforms in mental hospitals that could be attributed to the movement. What the movement did was to bring greater public attention to the issues of mental health, and that raised consciousness beyond the short tenure of the NCMH. Sadly, Beers once again suffered from major depression and in 1939 was placed in the Butler Hospital in Providence, Rhode Island, a private mental hospital that had opened in 1847. He remained there until his death in 1943 at age 67.

Morton Prince and Clinical Psychology

Morton Prince (1854–1929) was a neurologist who acknowledged the value of psychology in the medical arena. He was interested in the problems of psychopathology and believed that psychologists should be involved in the study and treatment of psychological disorders. In 1906, Prince founded the *Journal of Abnormal Psychology*, which published the early research and case studies on psychopathology, emphasizing psychic causes of mental disorders. (Prince later donated that journal to the APA and it is still published today.) Prince's journal proved to be an important outlet for psychologists, publishing, for example, articles by American psychologists such as Boris Sidis, Harvey Carr, Knight Dunlap, Joseph Jastrow, Hugo Münsterberg, Walter Dill Scott, Robert Yerkes, and many others, and advancing their presence in what most psychiatrists had considered to be their exclusive domain. Prince made other important contributions to psychiatry and clinical psychology including his most famous book, *The Dissociation of a Personality*, published in 1905, one of the earliest and most complete descriptions of a case of multiple personality (dissociative identity disorder). Prince's lifelong commitment to psychologists' place in psychopathology was indicated by his role in the opening of Harvard University's psychology clinic. When an anonymous donor gave Prince funds in 1926 to establish a psychology clinic at Harvard, Prince placed it in the Philosophy Department, where psychology was located, as opposed to locating it in Harvard's medical school.[34]

Elwood Worcester and the Emmanuel Movement

In 1889, Elwood Worcester (1862–1940) completed his doctorate with Wundt at Leipzig; his dissertation was on John Locke's religious opinions. He worked briefly as chaplain and psychology professor at Lehigh University where his interests in clinical psychology began. Consistent with the

New Thought Movement then prevalent, especially in the East, Worcester came to believe that many physical ailments had psychological or spiritual causes, which led him to consider the role that religion might play in healing. He left Lehigh in 1904 to become rector of the Emmanuel Church in Boston, and he remained there until his retirement in 1929. In his new position Worcester gained national fame for a philosophy of healing that proposed to cure disease through mental suggestion. Worcester differentiated his brand of religious healing from others of the time, noting that his approach blended medical diagnosis and spiritual advice. The program became known as the Emmanuel Movement, and it soon spread to other cities from New York to Seattle.

The movement began in 1906 when Worcester announced in a public lecture for his parishioners that he would be willing to meet the next morning with anyone who had moral or psychological problems they wanted to discuss. He expected that a few might show up, but was astounded when nearly 200 appeared. In the next few months Worcester worked out a program of treatment that included a medical examination. Based on that exam and his own interviews with the parishioners, individuals were selected to receive psychological treatment. The treatment was, in essence, psychotherapy, with a mix of hypnosis and relaxation training. The patient, seated in a comfortable chair, "is taught by rhythmic breathing and by visual imagery to relax the muscles, and is led into the silence of the mind by tranquilizing suggestion. Then in terms of the spirit, the power of the mind over the body is impressed upon the patient's consciousness, and soothing suggestions are given for the relief of specific ills."[35] These treatments typically lasted from 15 minutes to an hour (see Figure 2-7).

Historian Eric Caplan has written that when psychotherapy emerged in the beginning of the 20th century, the medical field had almost no interest in it. The success of the Emmanuel Movement changed that. By 1908 physicians began to attack the movement arguing that psychotherapy was a form of medical treatment and should be practiced only by physicians. After Freud's visit in 1909 and the growth of interest in psychoanalysis, there were additional pressures to wrest psychotherapy from lay practitioners.

There was much dissatisfaction with the Emmanuel Movement from the psychology community as well. Henry Rutgers Marshall (1852–1927),

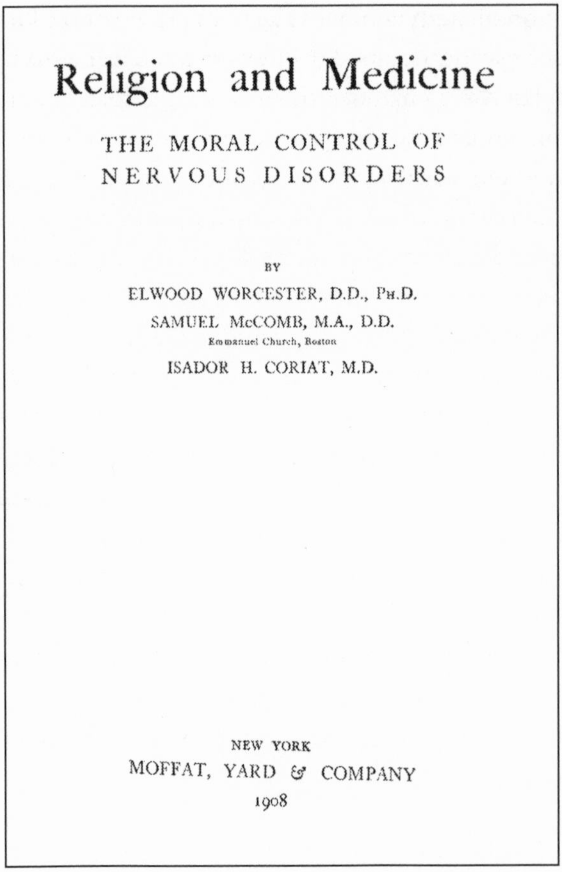

Religion and Medicine

THE MORAL CONTROL OF
NERVOUS DISORDERS

BY

ELWOOD WORCESTER, D.D., Ph.D.
SAMUEL McCOMB, M.A., D.D.
Emmanuel Church, Boston
ISADOR H. CORIAT, M.D.

NEW YORK
MOFFAT, YARD & COMPANY
1908

Figure 2-7. *Title page from Worcester's 1908 book, describing the philosophies and methods of the Emmanuel Movement.*

a philosopher and architect and former president of the American Psychological Association, attacked the movement, arguing that ministers were unqualified in the use of psychotherapy.[36] Witmer agreed, stating "Whatever Dr. Worcester's practice may be in his own church clinic, the principles of psychotherapy to which he and his associates adhere, are based upon neither sound medicine, sound psychology, nor to our mind, upon sound religion."[37] In his book on psychotherapy, published in 1909, Harvard psychologist Hugo Münsterberg (1863–1916) wrote, "The only safe basis of psychotherapy is a thorough psychological knowledge of the human personality."[38] As the self-appointed representatives of the science of human personality, psychologists were to provide that knowledge. Yet the practice of psychotherapy lay elsewhere according to Münsterberg. Concerned about the Emmanuel Movement, Christian Science, and other mental healing approaches, he wrote, "Scientific medicine should take hold of psychotherapeutics now or a most deplorable disorganization will set in, the symptoms of which no one ought to overlook to-day."[39] By 1910 the Emmanuel Movement was effectively at an end. Medicine was successful in usurping psychotherapy as a medical practice and it became the domain of psychiatry. Psychologists would have to battle psychiatry after World War II to add that tool to their own therapeutic bag.[40]

Clinical psychologists were not yet ready to offer psychotherapy as part of their professional services, but the popularity of psychoanalysis with the American public, the increased public awareness of mental health issues spawned by the Mental Hygiene Movement, the support of psychologists' involvement in issues of psychopathology provided through Prince's journal, and the attention afforded psychotherapy through the Emmanuel Movement were key elements in building a larger base for mental health issues in America. The growth of the field would soon outstrip the personnel resources of psychiatry. Public demand would open the doors for other mental health professionals.

Clinical Psychology: Organization, Certification

The experiences of psychologists during World War I increased interest in applied psychology, particularly for those interested in applying psychology to the treatment of psychological disorders and to the problems of business and industry. At the beginning of the war most psychologists were employed in college and university settings, largely engaged in teaching and research. Some academic psychologists did consulting work, sometimes in the form of applied research, and some psychologists, as we have noted, were employed full-time in nonuniversity settings such as juvenile courts, hospitals, businesses, and schools. These were the early professional psychologists, trained in the new science of psychology and eager to apply that knowledge to problems outside of the universities. Their competition was not from psychiatry at that time but from the same pseudoscientific practitioners who had provided psychological services to the public for the past century.

The new professional psychologists were concerned that the public could not differentiate the "real" psychologists from those practicing without training in scientific psychology. Consequently, in 1917, a handful of these applied psychologists, led by J. E. Wallace Wallin (1876–1969), who worked in the public schools with children suffering from intellectual disability, formed the American Association of Clinical Psychologists (AACP). The assumption was that membership in this association would serve as a kind of credential identifying the individual as a legitimate psychologist. But most of the public did not make such a distinction in seeking psychological services. Physicians and engineers, the two professional groups most often mentioned when psychologists discussed psychology as a profession, were licensed by the states, thus restricting practice, at least in principle, to individuals who held the proper credential. These two professions also had specialized university or professional school curricula for training. Individuals within the leadership of AACP explored the possibilities for similar credentialing and specialized training for clinical psychology.

Leta Hollingworth (1886–1939) wrote in 1918 that "certification in the clinical field seems feasible and necessary at this time."[41] She called for the APA to establish a standing committee that would

> prepare a list of departments of psychology, where prescribed training has been made available. This list should be published annually, and printed in the report of the A.P.A., and in the technical journals, and posted in departments of psychology. Then, for the immediate present, let the certified institutions certify individuals, by conferring upon qualified persons the prescribed diploma. In this there would, of course, be nothing legally mandatory. Ultimately the legal certification of individuals must be brought about, but in my judgment this will not be practicable until the courses of study have been standardized, and have actually been offered for three of four years at the university.[42]

She argued further that the doctoral degree should be the minimum level of training for clinical psychologists, whereas some psychologists had argued that a master's degree would suffice,[43] and she proposed that a new degree—"Doctor of Psychology"—be created for clinical psychologists, including a year of "apprenticeship."[44] Leta Hollingworth believed that ultimately certification of individual psychologists would occur but that it should begin with a standardized professional curriculum that would allow institutions to be certified.

As an activity, the application of science has historically been less valued than practicing the science itself. So it is not surprising that the activities of clinical psychologists made many of the university-based psychologists uncomfortable, some of whom felt that psychology was venturing into a field that was more properly the domain of another discipline, namely medicine. The medical community, too, had become uncomfortable with the activities of clinical psychologists. In 1916 the New York Psychiatrical Society appointed a committee to "inquire into the activities of psychologists and more particularly of those who have termed themselves 'clinical psychologists' in relation to the diagnosis and treatment of abnormal conditions."[45] When the committee report was prepared in 1917, it was sent to the leading medical and psychology journals for publication. The report acknowledged the utility of psychological tests in certain applications, largely in education (measuring individual differences) and business (in advertising and sales). Yet it warned of the dangers of the use of these tests in clinical settings, especially where there was not close supervision by medical personnel.

Organized medicine and psychiatry had reason to be concerned about the encroachments of clinical psychology on what they viewed as their domain. By 1917 two states had passed laws permitting judges to commit individuals to mental hospitals based on the expert testimony of clinical psychologists and without corroboration from medical experts. Even among physicians who recognized the value of psychological tests in assessing psychiatric patients, many wanted the actions of the clinical psychologist to stop with the assessment and not include participation in the diagnoses, much less treatments. That is, psychologists could administer and score the tests, but physicians would interpret the data for diagnostic purposes. Psychologists were reminded that whether people were sick in mind or body, the only personnel qualified to treat them were those certified by the state as a qualified medical practitioner. The report concluded:

> We recommend that the [New York Psychiatrical] Society express its
> disapproval of psychologists (or of those who claim to be psychologists as
> a result of their ability to apply any set of psychological tests) undertak-

ing to pass judgment upon the mental conditions of the sick, defective
or otherwise abnormal persons when such findings involve questions of
diagnosis, or affect the future care and career of such persons.[46]

It is no surprise that psychologists responded quickly and loudly to this
attempt by psychiatry to restrict the domain of psychopathology solely
to medical practitioners. In responding, psychologists touted their role
in developing diagnostic instruments and argued that they were the ones
qualified to assess questions of mental functioning and abnormality.[47]

The APA was concerned that the activities of clinical psychologists and
the AACP could lead to a rupture in organized psychology. There were those
in APA who believed they could exert more control over AACP if the organization were part of APA, and there were those in AACP who believed
that their organization might have more authority as part of APA. On the
other hand, some of APA's leaders argued that the APA bylaws made clear
the goals of the association—to advance psychology as a science—and that
professional issues were just not appropriate for APA. Furthermore, some
members of AACP worried that their agenda could be thwarted if they were
part of APA. In 1919, after intense negotiations, AACP agreed to dissolve
as a separate organization and become part of APA as the Section on Clinical Psychology.[48] The section identified three immediate goals: "promoting
better working relationships within clinical and within allied fields, developing professional standards for practitioners, and encouraging research and
publication on topics in clinical psychology."[49] Two years later, after arguing
that the public was being duped by "consulting psychologists" who were not
trained as psychologists, the section convinced APA to begin a certification
program for consulting psychologists. After several years, when only about
25 psychologists had paid the $35 fee to become certified, APA abandoned
the program, thus ending what had been its first formal credentialing effort.[50]

An Outbreak of Psychology: The 1920s[51]

There was a public euphoria in America in the 1920s, the "Roaring Twenties." America had helped win the Great War in Europe, democracy had tri-
umphed, the economy was good in contrast to the turmoil in the European
economies devastated by the war, and after nearly 150 years of existence

the United States finally had granted women the right to vote. Cities were growing, immigrants were coming to America to fill the new jobs in factories, and new technologies were changing the way people lived, presumably for the better. It was a decade of great optimism, at least before the stock market crash in the fall of 1929. Psychology was more popular than ever, and for good reason: the media regularly touted the benefits that could be gained from psychologists. A journalist wrote: "Men and women never needed psychology so much as they need it to-day... You cannot achieve [effectiveness and happiness] in the fullest measure without the new knowledge of your own mind and personality that the psychologists have given us."[52] A dozen or more magazines about psychology joined the ranks of popular magazines in the 1920s. One of the most popular began monthly publication in 1923 and was entitled *Psychology: Health, Happiness, Success*. It promised to translate the new science of psychology for practical use so that people could ensure themselves a lifetime of health, happiness, and success.[53]

Writing for the public in 1925, the founder of behaviorism, John B. Watson (1878–1958) explained why psychology was so critical for child rearing:

> Give me a dozen healthy infants, well-formed, and my own specified world to bring them up in and I'll guarantee to take any one at random and train him to become any type of specialist I might select—doctor, lawyer, artist, merchant-chief and, yes, even beggar-man and thief, regardless of his talents, penchants, tendencies, abilities, vocations, and race of his ancestors.[54]

Surely this was the American dream, to believe that one's children could be raised to great achievements regardless of the supposed limitations of heredity. Watson's radical environmentalism offered the kind of optimism that characterized America in the 1920s. Consequently, public demand grew for psychological services. Businesses wanted the help of psychologists, parents wanted the help of psychologists, and everyone wanted the better life that was promised to them through psychology. Where there is demand, someone will provide the requested services. In the 1920s there was much public demand and few trained psychologists. It was that situation that had prompted the certification effort by the APA Section on Clinical Psychology in the 1920s.

The Roaring Twenties were not without problems, including some that were made more manifest in the overcrowding of the cities and the acculturation and poverty of new waves of immigrants. Juvenile delinquency, which had been a concern before the war, grew more problematic in the 1920s. A national reform movement began in 1921 with the opening of the first child guidance clinic. By 1927, more than 100 clinics had been funded by the Commonwealth Fund, a private foundation engaged in charitable work. By the 1940s there were more than 200 such clinics, many of them funded by the states. The purpose of these clinics was clearly stated by the Commonwealth Fund: the prevention of delinquency. Children with intellectual problems or conduct disorders were to be identified early, and they and their families were to be provided with the means necessary to help them become productive, decent citizens.

The staffs at these clinics typically consisted of a psychiatrist, a clinical psychologist, and several psychiatric social workers. The psychiatrist served as administrator, the psychologist as assessment specialist, and the social workers as case managers. Decisions about a course of action for individual children were made as a team, but it was the social worker who usually carried out all interventions, meeting with the children, the families, and the schools. The Child Guidance Movement, as it is often called, had its greatest impact from its inception in 1921 until the end of World War II. However, its clinics continued to function well into the 1980s and some still operate today. Throughout their history they have been a major employer of clinical psychologists.[55]

Because of the exposure to applied work, including clinical psychology, during World War I, and because of the increased professional opportunities for psychologists in the 1920s, for example, in the child guidance clinics, the ranks of clinical psychology grew considerably. As their numbers grew, professional psychologists had need of a professional organization. By 1930, if not earlier, it was abundantly clear that APA was not going to be that organization.

An Organization for Professional Psychology

During the 1920s, more than a dozen professional psychology groups formed, most of them state psychological associations. They were created to provide a place where professional psychologists could meet to discuss issues of mutual interest, such as standards for training, certification by the state, and a code of professional ethics. The largest of the state associations was the New York State Association of Consulting Psychologists, which was founded in 1921. In 1930, Douglas Fryer (1891–1960), a psychologist at New York University, led a reorganization of the New York association, renamed it the Association for Consulting Psychologists (ACP), and extended its geographical boundaries to include the entire United States. Thus the ACP became the first national association for professional psychologists. In 1933 it published a code of professional ethics, the first such document for psychologists and a standard that many psychologists had long touted as critical if psychology was truly to be a profession. In 1937 ACP founded a journal, the *Journal of Consulting Psychology*, which was arguably the first professional psychology journal. Its title still exists today in a journal published by the APA: the *Journal of Consulting and Clinical Psychology*.

Although ACP tried to recruit members from across the country, it remained largely an organization of New Yorkers. So in 1935 ACP initiated a plan to create a federation of all of the existing professional psychology groups, which would have included the extant state psychological associations and the Clinical Psychology Section of APA. When it became clear that the federation idea was not popular, a wholly new organization was proposed. Thus was born the American Association for Applied Psychology (AAAP), founded in 1937. Both the ACP and the Clinical Psychology Section of APA voted themselves out of existence to become part of the new organization. The ACP's journal became the official organ of the new association. The AAAP began with four sections: clinical, consulting, educational, and industrial psychology. Clinical was the largest of the four with an initial membership of 229. The total membership was approximately 410 in its first year. Fryer, who had been key in the organization of both ACP and AAAP, became the first president of AAAP. He was followed a few years later by other distinguished individuals such as industrial psychologist Walter Van Dyke Bingham (1880–1952) and clinical psychologist Carl Rogers (1902–1987). Within AAAP, each section wrote its own bylaws, elected its own officers, formed its own committees, and planned its own program at the annual meeting of AAAP. Table 2-1 shows the 1938 AAAP program for the Clinical Section. It illustrates a mix of clinical research and practice.

TABLE 2-1. EXCERPT FROM THE 1938 AAAP PROGRAM

SECOND ANNUAL MEETING OF THE AMERICAN ASSOCIATION OF APPLIED PSYCHOLOGISTS

Program of the Meetings
At the Ohio State University, Columbus, Ohio
September 5, 6, 7, 8, 1938
Program of the Clinical Section

September 5

3:00–5:30 **Round Table: The Work and Training of Psychologists in State Hospitals**. Andrew W. Brown, Chairman
Panel: Edgar A, Doll, Elaine F. Kinder, Carney Landis, Emmett L. Schott, David Shakow, Lee E. Travis, Mary P. Wittman

September 6

9:00–10:30 **Symposium: The Work of Psychologists in Institutions and Child Guidance Clinics**. Andrew W. Brown, Chairman
Psychological Work in Prisons. James Q. Holsopple
Psychological Work in Schools for Delinquent Boys and Girls. Augusta T. Jameson
Psychological Work in Institutions for the Feebleminded. Elaine F. Kinder
Psychological Work in Child Guidance Clinics. C. M. Louttit

1:30–3:00 **Business Meeting of the Section of Clinical Psychology**. Andrew W. Brown, Chairman

3:00–4:30 **Symposium: Psychology and Mental Hygiene**. James B. Miner, Chairman
The Mental Health Program in the United States Health Service. L. M. Rogers
Mental Hygiene and Family Adjustment. H. Meltzer
Mental Health Problems in College. Harriet E. O'Shea
Psychological Concepts and Therapy in Mental Hygiene. Saul Rosenzweig

September 7

9:00–11:00 **Research Program on Clinical Psychology**. Edgar A. Doll, Chairman
Some Techniques and Pitfalls of Psychological Tests of Criminals. Lowell S. Selling
Preliminary for a Study of Disciplinary Problems in Prison. L. M. Hanks, Jr.
Some Technological Aspects of Counseling Adult Women. Rose G. Anderson
A Statistical Evaluation of Specified Cues Related to the Moment of Stuttering. Wendell Johnson
Treatment of Enuresis by the Conditioned Reaction Technique. John J. B. Morgan
A Mongolian with Superior Attainment in the Language Arts. William H. Thompson
Illustrative Techniques for Differential Diagnosis and the Measurement of Individual Improvement. Florence Mateer
The Experimental Use of Drugs in Psychopathology, Past and Future. M. M. Parker

Professional psychologists finally had their own organization, one that could be expected to work on behalf of their interests. But it was to be short-lived. When America became involved in World War II, the federal government put pressure on the various psychological organizations to join together in one voice for the national good. The result was a reorganization of APA in 1945, which included a divisional structure borrowed from the sectional structure of AAAP and a promise from the leadership of APA to work on behalf of professional as well as scientific interests.[56] The APA bylaws were revised to reflect the new commitment to professional psychology. Clinical psychology became Division 12 in the new APA.

Between the Wars: The Rise of Clinical Assessment

During World War I, psychologists were involved in two large-scale assessment programs. One, as mentioned earlier, was the measurement of intellectual functioning using the Army Alpha and Army Beta tests, under the direction of Robert M. Yerkes (1876–1956). The second was a program of personnel classification headed by Walter Dill Scott, whose advertising work we mentioned in the previous chapter. Before the war, Scott had developed a "Rating Scale for Selecting Salesmen." He believed that psychologists should be involved beyond just the assessment of intelligence and pressed his case for personnel selection with the US Army, an effort to assess individuals in terms of their suitability for various military jobs. His arguments were successful and he became head of the Committee on the Classification of Personnel in the Army. By the end of the war, his team had generated more than 100 different selection tests for more than 80 jobs and had tested 3.5 million soldiers. Given its short time frame and its massive scope, it was psychology's most impressive and most successful work on behalf of the war effort. For this work Scott was awarded the Distinguished Service Medal in 1919, the highest recognition a civilian can receive in wartime; he was the only psychologist to be so honored in World War I.[57]

Shell Shock Cases

The war also provided psychologists with considerable exposure to psychiatric cases. There were 40 Army hospitals by the end of the war and psychologists were stationed at each one. Army captain and psychologist

Harry Hollingworth was in charge of the psychology service unit at the Army hospital in Plattsburg, New York, a hospital "where soldiers with persistent psychoneurotic symptoms were assembled for further observation and diagnosis, care and treatment."[58] These soldiers were diagnosed with "battle fatigue" or "shell shock," a condition known today as Post-traumatic Stress Disorder (PTSD).[59]

The term *shell shock* first appeared in a medical journal article written by Charles S. Myers (1873–1946) in 1915. Myers, a physician who had founded the first experimental psychology laboratory at Cambridge University in 1912, was assigned to the British medical corps during WWI. He was particularly interested in the psychiatric casualties of the war, men who exhibited symptoms similar to a diagnosis of hysteria. Because he believed the disorder was caused by close proximity to exploding gun shells, he labeled the condition "shell shock," a term he had heard the soldiers use. He recognized it as a genuine psychiatric condition and urged humane treatment for affected soldiers. However, military leadership typically viewed these soldiers as constitutionally weak and as cowards. More than 300 British and commonwealth soldiers were executed during or shortly after WWI, based on charges of cowardice or desertion. Tragically, it is likely that many of those individuals suffered from PTSD.[60] In 2006, the British Parliament issued pardons for all of those executed soldiers.

Military attitudes toward shell-shocked soldiers in WWI in the United States Army mirrored those of their British counterparts. In fact, the US Army had hoped that psychologists could develop psychological tests that would screen these individuals during recruitment, and Robert Woodworth tried unsuccessfully to construct such a test. Like Myers, some psychologists and psychiatrists argued that these cases did not represent "weak" individuals as the Army believed, but that they were ordinary individuals whose mental disorder was the result of exposure to horrific conditions.

In these Army hospitals, psychologists typically administered a test battery to the soldier at the time of admission. It usually included a measure of intellectual functioning, some measure of reasoning and decision making, tests of vocational interests and aptitudes that might serve as a basis for recommendations in occupational therapy, and an assessment of "attitude" or what today might be called morale. Here is how Harry Hollingworth described the role of the clinical psychologists in these hospitals:

> [T]he work of the psychological service in a neuropsychiatric hospital...has been the following: Through the intelligence examination to throw light on the clinical condition, the complete diagnosis, the proper disciplinary measures, the military or civil serviceability, and the most effective and expeditious disposition of patients. Through the further analysis of such data to make at least a suggestive contribution to the study of the factors operative in the production of the psychoneuroses. Through the inventory of the patient's special aptitudes and educational equipment, to place him effectively for maximal therapeutic occupation. In a similar way to afford him aid in vocational adjustment and in the development of purposiveness and aim, in an effort to make of him a more balanced and a better adjusted personality. Through graphic records of the increments of functional capacity under physio- and mechano-therapy, to portray for his own encouragement and for the information of the physician the course of progress. Through intensive individual reeducation to direct and stimulate the patient in his recovery from specific symptoms and disabilities, thereby improving his general morale and his attitude toward the hospital and the service. Finally, through special experimental technique, to demonstrate the degree of rehabilitation and the approach to complete recovery in particular cases, in exact and comparable terms.[61]

We have included this lengthy quotation to show the breadth of contributions by psychologists serving in these Army hospitals. It is clear that the principal work involved psychological testing, whether the attempt was to measure intelligence, vocational aptitude, attitude, or progress achieved in various physical treatment programs.

If there is anything that defines American psychology in the 20th century it would be psychological testing. Functionalism, America's first "school" of psychology, emphasized the study of individual differences in the tradition of Francis Galton. Mental measurement, through the work of Cattell,[62] Goddard, Witmer, Yerkes, Scott, Terman, Harry Hollingworth, and many others, became the sine qua non of American psychology. And for approximately the first 50 years of its existence, it was the means by which most clinical psychologists earned a living. Motivated by their experiences during the war and reinforced by the successes they perceived from their work, clinical psychologists worked to expand and refine their repertoire of assessment instruments. They had begun with measures of intelligence, but by the 1920s were working to add measures of personality—instruments that would measure both normal and abnormal personality. It was this shift toward personality assessment that would lead to even greater conflicts between psychology and psychiatry in the years to come and would move the field of clinical psychology closer toward the provision of psychotherapy.

Early Personality Testing

Likely the first personality test to be used by clinical psychologists was based on the word association technique that Jung had introduced to American psychologists, first through an article he published in Prince's *Journal of Abnormal Psychology* in 1907 and second through the lectures he gave at the Clark Conference in 1909, which were published in the *American Journal of Psychology* in 1910.[63] Grace Kent (1875–1973), a psychologist, and Aaron Rosanoff (1878–1910), a psychiatrist (who apparently contributed very little to the study but was listed because he was her "supervising" physician), used Jung's method to create a test of personality by getting word associations on 100 words from 1,000 normal subjects, and, for comparison, 247 patients in mental hospitals. The frequency tables produced by the associations from the normal subjects resulted in the Kent-Rosanoff Association Test and was used to make clinical judgments of abnormality, in terms of deviation from their word association norms.[64]

Probably the first paper-and-pencil personality test to have clinical use was the Personal Data Sheet (PDS) constructed by Robert S. Woodworth (1869–1962) and published in 1919. Woodworth, who was one of Harry Hollingworth's mentors at Columbia University, created the test at the request of the military as an instrument that would predict which soldiers would be susceptible to shell shock. The test, based on symptoms and situations associated with neuroses, consisted of 116 yes-no items such as "Do you feel that nobody quite understands you?" and "Do you usually sleep well?" It was used by Hollingworth to collect data on soldiers at the Plattsburg Army Hospital. (Today this test would be labeled a measure of neuroticism.) Soon, other paper-and-pencil personality inventories were created, some for research, and some for clinical work.

Projective Personality Testing

In 1921, psychiatrist David Levy (1892–1977) returned from a European trip, bringing with him 10 inkblot cards that had been developed by a Swiss psychiatrist, Hermann Rorschach (1884–1922). The pictures on the cards were symmetrical, ambiguous shapes. Most blots were black and white with some shading differences. A few blots contained color. Subjects were asked to say what they saw in the blots and later to identify where the perceived images appeared in the blots (see Figure 2-8). Thus began the era of projective testing in America (although word association tests would be viewed later as projective as well). As psychoanalysis grew in influence, so too did the idea that personality, especially abnormal personality, could be better measured by tests that tapped the unconscious. The belief was that in the self-report technique of objective personality tests it was easier for the person to hide personality characteristics, whereas the ambiguous nature of the blots elicited responses from the unconscious that were not blocked by the defense mechanisms that would be operating in objective tests. By the 1930s, the Rorschach Test was a key assessment instrument in the arsenal of clinical psychologists, and it grew more popular in the 1940s with the addition of new scoring systems developed by psychologists Samuel Beck (1896–1980) and Bruno Klopfer (1900–1971), who produced methods that allowed extraction of more clinically relevant information. The use of the Rorschach may have changed the image of the clinical psychologist, if not the role. Ernest Hilgard described the change as follows:

> The appeal of the test to clinical psychologists rested in part on a practical advantage it gave them. Before World War II, the practice had developed in child guidance clinics of a weekly staff conference on ongoing cases in which the "team" of workers met together, usually under the chairmanship of a psychiatrist, but including the psychologists (who gave the tests) and the psychiatric social worker (who participated in

the therapy).... The practice gradually extended to adult cases as well. In case review conferences, the psychologist was usually called upon for IQ scores, and perhaps numerical scores on an inventory such as the Bernreuter test [a personality test]; and then was either dismissed or expected to keep quiet. However, if the psychologist was an expert on the Rorschach, which required subtle interpretation, the psychologist had secrets to share and was listened to with some deference because the psychologist now made clinical diagnoses that had been previously disallowed. To be able to talk of free-floating anxiety and colorshock based on the patient's responses commonly caused many heads about the table to nod in assent as others on the staff recognized something that had been seen in the patient. This was worth a great deal to the self-image of the psychologist, even though doubts arose over the accuracy of the test by statistical standards.[65]

The Rorschach Test began to lose its place of prominence in the 1970s as questions of reliability and validity continued to plague the test, as alternative objective methods were developed, and as behavioral techniques in clinical psychology became more prominent. Although no longer dominant in the clinical assessment arena, it remains in frequent use today and is still a part of many clinical psychology training programs.[66]

A second important projective test, the Thematic Apperception Test (TAT) appeared in 1935, developed by Christiana Morgan (1897–1967) and Henry Murray (1893–1988), the director of Harvard's Psychology Clinic. The TAT consisted of a series of somewhat ambiguous pictures, shown to the person one at a time. The person was asked to tell a three-part story of what events had preceded the picture, what was going on in the picture, and what would happen in the future. With the Rorschach and the TAT, projective testing dominated personality testing in clinical psychology in the 1940s, even though objective tests had not disappeared.[67]

The Minnesota Multiphasic Personality Inventory (MMPI)

The status of objective personality tests changed dramatically in the 1940s with the construction of the Minnesota Multiphasic Personality Inventory, better known as the MMPI. It was developed by two faculty members from the University of Minnesota, psychologist Starke Hathaway

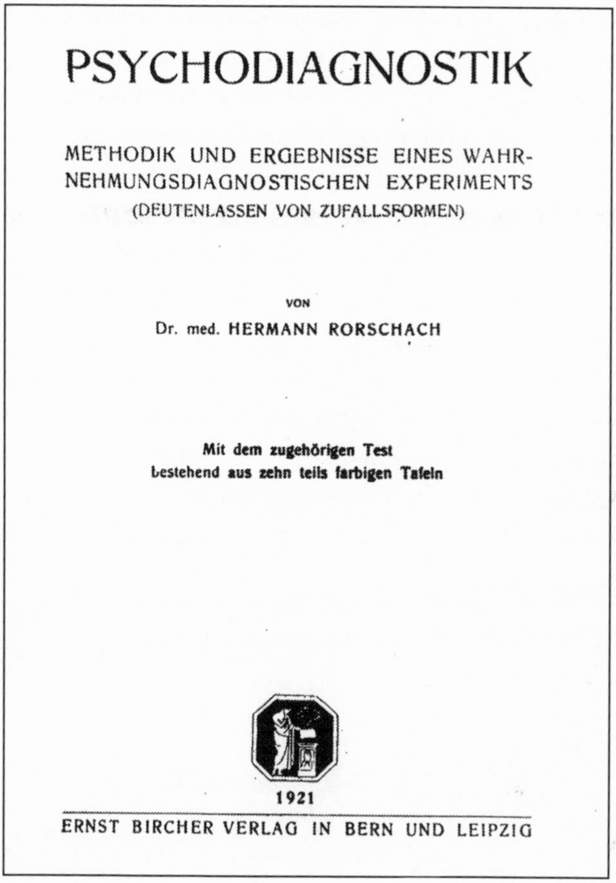

PSYCHODIAGNOSTIK

METHODIK UND ERGEBNISSE EINES WAHR-
NEHMUNGSDIAGNOSTISCHEN EXPERIMENTS
(DEUTENLASSEN VON ZUFALLSFORMEN)

VON
Dr. med. HERMANN RORSCHACH

Mit dem zugehörigen Test
bestehend aus zehn teils farbigen Tafeln

1921

ERNST BIRCHER VERLAG IN BERN UND LEIPZIG

Figure 2-8. *Title page of Hermann Rorschach's 1921 book which described his research with inkblots.*

(1903–1984) and psychiatrist J. Charnley McKinley, with funding from the Works Progress Administration. The paper-and-pencil test was published in 1943 and consisted of 561 items (later reduced to 550), such as "I believe I am being followed" or "I am an important person" or "I like mechanics magazines." Eventually the test was standardized on a group of normal subjects, as well as on psychiatric patients in nine different diagnostic groups, such as depression, hypochondriasis, and schizophrenia. This procedure allowed scales to be constructed that consisted of item-response patterns characteristic of patients in the various categories. Thus the test could be used with clients to identify response patterns in the test that were similar to those in one or more of the psychopathological groups. This test not only became widely used as a diagnostic device in clinical psychology, in which a large number of subscales were developed for more accurate diagnoses, but it also became an important research tool in studies of normal personality. In 1989 the MMPI was revised and updated, creating the MMPI-2.[68]

Since the earliest days of Cattell's anthropometric work, psychologists have looked for behavioral correlates to psychological tests. As that work progressed, psychologists found themselves employed in assessment jobs in schools, businesses, hospitals, and other clinical settings. Psychologists began with intellectual assessment and then added measures of personality assessment, intellectual impairment, interests, aptitudes, and achievements, adapting or creating many of these instruments for clinical work.[69] Psychologists constructed these measuring instruments, used them in research to understand better their potential, and employed them in a great variety of applied settings. Beginning in the assessment business, psychologists eventually played more of a role in diagnosis. But they were still second-class citizens in the mental health field. Roderick Buchanan has described the assessment-oriented field of clinical psychology between the world wars, noting that "Clinical psychologists were largely relegated to subservient roles and remained dependent in the final instance on the benevolence of psychiatrists."[70] For years clinical psychologists had been observers to psychotherapy, something that physicians had made abundantly clear was the exclusive domain of medical practice. That sacred turf was about to be invaded.

World War II and Clinical Psychology

Psychologists had been caught napping when World War I broke out, perhaps because they believed that President Woodrow Wilson would keep his promise that American troops would not enter the war in Europe. So when they found themselves pressed into service quickly in 1917, they were not prepared. That mistake would not be repeated for World War II. Both APA and AAAP had committees in place in 1939 to plan psychology's contributions to the war effort should the United States enter the war. When the time came, more than a thousand psychologists participated in jobs such as recruitment, selection, training, equipment design, propaganda, attitude surveys, interviewing and testing prisoners of war, morale studies, intelligence work, and personality studies, including an analysis of Adolf Hitler that attempted to predict his actions in the final years of the war.[71] The appraisal by the government and the public of psychology's role in the war was a very positive one, and the legacy of that assessment was unprecedented growth in graduate programs in psychology and in scientific and professional opportunities for psychologists. Whereas all of psychology experienced growth after World War II, no group benefited more than clinical psychology (recall Figure 2-1 at the beginning of this chapter).[72]

Early in the war the federal government began making plans to meet the mental health needs of returning military veterans. It was clear that the pool of psychiatrists was far too small to meet the anticipated needs; thus the government went looking elsewhere for acceptable practitioners. In 1942 the federal government mandated that the Veterans Administration (VA) and the United States Public Health Service (USPHS) expand the available pool of mental health professionals. That directive was translated into increasing the availability of clinical psychologists. The VA and USPHS worked with the newly organized APA to develop doctoral programs in clinical psychology and to identify programs of acceptable quality. The former goal led APA to work with university psychology departments to improve the extant clinical psychology training programs and to encourage departments not engaged in clinical training to initiate such programs. The latter goal led to the creation of APA's accreditation program that began accrediting doctoral training programs in clinical psychology in 1946. The USPHS promised funds to psychology departments training clinical psychologists and the VA promised funding for practica and internship training.[73] Because the GI Bill had been altered in the final stages of its debate in Congress to include funds for graduate study, money was also available from that program to support veterans, and, not surprisingly, many veterans were interested in graduate study in clinical psychology. As it turned out, the federal government was accurate in its forecast of a great need for mental health services for veterans. On April 1, 1946, a few months after the end of World War II, 74,000 patients were being cared for by the Veterans Administration. Of that number, 44,000 (nearly 60%!) were classified as neuropsychiatric patients.[74] The need for clinical psychologists was evident and immediate.

Although some universities were offering doctoral programs in clinical psychology and an accreditation process was in place at APA by 1946, there was no agreed-upon curriculum for how clinical psychologists should be trained. In 1918, Leta Hollingworth had written that the training model would be the first step in identifying a profession of clinical psychology, yet here it was, nearly 30 years later and still that question had not been answered. David Shakow (1901–1981) proposed such a curriculum in a report that he prepared for AAAP in 1941. Five years later he was asked by APA to chair a committee to

(a) formulate a recommended program for training in clinical psychology;
(b) formulate standards for institutions giving training in clinical psychology, including both universities and internship and other practice facilities;
(c) study and visit institutions giving instruction in clinical psychology and make a detailed report on each institution.[75]

Shakow and his committee published their report in 1947[76] and two years later it became the framework for the organization and discussion at a conference funded by the newly founded National Institute of Mental Health (NIMH) to reach agreement on a national training model in clinical psychology (see Figure 2-9).

Clinical Psychology and the Scientist-Practitioner Model

Reaching agreement on a model curriculum for clinical psychology was not an easy task. University departments were reluctant to have an external agency (APA, NIMH, or the VA) dictate a curricular model to them. These same departments feared a loss of control over such programs, a situation that they believed could be exacerbated by the fact that NIMH funds would be partially supporting these programs, thus giving NIMH another level of authority in determining what would take place in psychology departments. In addition, many psychology faculty members did not support the development of applied psychology programs, particularly clinical psychology, and believed that any curriculum that emphasized professional issues would by necessity weaken the training in scientific research that was the traditional mainstay of a doctoral education in psychology.

With the Shakow committee report as a starting point, 73 individuals (mostly psychologists, but a few representatives from psychiatry, nursing,

Figure 2-9. *David Shakow was one of the most influential clinical psychologists of the twentieth century and the architect of the Boulder Model.*

and social work as well) were invited to spend two weeks at the University of Colorado in August–September 1949 to try to reach consensus on a model for training clinical psychologists. The agenda was loaded with complex issues. The participants discussed

> the core curriculum; clinical specialties; private practice; master's level psychologists; postdoctoral training; undergraduate student access to clinical courses; standards for agencies beyond the university that offered practicum and internship work; student characteristics for selection; financial aid for clinical students; training in ethics; the relationship of clinical psychology to other fields such as medicine, social work, and vocational guidance; licensing and certification; accreditation of programs; federal government involvement with clinical training; training of clinical faculty; placement of the internship (predoctoral or postdoctoral,

in the university or outside of it); society's needs for clinical services; training in psychotherapy and other skills; and training for research.[77]

It is almost impossible to imagine that the participants, who represented so many different viewpoints, could reach any kind of consensus on such diverse and complex issues in a two-week period. But that is exactly what they did. They agreed to approximately 70 resolutions that created a model of professional training that they called the "scientist-practitioner" model.[78] Today it is known by that name but also referred to as the "Boulder model." It designated core skills that the professional psychologist should have that were beyond the typical training of doctoral students in psychology. It required practicum training, ideally in multiple sites, that would prepare the student for a required one-year internship in an appropriate setting. And the student had to be trained as a researcher as well; preparation of a research dissertation was part of the program, as the program developers believed that the profession of psychology should be based on an understanding and use of its science. The agreement on the model represented a monumental achievement in terms of debate, compromise, and trust. It is still the dominant training model today in clinical psychology programs as well as other professional specialties, although since its inception in 1949, psychologists have debated exactly what was meant by the model and how appropriate it is, given the changes in psychology, medicine, and the world over the past 50 years.[79]

Psychologists and Psychotherapy

In the military, it is said that rank has its privileges. One pays attention to chain of command and pecking order. Psychiatrists and clinical psychologists had been at odds since the turn of the 20th century when psychiatry perceived psychology as overstepping its authority in venturing into the psychiatric domain of mental health. Shots had been fired from both camps. Psychiatrists sought to limit psychologists solely to testing and ensuring that the testing was viewed as assessment and not diagnosis, the latter being reserved for psychiatry. Psychologists had developed their tests and believed they were the best qualified individuals to interpret their meaning. They also believed that their science gave them insights about treatment programs that would be more or less successful with certain kinds of patients; thus they were not content to serve merely as psychometricians. When the military joined psychiatrists and psychologists in what were called psychiatric teams during World War II, it was inevitable that professional jealousies would arise. Yet war is a crisis situation and it often brings out the best in people as they work together to solve problems that have human importance and urgency.

In 1944–1945, psychologist William A. Hunt (1903–1986) was in charge of the clinical psychology program in the US Navy. Hunt described clinical psychology in the WWII military as follows:

> We learned by doing. The job was bigger than we were and we needed all the help we could get, from whatever professional or personal sources were available. Professional distinctions and professional politics were confined largely to the Washington level. In the field they faded before the immensity of the task. I remember one psychiatric chief of service who wrote me in the Bureau of Medicine and Surgery and asked that I send him two psychologists "to do psychotherapy." "If you send psychiatrists," he said, "they'll be caught up in all sorts of extra medical administrative duties, but you psychologists as non-medical people are free of these, and can work with patients."[80]

During the war, more than 400 clinical psychologists served in the military's neuropsychiatric services. The majority of them were engaged, at least part of the time, in delivering psychotherapy. And most of them received their psychotherapy training on the job. It was a watershed event for the profession. The psychologists had seen Paris; they were not going back to the assessment farm.[81]

Clinical psychologists had been around psychotherapy in a variety of settings, such as state hospitals and child guidance clinics, and they had been using psychotherapy in university counseling centers since the 1920s. A few psychologists, trained as psychoanalysts, had even developed private practices as psychotherapists as early as the 1920s.[82] But the door was largely opened by the military, which allowed psychologists to be put to the test as psychotherapists. Once opened, psychiatry found it impossible to close.

We have mentioned the role of the VA in encouraging the APA to develop an accreditation system for clinical psychology and in encouraging psychology departments to develop clinical training programs. The training funds offered by the USPHS and the VA meant that doctoral students could get considerable financial support for their clinical education. The VA also became the major employer of clinical psychologists, so many new psychologists went directly from their internships into jobs with the VA. The VA used psychologists in assessment roles, but also expected them to serve as psychotherapists. Consequently, courses in psychotherapy became commonplace in clinical training programs and clinical students were expected to have completed them before beginning their practicum training at the VA, usually in their third year of graduate study.

When these VA psychology training programs were being established, the chief psychologist at the VA Central Office in Washington, DC was James G. Miller (1916–2002) who had earned an MD degree as well as a PhD in psychology. He established parity for psychologists and psychiatrists in the VA with regard to government service rating and thus salary (although later changes would provide greater salaries for psychiatrists). Such equality was important for psychologists, but ultimately what mattered was whether they could provide quality services to VA patients. That would determine the level of respect they were shown.

Models of Psychotherapy

In the 1940s, psychiatrists were still in charge in the state hospitals and were owners of the somatic treatments popular during that time. There was insulin coma therapy (also called insulin shock therapy) used primarily to treat schizophrenic patients. There was electroshock therapy, used for many kinds of psychiatric patients but especially those suffering from depression. And if the insulin did not work on the schizophrenic patients, then one could try prefrontal lobotomy, a procedure that destroyed a portion of the frontal lobes of the brain, for which its inventor, Egas Moniz (1874–1955), won the Nobel Prize in Medicine and Physiology in 1949. The procedure was discontinued in the 1960s as evidence mounted about the serious brain damage done by many lobotomies and because of the effectiveness of new antipsychotic drugs, such as Thorazine (chlorpromazine).[83] Of course such techniques were not available to clinical psychologists.

Among the extant psychotherapy models there was classical psychoanalysis, as had been practiced by Freud, in which the patient was often
seen daily, or a modification of it, psychoanalytic psychotherapy, in which
the patient might be seen once or twice a week. In fact, Freudian psychoanalysis enjoyed little popularity as a therapeutic tool for clinical psychologists. There were, however, other derivations of psychoanalysis including,
but not limited to, the analytic psychology of Carl Jung or the individual
psychology of Alfred Adler (1870–1937), part of the group of neo-Freud-
ians whose ideas had greater impact on American clinical psychology.
These individuals redefined the ego, removing it from its service to the
id and endowing it with a broader role in determining behavior and personality. They shifted the focus from the intrapsychic conflict that Freud
emphasized to interpersonal conflicts focusing on both environmental and
interpersonal factors, and from psychosexual emphases to a focus on psychosocial processes. Group therapy approaches, pioneered by psychiatrist
Jacob L. Moreno (1892–1974) and developed further during the war, were
also used. In 1942, Carl Rogers (1902–1987) published a book describing
what was initially called nondirective therapy, later called client-centered
therapy, and finally person-centered therapy. Rogers's therapeutic approach
dominated the university counseling centers and indeed was crucial in the
modern development of counseling psychology (see chapter 5). For clinical psychologists, however, psychodynamic theories dominated clinical
practice in the 1940s and 1950s, even if psychoanalysis as a therapeutic
method did not. Psychologists were, in general, eclectic in their approach,
albeit directed toward helping the patient resolve interpersonal and intrapsychic conflicts.

Psychotherapy had been mired in controversy since its origins. In the
middle of the 20th century, experimental psychologists were often critical
of what seemed like a mystical if not magical process. Clinical psychology
was supposed to be a profession based on science and that meant using
therapeutic techniques that could scientifically be shown to be effective.
But psychotherapy research was difficult to do. Treatment components
were not well defined, there was great variability across therapists, patients
could not be categorized neatly for design purposes, appropriate control
conditions were difficult to arrange, no-treatment control groups seemed

clearly unethical, and it was difficult to reach agreement on outcome measures (measures of recovery). But clinical psychologists and psychiatrists defended the quality of their practices, acknowledging that success in therapy stemmed largely from the relationship of the therapist and patient, a relationship that was admittedly difficult to assess.

In 1952, psychologist Hans Eysenck (1916–1997) published an article that was exceptionally critical of psychotherapy. In a review of the extant outcome research, he argued that there was little scientific support for its effectiveness.[84] Although his criticism had little, if any, immediate effect on the practice of psychotherapy, it rang the bell in the first round of a fight between the behaviorists who dominated academic psychology and the more insight-oriented practicing clinical psychologists.

Behavioral Therapies

At the end of the 1950s and through the 1960s a new form of psychological therapy emerged that would have considerable impact on clinical practice: behavior therapy or behavior modification. Academic psychologists were generally supportive of these therapies because they viewed them as grounded in the animal studies of psychology's learning laboratories and thus part of American psychology's long love affair with behaviorism. It was a textbook example of the belief that experimental psychology would make the discoveries and that clinical psychologists would then put them into practice. Two individuals were especially influential in this movement: Joseph Wolpe (1915–1997) and B. F. Skinner (1904–1990).

Wolpe published his therapeutic methods in 1958, drawing on the work of Russian physiologist, Ivan Pavlov (1849–1936), or what would be called classical conditioning.[85] Among Wolpe's most popular methods was systematic desensitization, a technique that paired incompatible states such as fear and relaxation. This method proved to be especially effective in treating phobias and other anxiety disorders. The method typically had the patient combine muscle relaxation with imaging of situations that would normally induce fear. If the relaxation was kept at a stronger level than the fear generated by the imagery, then with repeated pairings, the fear would be desensitized. [This technique was anticipated in the work of Mary Cover Jones (1896–1987) in a study she published in 1924 in which she deconditioned a fear in a young boy. Because of this pioneering work, she has been referred to as the "mother of behavior therapy."][86]

Skinner's work in operant learning had begun in the 1930s, but its use in clinical settings emerged in the 1950s and was quite prominent in the 1960s. It was incorporated by clinical psychologists in state hospitals, in private clinics, in prisons, in programs for children with intellectual disability, in sheltered workshops for adults with intellectual disability, and in private practice. It included programs in aversive conditioning (using punishment to suppress behaviors that did not appear amenable to extinction methods), token economies, and especially treatment programs based on shaping desired behaviors through positive reinforcement procedures.[87]

Part of the appeal of behavior therapy techniques was that they moved clinical psychology away from the medical model of which it had always been a part, a disease model that assumed that symptoms were indicative of underlying causes that had to be treated if the problem was to be eliminated (cause-symptoms-treatment). Many behavior therapists, on the other hand, did not search for causes. Instead they treated the symptoms as behaviors to be eliminated, using therapeutic techniques that were designed to suppress or extinguish undesirable behaviors. Thus a clinical psychologist as behavior therapist might say, "I don't care why you are afraid of the dark. I don't need to know the cause and might spend years in therapy with you trying to find it. Instead I can treat this fear and make it go away." Psychiatrists and clinical psychologists who were psychodynamically inclined argued that if a therapist treated only the symptoms and failed to deal with the cause, then other symptoms would appear, an occurrence known as symptom substitution. Yet the research indicated that symptom substitution was a very rare occurrence. Behavior therapy proved effective for the treatment of some disorders, wholly inapplicable to many others, and naïve in its narrow conceptualization of psychopathology, based as it was on the restrictions of behaviorism. It did serve to remind the profession of its grounding in the science of psychology, and it paved the way for better outcome studies, leading eventually to the contemporary work labeled "best practices" and "empirically supported treatments." It also led to cognitive therapies in the 1960s and beyond, as psychologists focused more on how inner experience, a taboo topic for the behaviorists, affected behavior.

Cognitive Therapies

Psychology's cognitive revolution in the 1960s, sparked by the development of the computer as machine and as metaphor for the mind, brought back topics of thinking, language, memory, consciousness, and emotion, topics that had been banished or at least ignored in the heyday of behaviorism. This was a critical factor in the rise of cognitive therapies; it provided the experimental grounding that would support cognitive approaches. Perhaps of greater importance, though, was the realization among clinical psychologists that there was more to psychological problems than problem behavior. How the clients perceived their world, how they learned, how they experienced emotion, and how they thought about themselves were often not addressed in behavior therapies. New cognitive therapies, the revamping of some older insight-oriented approaches, and some new humanistic therapies would dominate psychotherapy in the 1970s.

Albert Ellis's (1913–2007) rational-emotive therapy, one of the earliest of the cognitive therapies,[88] stated that psychological problems were often the result of irrational beliefs that people held. The goal of therapy was thus to restructure the patient's thought patterns to eliminate those irrational thoughts. Another of the cognitive approaches was Aaron Beck's (b. 1921) cognitive therapy, which also worked to restructure the way patients think.[89] Beck's therapy grew out of his work in depression in which he saw much evidence of patients with unrealistic thoughts. In his technique, patient and therapist worked together to identify the problematic thought patterns and to gather evidence of their unrealistic nature.[90] Other cognitive therapies have emerged, some labeled cognitive-behavior therapies. Initial therapies were concerned primarily with depression, but more recent successes have dealt with anxiety disorders, eating disorders, and panic disorder.

Humanistic Therapies

The humanistic therapies, which encouraged self-exploration and self-determination, emerged in America in the 1960s, a decade of drugs, sexual exploration, and self-discovery. Humanistic psychology is sometimes called "third force psychology," contrasting it with the philosophies of behaviorism and psychoanalysis. The label is an overstatement, because humanistic psychology never became a force in American psychology to compare with the other two. The movement is most often associated with the ideas of Abraham Maslow (1908–1970) and Carl Rogers. These psychologists emphasized the goodness of people and the potential for human growth that presumably is part of the life goals of everyone. They spoke about individuals striving for self-actualization or self-realization. Maslow objected to the determinism of psychoanalysis (behavior is determined by unconscious intrapsychic conflicts) and behaviorism (behavior is dictated by a life history of reinforcements and punishments), arguing instead that individuals had considerable control over their lives. The goal of humanistic therapy was to help them discover their potential and to be able to pursue life as they wished. Further, Maslow and Rogers wanted individuals to have more control over the therapy process (thus the nondirective approach of Rogers).[91] Although humanistic therapies have declined considerably since the 1980s, Rogers's influence on psychotherapy is still seen in clinical and counseling psychology today. We say more about the evolution of psychotherapy and clinical psychology, in terms of such subjects as managed care, prescription privileges, brief therapies, empirically supported treatments, and additional professional specialties, in chapter 6.

Further Evidence of a Profession

The markers of a profession include such things as certification and licensure, a code of ethics for standards of practice, journals for communication of professional issues, national organizations, and standardized training programs (often in professional schools). We have already mentioned all of these with regard to clinical psychology. The Boulder Conference of 1949 described a training model for professional psychologists, both ACP and AAAP served as national associations for applied psychologists (which APA agreed to do as well after the merger of APA and AAAP in 1945), the *Journal of Consulting Psychology* was founded in 1937, APA mounted a certification program for consulting psychologists in 1921 (although it failed), and ACP published a code of ethics in 1933. Although these were important events, they were often temporary measures, or at least measures in need of revision as the profession of psychology developed.

Licensure for Professional Psychologists

Certification is a process by which a title is protected, such as the title "psychologist." Licensure is more encompassing because in addition to the title, licensing defines a list of practices that make up a particular occupation. In 1945, Connecticut was the first state to certify psychologists, and the following year Virginia passed the first psychology licensing law, thus defining the nature of psychological practice and restricting those activities to qualified psychologists who would obtain licensure in Virginia. Licensure was exceptionally important for psychologists, not just to prevent nonpsychologists from practicing psychology, as they had always been able to do, but to have the state government acknowledge officially that "psychology is a profession." Psychologists worked for decades, principally through their state psychological associations, on obtaining licensure laws across the country. The APA also helped in those efforts. Eventually all 50 states passed licensure laws, the last being Missouri (the "show me" state) in 1977. Tied to the licensing laws were state examination boards, established to review the credentials of candidates and to determine their worthiness for licensure. Many of the psychology licensing laws are quite similar and all call for passage of an exam intended to measure competency in psychology and its applied areas.[92]

Licensing laws and state examination boards were established to ensure some minimal competence. Professional psychologists wanted something more, along the lines of the board-certified diplomas that the field of medicine awarded to practitioners who had demonstrated exceptional competence. In 1947 the American Board of Examiners in Professional Psychology (ABEPP originally, now just ABPP) was established to examine the credentials of professional psychologists who had demonstrated advanced competency. Today, ABPP diplomas are given in 12 areas, including clinical psychology, clinical neuropsychology, family psychology, health psychology, psychoanalysis, school psychology, counseling psychology, and forensic psychology.

Professional Ethics

Psychologists are expected to abide by a code of ethics. The APA published its initial ethics code in 1953 and has revised it several times since, most recently in 2002, with amendments on human rights added in 2010. It is entitled *Ethical Principles of Psychologists and Code of Conduct* and contains sections on such topics as evaluation and assessment, advertising, privacy and confidentiality, and therapy. Under therapy it deals with structuring the relationship, informed consent, sexual intimacies with current and former patients, and terminating the professional relationship. APA also established an Ethics Office and a Committee on Ethics whose job it is to monitor complaints that the APA may receive about members who are accused of violating APA's ethical principles.

Professional Journals

As noted earlier, the *Journal of Consulting Psychology* is still published today as the *Journal of Consulting and Clinical Psychology*. But what began as a professional journal evolved into a research journal. When the APA reorganized in 1945, the agreement with AAAP called for the establishment of a new publication that would be a professional journal. The *American Psychologist* began publication in January 1946 and its masthead carried the subtitle "The Professional Journal of the American Psychological Association." But it was never really a professional journal and in 1957 the word "professional" disappeared from the subtitle.[93] In 1969, APA and its Division on Clinical Psychology (Division 12) began publication of a new journal, *Professional Psychology*. Published today as *Professional Psychology: Research and Practice*, it continues to function as a journal attuned to professional issues.

Professional Psychologists and the APA

The APA began as an organization dedicated to one goal, the advancement of science. In 1945 the bylaws were changed to read, "The object of the American Psychological Association shall be to advance psychology as a science, as a profession, and as a means of promoting human welfare."[94] Certainly from its founding in 1892 to its reorganization in 1945, APA showed little understanding of or interest in professional issues. Even after the reorganization in 1945 when APA's leadership made promises to promote the interests of professional psychologists, this did not happen not, that is, until the profession grew so much that the professional psychologists outnumbered the academic/research psychologists, probably some time in the early 1970s. Today APA is clearly an organization dedicated mainly to those psychologists engaged in professional practice. In the late 1980s a large number of academic/research psychologists called on APA to devise a governance structure that would give them more of a political voice in APA, a voice they had lost because of their smaller percentage of membership. APA made no such changes and so the dissenters left APA to form a rival organization in 1988, the American Psychological Society (APS), now the Association for Psychological Science. Although there are many smaller specialty professional psychology associations in existence today, including all of the state psychological associations, the APA, with a current membership of approximately 134,000,[95] remains the largest and most effective voice for issues involving the practice of clinical psychology and other professional specialties. The APA also includes many divisions today that are related to clinical psychology, in addition to Division 12; examples are 29—Psychotherapy, 38—Health Psychology, 39—Psychoanalysis, 40—Clinical Neuropsychology, 42—Psychologists in Independent Practice, 43—Family Psychology, 49—Group Psychology and Group Psychotherapy, 53—Clinical Child Psychology, and 54—Society of Pediatric Psychology.

Professional Schools of Psychology

The standards for professional education and training in psychology are part of the criteria for the accreditation of doctoral programs, as established by the Council of Representatives of the APA and maintained through its Committee on Accreditation and Office of Program Consultation and Accreditation. The APA's accreditation program accredits doctoral programs in three professional specialty areas only: clinical, counseling, and school psychology. These criteria are revised periodically, most recently in 2006.[96]

Over the years the models for professional training have been debated. Consequently, different kinds of training programs began to appear. Decades of position papers, conferences, and meetings made it clear that training psychologists as practitioners was needed and desired but would require substantial momentum to overcome the dominance of the scientist-practitioner model laid out in 1949. Closely on the heels of Boulder, professional psychologists were pushing the system and organizing efforts for change. Under the direction of Gordon Derner, Adelphi University achieved APA accreditation in 1957 for a clinical psychology program that focused on the development of practitioners. Further advancing the cause the clinical psychology program at the University of Illinois offered a new degree, the doctor of psychology (PsyD) in 1968.[97]

The first freestanding professional school of psychology, one not associated with a university and dedicated to the training of psychological practitioners, was the California School of Professional Psychology, which opened two campuses in San Francisco and Los Angeles in 1970. The school was founded principally through the efforts of Nicholas A. Cummings (b. 1924), a graduate of the Adelphi program. The California school was established because at the time only two universities in California trained clinical psychologists and together graduated fewer than 20 students each year. In order to facilitate the growth of these schools and to enhance the quality of professional training, Cummings also founded the National Council of Schools of Professional Psychology (NCSPP) in 1976.[98] The NCSPP continues to provide leadership and direction for the development of professional psychology programs.[99]

A national conference on clinical training at Vail, Colorado, in 1973 codified the movement to train professional psychologists more fully in professional issues and skills, with a minimum focus on research training.[100] The conference endorsed the degree of Doctor of Psychology (PsyD); a degree that had been in place at the University of Illinois since 1968 and a proposal that Leta Hollingworth had made in 1918 (see Figure 2-10)!

PsyD programs have grown in number since the Vail Conference. In 2012, APA accredited 235 programs in clinical psychology. Of that number, 62 offered the PsyD degree.[101] Furthermore, the number of doctorates awarded by professional schools has grown substantially, PsyDs in clinical psychology increased over 300% during the 20 year period from 1987–2007. In 2007 professional schools accounted for a greater proportion of clinical doctorates (PsyD and PhD) than was the case in 1987 (55% vs. 37%, respectively).[102]

All of this information points to the immense growth of professional psychology, but especially of clinical psychology in the past 40 years.

Figure 2-10. *Leta Stetter Hollingworth (1886–1939) was an important figure in studies of gender differences, in developing programs for gifted children, and in the development of clinical psychology as a profession.*

Clinical Psychology in the 1960s

James Capshew wrote, "The notion that Americans lived in a 'psychological society' took hold rapidly in the 1950s and had become commonplace by the 1960s."[103] The 1960s were a time of great social turmoil in America. There were riots in cities related mostly to issues of civil rights. There was an unpopular war in Vietnam that greatly divided Americans and brought violence to college campuses. A US president, John F. Kennedy, was assassinated, as was his younger brother, Robert Kennedy, while campaigning for the same office. The leader of the civil rights movement, Martin Luther King, Jr., who strongly advocated nonviolence as a force for social change, was murdered. Sex, drugs, and rock and roll divided generations who seemed unable to communicate with each other. In the midst of all this tragedy there was a sense of hope that all could be better, that racism, poverty, and war could be ended. It was a decade focused largely on social issues; thus it is no surprise that psychology would be a subject of considerable interest during this time. The success of a new popular magazine begun in 1967, *Psychology Today*, was indicative of the public's enhanced interest in social and behavioral issues.

Community Mental Health Centers

Professional opportunities in psychology, stimulated by the continued impact of post-World War II growth and by the national mental health acts of 1963 and 1964, continued to increase at dramatic rates. The mental health acts of the 1960s were designed to end large mental asylums and to serve psychological patients as outpatients in community mental health centers (CMHCs); these centers were to be spread across the nation, located in any community with a population of 30,000 or greater. The belief was that many of the state hospital patients would be released to families who would assume primary care for them and that the CMHCs would be there to deal with any crisis or acute needs, to provide outpatient psychotherapy, to help in the management of medications, and to arrange for hospitalization when necessary. The intentions were good; the logic was horribly flawed. Eventually more than 700 federally funded CMHCs were built, virtually all of which employed clinical psychologists as psychotherapists on a part-time if not full-time basis. For many communities in America, the CMHCs provided the first mental health services those communities had ever seen. Still, the number of centers was far short of what was needed to meet the goals of the program. These centers were often understaffed and generally underfunded, and in the 1980s they lost their federal funds, thus further reducing their services. Many of the patients from the state hospitals who were to be served by the centers never showed up, and when they did, many of them did not return. The belief in family care turned out to be a gross miscalculation; more than 60% of the released state hospital mental patients had no family members to care for them. In the 1970s and 1980s many of these former mental patients swelled the ranks of America's homeless.

Independent Practice

Despite continued opposition from psychiatry, 26 additional states began licensing psychologists in the 1960s, making the total 41 by the end of the decade. For the first time, states passed "freedom of choice" laws requiring health care insurance providers to allow policyholders to choose among several mental health practitioners, including licensed psychologists. That meant that a person could seek the services of a clinical psychologist directly, and that the psychologist could be reimbursed directly by the insurance company without having a referral from a psychiatrist, as had been the case in the past.

We mentioned earlier that a few clinical psychologists had begun private practices in the 1920s, principally as psychoanalysts, often with master's degrees. Albert Ellis, who began a psychoanalytic private practice in 1943 with a master's degree in clinical psychology, was typical of these early independent practitioners.[104] Their numbers increased somewhat after World War II, but continued to be a very small part of clinical practice in psychology, first because of the plentiful opportunities in the VA and child guidance clinics, and later because of expanded openings in CMHCs. By the end of the 1960s though, bolstered by licensing laws and freedom of choice laws, there was a noticeable trend for clinical psychologists to hang up their own shingles. Psychodynamic approaches no longer dominated the psychotherapy in these practices.

In 1969 a private practitioner, Robert M. Hughes (b. 1913), helped to organize Psychologists in Private Practice, which published a newsletter entitled *The Private Practitioner*. In 1974 the name of the organization was changed to the American Society of Psychologists in Private Practice (ASPPP). The reach of ASPPP was not national and the small organization, around 600 members in the late 1970s, had trouble growing, even though there was ample evidence that the number of psychologists in private practice was increasing. Furthermore, members recognized that as an independent organization of independent practitioners they had little political clout to address the issues that were important to them. Consequently, in 1977 they explored the possibility of becoming a division of the APA. A petition by ASPPP was rejected by APA in 1980 but approved the following year. On January 1, 1982, ASPPP dissolved and became Division 42 of the APA, Psychologists in Independent Practice, with an initial membership of 650. Two years later the Division 42 membership numbered more than 5,000. By 1995 it had topped 10,000 members.[105] It remains the largest of the APA divisions today, yet its numbers have dropped considerably as has the membership of most APA divisions. This does not reflect a reduction in the number of independent practitioners; those numbers continued to rise as the demands for psychotherapy increased. It is estimated that by 1990 at least a third of the American population had used psychotherapy. And as the social stigma associated with psychological and psychiatric care diminishes, and as people have firsthand experiences that demonstrate the benefits of mental health care, the percentage of individuals partaking of such services will continue to grow.[106] Although the restrictions of managed care[107] have reduced the ranks of independent practitioners most recently, an issue we discuss in chapter 6, the majority of clinical psychologists in America today still earn their living in private practice.

Conclusion

In this chapter we have provided a brief and selective history of clinical psychology in America, the largest of psychology's professional specialties, from the beginnings of the psychiatric profession in mental asylums to the explosive growth in private practice. It has been impossible to tell this story without also describing the development of the profession overall, that is, developments that included practitioners in school psychology, industrial/organizational psychology, and counseling psychology, the subjects of our next three chapters. Clinical psychology continues to evolve as a profession, affected by changing American demographics, discussions about training models, debates over treatment effectiveness, changes in health insurance practices, and changes in federal and state laws regarding practice. We continue this story in terms of more recent developments in the final chapter of this book.

Chapter 3
School Psychology

A unique and defining characteristic of school psychology is its focus on children. The interaction, synthesis, and application of psychological and educational principles and practices in service to children at all levels of functioning has been a constant in the development of school psychology from its origins in the late 19th century to the present day.

Many associated with the new applied psychology of the early 20th century found a calling in psychological work with youth, often in connection with public and special schools. Many of the psychologists introduced in the previous chapter were involved in some aspect of the assessment and treatment of children. As we will see, much of the pioneering work and many of the pioneers who provided the historical background for school psychology also served the historical record of allied areas such as special education, child development, clinical psychology, and educational psychology. Surprisingly, even though it shares a history as old as other areas of applied psychology, an independent identity for school psychology as a profession would not be achieved until the 1970s. In this chapter we will review the development of school psychology from its diverse beginnings in psychology and education through its sanctioning as a profession.

Education and Democracy

The beginning of the 20th century in America was marked by high hopes and wishful optimism. It made no difference if one was a citizen of the Midwest or an immigrant from overseas, the wish was the same; a better life. America offered that possibility. The allure of freedom, particularly the freedom to pursue a better life, inspired in many a democratic ideal of what America could become. The industrial revolution made much of the dream possible. A growing population, one that was increasingly urban and foreign born, matched America's dramatic increases in goods and services. Immigration and migration brought a variety of cultures, languages, and customs to cities like New York, Philadelphia, and Chicago, making them worlds unto themselves. Diversity was omnipresent, simultaneously stimulating and staggering.

Against the backdrop of a rapidly changing social order, the public school emerged as the social institution most likely to achieve unity within the diversity that was America. Philosophically this was captured in the thought of John Dewey (1859–1952) whose 1916 book *Democracy and Education: An Introduction to the Philosophy of Education*[1] expressed the belief that school was a place for children to learn the necessary skills to take their place in a democratic society. This could be accomplished by developing skills of complex reasoning, problem solving, and critical thinking. He emphasized learning by doing, encouraging teachers to allow students to pursue their own interests and direct their own efforts. As a result Dewey became closely associated with the progressive education movement in America.[2]

Progressive education was part of a larger focus on youth and children that emerged in the late 19th century. Children, as the salvation of the race, is an old theme and one that was particularly relevant to the new American society. The caldron of change stirred by industrialization and immigration caused an unease and discomfort that many believed (and hoped) would be allayed by time. Perhaps the next generation would inherit a better world, one that was more comfortable, familiar, and routine. The hope invested in youth brought with it a corresponding expectation that education offered the promise of true democracy. The child of the banker could learn alongside the child of the laborer, shoulder-to-shoulder on a level playing field with all inculcated into the ideals of American culture and democratic living. As a philosophy or point of view there was not much to argue with, however, the reality was altogether different. Urban schools were desperately overcrowded. More often than not, English was not the primary language of the students. Health problems were rampant.

Students frequently left school by the 6th grade to work in factories. Rural schools too had problems. Finding teachers was difficult and the one room schoolhouse had to accommodate all children, regardless of age or ability. Schools for African American, Native American, and Hispanic American children, rural or urban, were most often segregated and inferior. It appeared to many that children were at risk both physically and spiritually, a situation exacerbated by the large impersonal and increasingly machine-dominated city. In this atmosphere, aid societies for children flourished, as did laws governing child labor and compulsory schooling. Together these efforts formed part of the movement known as child saving.[3]

Child Development and the Legacy of G. Stanley Hall

The interest in children evident during the child saving movement was also evident in the emergent applied psychology of the times. Evolutionary theory had suggested the notion of development over time, a concept that very much interested psychologist G. Stanley Hall (1844–1924) (See Figure 3-1). A complex man, Hall did much to advance applied psychology in America.[4] According to Sheldon White:

> Because Hall was active and influential at just the right time, he compiled many firsts and foundings—as Wundt's first American student, first American professor of psychology, founder of what some say was the first American psychology laboratory, founder of the *American Journal of Psychology*, first president of Clark University, founder and first president of the American Psychological Association, leader of the child study movement, founder of the [journal] *Pedagogical Seminary*, and so on. Hall invited Freud to Clark University in 1909 and thus helped psychoanalysis get international recognition.[5]

Hall actively studied the development of children, relying heavily on the questionnaire method. He gathered data from parents, teachers, and children across America, aided in his efforts by a close association with parent and teacher organizations. In 1904 he published detailed accounts of his researches in a massive two-volume tome titled, *Adolescence: Its Psychology and Its Relation to Physiology, Anthropology, Sociology, Sex, Crime, Religion and Education.*[6]

Figure 3-1. *G. Stanley Hall.*

An early primer on child development, the book contained Hall's recapitulation theory. A variant of Haeckel's biological maxim, ontology reca-
pitulates phylogeny, Hall's theory asserted that during their development
children repeat the history of the race. It was a theory that drove many
of Hall's ideas about development and by extension his views on topics
such as parenting and education. It was also a theory filled with biological determinism, a position that brought Hall to regard some races as less
developed than others. He made frequent reference to the deficiencies
of African Americans, calling them an adolescent race and writing that:

> Religious excitement is often ascribed as one cause of insanity, and while
> this is sometimes true of the negroes, the relation of cause and effect is
> often just the reverse if this. His disease expresses itself often through his
> highly emotional, religious nature. Perhaps history presents no parallel
> to the sudden creation of a nation in a day by the proclamation of eman-
> cipation, but the fact of mental inferiority according to the established
> standards of measuring culture and civilization is unquestionable.[7]

Likewise, Hall viewed male and female development through the lens of evolutionary and recapitulation theory. He argued against coeducation, believing that females were best suited to reproductive and maternal roles. Given Hall's view on race and gender, it is ironic to consider that he graduated the first African American PhD in psychology (Frances Cecil Sumner, 1895–1954) in America, as well as a substantial number of women PhDs.[8]

Recapitulation theory was generally assailed and the child study movement ended early in the 20th century. Hall had nonetheless popularized and promoted child development. He advanced normative child development, urging teachers and parents to consider developmental and contextual factors in the education and rearing of children. As historian Henry Minton noted:

> He was an ardent evolutionist who believed that heredity was a more significant determining factor than environment. By 1903 he was acknowledged as a leader of the child-centered philosophy of education, a point of view that emphasized the need for schools to adjust their curriculum to the needs and inherent nature of children. According to Hall, the traditional nineteenth century emphasis on academic subjects with regimented drill was inappropriate. Instead, he championed industrial training, moral education, physical training, and health. He also favored individualized instruction and believed that gifted children, who he assumed came primarily from the middle class, should be singled out for academic training by the time they reached adolescence.[9]

Many of Hall's academic offspring made substantial contributions to the emergence of school psychology, including Henry Goddard (1866–1957), Lewis Terman (1877–1956), and Arnold Gesell (1880–1961). Most would adopt Hall's biological determinism, especially as it related to the inheritance of intelligence. This was especially true of Goddard and Terman who almost single-handedly introduced intelligence testing into American culture and society.

Estimating IQs

Goddard, who received his PhD under Hall in 1899, became interested in intelligence testing in 1906 when he was appointed the director of

FEEBLE — MINDED CLUB MAY 27, 1916

Figure 3-2. *Henry Goddard (first row, extreme right) seated with the Feeble-Minded Club (1916). Goddard and assorted colleagues would gather twice a year to discuss issues of intellectual disability.*

research at the New Jersey School for Feebleminded Boys and Girls (now known as the Vineland Training School) in Vineland, New Jersey (see Figure 3-2). As described in chapter 2, Goddard was the first to translate the Binet scales into English, a development that helped to make the intelligence test the centerpiece of 20th century psychological assessment. Terman, a 1905 graduate of Clark University, was also interested in the testing of intelligence. Accepting a faculty position at Stanford University in 1910, Terman began to investigate the work of Binet and Goddard. Along with a cadre of graduate students, Terman worked on revising and extending the Binet scales. In 1916, he released the Stanford revision of the Binet-Simon Scale, more widely known as the Stanford-Binet. Among the many popular features of the new scale was the introduction of the

Intelligence Quotient (IQ). Adopted from the work of German psychologist William Stern (1871–1938), the IQ provided a convenient method for expressing the relation between mental age and chronological age. To calculate the IQ, Terman divided mental age by chronological age, and multiplied by 100 (thus removing the decimal place). For example, if a 10-year-old obtained a mental age of 9 years on the Stanford-Binet, the IQ would be 90 (10 divided by 9 = .9, multiplied by 100= 90). Terman's new scale and its subsequent revisions captured the intelligence testing market for decades. Shortly after release of the 1916 Stanford-Binet, Goddard and Terman collaborated on the development of the Army Alpha and Beta tests, an event that played a crucial role in the rise of professional psychology (discussed in greater detail in chapter 2).

Goddard and Terman would go on to make their mark on American psychology, each studying an extreme of the IQ distribution they had helped to engineer. Goddard focused on the lower end, Terman, the higher. Both reflected the hereditarian point of view. Goddard employed intelligence tests in the identification and classification of the intellectually disabled. He believed in the humane and caring treatment of the intellectually disabled, but preferred this be done in institutions where behavior could be controlled and directed.

Terman turned his attention to the study of the gifted, assuming their talents appeared early in life. In a series of studies he used retrospective reports to discern the IQs of eminent men. One of his first subjects was Francis Galton. According to historian of psychology Raymond Fancher, "Terman estimated that young Galton's more spectacular exploits occurred at about half the age at which normal children can do them; this suggested a childhood IQ of close to 200. In a 1917 paper, Terman reported that this figure exceeded by far any single IQ yet obtained from the thousands of California schoolchildren who had taken the Stanford-Binet, and concluded that Galton had been an extraordinary child genius."[10]

One of Terman's graduate students, Catherine Cox (1890–1984), used this method for her dissertation. She identified 300 historical figures considered to be geniuses and searched their childhood histories for signs of precocious activity and development. She concluded that the average IQ of the group was 155, well above the normal distribution average of 100. This was important to Terman as it demonstrated that giftedness could be identified in childhood. It was one thing to reconstruct intelligence scores, another to test actual children with actual tests and follow their development over time. Recognizing this, Terman began his genetic studies of genius, a longitudinal study of near mythic proportion that continues to this day.

It was rather clear to Terman—intelligence was inherited and fixed. The brightest in society should be identified and encouraged. Terman went so far as to endorse practices such as the forced sterilization of the intellectually disabled. There were those who took exception with Terman and his point of view. In an article about Terman, writer Mitchell Leslie wrote:

> IQ tests and the social agenda of theory advocates roused critics right from the start. To the journalist Walter Lippmann, the intelligence-testers were "the Psychological Battalion of Death," seizing unparalleled power over every child's future. Lippmann and Terman dueled in the pages of the *New Republic* in 1922 and 1923. "I hate the impudence of a claim that in 50 minutes you can judge and classify a human being's predestined fitness in life," Lippmann wrote. " I hate the sense of superiority which it creates, and the sense of inferiority it imposes." In a sarcastic rejoinder, Terman compared Lippmann to the creationist William Jennings Bryan and the other opponents of scientific progress, then attacked Lippmann's writing style as "much too verbose for literal quotation." Though he could never match Lippmann's eloquence, in the end Terman won the war: intelligence testing continued to spread. By the 1930s, kids with high IQs were being sent into more challenging classes to prepare for high-earning jobs or college, while low scorers got less demanding coursework, reduced expectations and dimmer job prospects.[11]

Arnold Gesell: The First School Psychologist

In 1915, Arnold Gesell became the first person in the United States to hold the title of school psychologist. Gesell, a classmate of Terman's at Clark and student of G. Stanley Hall, received his PhD in 1906 (see Figure 3-3). Upon graduation he held a number of jobs and stayed in close contact with classmate Terman. He visited Lightner Witmer (1867–1956) and toured the psychological clinic at the University of Pennsylvania,

Figure 3-3. *Arnold Gesell, MD, PhD, was the first person in the United States to hold the title of school psychologist.*

and met on numerous occasions with Henry Goddard at the New Jersey School for Feebleminded Boys and Girls. With plenty of new knowledge about children with various forms of what was then termed "mental and moral retardation," he returned to school to pursue a medical degree. After a year at Wisconsin, he accepted a part-time faculty appointment at Yale University and continued his medical studies. As he moved closer to graduation he was recruited to Stanford by Terman. Yale did not want to lose him, offering a full professorship and a position as State Director of Child Hygiene for the Connecticut Board of Education. He accepted Yale's offer and in 1915 completed medical school, became a full professor and director of the Clinic of Child Development at Yale, and worked part-time for the Board of Education as the nation's first official "school psychologist." According to school psychology historian Thomas Fagan:

> In terms of the general nature of this position, it is important to verify that this was not a full-time, district-based school psychological practitioner position as we would conceptualize such today and which did exist (under titles other than school psychologist) at that time in selected settings outside of Connecticut. It was instead, a half-time, contractual position directly responsible to the State Board of Education [SBE], serving many settings in Connecticut including rural and urban districts, some of considerable distance from New Haven. His role was a mix of research, consultation, case study, and inservice education, akin to both contemporary practitioners and SBE consultants, but more like SBE school psychological employees of the era 1930–1960 that served entire regions of particular states.[12]

Gesell's appointment with the Connecticut State Board of Education ended in 1919, although he stayed on for a number of years as a consultant. Turning his attention to his Yale work, Gesell made his mark as a child development specialist. At the Clinic for Child Development (renamed the Gesell Institute of Human Development in 1950), Gesell studied children using observational methods. Reflecting a variation of the hereditarian views of Hall and his classmates at Clark, Gesell stressed that maturation unfolds in a uniform manner. Given a normal environment, parents could expect their children to progress through an orderly sequence of development. Timetables and schedules of development published by Gesell and his associates enjoyed considerable and lasting popular appeal.

Individual Case Study and the Legacy of Lightner Witmer

At about the same time that G. Stanley Hall was developing his nomothetic principles of child development, Lightner Witmer was refining his idiographic approach to the study of individual differences in children pre-senting with learning, behavioral, and emotional problems. The founding of the psychological clinic at the University of Pennsylvania in 1896 was a watershed event in the history of both school and clinical psychology.[13] The reasons will become obvious.

New Work in Applied Psychology

Witmer was able to see the possibilities of new work in applied psy-chology and at the 1896 annual meeting of the American Psychologi-cal Association he outlined a plan of what he termed "practical work in psychology." Using the labels of that time, the plan comprised four areas: (a) investigation of mental and moral retardation by means of statisti-cal and clinical methods, (b) establishment of a psychological clinic and hospital school for children suffering from retardation or physical defects that inhibit academic progress, (c) creation of opportunities for those in teaching, medicine, and social work to observe and work with retarded and normal children, and (d) training of psychological experts to work with mentally and morally retarded children in the school system or with the practice of medicine.[14]

To his credit he was able to make progress in all areas. He investigated mental and moral retardation largely through intensive individual assess-ment, often doing the testing himself. Witmer was interested in behavior, noting, "If psychology is a science of behavior and the unit of observation is a performance, and every performance may be analyzed into the opera-tions of qualitatively discriminated abilities, then psychology may also be defined as the science of competency."[15] He insisted that test results were meaningless unless the examiner witnessed and understood the test-taking behavior of the child. Performance measures were popular at the clinic, with Witmer modifying tests such as the Seguin Form Board and the Mon-tessori Cylinders to meet his needs. By 1915 there were over 30 tests in use at the clinic, the most popular being the form boards, the Binet-Simon, tests of arithmetic and writing, copying with pencil or crayon, color nam-ing and discrimination, and general observation.[16]

Completion of the second area came with the opening of the psycho-logical clinic in 1896 and the hospital school in 1907. In essence, the hospital school was an extension of the clinic. For children who required extended observation before a diagnosis was made and a treatment plan offered, a period of stay at the hospital school was arranged. The hospital was established through a private donation and Witmer named it the Orthogenic School. In doing so coined the term orthogenics, which he defined as, "the name for that branch of science which investigates retardation and deviation and the methods of restoring to normal condition those who are found for one reason or another to be retarded or deviate."[17]

The third area, practical work for those in teaching, medicine, and social work, was a point of particular emphasis. Witmer was refreshingly candid in his willingness to admit when he did not know something, and in the case of medicine, social work, and teaching he claimed no expertise. Rather, he understood the value in assembling those specialists and professionals who could best aid in the assessment and diagnosis of the children referred to the clinic. Witmer welcomed these specialists into the clinic. Social workers conducted home visits and maintained contact with families outside the clinic, and physicians provided medical evaluations and treatment. Often this included removal of adenoids and tonsils (diseased and healthy), as it was commonly believed that infections of these tissues caused learning problems. Teachers were particularly important to Witmer because in the process of instruction much could be gleaned about the nature of a child's learning problems. He formalized this into what he termed diagnostic teaching, a procedure that was always an important part of both diagnosis and treatment.

Above all else Witmer was a psychologist. He believed that departments of psychology should be responsible for the education and training of the new specialists who would work with problem children using his clinical method. Just as experimental psychology linked lecture and lab, so too did Witmer offer coursework in child psychology which offered work experience in conjunction with coursework in child psychology.[18] The opportunities for practical work also created an atmosphere of innovation at the University of Pennsylvania where a host of specialty clinics appeared, all headed by Witmer students. This included a vocational guidance clinic directed by Morris Viteles (1898–1996), a speech clinic started by E. B. Twitmyer (1873–1943), and a personnel clinic headed by Robert Brotemarkle (1892–

1972). Through his efforts Witmer hoped to train students as psychological experts "who should find [their careers] in connection with the school, through the examination and treatment of mentally and morally retarded children, or in connection with the practice of medicine."[19]

Obviously Witmer's clinical psychology contained equal elements of clinical and school psychology. Such labels did not matter to Witmer, who was much more concerned with the work and its role in society (see Figure 3-4). Indeed, his vision and definition of clinical psychology encompassed virtually all of the professional areas in psychology,

> Clinical psychology is derived from the examination of many human beings, one at time. The analytic method of discriminating mental abilities and defects develops an ordered classification of observed behavior by means of post analytic generalizations. Diagnostic education is the orthopedic treatment of human beings as individuals, in order that each may realize his indicated potentiality of performance. The psychological clinic is an institution for social and public service, for original research, and for the instruction of students in psychological orthogenics, which includes vocational, educational, correctional, hygienic, industrial, and social guidance.[20]

The clinical method treated each child as an individual. This was in opposition to much of the emphasis on normal development and group data typified by Hall and the child study movement. Another difference between the approaches of Hall and Witmer involved the nature-nurture issue. Hall and his students, including Terman and Goddard, embraced a hereditarian view of intelligence. Witmer maintained a stance much closer to the nurture point of view. Although he believed that intelligence was fixed and not increased through training, he maintained that environmental influences could serve to advance or retard the expression of intelligence. Taking an antieugenicist stand Witmer proclaimed, "The more mongrel a people, the more intelligent; the purer the blood, the more stupid."[21]

Witmer found the environmental point of view more conducive to treatment and commented:

> Who can improve a man's inheritance? And what man's environment cannot be bettered? In place of the hopeless fatalism of those who con-

Figure 3-4. *Issue of Lightner Witmer's journal* The Psychological Clinic.

stantly emphasize our impotence in the presence of the heredity factor, we prefer the hopeful optimism of those who point out the destructive activity of the environment. To ascribe a condition to the environment is a challenge to do something for its amelioration or cure; to ascribe it to heredity often means that we fold our hands and do nothing.[22]

But there is more to the story. If Witmer determined a child was morally or mentally retarded due to environmental factors, something could be done. For those whose retardation was due to heredity or unreachable by environmental means, then the options were much fewer and more severe. Referring to such cases Witmer and colleagues noted that, "the school authorities ought to lend their every assistance to obtain legal sanctions for the segregation of these children in special institutions, in order that they may not pass their lives among normal children, with the danger of moral contagion and the possibility of propagating their kind."[23] Included in this group were children with severe cases of epilepsy, contagious or infectious disease, and those "helplessly crippled or suffering from revolting physical deformity."[24] It is easy to cast aspersions at such declarations but again as history teaches us, Witmer and his contemporaries were part of a time and place where such attitudes, beliefs, and values were commonplace.

Witmer's legacy to school psychology remains a visible one. Division 16 (School Psychology) of the American Psychological Association offers an annual Lightner Witmer Award to recognize exceptional scholarship early in the career of a school psychologist. Vestiges of Witmer's clinical method, the treatment team approach, diagnostic teaching, and field experience can still be seen in the preparation and practice of school psychologists.

Special Education and School Psychology

Witmer's founding of the psychological clinic in 1896 was a concept whose time had come. In a short period of time clinics were established in major cities across America. Many, like Witmer's clinic, were on university campuses and provided services to schools on essentially an outpatient basis with referred children usually seen at the clinic, not at their school. As a result of such things as compulsory attendance laws, immigration, and child saving, school enrollments skyrocketed in the early decades of the 20th century. This meant that many more students with disabilities entered and remained in the public education system.

For those children who did not progress in the regular curriculum, special education classes were developed and implemented. By 1911 it was estimated that about 4% of school children were feebleminded, with another 33% considered slow and incapable of making progress in a program of regular education.[25] The term, "exceptional children" was used to describe the population of children who needed something other than the resources of the regular classroom, it included the deaf and blind, those with learning and emotional problems, and those identified as gifted. In a large city school system there might be 500,000 children, and if nearly

40% were in need of special education services, a university-based clinic like Witmer's would not be able to meet the demand. The answer would come in the development of clinics that operated within the schools.

Psychology in the Schools

In 1899 the Chicago Board of Education authorized the establishment of the Department of Scientific Pedagogy and Child Study (renamed the Bureau of Child Study and later the Division of Child Study), the first psychological clinic in the United States located in a public school system. Inspired by Dewey's concept of the role and function of education and Hall's child study, the Chicago clinic offered a range of services including: (a) the collection of anthropometric and physical measurements for the establishment of age norms, (b) the application of scientific methods to the study of educational problems, (c) the examination of individual problem children, and (d) the training of teachers and principals.[26]

Within a short period of time the Chicago clinic abandoned much of its anthropometric and physical measurement (and the child study method in general) in favor of individual psychological assessment, much in the tradition of Witmer's clinical method. The Chicago clinic was a sign of things to come. The recognition of the need of special education services also made clear the need for trained personnel. In addition to teachers, qualified examiners were needed, people familiar with both child development and the assessment of individual differences. In 1914 J. E. Wallace Wallin (1876–1969), a pioneer in school psychology and special education,[27] reported data on the availability of school psychology services in the United States (see Figure 3-5). He identified 19 school-based clinics established between 1899 and 1914 and offered data on 155 examiners working in those clinics.[28] Even though school psychological services were on the rise, the personnel providing those services varied widely in terms of training and preparation. Commenting on the first generation of school psychology personnel Fagan and Wise noted:

> School psychological services existed only to a limited extent and were delivered directly or indirectly to children by agencies inside or outside the school. They were based on available methodologies of child study and clinical psychology, and were provided by the pioneers in these new

fields. It is reasonable, therefore, to hypothesize that among the primary reasons for securing and employing school psychologists was the specific notion of having them help educators sort children reliably into segregated educational settings where they might be more successful individually and where their absence would help the system itself function better for the masses of "average" children. In essence, pupil personnel services that included school psychologists were not central to the system of schooling; rather, the services furthered the system's goals of educating the masses more efficiently while dealing with the problems such goals presented...The concept of the school psychologist, therefore, as an ancillary member of the system, and as a "gatekeeper" for special education has a long historical precedent.[29]

The school psychology movement was on its way, pushed forward by increasing special education enrollments, the refinement of testing procedures, and the growth of applied psychology.

Organization and Identity

For those psychologists engaged in the testing of children, opportunities were available in a growing number of settings, including the juvenile justice system, state institutions, research and guidance bureaus, and the public schools. Common to all was an interest in the development and application of an ever-expanding domain of psychological tests. However, it was a group without a home. As was the case for many of the pioneers in the professional areas, the APA of the early 20th century did not represent their interests or activities. Two psychologists close to the nascent school psychology movement, J. E. W. Wallin and Leta Stetter Hollingworth (1886–1939)[30] sought to remedy the situation by founding the American Association of Clinical Psychologists (AACP) in 1917 at the Carnegie Institute of Technology (site of the nation's first department of applied psychology). As discussed in chapter 2, the group promoted training and certification standards for the practice of clinical psychology. Again it is important to keep in mind that the term clinical psychology was used in 1917 to represent a broad range of activities best described as applied psychology.

Figure 3-5. *J. E. Wallace Wallin was a pioneer in school psychology and special education. He employed a variety of measures to assess the functioning of schoolchildren. Here he is assessing auditory acuity in a school-age child.*

Wanting to avoid conflict and keep psychology unified, the APA sought to bring the AACP into the organization. This was accomplished in 1919 through creation of the Section of Clinical Psychology, the APA's first special interest division. Early on the new section sought to establish standards for the credentialing of consulting psychologists. Apparently it was believed that the term clinical psychology was too restrictive and failed to capture the work of applied psychologists who might be found in hospitals, child guidance clinics, employment bureaus, industry, elementary and secondary schools, and colleges and universities. The attempt at certification failed and the effort was ceased in 1927. During that time only 25 psychologists were certified. This included 17 who listed a university affiliation, four from the public schools, one working in a psychiatric hospital, and three in private practice.[31] The clinical section quickly languished. Beyond presentations at the annual APA meetings, the group was never very active.

It seemed that the APA could not or would not work in the interest of the applied psychologists in its ranks. This was evident in the growth of grass-roots associations of consulting psychologists, many of which coalesced to form the Association of Consulting Psychologists (ACP) in 1930.

Centered in New York City, the ACP attracted many members of the APA's clinical section, including Gertrude Hildreth (1898–1984). Hildreth was a member of the pioneering generation of school psychologists. She had worked as a school psychologist in Oklahoma before heading east in 1925 for her doctorate at Teachers College, Columbia University. Later as a faculty member at Teachers College, and then at Brooklyn College, she supported the growth of professional psychology, helped define school psychology, and developed the widely used and highly popular Metropolitan Readiness Tests.[32] In 1936 as president of the ACP she appointed a committee to consider the development of a national program of consulting psychologists. The following year ACP, along with several other groups with applied interests, merged to form the American Association for Applied Psychology (AAAP). The AAAP was comprised of four sections, business and industrial, clinical, consulting, and educational psychology. School psychologists could be at home in any of the latter three, although the educational section claimed school psychology as part of its domain. Many closely associated with school psychology were officers of the clinical section of the AAAP including Gertrude Hildreth, Bertha Luckey, J. E. W. Wallin, and Wilda M. Rosebrook. As an interesting aside, Carl Rogers chaired the Committee on Psychological Service in School and College, a subcommittee of the Educational Section.[33]

By now, the number of applied psychologists was growing at a rapid pace. Membership in the AAAP increased steadily, making it the largest association of psychologists outside of the APA. The need for psychologists created by World War II led the federal government to pressure the APA to unite psychology. In negotiations with the AAAP, the APA reorganized in 1945.[34] As a part of that process Division 16, School Psychologists was formed.

Of the time, Thomas Fagan noted:

> For school psychologists, the creation of a separate division was a long-awaited recognition of the uniqueness of their services to school settings and children. Although school psychologists were previously represented

within the AAAP's sections for clinical and educational psychology, they did not have the identity they preferred and were dissatisfied with having to share their representation with academics. Archival records indicate the lines of tension then extant and provide an explanation for the creation of Division 16, which in its first years limited membership to practitioners in school settings (Symonds & English, 1938). These records strongly suggest that an APA division for school psychologists evolved out of the AAAP, principally from the Education Section (Fryer, 1937).[35]

Division status brought with it an infrastructure and organizational identity that helped to foster communication among school psychologists throughout the country. Programming at annual meetings of the APA brought the membership together and the division newsletter kept the membership informed about developments throughout the year. The dissemination of research, theory, and practice through professional journals began in the 1960s with the publication of the *Journal of School Psychology*. Originally a publication of the Ohio Department of Education, and intended as a free biannual publication for Ohio school psychologists, it became a national journal in 1963, and continues as a quarterly publication. The independent journal *Psychology in the Schools* appeared in 1964, and is published bimonthly. It was not until 1986, with the publication of *Professional School Psychology* (now *School Psychology Quarterly*), that Division 16 began its own regular journal publication.[36]

Recognition

No doubt the establishment of Division 16 reserved a place for school psychology among the new specialties in psychology. Beginning with about 100 members in 1947, Division 16 membership rose to 276 by 1950, and by 2010 stood at more than 1,300.[37] From the start identity issues were plentiful. Reflecting the earlier affiliation with the AAAP, about one-third of Division 16 members were also members of Divisions 12 (Clinical and Abnormal Psychology) and 15 (Educational Psychology). In addition, most school psychologists were not members of Division 16, let alone the APA. The requirement of the doctoral degree in psychology for full membership (fellow) status in Division 16 and the APA, kept away many subdoctoral personnel. For those with the equivalent of a master's degree or some graduate work and experience in a school setting, membership in Division 16 and APA as an associate was possible. About two-thirds of Division 16 members were associates.[38]

The entry-level issue was a big one. Throughout the early years school teachers, administrators, physicians, or psychologists might provide school psychology services. Training standards were nonexistent. Many services were provided by examiners who Wallin referred to as "Binet testers." Their training he noted:

> consists in having taken normal school, college or university courses in the usual branches of education and psychology, and a summer course on mental tests and on feeble-minded children or in having taken a regular medical course on mental tests and on feeble-minded children; or in having taken a regular medical course and then reading literature on feeble-minded and backward children, learning to give the Binet system, or paying a visit to a psychological clinic. Even if we concede that it is possible thus to prepare psycho-educational testers, the conclusion remains true: that such testers are not expert psycho-educational diagnosticians, and that to prepare expert psycho-educational diagnosticians, requires three to four years of technical training and clinical experience.[39]

The term psycho-educational highlighted the problem. For those with a background in education the bachelors' degree was sufficient for the practice of education, that is for being a teacher in the classroom. In most cases the master's degree was the terminal degree for educational practice. Psychology and the practice of psychology was another matter. As early as 1918, applied psychologists were warming to the idea of the doctoral standard for the practice of psychology, a standard that by midcentury became the norm in professional psychology. Because so many associated with the school psychology movement were in education, the doctoral standard was not seen as a necessary requirement for the practice of school psychology. In addition, state education boards often credentialed school psychologists, obviating the need for APA accreditation. In the mid-1920s, the New York City schools introduced an examination for employment as a school psychologist. In order to take the exam a master's degree in psychology and a year of experience were required. Such action helped to create a market for school psychologists, a development that was matched by university programs of preparation. In 1929, New York University became the first university in America to offer a program of preparation in school psychology.[40] Teachers College, Columbia University followed soon after, and in 1935 New York State was the first to offer certification for school psychologists.[41] As similar developments occurred throughout the country school psychology began to take shape and definition. In 1930, Gertrude Hildreth published *Psychological Service for School Problems*, considered the first book on the topic of school psychology. In it she described the new profession:

> In many progressive public school systems and private schools the educational specialists employed are known as school psychologists. Such specialists are regular members of the staff not wholly identified with the teachers, principals, or supervisors. In cooperation with others, they carry on general functions of child study and adjustment; and they employ scientific techniques, so far as these are available, in obtaining information of an objective sort about children, using such information in cooperation with teachers and supervisors for purposes of educational guidance. They undertake the diagnosis of pupil maladjustment by all available means, and their offices serve as clearing bureaus for teachers, administrators, and laymen seeking assistance in the study of pupil problems.[42]

Hildreth's book provided a detailed description of school psychological services, including the description of a typical work day (see Table 3-1).

Further recognition came in 1942 when Percival Symonds, editor of the *Journal of Consulting Psychology*, and a colleague of Hildreth's at Teachers College, Columbia University, devoted an entire issue to school psychology. In the introduction to the issue he wrote:

> This issue of the *Journal of Consulting Psychology* devoted to the *school psychologist* focuses merited attention on one of the most widespread and effective services which applied psychology has to offer. A school psychologist is a *psychologist in a school*—that is, one who brings to bear on the problems of the school and its administrators, teachers, and pupils the technical skill and insight which the science of psychology can provide. The school psychologist is a specialist in human relations, and by virtue of his understanding of the principles of motivation, learning, and individual differences, and his skill in applying this knowledge to educational

> problems, occupies the position of technical expert in the school similar
> to that of the engineer in an industrial enterprise.[43]

Much like Hildreth's 1930 book, the articles contained in the journal covered a range of topics in school psychology. In essence they provided a snapshot of the best practices of the time.

As school psychology approached midcentury, there was a sense that roles were expanding. The debates over levels of training, certification, and the like were helpful in giving shape and substance to the work of the school psychologist. No longer did school psychologists see themselves merely as "Binet testers." Many saw the potential to do much more as indicated by the diversity of roles and functions contained in both the special issue of the *Journal of Consulting Psychology* and Hildreth's *Psychological Service for School Problems*.

The growth in the technology of applied psychology lent support to role expansion for school psychologists. Halfway into the 20th century, school psychologists had at their disposal an armament of assessment tools capable of providing a myriad of data to describe the functioning of the individual child. Increased dimensions and domains of assessment moved school psychologists beyond the narrow confines of intelligence test administration and into roles as assessment experts who utilized a multitrait, multimethod approach to assessment. It was now possible for school psychologists to conduct diagnostic interviews with parents and teachers and make behavioral observations of children in classrooms. They could coordinate special services, and in essence do all those things that Lightner Witmer had advocated at the beginning of the century. More important, they were moving closer toward claiming an identity as professional psychologists.

School Psychology at Midcentury

By 1950 school psychology had achieved a recognized place in what was becoming the new applied order in American psychology. Visibility was gained by the formation of Division 16, serials and monographs introduced the school psychology movement to a wider audience, training programs and faculty appeared in large and prominent universities, and an increasing base of professionals working in public and private schools provided services to thousands of children. Taken together these developments sug-

TABLE 3-1. A SCHOOL PSYCHOLOGIST'S DAY*

Morning

Examination with the Binet test of a child applying for admission.

The administration of group tests to a small group of absentees who missed the test during the recent testing survey.

Conference on a problem child in the high school.

Conference on a problem child in the elementary school.

Answering correspondence and making requisitions for the tests to be used in the next survey.

Afternoon

Completion, for the principal, of reports of a group of seventh-grade children whose achievement was found to be deficient on recent tests.

Further work on the construction of reading and arithmetic readiness tests for the primary grades.

Instructions to an assistant for making a set of flash cards for diagnostic work in reading.

Partial diagnosis of the reading difficulties of an upper elementary grade pupil.

Study of the reading progress of a French child who had recently entered the school.

Conference with a high school teacher.

This day began at 8:30 and closed at 5:45, with half an hour's recess at noon.

The rank order of activities engaged in by the same psychologist, arranged according to the amount of time consumed in their performance during the year, is approximately as follows:

1. Conferences with school staff members, parents, visitors, psychologists in training.
2. Individual testing of pupils.
3. Group testing.
4. Test scoring.
5. Tabulation of results and the construction of graphs and charts.
6. Diagnostic work with individual pupils.
7. Research including test construction and conferences with staff members conducting research.

*Taken From: Hildreth, G. H. (1930). *Psychological service for school problems.* Yonkers, NY: World Book Co.

gested that school psychology was in a position of ascendancy, however, such was not the case. Conflicts over subdoctoral practitioners and identity diffusion were working against the unification of school psychology, issues that paled in comparison to the implications of the torrid pace of development of the provision of mental health services to adults.

The National Institute of Mental Health and School Psychology

World War II made painfully clear the significant gaps in America's mental health safety net. Essentially there was no net at all. Before the war, advocates for the mentally ill came almost exclusively from grassroots organizations, including many who had witnessed firsthand the horrors and deprivations resulting from far too few treatments and less than adequate institutional care. A science and practice of mental health care was all but nonexistent. The federal government now charged with the care of significant numbers of returning veterans, many crippled physically and mentally by their war experience, was quick to realize that the available supply of mental heath professionals was woefully inadequate to meet the anticipated need. The realization of the magnitude of the problem brought about the National Mental Health Act of 1946, an event that had an immense and far-reaching impact on professional psychology (see chapter 5 for an extended discussion). Within the short span of six years between 1946 and 1952, both clinical and counseling psychology managed to establish, with the financial resources provided by the National Institute of Mental Health (NIMH) and the Veterans Administration, doctoral training programs in professional psychology. Soon, a steady stream of doctoral-level psychologists were providing a wide range of inpatient and outpatient services to returning soldiers and other veterans. The process created an entirely new generation of psychology faculty and programs of study. School psychology, admittedly late to the game, was able to share only a small amount of the new largess.

The Thayer Conference

The National Mental Health Act was intended to provide a national program of mental health. Whereas much of the attention and money was focused on services to adults, public school personnel were vigilant in seeking inclusion of services to children and families through school-based initiatives. At the urging of the National Association of School Social Workers, the NIMH appointed a subcommittee in Mental Hygiene Personnel in School Programs, which released a report in November 1949.[44] The report offered limited support to school social workers and allied professionals. They offered no major funding initiatives nor was school psychology invited to join the tenured and privileged ranks of psychiatry and clinical psychology.

In 1953, school psychologists pushed the same issue that counseling and clinical psychologists had years earlier, that of supply and demand. Only now the equation was applied to children. There were plenty of school children in need and far too few school psychologists to serve them. Not only were there dramatic shortages of trained personnel, there were corresponding deficits in recognized training programs. In 1953 there were only two doctoral training programs in school psychology, one at the Pennsylvania State University (organized in the 1930s), and a newly organized program at the University of Illinois.[45]

The NIMH had provided the funds for clinical psychology to hold the Boulder Conference in 1949, and for counseling psychology to convene the Northwestern Conference in 1951, conferences that assisted each area in establishing standards for doctoral training programs. School psychology was ready for its turn.

Like its predecessors in clinical and counseling, school psychology made an application for NIMH funding through the APA's Education and Training (E & T) Board. The board chair, E. Lowell Kelly, appointed a steering committee composed of five persons nominated by the board and five persons nominated by Division 16. The committee was successful in securing NIMH funding and set about planning for 48 participants to convene at the Hotel Thayer in West Point, New York, from August 22 to August 31, 1954, just prior to the convening of the annual meeting of the APA in New York City. Table 3-2 provides a list of the participants. Reading over the list reveals the wide range of services and service providers that gathered under the umbrella of school psychology. Here were representative groups concerned with the welfare and well-being of children, and all interested in the single largest setting where American children could be found, the schools.

Using the Boulder Conference as a model, the participants set about discussing the needed architecture to formalize the role of the school psychologist in the ranks of professional psychology. The document produced by the Thayer Conference, *School Psychologists at Mid-Century: A Report of the Thayer Conference on the Functions, Qualifications and Training of School Psychologists*,[46] outlined the shape and substance of school psychology, and offered a guide to training that was approved by the membership.

The director of the NIMH was psychiatrist Robert Felix. A friend to psychology, he was a passionate believer in community mental health and saw the school as an institution that played an especially important role in American life. Writing in the introduction of the Thayer Conference report

TABLE 3-2. THAYER CONFERENCE PARTICIPANTS*

Ackerly, S. Spafford, MD, Chair of Department of Psychiatry and Mental Hygiene, and Director of Louisville Child Guidance Clinic, University of Louisville, School of Medicine, Louisville, Kentucky.

Bice, Harry V., Consultant on Psychological Problems, New Jersey State Crippled Children's Commission, Trenton, New Jersey.

Birch, Jack W., Director of Special Education, Board of Public Education, Pittsburgh, Pennsylvania.

Bobbitt, Joseph M. (Guest), Chief, Professional Services Branch, National Institute of Mental Health, USPHS, Bethesda, Maryland.

Bordin, Edward S., Associate Professor of Psychology, University of Michigan, Ann Arbor, Michigan.

Boston, Opal, Supervisor, School Social Workers, Indianapolis Public Schools; President, National Association of School Social Workers.

Burdette, Esallee, Washington High School, Washington, Georgia; representing the National Education Association Department of Classroom Teachers.

Carter, Jerry W., Jr. (Guest), Chief Clinical Psychologist, Community Services Branch, National Institute of Mental Health, USPHS, Bethesda, Maryland.

Cook, Walter W., Dean, College of Education, University of Minnesota, Minneapolis, Minnesota.

Cornell, Ethel L., Associate in Educational Research, State Education Department, Albany, New York.

Cutts, Norma E., Professor of Psychology and Education, New Haven State Teachers College; Lecturer in Educational Psychology, Department of Education, Yale University.

Driscoll, Gertrude P., Professor of Education, Teachers College, Columbia University, New York, New York.

Dunlap, James M., School Psychologist, University City Public Schools, University City, Missouri.

Elliott, Merle H., Director of Research, Oakland Public Schools, Oakland, California.

Fite, Mary D., Psychologist, Gilbert School, Multonomah County, Oregon. Address: 12500 S. E. Ranona, Portland, Oregon.

Gates, Robert, Consultant, Education for Exceptional Children, State Department of Education, Tallahassee, Florida.

Gowan, May Seagoe, Professor of Education, University of California, Los Angeles, California.

Gray, Susan W., Associate Professor of Psychology, George Peabody College, Nashville, Tennessee.

Harris, Dale B., Professor and Director, Institute of Child Welfare, University of Minnesota, Minneapolis, Minnesota.

Hobbs, Nicholas, Chair, Division of Human Development & Guidance, George Peabody College, Nashville, Tennessee.

Kelley, Noble H., Chair, Department of Psychology, Director of Psychological Services, Southern Illinois University, Carbondale, Illinois.

Kirk, Samuel A., Professor of Education and Director, Institute for Research on Exceptional Children, University of Illinois, Urbana, Illinois.

Krugman, Morris, Assistant Superintendent of Schools and in Charge of Guidance, Board of Education, City of New York.

Langhorne, M. C., Chair, Department of Psychology, Emory University, Georgia.

Lantz, Beatrice, Consultant, Division of Research and Guidance, Los Angeles County Schools, California.

(Continued)

Levin, Max M. (Guest), Psychologist, Training and Standards Branch, National Institute of Mental Health, USPHS, Bethesda, Maryland.

Luckey, Bertha M., Supervisor, Psychological Service, Cleveland Board of Education, Cleveland, Ohio.

McCandless, Boyd R., Professor and Director, Iowa Child Welfare Research Station, State University of Iowa, Iowa City, Iowa.

Magness, Guy N., MD, Director, School Health Service of University City Public Schools, University City, Missouri. (School Physician)

Mathews, W. Mason, Chair, Laboratory Services (School Services), Merrill-Palmer School, Detroit, Michigan.

Moore, Bruce V., Executive Officer, Education and Training Board, American Psychological Association, Washington, D. C.

Mullen, Frances A., Assistant Superintendent of Schools in charge of Special Education, Chicago Public Schools, Chicago, Illinois.

Myers, C. Roger, Professor of Psychology, University of Toronto, a Psychologist, Department of Health, Toronto, Ontario, Canada.

Newland, T. Ernest, Professor of Education, University of Illinois, Urbana, Illinois.

Ojeman, Ralph H., Professor of Psychology and Parent Education, Iowa Child Welfare Research Station, State University of Iowa, Iowa City, Iowa.

Olson, Willard C., Professor of Education and Psychology, and Dean, School of Education, University of Michigan, Ann Arbor, Michigan.

O'Shea, Harriet E., Associate Professor of Psychology, Purdue University, Lafayette, Indiana.

Raimy, Victor C., Chair and Professor, Department of Psychology, University of Colorado, Boulder, Colorado.

Roberts, S. Oliver, Professor of Psychology and Education, Chair, Department of Psychology, Fisk University, Nashville, Tennessee.

Robinson, Francis P., Professor of Psychology, Ohio State University, Columbus, Ohio.

Rodnick, Eliot H., Chair, Department of Psychology, Director of Clinical Training, Duke University, Durham, North Carolina.

Saffir, Milton A., Director, Chicago Psychological Guidance Center; Principal of Marshall Elementary School, Chicago, Illinois.

Skodak, Marie, Director, Division of Psychological Services, Dearborn Public Schools, Dearborn, Michigan.

Strother, Charles R., Professor of Psychology, Professor of Clinical Psychology in Medicine, University of Washington, Seattle, Washington.

Tulchin, Simon H., Consulting Psychologist, 30 East 60th Street, New York, New York.

Wall, William D., Department of Education, UNESCO, Paris, France.

Weiss, Emalyn R., Supervisor of Special Education, Berks County Schools, Reading, Pennsylvania.

Young, Albert T., Jr., School Psychologist, City of Falls Church Public Schools, Falls Church, Virginia.

Visiting the Conference

Ewalt, Jack R., MD, Commissioner, Department of Mental Health, Massachusetts, and Professor of Psychiatry, Harvard Medical School.

Ewing, Palmer L., Superintendent of Schools, Buffalo, New York.

Kelly, E. Lowell, Professor of Psychology, University of Michigan, Ann Arbor, Michigan; President-elect, American Psychological Association.

Sanford, Fillmore H., Executive Secretary, American Psychological Association, Washington, D. C.

*Taken from: Cutts, N. E. (Ed.) (1955). *School psychologists at mid-century: A report on the Thayer conference on the functions, qualifications, and training of school psychologists*. Washington, DC: American Psychological Association.

he noted that the roles of the schools, "have long been recognized as an influence second only to the home in determining the degree to which our citizens achieve that adult goal which the layman calls adequacy or happiness or self sufficiency and which the psychiatrist calls maturity. The schools have long shown that they are sensitive to this responsibility, as indicated by their increasing utilization of specialized personnel such as counselors, school social workers, guidance personnel, and school psychologists."[47]

The recommendations for training school psychologists bore resemblance to those of clinical and counseling psychologists. A major difference was in the open endorsement of master's-level practitioners. Clinical and counseling psychologists had dealt with the topic at their respective training conferences and both upheld the doctoral degree as the standard for entry into the profession. Attendees at the Thayer Conference also struggled with the issue and chose to reserve the title *school psychologist* for those with doctoral training, while supporting the master's-level practitioner through the title of psychological examiner. Although there was much debate about the proper title for those with training at the master's level, a curriculum was offered in the report with the general content approved by the attendees. Publication of training guidelines appeared in the *American Psychologist* in 1963.[48] The assumptions upon which these standards were based were outlined as follows:

1. School psychologists are dually oriented professionals who need to be well educated in both psychology and education. The objective of training is to develop psychologists who are interested in and knowledgeable about schools, whose contributions are meaningful to and utilized by the teacher because they are based on understanding of the classroom situation and teacher problems as well as on sound psychological knowledge and skills.

(a) The development of competencies needed by a fully qualified school psychologist requires at least the education represented by a doctoral degree or 3 years of graduate training in a planned sequence of course, laboratory, and supervised work experiences offered by a recognized training institution.

(b) There are several alternative ways to achieve the desired objective of appropriate attitudes toward and understanding of the educational environment in which the school psychologist functions as a psychologist. Teacher training and certification and teaching experience are often effective. A program of training in school psychology, oriented as it is toward schools and including graduate work in education and supervised experience in a school setting, is considered to be an equally effective means of attaining the objective.

The discussion went on to describe the training of subdoctoral personnel,

3. There are psychological services that can be provided satisfactorily by people with less training than that considered essential for a school psychologist.

(a) Because of the knowledge and understanding needed for the judgments involved in psychological services, individuals with less than the minimal training as stated in 1a above should be employed only when there is provision for adequate supervision by a qualified school psychologist.

(b) The certificate and title under which these services are performed should help the school and the professional worker recognize training and function limitations.[49]

Like its predecessors, the Thayer Conference set forth an allegiance to the APA by endorsing the doctoral standard as the requisite degree for calling oneself a school psychologist. In doing so, Division 16 helped to ensure recognition and accreditation of school psychology as a professional area by the APA, even though the first program certification did not come until 1971 when it was awarded to the University of Texas.[50] The dividends also included recognition of school psychology as a professional area specialty by the American Board of Examiners in Professional Psychology (ABEPP) in 1969.

Expansion

Like clinical and counseling psychology, school psychology enjoyed considerable growth and expansion in the years after World War II. In point of fact, school psychology was one of the fastest growing areas of psychology.[51] The increasing attention and funding given to mental health issues was not lost upon school psychologists, who saw in the issue a place for school psychology to utilize its expertise. In her 1957 Division 16 presidential address, Gertrude Driscoll called for school psychologists to play a major role in the prevention of mental illness (see Figure 3-6):

Prevention implies a start at the beginning of a situation that produces a disease. In our secondary schools we have the parents of the next generation. In our kindergartens we have children who are young enough to respond in general to opportunities for healthy growth. The children who at this early age give evidence of maladjustive reaction patterns can be re-educated more easily than at a later age. We must never underrate the fact that as school psychologists we have available to us all educable children in the country. This fact is indeed a challenge. If we as school psychologists accept the challenge we may in the next decade change into quite a different breed of professional worker.[52]

The concept of prevention was popular with the NIMH, which supported various efforts by school psychologists to play a role in the mental health of children, an activity that was increasingly represented in the training and preparation of school psychologists.[53] NIMH funding sponsored publications such as the *Mental Health Monographs*,[54] provided standards for doctoral students in school psychology, and continued the established practice of funding training conferences.

After the Thayer Conference, NIMH monies supported the Peabody Conference on the Internship in School Psychology, held at George Peabody College for Teachers in Nashville, Tennessee, March 21–23, 1964.[55] The conference helped to establish guidelines for internship training for doctoral students in school psychology much in the same way that clinical and counseling psychology had in previous years. Close on the heels of the Peabody Conference, NIMH sponsored the New Directions in School Psychology Conference from June 22–24, 1964 in Bethesda, Maryland.[56] T. Ernest Newland (1903–1992), a participant of both the Boulder and Thayer Conferences, described the New Directions Conference:

Prompted in part by the desire to hold a 10-year follow-up of the Thayer Conference, in part by new personnel in the NIMH, and probably in part by the restlessness and self-searching of the 1960s, a smaller and shorter meeting was funded by the NIMH. The focus of this was to be "new directions." Those attending constituted a mix of "oldhands" and of some who were quite new to the field. We old hands regarded the meeting as having little basic impact upon the field. Most of what was advocated by

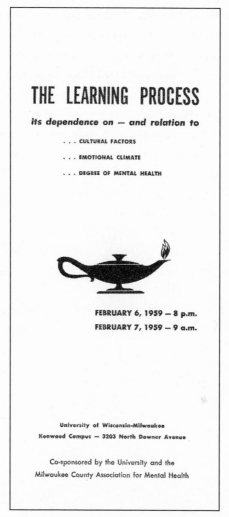

Figure 3-6. *Brochure for a mental health conference for teachers.*

the more recent members, in their own new terminology, was what we had been advocating for years. Essentially the wheel was rediscovered. As so often happens, many were seeking the new without having first even understood the old.[57]

Other activities of the NIMH impacted school psychology, albeit less directly. With the urging and support of the NIMH, the Mental Retardation Facilities and Community Mental Health Centers Construction Act was passed into law in 1963. It provided grants for assistance in the construction of community mental health centers nationwide. As community mental health centers appeared across America, they provided a new set of services to children and families. In many cases these services complemented the activities of school psychologists and served as referral sources for services that were beyond the scope of the public school system.

Other forms of federal legislation also played a role in supporting school psychology services. The National Defense Education Act (NDEA) of 1958, a direct response to the Russian launch of the satellite Sputnik, directed substantial resources toward the identification and guidance of students who showed promise in math and science. Massive programs of school guidance and testing were instituted as a result of the NDEA, a development that raised awareness of the need for psychologists and psychometricians in the schools.

The most sweeping legislation impacting school psychology was Public Law 94-142, the Education for all Handicapped Children Act enacted in 1975. The act mandated a free and appropriate public education for all handicapped children between the ages of three and twenty-one. It outlined a series of steps to be taken to identify, evaluate, and educate children with handicapping conditions, and mandated that special education and related services be provided in the least restrictive environment (LRE). The impact upon school psychology was substantial. Demand for school psychologists increased dramatically, as did the number of rules and regulations. In 1978, federal funds were provided for the creation of the National School Psychology Inservice Training Network (NSPITN) at the University of Minnesota. In existence for only six years, NSPITN played an important role in training school psychologists in the intricacies of Public Law 94-142 and in shaping the debate over the future of school psychology.

Public Law 94-142 was amended in 1986, expanding eligibility criteria to include children from birth to two years of age. In 1990, the name of the law was changed to the Individuals with Disabilities Education Act (IDEA) and then again in 2004 to the Individuals with Disabilities Education Improvement Act (IDEIA). It remains the most important piece of federal legislation upholding the rights of disabled children. It also helps to maintain the school psychologist at the center of the identification, assessment, and placement of special needs children.

Back to the Future

The trio of professional programs accredited by the American Psychological Association, clinical, counseling, and school psychology, have all struggled with the issue of subdoctoral training during their history. Of these, school psychology has been the most declarative in supporting and encouraging the training of subdoctoral personnel. Such support was demonstrated in the published training standards of 1963, an outgrowth of the Thayer Conference of 1954.

As school psychology doctoral training programs grew, so too did the gulf between doctoral and subdoctoral personnel. The leadership of Division 16, once populated mostly by practitioners, was coming to be dominated by faculty members from university (doctoral) training programs. The division wished to include more subdoctoral colleagues, but their efforts were not enough. In 1968, the Ohio School Psychologists Association (OSPA) played host to a national conference in Columbus, Ohio, where practicing school psychologists from across the country gathered to survey the condition of school psychology. Very quickly a call was made for a new national organization for school psychology.[58]

The National Association of School Psychologists

The meeting at Columbus was eventful. The majority of school psychologists were practitioners, most with subdoctoral training. There was a clear consensus that Division 16 was not representing all school psychologists, and not promoting the interests of practicing school psychologists who saw themselves as precariously behind in federal funding. A raw nerve had been exposed and the action taken was swift and decisive. The decision was made to organize and on March 14, 1969, the National Association of School Psychologists (NASP) held its first conference. The new organization was an immediate success. Interest in the organization, and attendance at meetings, was strong. Addressing participants at the second conference in Washington, DC, William Farling, an architect of the NASP, announced:

When we refer to developments in NASP as having meaning *to* and *for* school psychology, we are reiterating the two-directional emphases of the Association's purposive service *to* school psychologists as practicing professionals and representation *for* school psychologists in the organizational, governmental, and public forums of the country.

Regarding services to professional school psychologists, it is important to keep in mind that NASP was born to devote itself to the practice of this profession—the continuation and improvement of that practice. The Association is committed to the facts of life practicalities and to the future of life potentialities of applied psychology in our schools.[59]

Starting on a strong note, the NASP has continued to grow. So much so that it is now the largest organization of school psychologists in the world, boasting a membership of more than 25,000 members.[60] It does what the framers intended; it provides a home for subdoctoral practitioners, and represents school psychologists in matters of public policy.

In many ways, the NASP was able to accomplish what Division 16 could not or would not do, establish a credential for subdoctoral school practitioners. For decades there was significant confusion and variation in credentialing requirements. In the 1980s the NASP put together the National School Psychology Certification System (NSPCS), which credentials school psychologists who meet a nationally recognized standard. Currently that standard requires: (a) completion of a sixth-year specialist degree in school psychology, (b) a total of 60 graduate (90 quarter) semester hours, (c) a supervised internship consisting of 1,200 hours, and (d) a passing score on the National School Psychology Examination.[61]

The NASP also developed a strong relationship with the National Council for Accreditation of Teacher Education (now known as CAEP; the Council for the Accreditation of Educator Preparation), the major accrediting body of professional school personnel in America. For many years CAEP has accredited school psychology programs at both the doctoral and nondoctoral level.

NASP and Division 16

The history of professional psychology tells us that there have been other times when the American Psychological Association was perceived as failing to provide for its applied members. Recall the formation of the American Association of Clinical Psychologists (AACP), the Association of Consulting Psychologists (ACP), and the American Association for Applied Psychology (AAAP). In all these cases the splinter group was eventually reincorporated into the APA. Such has not been the case with NASP and Division 16. Both maintain cordial working relations, working together on issues of mutual concern, and sharing many members in common. The cooperation of the two groups (along with National School Psychology Inservice Training Network) allowed for the convening of the Spring Hill Symposium on the Future of Psychology in the Schools in 1980, the Olympia Conference of 1981, and the 2002 Multisite Conference on the Future of School Psychology. These meetings provided a forum for a variety of interests in school psychology to unite and consider future needs, demands, and opportunities for school psychology.[62] An important link between the APA and the NASP was the interorganizational committee. Formed in 1978 as the APA-NASP Task Force on Accreditation and Credentialing, it sought to improve communication and relations between the APA, Division 16, the NASP, and the NCATE. More effective perhaps in word than deed, the APA dropped its support for the interorganizational committee in 2002 and it disbanded.

Thomas Fagan, a historian of school psychology and a past president of the NASP, offers a first person view of the relations between the NASP and Division 16:

> So long as there are two national groups for school psychology (NASP and Division 16), there will be two national voices unless they can reach agreement on how they will proceed together. They have not achieved such agreement. Thus, NASP has yet to become *the* official voice of school psychology at the national level even though it is the most representative organization. Second, NASP has yet to link as effectively with the broader arena of psychology as it has with the broader arena of education. It needs a direct pipeline into psychology, and Division 16 is certainly capable of facilitating that process. Furthermore, NASP neither has not gained the scientific respect accorded Division 16. NASP continues to be seen as primarily a practitioner-oriented organization less

dedicated to the scientific ideals of psychology as defined by APA or more recently by the APS. NASP has a scholarly journal that exudes scientific ideals, and its conventions are certainly diverse and successful; but it is not perceived as a scientific organization. To effectively interact with the psychological community, it is important for NASP to be perceived as having greater scientific interests. NASP may have as much trouble overcoming that perception as Division 16 had in the 1960s overcoming practitioners' perception of it as narrowly scientific in emphasis. Finally, NASP has yet to capture respect for representing doctoral and university training issues in school psychology. Most trainers belong to Division 16 and NASP. They remain with Division 16 because of its accreditation status and its identification with the world of psychology. There is still the lingering doubt for many school psychologists and trainers about the capacity of NASP, or any group outside the APA household, to give them the respectability as "real psychologists."[63]

Conclusion

The work of school psychologists today is surprisingly similar to that of 100 years ago. The tools and the theories may change, but in the provision of services, school psychologists continue to focus on children and learning environments. They assess, consult, educate, and coordinate a range of services designed to improve adjustment and the quality of life of the children they serve.

Like all of the professional areas discussed in this book, school psychology has passed through a series of developments on its way to recognition and acceptance as a profession. Along the way it offered opportunities for women in psychology where few had previously existed. It helped to shape and implement federal policies that have affected the lives of millions of children, and highlighted the help and hindrance of the measurement of individual differences.

School psychology is rooted in the traditions of 20th century education and psychology, which early in the century enjoyed a more seamless relationship than is the case today. Throughout, school psychologists have had to walk a fine line to maintain a balance between the two. As a profession, education has a much longer history than psychology. Teachers were trained, examined, and certified well before the first license was issued to a professional psychologist. The school psychologist has had to exist in both worlds, often faced with disparate expectations and requirements. Despite ambiguity, conflict, and confusion, school psychology has grown and matured. Today in the United States there are over 240 training programs and over 35,000 school psychologists.[64] School psychologists are represented by two national organizations, numerous state associations, and a growing international organization (the International School Psychology Association founded in 1982).

So what is the future for school psychology? From the past we can perhaps glimpse some sign of the future. We see that in choosing to become health service providers, many clinical and counseling psychologists tied their fate to the promise of federal and private insurance dollars in support of the mental health services they provided. As institutions deinstitutionalized and managed care filled its provider lists with Licensed Professional Counselors and other allied professionals, psychologists found themselves increasingly on the outside looking in. Likewise, as American business and industry changed its collar from blue to white, industrial psychology transformed itself into organizational psychology. School psychology has been an exception, swayed less by circumstance, and maintained more by tradition. For as we have seen, wherever you find children and schools, you will find school psychologists.

Chapter 4
Industrial/Organizational Psychology

In the early evening of October 20, 1909, agents of the US government stopped a truck outside Chattanooga, Tennessee, and under federal
authority over interstate commerce, seized its freight. The "contraband"
consisted of forty barrels and twenty kegs of Coca-Cola syrup on its way
from the headquarters plant in Atlanta, Georgia, to the bottling plant in
Chattanooga. The seizure was ordered from Washington, DC, under the
authority of the recently passed Pure Food and Drug Act. In the lawsuit
that was to follow, the Coca-Cola Company would be charged with marketing and selling a beverage that was injurious to health because it contained a harmful ingredient, caffeine.

As the Coca-Cola Company prepared for trial in the spring of 1911, its
scientists realized that their research evidence on caffeine consisted primarily of studies on physiology, with almost nothing on behavior other than
a few experiments on animals. Human behavioral studies were needed,
and soon. The company approached Harry Hollingworth (mentioned in
chapters 1 and 2), a psychologist at Barnard College in New York City,
who had earned his doctorate only two years earlier. Hollingworth was
cautious about accepting the research assignment. He was aware that others, more senior than he, had already turned down Coca-Cola's offer. He
was concerned as well about questions of scientific integrity that would
be raised by a large company's spending a lot of money for research that it
hoped would be favorable to its legal and commercial needs. Hollingworth
sought to minimize that concern in his contractual arrangement with the
Coca-Cola Company. The contract specified that he would be allowed to

publish the results of the studies regardless of their outcome, and that the results of the research would not be used in any Coca-Cola advertising.

Hollingworth designed a series of studies that he carried out with his wife, Leta Hollingworth (whose role in clinical and school psychology was discussed in chapters 2 and 3). These studies involved a scope of testing and a sophistication of methodology that had not been seen before in applied psychology. The research was designed to test the effects of caffeine on sensory, cognitive, and motor functioning in humans. A battery of 30 different tests was given to participants under differing drug dosages and at different intervals. Some of the control procedures used in this carefully conducted research included presenting tasks in all possible orders, giving some participants inactive substances to assess placebo effects, and keeping participants (as well as experimenters) "blind" to which participants received what substances (double-blind testing).

The results indicated that even high doses of caffeine (much higher than would ever be consumed by heavy drinkers of Coca-Cola) had no ill effects on behavioral or cognitive performance. The data were some of the most impressive scientific evidence presented at the trial in Chattanooga, but although the court found in favor of Coca-Cola, the company eventually lost the case in the Supreme Court. The company was required to pay court costs, and, on its own, it reduced the caffeine content of its soft drink.

Hollingworth's research for Coca-Cola was important on several levels. It marked perhaps the earliest example of funding by a large corporation for psychological research. The success of the research advanced Hollingworth's reputation in the business community and resulted in many other business research opportunities that led to a very successful career for him as an applied psychologist. Of greatest significance, though, was that the work helped bridge the gap between academic psychology and the business world, opening doors for psychologists seeking to consult with businesses and showing psychologists how they could use their science in service to the workplace.[1]

The Salience of the Workplace

Work is a defining part of life. It is the means by which societies exist. It can bring great satisfaction or it can bring considerable stress. For individuals and families, work puts food on tables, clothes on bodies, and shelter over heads, but it also provides for communal needs such as schooling, medical care, mutual defense, and places of recreation. Virtually everyone has had or will have some kind of job, whether it be as a parent, a migrant worker picking fruit, a corporate executive, a software developer, a homemaker, a salesperson, a schoolteacher, a coal miner, or a professional athlete. Assuming that they are mentally and physically capable, people are expected to work. They are expected to be productive, to contribute to their society in some way.

Work occupies much of our lives. It is not uncommon for people to work 50 or 60 years or more before taking retirement, and for many, retirement is never an option. Many people are fortunate enough to have choices about the kinds of work they will pursue, choices that can mean high wages and good working conditions. Others are not so fortunate, however, and spend their lives in jobs that are low-paying and often dangerous to their health. Because individuals spend so much of their lives in the workplace, it is not surprising that psychologists have been interested in applying their discipline to issues of work.

Business is king in the United States. Although the United States has only 7% of the world's population, it generates nearly 40% of the world's income.[2] Psychologists have long been a part of that economic production. Today the field that brings psychology to business and industry is called industrial/organizational psychology, and it is one of the specialties in professional psychology. Industrial/organizational psychologists, or I/O psychologists as they are often known, work in universities, government offices, research and development entities, and virtually every kind of business one could imagine. Some of the problems they pursue are old ones, for example, assessing the components of a job or assessing the skills and performance of a worker. These are the personnel issues that make up the "I" side of the field. Many of the problems are newer, such as redesigning organizational structures that are more efficient and create better employee morale, and are part of the "O" side. Although most I/O psychologists typically specialize in activities on one side or the other, they are usually trained on both sides, and for good reason; issues in the workplace are rarely, if ever, solely in one domain or the other. I factors influence O factors and vice versa. This chapter tells the story of the growth of I/O psychology from its beginnings in the late 19th century to its place of prominence in psychology and business today.

The New Psychology and the Business of Advertising

As we noted in chapter 1, phrenologists, physiognomists, and other 19th-century practitioners offered their services to businesses and individuals, helping businesses hire the right kind of person for the job and helping individuals learn their talents and how those talents might be best applied in the world of work. When the science of psychology arrived in the United States in the 1880s, it would not take long for the new psychologists to get involved in the same questions. Also in chapter 1 we discussed briefly the work of Walter Dill Scott in the psychology of advertising. Yet Scott was not the first psychologist to venture into the world of business. His predecessor was another of Wundt's American doctoral students, Harlow Gale (1862–1945), who in the fall of 1895 sent a questionnaire to 200 businesses in the twin cities of Minneapolis and St. Paul, asking them about their advertising views and practices. In his cover letter, Gale wrote: "At the University of Minnesota we are making a psychological investigation of advertisements. It is an entirely new field for psychological work and one of great and increasing importance. It is our aim to find the mental processes which go on in the minds of customers from the time they see the advertisement until they have purchased the article advertised."[3]

It is no accident that the new psychology's initial venture into the business world was in the field of advertising. American business, like America, was undergoing substantial changes at the turn of the 20th century. Advertising was no exception. Advertisers, long content to pitch their products to local markets, now looked at the expanded markets created by growth of the railroads and the telegraph, and by the rise of national magazines. New technologies in many fields had created the capacity for surplus production that required broader markets to sell that surplus. Business historians Keith Bryant and Henry Dethloff described it as follows:

> Advertising became increasingly important after the 1890s as manufacturers reduced price competition and stressed product differentiation. As manufacturing capacity came to exceed demand, firms used advertising to create additional markets. Profit levels provided for ever-expanding

advertising budgets and for the hiring of experts in advertising techniques as well as in sales.... In an economy of excess, advertising became the means to dispose of an oversupply. The effect, in the long run, was the development of a consumer society with advertising as one of its major institutions.[4]

Although Harlow Gale's questionnaire on advertising generated little enthusiasm in the business community in 1895 (he got a return rate of only 10%), by the first decade of the 20th century advertisers were more interested in the expertise of the new psychologists. The new sentiments were expressed in 1908 by advertiser David Gibson who wrote:

> Most advertising would be a great deal better investment if there were more psychology in it... Instead of finding out by cut-and-try methods, wouldn't it pay to listen to the college professor's say so on such subjects as attention, interest, association, desire, and all the other things that bear directly upon the success of advertising copy?[5]

When advertising firms went looking for experts to hire, psychologists like Walter D. Scott and Harry Hollingworth offered to help. The research questions were interesting and the pay was good, even if some academics felt that the work, because it was applied, was tainted. Indeed, reflecting awareness of the common prejudices held within universities against those colleagues in the sciences who worked on problems funded outside the academy, Hollingworth, tongue in cheek, described such work as a career for those "with no sanctity to preserve."[6]

Scott and the Power of Suggestion

Although Gale was the first American psychologist to work on the subject of advertising, he did not continue that work. Instead, the psychology of advertising was pioneered by Walter Dill Scott. By 1903 Scott had published his first book on advertising psychology and was engaged full-time in business research. Mostly he pursued research problems that were supplied to him by businesses that were willing to pay for the research, largely in the field of advertising. In his writings, Scott stressed the power of suggestion. Historian of psychology David Kuna has written that Scott viewed the consumer as "a nonrational, suggestible creature under the hypnotic influence of the advertising writer."[7] Scott wrote, "Man has been called the reasoning animal but he could with greater truthfulness be called the creature of suggestion. He is reasonable, but he is to a greater extent suggestible."[8]

Scott advocated two advertising techniques in particular: the direct command and the return coupon. Both drew on the power of suggestion. The first suggested a direct action—for example, "Use Sullivan's Cold Remedy"—whereas the second suggested a course of action that involved filling out the coupon, clipping it, and mailing it in to the company. Both techniques relied on Scott's belief that many individuals were compulsively obedient.

There was not much research to validate Scott's claims but there was substantial anecdotal evidence to give him credibility. By 1910, advertising magazines contained numerous testimonials to the effectiveness of Scott's advertising theories. So accepted and influential were his ideas that "suggestive advertising" was by then considered a redundant phrase. His impact on what was to become the field of industrial psychology cannot be overstated.[9] Scott gave scientific credibility to psychology's involvement with advertising and opened the doors for other psychologists who would enter the advertising field, such as Harry Hollingworth and John B. Watson (1878–1958).

Harry Hollingworth and the Effectiveness of Advertising

Hollingworth, who began his advertising work around 1910 when the zeitgeist in American psychology was changing, adopted a less mentalistic view of advertising, emphasizing instead human motives, especially as they were manifested in wants and needs. He began research that tested the relative effectiveness of advertising appeals. According to Hollingworth, advertisements were meant to do four things: get the person's attention, hold it to the message of the advertisement, fix the message in the person's memory, and motivate the person to take the desired action. If the fourth of those did not occur, then the advertisement was ineffective.

Hollingworth began to pretest the effectiveness of advertisements in a series of studies that allowed the isolation of individual components of the ads. Such testing allowed advertisers to use only the most effective ads, thus preventing considerable waste in advertising budgets. In order to demonstrate the validity of his approach, he tested multiple advertisements for a variety of products such as soaps, electric lights, and facial powders, advertisements that were sent to him by several companies whose sales data indicated the relative effectiveness of their ads. The companies did not share their sales data with Hollingworth who tested each of the ads and determined his own ranking of relative effectiveness. When his rankings were compared to the sales data from the companies, the correlation was an amazingly high .82.[10]

Hollingworth's laboratory testing focused on identifying those stimulus elements of the advertisement that seem most related to the four components of the ad. That is, what components functioned to attract attention, to hold attention, to aid memory for the ad's message, or to produce the desired behavior? This stimulus-response approach that defined Hollingworth's research became the dominant research paradigm for other advertising psychologists such as Daniel Starch, Edward K. Strong, Jr., and A. T. Poffenberger.

The demonstrated efficacy of the procedures strengthened the role of consulting psychologists in their work with businesses and further demonstrated to experimental psychologists the applicability of their methods to problems in the world outside of the academy. Eventually this work evolved into marketing research in which the laboratory was replaced by external settings, but the testing methods remained much the same. Further, Hollingworth's objective approach to advertising and the success of the laboratory and market-based studies paved the way for advertising firms to employ psychologists as full-time researchers.[11]

Watson's Behavioristic Approach to Advertising

By the 1920s, the American advertising community employed several psychologists, including John B. Watson, founder of behaviorism, and formerly a professor at Johns Hopkins University. After Watson's dismissal from Johns Hopkins, due to a scandalous divorce,[12] he went to work for one of New York City's largest advertising agencies, J. Walter Thompson (see Figure 4-1). There he initiated a scientific approach that collected market research data and focused on targeting advertising campaigns for particular consumer markets. He promoted the use of testimonial advertisements featuring celebrity endorsements of products, and employed indirect testimonials in which advertising appeals used one of what Watson considered

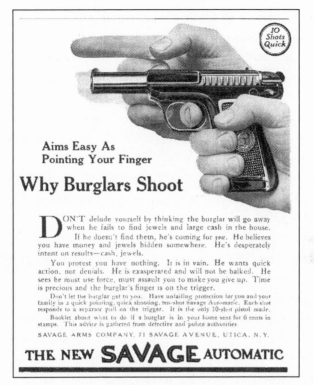

Figure 4-1. *Sample ad from Harry Hollingworth's handgun advertising research.*

the three innate emotions—fear, rage, and love—to motivate buying; for example, his ads sold toothpaste, not because of its dental hygiene benefits, but because whiter teeth would presumably increase an individual's sex appeal.

Scott, Hollingworth, and Watson paved the way for many psychologists who contributed to the advertising field by the 1930s, including the following who wrote books on the subject: Henry Foster Adams, Charles E. Benson, Joseph V. Breitweiser, Harry D. Kitson, Albert T. Poffenberger, Carl E. Seashore, Daniel Starch, and E. K. Strong, Jr. By the 1930s, the mentalistic approaches of Gale and Scott that emphasized suggestion had given way to the more objective approaches of Hollingworth and Watson, which relied on the discovery of stimulus-response relations and the role of motives and emotions in consumer behavior. The success of advertising psychologists in the Great Depression led to an escalation of psychologists in that field following World War II and continuing through the prosperity of the 1950s and 1960s. The psychology of advertising remains strong today, as evidenced by the important presence of psychologists who work in the fields of advertising, marketing, and consumer research.

Hugo Münsterberg and the "Founding" of Industrial Psychology

Several psychology textbooks and articles list Harvard University psychologist Hugo Münsterberg (1863–1916) as the founder of industrial psychology. Münsterberg's initial published work in industrial psychology was a 1909 article promoting the applicability of scientific psychology to the problems of the business world,[13] an article published after the appearance of both of Scott's books on advertising and at a time when Scott was well known for his contributions in business psychology. Thus the label of founder for Münsterberg is surely not merited. So why has he so often been given this honor, even if undeserved?

Münsterberg published two books on industrial psychology, the first in 1913, the second in 1915.[14] The first, *Psychology and Industrial Efficiency* (which had appeared a year earlier in a German-language edition), was for a time on the best-seller lists. In the early 20th century, efficiency was a buzzword for American business. Efficiency meant more effective advertising, better training of workers, scientific management, better employee selection procedures, better accounting methods, better performance from employees, and higher quality of work products. Münsterberg was interested in many fields of applied psychology, as evidenced by his books on psychotherapy, forensic psychology, educational psychology, and industrial psychology.[15] Yet the last of those was of greatest interest. His biographer, Matthew Hale, Jr., has written that "no questions in applied psychology attracted [Münsterberg] more than those of industrial organization and efficiency. For more than half a decade...he extended his view to the entire range of economic psychology: vocational guidance, advertising, personnel management, mental testing, fatigue and monotony, motivation, and the 'mind' of labor."[16]

Münsterberg promoted psychology as the science of human efficiency. The key to business efficiency was matching the skills and talents of the worker to the requirements of the job. A good match of worker and job meant a more satisfied worker and a better work output. According to

Münsterberg, the science of psychology had the tools to discover a perfect match by determining the mental and physical traits required for any job and by measuring those traits in workers. Indeed, Münsterberg was so enthusiastic about the possibilities for psychology to assist businesses that he urged the federal government to establish experimental extension stations through the Department of Commerce and Labor that would offer psychological expertise to local businesses and industry.[17]

Münsterberg's 1909 article on business psychology, which had appeared in a popular magazine, brought him several consulting opportunities with various businesses. He was, for example, asked by the San Francisco and Portland Steamship Company to devise tests to select ship captains (six months before the sinking of the Titanic) and, after a series of fatal accidents involving pedestrians, by the Boston Elevated Railway Company to develop tests to select competent trolley car operators. These studies, and several others, became the basis for his best-selling book on industrial psychology in 1913. Münsterberg conducted several such studies on behalf of businesses, but his career in industrial psychology was short-lived. Although he might not be considered the founder, he clearly was a great promoter of industrial psychology. At the time of his 1913 book he was one of the most visible psychologists in America, largely because of the many articles that he published in popular magazines and the many books that he wrote for public consumption. His voice had wide reach. Thus his industrial psychology book had great impact, partly because of its timing in relation to American business's growing interest in science (fueled in part by Frederick Taylor's scientific management, which we discuss later), but also because of the popularity of Münsterberg. Without a doubt, his book had more impact on the development of the field of industrial psychology than any earlier book. That book made him a force in industrial psychology. It would be another 20 years before the field would see a contribution of similar magnitude.[18]

Carnegie Tech's Division of Applied Psychology

In 1914, Arthur Hamerschlag was president of the Carnegie Institute of Technology (CIT) in Pittsburgh, Pennsylvania, a technical university founded with funds from steel magnate and philanthropist Andrew Carnegie about 10 years earlier. Carnegie envisioned a university that would combine the liberal arts with practical job training. Influenced by Münsterberg's book on industrial psychology, Hamerschlag attended the annual meeting of the American Psychological Association in 1914 because he was interested in what psychology might be able to add to instruction at his university. There he encountered a young psychologist from the faculty of Dartmouth College, Walter Van Dyke Bingham (1880–1952), and he invited Bingham to visit CIT as a consultant. Bingham made the visit early in 1915 and afterward sent Hamerschlag a report of what he saw as the potential contributions for psychology at CIT. In the report, Bingham recommended a psychologist, Guy M. Whipple, as someone who could meet the needs at CIT. Hamerschlag interviewed Whipple but then offered the job to Bingham instead. In September of that year, Bingham joined the CIT faculty as director of the Division of Applied Psychology. It was to be a program unlike any other in the country.

In his report to Hamerschlag, Bingham had listed two broad emphases in which psychology could be practical at CIT: (a) help students identify their talents and match those talents to the jobs for which they were best suited, and (b) teach students to use psychology to be able to understand human behavior and to be able to influence it. The first of those reflected the growing popularity of vocational guidance stimulated in part by the influence of Frank Parsons (we discuss this topic more fully in chapter 5). The second emphasis reflected the work of Scott, Hollingworth, Münsterberg, and others in the use of psychology in advertising and sales. These two emphases defined the early work of the CIT psychology division (see Figure 4-2).

Bingham opened the division with a staff of four. Two were existing faculty, both with master's degrees in psychology and education, but the other two were new hires, both psychologists: James Burt Miner (1873–1943) who received his PhD with Cattell at Columbia University, and Louis L. Thurstone (1887–1955), who had worked a summer with Thomas Edison and would soon complete his doctorate at the University of Chicago. Miner initiated studies of student interests and developed an interest test that E. K. Strong, Jr., would later form into the Strong Vocational Interest Blank.[19] Thurstone began research on the learning involved in linotype operations, part of the printing process at that time. Bingham and the rest of the staff were involved with the development of other tests, including tests of spatial abilities that were important in such occupations as archi-

Carnegie Institute of Technology
PSYCHOLOGICAL EXAMINATION
READING TEST

Full Name...
            Last Name   Given Names

High School.. City..

Age .... Date ....

Do not open this pamphlet until you are told to do so by the examiner.

This is a test to see how quickly and accurately you can think. The result of the test will be used by your advisers in order that they may know more about your abilities.

Read the following sentence and interpret what it means.

A small leak will sink a ship.

This means that small and unimportant things may ruin or damage large and important things. This meaning can be stated in different ways. Read the four following sentences and find two sentences which have nearly the same meaning as the statement above. Make a check mark before each of these two sentences. **Check only two sentences.**

1)........A spark may start a great fire.
2)........When the cat is away the mice will play.
3)........Reputation may be ruined by a word.
4).......Untempted virtue is easily retained.

Check the **first** and **third** sentences because they represent nearly the same meaning as the given sentence.

Read the following sentence and interpret its meaning.

Don't put all your eggs in one basket.

Check two of the following statements with nearly the same meaning as the above statement.

........The mouse that has but one hole is soon caught.
........Catch the bear before you sell his skin.
........The proof of the pudding is in the eating.
........Put not all your crocks on one shelf.

Check the first and fourth statements because they have nearly the same meaning.

In this test you will be given a series of questions like this. Read the first sentence carefully to see what it means and then check **two** of the remaining sentences that have the same meaning.

Do not ask any questions. If you come to a problem that you do not understand, go to the next problem.

You will be given thirty minutes. You should solve all the problems in that time. Hand in your paper when you have finished.

DO NOT TURN THIS PAGE UNTIL YOU ARE TOLD TO BEGIN

No. 40010 Thurstone test.   C. H. Stoelting Co., Chicago, Ill., U. S. A.

Figure 4-2. *Psychological Examination Reading Test from the Carnegie Institute of Technology.*

tecture, sheet metal work, and costume design. Furthermore, Bingham began a program of mental testing that involved all incoming CIT students. They were given tests of intelligence, memory, reasoning, language ability, manual dexterity, and spatial ability. It was hoped that these data could be used to predict successful performance in various college majors but could also be extended to predict success in various jobs. In addition to the test development programs, the psychology division initiated a series of courses designed to help students apply psychology—for example, educational psychology, applied psychology, and vocational psychology.

The Bureau of Salesmanship Research

In 1916, Bingham began an ambitious program to establish a Bureau of Salesmanship Research within the psychology division. The bureau was to be supported by contributions from local businesses such as the Equitable Life Assurance Society, Heinz Foods, and Carnegie Steel. By March of 1917 there were 30 business partners. These business partners, via participation on an oversight board, had some influence on the research questions that would be investigated by the bureau. Further, the bureau would conduct occasional workshops on various business subjects for employees from the partner businesses. It was an arrangement that was unique in psychology, and it established formal linkages between academic psychology and the business world. To start the bureau, Bingham hired the psychologist who had by then done the most work in the business field, namely, Walter Dill Scott, who by 1916 had published two additional books on the psychology of business.[20] With funds supplied by the business partners, Scott was able to hire five research assistants, several of whom would be graduate students in the psychology program. Among that initial group was some exceptional talent that included Edward S. Robinson (1893–1937), later a professor of psychology at Yale University, and Dwight L. Hoopingarner, whose expertise on labor relations made him a member of President Franklin D. Roosevelt's four administrations.[21]

The bureau wasted no time in supplying their partners with useful information and in using their partners as part of the research process. In 1916, Scott published a booklet, *Aids in the Selection of Salesmen*, which was distributed to the business partners.

> The booklet included a "personal History Record" to be filled out by the salesperson; an "Interviewer's Scale" in which the interviewer rated the candidate on such traits as convincingness, industry, value to the firm, and appearance; a "Range of Interest" form developed by Robinson that assessed the candidate's knowledge of such diverse subjects as Chopin, crank shafts, Rodin, silos, mimeographs, mayonnaise, Bismarck, colan-

ders, and Rhode Island Reds; a paper-and-pencil adult intelligence test; and other tests and forms, all copyrighted by the Bureau.[22]

The business partners were to administer the tests to their salespersons and return those data to the psychology division along with evaluative data about the sales performances of the individuals. Those data were to be used by Scott and his colleagues to develop better measures of predicting sales success.[23]

The End of the Division of Applied Psychology

A few years later the psychology division added a Research Bureau for Retail Training dedicated to studying personnel selection, training, and supervision. This bureau was initially supported by six of Pittsburgh's largest department stores. By 1920 the division included a Department of Vocational Education and a School of Life Insurance Salesmanship. At its peak in 1923, the faculty and staff in the Division of Applied Psychology numbered 25, not counting research fellows. Despite the rapid growth of this unique program and its service to the business community, by the summer of 1924 it had essentially disappeared. The reasons for its demise are complex.[24] The short answer is that CIT replaced Hamerschlag as president and the new president did not envision psychology as one of the prominent programs in what he viewed as an engineering university. Bingham and the rest of his talented staff quickly dispersed to other jobs: Thurstone to the University of Chicago, Strong to Stanford, Miner to Kentucky, and Scott to Northwestern. Bingham continued his work in industrial psychology in the private sector and in government work. Although the CIT Division of Applied Psychology and all of its business-oriented units no longer existed, its legacy continued through the more than 65 doctoral students it trained, some of whom pursued careers in industrial psychology. Futhermore, its faculty largely continued to work in the psychology of business, spreading the influence of this applied specialty.[25]

The One Right Way: Scientific Management

By 1913 both Scott and Münsterberg had written books on increasing efficiency in industry. These books did not initiate this emphasis in business;

rather, as noted earlier, they were a reaction to management's obsession that characterized American business at the turn of the century. In the late 19th century, labor unions had grown in power, and frequent strikes proved a significant hindrance to production and profits. Management needed some way to regain its power. A mechanical engineer, Frederick Winslow Taylor (1856–1915), would provide that. Taylor recognized the inherent conflict in industry between employer and employee. Employees wanted higher wages; employers wanted cheap labor. Employers also wanted production, ideally more efficient production, which meant less time required to produce goods. Taylor argued that efficiency resulted only when management and workers understood that mutual cooperation was mutually beneficial.

Taylor developed a system of management that he labeled "scientific management," which later became known as "Taylorism." Scientific management began with an analysis of a job to determine the best way to do that job, whether it was carrying iron, laying bricks, shoveling coal, or building cabinets. These proponents of scientific management were known as "efficiency experts," a label that was despised by labor. They began by studying a particular job, observing workers on the job, breaking workers' actions down into individual movements, and timing each of those movements with a stop watch (later they used film in what were called "time and motion studies" of work). From these observations, the efficiency experts were able to describe *the* one right way to do a job (and according to them there was only one right way). Once the right way to do the job was determined, it was possible to determine what a productive work output would be (see Figure 4-3). In other words, once one knows the best way to make a cabinet, one can know how long it takes to make a cabinet and thus how many cabinets should be produced by a worker in a day. Taylor encouraged managers to use this information to establish production expectations and to set wages to reinforce those workers who met or exceeded quotas and punish workers whose performance did not measure up to the established standards of production. Indeed, workers could be paid an amount for each cabinet they made, a procedure known as piece-rate work. Taylor believed that this approach would please both management and worker because it would ensure management a reasonable rate of production tied to wages and it would also ensure that the best workers received the highest wages.[26]

Instruction Card
for Finishing a Piston Rod

Detailed Instructions	Tool Used	Depth of Cut in Inches	Feed in Inches	Spindle RPM	Speed in Feet per Minute	Minutes Allowed
Set up and clamp rod						5.0
Set tool						1.0
Rough turn body and cross head fit	PRSE	1/4	3/32	44	40	10.5
Change and set tool						1.5
Rough turn cross headfit and collar		1/4	1/8		40	3.0
Reverse and reclamp rod						2.5
Rough turn piston clearance boss		1/4	3/32		48	7.0
Remove						2.5
				Total minutes		33.0
				Total hours per piece		0.55

Figure 4-3. *Instruction cards like this one were a key component of scientific management. They were developed for thousands of field and factory jobs. They were not suggestions for how the job should be done; they were exact prescriptions for the "one best way." Note that this example specifies the tool to be used, the order of the steps to finish the metal rod, the specific tasks to be accomplished at each step, the time required to complete each step, and the time required for the total job.*

Taylor described the benefits of his system as follows:

> The general adoption of scientific management would readily in the future double the productivity of the average man engaged in industrial work. Think of what this means to the whole country. Think of the increase, both in the necessities and luxuries of life, which become available for the whole country, of the possibility of shortening the

hours of labor when this is desirable, and of the increased opportunities for education, culture, and recreation which this implies. ... Scientific management will mean, for the employers and workmen who adopt it ... the elimination of almost all causes for dispute and disagreement between them. What constitutes a fair day's work will be a question for scientific investigation, instead of a subject to be bargained and haggled over. ... The great increase in wages which accompanies this type of management will largely eliminate the wage question as a source of dispute. But more than all other causes, the close, intimate cooperation, the constant personal contact between the two sides [management and worker], will tend to diminish friction and discontent.[27]

It was a grand vision, but one that shared little with its reality in practice. The science of human behavior is never so easily realized, although engineers, scientists, and managers at the beginning of the 20th century could be forgiven for not understanding that.

Problems with Scientific Management

Initially, scientific management was well received, not only within the ranks of business owners and managers but also in government agencies and the popular press where it was presented as a scientific approach to business that would promote fairness in the treatment of workers while ensuring the production goals of business. But the bloom was soon off the rose. Although the system was popular with managers, it did not please workers. Workers had no input into this system. Individuals who might have been building cabinets for 25 years would be told the best way to build a cabinet by an efficiency expert who had watched perhaps one cabinet being built. Workers believed that management would use scientific management to increase production, and thus profits, without increasing wages; that is, the workers would not share in the extra profits. Or that wages would increase, but production would increase at an even greater rate meaning management would earn disproportionately more. Mostly they were right in their suspicions. Having been left out of all decision making, workers began to raise their voices. A strike at a Massachusetts arsenal in 1911 led to a congressional investigation of scientific management, which resulted in a ban on piece-rate incentive programs and the use of time measurement approaches to job performance in any government work. Other government hearings led to further restrictions of Taylor's system in government work.[28]

With the loss of endorsement by the US government, it is no surprise that the system was in trouble in the business world as well. Some of Taylor's followers sought to fix the system with greater attention to the concerns of workers. For example, Lillian Gilbreth (1878–1972), who earned her doctorate in psychology in 1915, wrote a book on the psychology of management in 1914 that promoted Taylor's system with modifications recognizing the experience of the worker and the role of the worker in the job-product equation. Gilbreth's book did not provide the fix that Taylorism needed, but it did recognize the psychology of the worker. Lillian Gilbreth, although trained as a psychologist, worked as an engineer and was married to an engineer (Frank Gilbreth, one of the leaders in scientific management and the principal promoter of time-motion studies as a way to define efficiency) (see Figure 4-4).[29] Whereas engineers paid little attention to the human equation in their efficiency studies, Lillian Gilbreth understood that workers needed a say in the workplace.

Workers Are Not Machines

One of Taylor's major failings was his mistaken belief that economic incentives were all that mattered to workers. He paid no attention to individual differences in workers, except in terms of piece-rate work. Historian Thomas Hughes has written that Taylor "proved naïve in his judgments about complex human values and motives."[30] He told workers not to question what they were told but to follow orders exactly as given to reap maximum financial benefits. Workers refused to be treated like machines. There were important issues to be raised, human issues. Those human issues were the domain of psychology, and psychologists were more than willing to bring their expertise to bear on the problems of efficiency. A world war was about to give them a chance to show what they knew about human differences and the relationship of those differences to ability.

World War I and Its Aftermath

In chapter 2 we discussed the role American psychologists played in World War I. In a word, they were involved with testing. Robert Yerkes

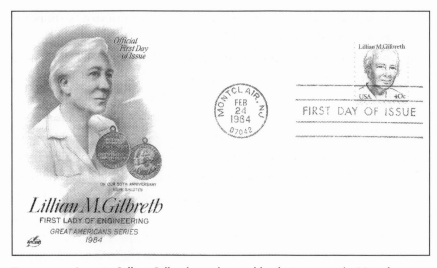

Figure 4-4. *In 1984 Lillian Gilbreth was honored by the issuance of a United States postage stamp (40 cents) featuring her portrait. The campaign to recognize her contributions was originated by the women's division of the American Society of Mechanical Engineers. She is the only American psychologist to appear on a US stamp, although some would argue that philosopher John Dewey (1859–1952), who received a stamp in 1968, could be considered a psychologist.*

headed the program to assess intelligence of military recruits and chaired the committee that developed the Army Alpha and Army Beta tests, used to test nearly 2 million military personnel and recruits. Bingham was one of the seven psychologists who served on that committee. His applied experience at CIT proved invaluable. Bingham and Scott also pressured the Army to establish a program for the selection of officers. You may recall from chapter 2 that Scott was selected to head this operation as chair of the Committee on the Classification of Personnel in the Army. Bingham served as executive secretary for the committee. The committee began its work by modifying some of the selection tests for salespersons that had been developed by Scott, Bingham, and others at CIT. Eventually the committee developed more than 100 selection tests for 80 different jobs. Approximately 3.5 million soldiers were assessed using one or more of these selection tests. The effort was seen as a great success by the military, and Congress concurred, awarding Scott the Distinguished Service Medal in

1919. As mentioned earlier, he was the only psychologist to be so honored for his military work during that war.[31]

Historians debate the impact of psychologists' contributions during the war, questioning especially the usefulness of the intelligence testing program.[32] There is, however, no denying that psychologists emerged from the war with a public image of important wartime contributions, and they were quick to use this image in promoting the applications of psychology to business. Historian of psychology Thomas Van de Water has written that "in the public eye...the government had validated psychology by accepting and funding its tests and commissioning its practitioners." Psychologists used this "seal of approval," suggesting that similar accomplishments "could be expected in peacetime applications for business."[33]

The postwar years saw the rise of mental testing in American business. Mental tests gradually became a part of business practices in measuring advertising appeals, management styles, consumer behavior, sales strategies, and particularly personnel issues, such as worker selection, job analysis, production, and efficiency. Whereas the Taylorists found themselves on the defensive regarding their lack of consideration for the worker, psychologists emphasized that their approach to efficiency did not embody the tenets of scientific management and its insistence on the one right way, but instead focused on the match of worker talents to job requirements.

Personnel issues became even more salient in the 1920s as companies grew and jobs became more specialized. To meet these changes, companies established personnel departments that were centralized offices for hiring and job placement. These departments sometimes included psychologists as consultants or as full-time employees who focused their work on employee testing and matching of job requirements and employee skills. Whereas the Taylorists, with their engineering backgrounds, had argued that the behavior of workers was due largely to workplace factors such as economic incentives, machine improvements, and plant reorganization, psychologists instead stressed the importance of human factors such as intelligence, personality, and motivation as key determinants in work efficiency.[34] The use of psychological testing in the business community was slow in developing but would eventually be widespread. It developed largely from the needs of personnel departments.

Personnel Psychology in the 1920s

A number of factors precipitated the growth of personnel psychology in the 1920s. Paramount was the international push for greater efficiency and the belief that the tools of science could serve that need. Further, as businesses evolved, growth in the sheer number of jobs and the increased specialization of those jobs called for a better match between worker and job. Within psychology, the successes of the selection work carried out by Bingham and his team at CIT and by Scott and his colleagues during World War I, as well as other mental testing efforts, interested some psychologists in personnel work.

Journal of Applied Psychology

In 1916, as the United States struggled to stay out of the war in Europe, plans were initiated for a new American psychology journal to publish the work of this new breed of consulting psychologist. The first issue of the *Journal of Applied Psychology* appeared in 1917 with G. Stanley Hall, John W. Baird (1869–1919), and Ludwig R. Geissler (1879–1932) as editors. Geissler would be the principal editorial force for the journal. The initial editorial in the journal described considerable breadth in the applied topics that it was expected to cover. It was made clear, however, that the thrust of the journal was expected to be the psychology of business. Regarding the application of the new science of psychology, the editors wrote:

> But perhaps the most strikingly original endeavor to utilize the methods and the results of psychological investigation has been in the realm of business. This movement began with the psychology of advertising...but it soon spread to the adjacent field of salesmanship.... Thence the attention of the applied psychologist turned to the more comprehensive and fundamental problem of vocational selection—the question, namely, of making a detailed inventory of the equipment of mental qualities possessed by a given individual, of discovery of what qualities are essential to successful achievement in a given vocation, and thus of directing the individual to the vocational niche which he is best fitted to fill.[35]

The editorial continued in its praise of the value of psychological applications to the workplace, echoing the words Lightner Witmer had used at the

APA meeting in 1896 in urging his colleagues to use their science to throw light on the problems of humanity.[36] The editors noted that the personnel questions now being addressed by psychology should appeal to every psychologist who wished to decrease "the number of cases where a square peg is condemned to a life of fruitless endeavor to fit itself comfortably into a round hole."[37] There was, indeed, a decidedly industrial theme to the journal's content, including many articles describing selection instruments for such vocations as firefighters, police officers, pilots, telegraphers, mill workers, and stenographers.[38]

Psychological Consulting Firms

The emphasis on personnel issues led Scott and several of his colleagues from his wartime personnel committee to found what was the first psychological consulting firm, the Scott Company. Founded in 1919, the company offered psychological services, largely in the form of job analysis and personnel selection, to the business community (see Figure 4-5). Scott served as president and chief fund-raiser for the company, relying heavily on the many contacts he had made during his wartime service. The company initially did well under Scott's leadership but began to falter soon after he left in 1920 to assume the presidency of Northwestern University. It ceased its operations in 1923.[39] A similar postwar effort at providing psychological consulting services to industry was the formation of the Psychological Corporation. Founded by James McKeen Cattell in 1921, the corporation's early years were not profitable. Eventually, however, it became a very successful publishing house and for many years has been the principal distributor for a variety of psychological tests. Today it is well known to psychologists and graduate students in assessment as the distributor of the ubiquitous Wechsler Scales of Intelligence.[40]

Although these early psychological consulting firms did not thrive, individual psychologists did find consulting opportunities or full-time employment in business and industry. They promoted testing, particularly tests for employee selection. Their hiring was supported by a growing literature extolling the value of psychological tests in business and industry and the need for qualified psychologists to administer and interpret those test results in, for example, Harry Hollingworth's *Vocational Psychology* (1916), Henry Link's

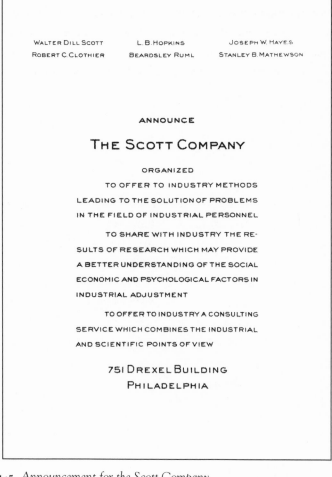

WALTER DILL SCOTT   L.B.HOPKINS   JOSEPH W. HAYES
ROBERT C.CLOTHIER   BEARDSLEY RUML   STANLEY B. MATHEWSON

ANNOUNCE

THE SCOTT COMPANY

ORGANIZED

TO OFFER TO INDUSTRY METHODS
LEADING TO THE SOLUTION OF PROBLEMS
IN THE FIELD OF INDUSTRIAL PERSONNEL

TO SHARE WITH INDUSTRY THE RE-
SULTS OF RESEARCH WHICH MAY PROVIDE
A BETTER UNDERSTANDING OF THE SOCIAL
ECONOMIC AND PSYCHOLOGICAL FACTORS IN
INDUSTRIAL ADJUSTMENT

TO OFFER TO INDUSTRY A CONSULTING
SERVICE WHICH COMBINES THE INDUSTRIAL
AND SCIENTIFIC POINTS OF VIEW

751 DREXEL BUILDING
PHILADELPHIA

Figure 4-5. *Announcement for the Scott Company.*

Employment Psychology (1919), Arthur Kornhauser and Forrest Kingsbury's *Psychological Tests in Business* (1924), Charles Griffiths's *Fundamentals of Vocational Psychology* (1924), and Donald Laird's *The Psychology of Selecting Men* (1925).[41] These texts, and others, emphasized the importance of selection, both for the company and for the worker. Henry Link (1889–1952), who would soon be president of the Psychological Corporation, explained:

> Other things being equal, both the employer and the employee gain in
> proportion as men work at a job for which they are more fit than any other

men are, and as each man is given the job for which he is better fitted than for any other job.... If sufficient ability and effort are expended it is possible to measure the comparative fitness of any number of men for any one given job, or the comparative fitness of any one man for any number of different jobs. These are the tasks of scientific personnel work.[42]

Psychologists and managers were not the only participants in personnel work. Recall the writings of Katherine Blackford, described in chapter 1, who promoted a personnel system based on the "science" of physiognomy, suggesting, for example, that businesses hire blonds for sales jobs because they were more likely to have convex faces indicating traits of aggressiveness and persistence. Physiognomic or characterological systems were very popular as selection methods in American businesses in the first third of the 20th century, and psychologists found themselves in a fight over authority for personnel work. In response to the work of those seen as charlatans, psychologists were consistent in their message to business executives: Psychological "tests are scientific instruments. Test work should be supervised by someone with thorough training in applied psychology. Otherwise it should be left alone.... As patent medicines, tests are dangerous."[43]

Establishing Scientific Legitimacy

Psychologists used several means to attempt to establish the scientific legitimacy of their work for the business world. The American Psychological Association began a program in 1921 to certify "consulting psychologists," a program intended to offer qualified doctoral-level psychologists a credential they could use in working with the public (see the brief discussion of this program in chapter 2). In the same year, Cattell founded the Psychological Corporation, in part as a kind of credentialing body to identify qualified psychologists who could do applied work. Also in 1921, while still at CIT, Bingham helped to found the Personnel Research Federation (PRF) in New York City, an organization whose purpose was to work with businesses and other entities (such as governments) "to find solutions [to] those crucial problems which center about personnel in industry...particularly the economic, social and generally humanistic aspects of the case."[44] PRF began publishing a scientific journal in 1922, entitled the *Journal of Personnel Research* (name changed to *Personnel Journal* in 1927), which

Bingham began editing in 1923. That journal and the *Journal of Applied Psychology* provided two important outlets for the expanding research in personnel psychology.

Industrial Psychology Monthly

Industrial psychologists recognized that business executives rarely read those scientific journals, nor were their comments welcomed for publication there (although the *Journal of Applied Psychology* did publish such commentaries in its first few years of existence). The solution was a new journal, more along the lines of a magazine that would speak directly to the needs of the business community in a language that it would find useful. *Industrial Psychology Monthly* began publication in January 1926. Its editor was Donald A. Laird (1897–1969), a psychologist at Colgate University and author of more than a dozen books on applying psychology to business, most of them written for a business audience. Laird's initial editorial board consisted of three managers from industry and four university-based psychologists. The authorship of his magazine articles reflected a similar balance. The first issue included an article on managing workers through their self-interests; it was written by a manager from the automobile industry. Another manager wrote about controlling office output, while a psychologist who consulted for the Yellow Cab Company of Chicago described a selection test for chauffeurs. In addition to the articles, each issue contained a notes and news section that provided brief synopses of relevant findings from psychological research and reviews of new books related to the psychology of business. The magazine took seriously its scientific charge and published several articles debunking the credibility of phrenological and physiognomic selection systems. Laird and his colleagues believed that they were providing an important service to industrial psychologists by publishing their work in a format useful for business executives and for the business community as well by providing it with valuable information about the application of psychology to their problems (see Figure 4-6). However, after only three years the magazine ceased publication.[45]

Steady Growth

Despite the failure of Laird's magazine, the 1920s witnessed a steady but slow growth of psychologists in the personnel industry, including some

---

Industrial Psychology Monthly

April 1926   Vol. 1, No. 4

Table of Contents

Women in Industry, by *Lewis W. Hine* 247

Women and the Industrial Revolution, by *Harry E. Barnes* 253

Where Women Work Today, by *Ruth Reed* 257

Recreation for Women Employees, by *Ruth I. Stone* 262

Job Tenure of Women Workers in Industry, by *Amy Hewes* 265

Nervous Women in Industry, by *Mary C. Jarrett* 271

The Selection of Girl Cashiers, by *Lorine Pruette* 277

Salvaging the Worker Through Work, by *H. W. Stevens* 280

Industry looks at the Married Woman Worker, by *Sadie M. Shellow* 283

The Woman Business Executive, by *Iva L. Peters* 288

Women in Industry, the Family, and the Home, by *Chase Woodhouse* 293

Editorial Comment 299

Notes and Items 302

New Books to Read 310

Figure 4-6. *Table of contents from the April 1926 issue of the magazine* Industrial Psychology Monthly, *a special issue of the magazine devoted to women in the workplace.*

female psychologists who found industry more accepting than academia. Marion Bills (1890–1970) worked for the Aetna Life Insurance Company in Hartford, Connecticut, for more than 30 years in personnel selection and sales research; and Elsie Bregman (1896–1969) served as personnel officer at Macy's Department Store in New York City for several years where she developed a battery of tests for employees, before taking a position with the Psychological Corporation.[46]

In the beginning, psychologists working in business had referred to themselves as consulting psychologists, economic psychologists, or business psychologists. But by the 1920s, "industrial psychologist" was the more likely label. Even so this was a small field. It is estimated that by the end of the 1920s the total number of industrial psychologists did not exceed 50. Approximately 60% of those worked in business and government settings, with the rest being employed in universities.[47] By the end of the 1930s the number of industrial psychologists would still be small, numbering around 100. The explosive growth in the field would await World War II. In the meantime, the field would witness the beginnings of its organizational side.

The Great Depression and the Beginnings of Organizational Psychology

During the Great Depression of the 1930s, more than a quarter of the American work force could not find jobs. Psychologists were in a difficult position as well. Doctoral programs had expanded in the prosperous 1920s and the new doctorates being turned out in greater numbers found themselves looking for jobs in a contracted market in which university jobs were particularly scarce, and the graduates were also competing for jobs with many recent émigré psychologists from Europe, most of them fleeing from the Nazi regime.[48] With the academic market limited, psychologists looked for opportunities in applied work.

The traditional personnel work of industrial psychologists met with mixed results in these times of economic woes. Most companies, because of significant layoffs, reduced or eliminated their personnel departments because hiring was essentially nonexistent. Yet some businesses saw the unemployment lines as a pool to be tapped for better talent, making selection skills even more important. Industrial psychologists would use this time to redefine their field.

Morris Viteles (1898–1996) was one of America's most important industrial psychologists.[49] He was a doctoral student with Lightner Witmer at the University of Pennsylvania, and while there he headed one of the earliest vocational guidance clinics in the United States, possibly the first of its kind.

He is best known, however, for the 1932 publication of a landmark book in industrial psychology, the most important book in the field since Münsterberg's text almost 20 years earlier. Entitled simply *Industrial Psychology*, this book surveyed the accomplishments of the field to that time and pointed the way to a plan for research and practice for the future. For more than 20 years, psychologists referred to it as the "bible" of industrial psychology.[50] According to Viteles, three forces shaped the foundation and development of industrial psychology: "economic, social, and psychological."[51] In reviewing the influence of Taylor's scientific management, Viteles wrote that Taylor and his disciples "establish[ed] firmly the economic objective of industrial psychology."[52] By this he meant that industrial psychologists recognized early on that their employment existed in the service of management. That is, psychologists who worked with or for businesses were hired, not by workers, but by owners and managers. They were hired to achieve some kind of economic goal, typically to increase profits. They were, as historian Loren Baritz described them, "servants of power."[53] This message was not lost on workers who saw psychologists, as they had the Taylor efficiency experts, as tools of management. It was a view that some psychologists wanted to change. But the reality was undeniable. Research funds, consulting funds, or salaries for the industrial psychologists were paid by management. It was clear where one's duty lay.

Economic factors were certainly the driving force for industrial psychology, but they were not the only ones. One can argue that many of the difficulties faced by the Taylorists, both with workers and the US Congress, was an almost singular reliance on seeing the workplace in terms of economic issues (e.g., wages and productivity). As an engineer, Taylor understood machines. Machines did their work one way, and (unless they were malfunctioning) they did their work that same way again, and again, and again. Taylor argued that workers needed to learn to do their jobs the one right way and to do it that way again, and again, and again.

Psychologists were willing to pay homage to the economic gods. They understood that necessity or they did not work in industry for long. Yet they also recognized other forces that were crucial in determining (and controlling) the behavior of humans, forces that Viteles labeled social and psychological. They understood that humans did not function like machines. Workers wanted to be respected as human beings, they wanted conditions of fairness in the workplace, and they liked to be asked for their opinions about how to do their jobs. Psychologists had witnessed the public relations fiasco of the Taylorists. They would not make the same mistakes.

The Hawthorne Studies

A series of studies in the 1920s and 1930s provided new insights into factors related to workplace productivity. In 1927, psychologist Elton Mayo (1880–1949) was head of Harvard University's Department of Industrial Research when he was invited to conduct some research for the Western Electric Company at its Hawthorne Works division in Chicago. The studies were to investigate factors contributing to productivity (a combination of efficiency and effectiveness) and worker satisfaction, and investigated such variables as workplace illumination, rest intervals, length of work day and work week, and wage incentives. The findings proved to be most unexpected. Productivity increased due to the manipulation of the variables just listed, but some of the increases occurred (or at least production did not decrease) in conditions in which the variables were reversed. This paradox led to additional experiments focusing on psychological and social factors (e.g., worker attitudes, worker-supervisor teams, group dynamics) in addition to the physical factors of the workplace. The conclusion was that the psychological variables proved to be of greater importance than the physical variables in affecting production. Giving special attention to workers and listening to them "was as important, perhaps more important, than the changes in working conditions."[54] This experimental finding has become known as the "Hawthorne effect."

There were other surprises in the Hawthorne studies, particularly from experiments that were known as the bank wiring studies. This research was designed to study the social processes governing production. A department was selected at the Hawthorne Works that manufactured electric switches in a series (a bank).

> A major discovery that the investigators made in the bank wiring room was that the workers were intimately involved in the most intricate social organization of their own ... their social organization prevented devi-ant behavior of the group members, and it protected the entire group from outside interference or control.... Adjusting the reports of their daily production, the wiremen controlled the amount of their work and

thus prevented management from imposing production quotas or other demands upon them. The group itself decided how much work was to be done, and regardless of the efforts of management, the sanctions of the informal organization were more effective than those of the formal organization. In other words, the small group, not management, determined the level of production.[55]

The researchers also found, to their amazement, that there was no correlation between the ability of an individual and that individual's performance. Individual work rates were not determined by the variable abilities of the individuals but by the social control pressures exerted by the group. Despite the fact that management offered incentives for higher production, the lure of those incentives was not enough to overcome the social pressures of the group. That meant that performance could not be predicted from ability. The implications of that finding for industrial psychology were monumental (see Figure 4-7).

> If the Hawthorne researchers were right, if performance and ability were unrelated, the industrial psychologists of the 1920's who had searched for the perfect psychological test had been wrong. ... From Hawthorne on, the problems of selection, training, efficiency, and control would never seem as simple as they had appeared to the testing psychologists of the 1920's.[56]

Baritz has called the Hawthorne studies "the single most important social science research project ever conducted in industry."[57] Although the interpretations of the Hawthorne studies remain controversial today, there is no denying their role in altering the focus of industrial research and practices toward recognition of the importance of human relations in the workplace.[58] The Hawthorne experiments demonstrated the importance of assessing worker attitudes, of interviewing workers,[59] of offering counseling programs in the workplace,[60] of allowing workers to have input into the establishment of workplace norms, and of encouraging workers and supervisors to develop teams in a collaborative way. Some historians see these studies as the beginning of organizational psychology.[61] Other studies would soon add to this new focus for industrial psychologists.

MANAGEMENT AND THE WORKER

An Account of a Research Program Conducted by the Western Electric Company, Hawthorne Works, Chicago

BY

F. J. ROETHLISBERGER

ASSOCIATE PROFESSOR OF INDUSTRIAL RESEARCH
HARVARD GRADUATE SCHOOL OF BUSINESS ADMINISTRATION

AND

WILLIAM J. DICKSON

CHIEF OF EMPLOYEE RELATIONS RESEARCH DEPARTMENT
WESTERN ELECTRIC COMPANY, HAWTHORNE WORKS

with the assistance and collaboration of
HAROLD A. WRIGHT

CHIEF OF PERSONNEL RESEARCH AND TRAINING DIVISION
WESTERN ELECTRIC COMPANY, HAWTHORNE WORKS

HARVARD UNIVERSITY PRESS
CAMBRIDGE, MASSACHUSETTS
1939

Figure 4-7. *Title page from* Management and the Worker *(1939).*

Attitudes, Leadership, and Worker Satisfaction

According to psychologists Raymond Katzell and James Austin, two other sets of studies from the 1930s deserve mention for the way they reflected changes in the nature of industrial psychology from its largely selection-oriented personnel paradigm.[62] The first of these was a series of studies of employee attitudes and morale at large companies, for example at Procter & Gamble and at Kimberly-Clark Corporation.[63] These studies were important, in part for their development of attitude assessment measures, but for our purposes, more so for their acknowledgement of the importance of getting feedback from workers about their jobs.

The second set of studies was conducted by German émigré psychologist Kurt Lewin (1890–1947). With World War II under way and the fascist regimes enjoying such military success, Lewin wondered about leadership style as it related to productivity. Using leadership style as an independent variable in research with groups of young boys, Lewin investigated the effect of each of three styles (democratic vs. authoritarian vs. laissez-faire) on production, quality of work, and satisfaction of the boys. The study showed that the democratic leadership style produced the work of the best quality and the best worker satisfaction, and that production remained high, even when the leader was not present.[64] Although the study may have been good news for democracy during a time when some may have questioned its relative effectiveness, the importance for industrial psychology was the clear demonstration of the powerful effect of a social psychological variable—namely, leadership—on traditional workplace outcome measures. Indeed, studies of the effects of leadership would become one of the principal areas of work in organizational psychology.

To those two sets of studies we would add a third, a book by Robert Hoppock (1901–1995) entitled *Job Satisfaction*, published in 1935.[65] Although job satisfaction did not become a mainstream focus of industrial/organizational psychology until after World War II, this landmark book and the research it inspired is indicative of the growing recognition among industrial psychologists in the 1930s that the attitudes of workers figured prominently in industry's goals of increased production and efficiency, and it is further evidence of the seeds of organizational psychology in the Great Depression.

As industrial psychology matured as a field of practice in the 1930s, its practitioners were clearly servants of power. But their work on social and psychological factors in business forced an American industrial empire still enamored with the promises of Taylorism to recognize the worker as part of the decision-making process in industry. Granted, the rise in power of labor unions in the 1930s did much to ensure that workers' voices would be heard, but the science of psychology was also a player in orchestrating the greater attention paid to human relations in American industry.

Organizing Industrial Psychologists

Today industrial/organizational psychologists meet together in several venues, most notably the Society for Industrial and Organizational Psychology (SIOP) and the Academy of Management. The beginnings of organizational efforts date to the 1930s. Industrial psychologists, particularly those working full-time in industry, were involved in the foundation of the Association of Consulting Psychologists (ACP) in 1930. They participated in the annual meeting of that group, offering programs each year for psychologists working in industry. In 1936, industrial psychologists within ACP formed a committee to "work for the improvement of status among industrial psychologists, and possibly develop a set of standards and code of ethics."[66] They did not develop a code of ethics but did produce a document outlining the coursework and training experiences students should have to work in industrial psychology. Moreover, they developed materials that described careers in industrial psychology for students and that were intended to recruit students to the field.[67]

As noted in chapter 2, the ACP dissolved in 1938 and became part of a new organization representing consulting and applied psychologists, the American Association for Applied Psychology (AAAP). This new organization established four sections, one of which was the Industrial and Business Section, or Section D. One of the products of this group was a list of professional services that members were willing to provide, a list published in a 1938 issue of the *Journal of Consulting Psychology*.[68] (That list is shown in Table 4-1.) The list is interesting because it provides a comprehensive catalog of the services that industrial psychologists believed they were competent in providing at the end of the 1930s. It offers evidence of both the traditional personnel work that characterized the beginnings of industrial psychology as well as services that would fit the developing emphases in organizational psychology. It also makes clear that Taylorism was not dead and that psychologists were willing to help find the one right way to do the job.

The industrial psychologists of Section D were busy with several tasks, including developing a code of ethical practice for their applied specialty and improving public relations. Part of the public relations campaign was an effort to inform businesses about bogus selection systems (e.g., selection

TABLE 4-1. AREAS IN WHICH INDUSTRIAL AND BUSINESS
SECTION MEMBERS WERE WILLING TO RENDER
PROFESSIONAL SERVICES (1938)

Area	Professional Service
1.	Study of the requirements of occupations
2.	Development and use of tests and other scientific techniques in the scientific placement of workers
3.	Formulation of the best methods of applying human energy at work
4.	Organization and systematization of training programs to insure the most complete development and most efficient use of individual ability
5.	Determination of the optimal conditions of work
6.	Analysis of characteristics of industrial organization for the determination of types best adapted to serve both the economic and social, and broadly, human objectives of industrial organization
7.	Examination and control of motivating forces in the case of both workers and management, which influence production and harmonious relationships in the industrial situation
8.	Analysis of human factors influencing the demand for and sale of commodities through the application of scientific techniques of market research

based on facial features) that were still popular in the 1930s. The public relations efforts were also intended to generate more business. Toward that end, Section D scheduled at least one public lecture each year as part of the program of AAAP. These lectures were well advertised to businesses in the cities where the meetings occurred and were intended to sell the services of industrial psychology.[69]

The AAAP was only seven years old when it merged with the APA in 1945, a merger necessitated by the war. The newly organized APA adopted the sectional structure of the AAAP, establishing 18 charter divisions representing the growing specialized interests of psychologists.[70] Several of those divisions were the applied groups from the AAAP, including Section D, which in the new APA became Division 14, the Division of Industrial and Business Psychology. The division would undergo several name changes—Division of Industrial Psychology in 1962, Division of Industrial and Organizational Psychology in 1973, and Society for Industrial and Organizational Psychology in 1983—reflecting changes in the nature of the applied specialty and, in the final case, a desire for some independence from the APA.[71] Psychologists from industry were well represented in Division 14 but the annual division programs at the meetings of the APA typically focused on research and not on the practical issues that were part of everyday life in the world of business. Consequently, psychologists from business settings formed their own groups, typically local or regional in nature. A group calling itself Industrial Psychologists Employed in Private Industry began meeting on the East Coast in the early 1950s. A midwestern group began meeting in 1951, calling itself the Dearborn Conference, and has met twice each year since that time.[72] A third group known as the No-Name Group began meeting in Hartford, Connecticut in 1955. Seven of its members would become presidents of Division 14.[73] These small groups were important for the social contacts among psychologists working in industry but also as a venue to discuss common problems and possible solutions. They also served to organize these industrial psychologists so that they were able to achieve leadership roles within the more formal organizations often dominated by academics.

World War II and Its Aftermath

American psychologists were ready for World War II. As discussed earlier, both the AAAP and the APA had committees in place by 1939 whose purpose was to explore the roles psychologists might play in wartime and to plan for the mobilization of psychologists in the event of America's involvement in the war. By 1940, the military began to employ psychologists. The US Army created a seven-person committee of psychologists to consult on matters of selection. Bingham was appointed chief psychologist in the Adjutant General's Office and assigned to chair the committee that developed the Army General Classification Test, the most widely used selection instrument in the history of the US military services. During the war, an estimated 12 million individuals were assessed with that test. Its success was even endorsed by First Lady Eleanor Roosevelt after she visited Bingham and the other psychologists involved in the classification and assignment of military personnel.[74] Other assignments relevant to the skills of industrial psychologists included studies of recruitment strategies, leadership, training, organizational design, interviewing, morale studies, and human factors work, involving equipment design.

As World War I had proved to be a boon to applied psychology, World War II was more so. In chapter 2 we described the phenomenal growth of clinical psychology after the war. Industrial psychology would also undergo considerable growth, both in numbers and in the breadth of the discipline and its practice. One way to see the growth of this field is in the membership numbers for Division 14. When the Division began in 1945 it had 130 members, and it mushroomed from there: 514 in 1955, 934 in 1965, 1,370 in 1975, 2,499 in 1985, and 2,700 in 2001.[75] Regarding the rapid growth of industrial psychology after World War II, historian Donald Napoli wrote:

> the military had given psychologists a chance to prove the effectiveness of selection, classification, and aptitude testing, and psychologists met the challenge successfully. Civilian employers also offered new opportunities, which grew largely from the labor shortage produced by wartime mobilization. Business managers, beset by high rates of absenteeism and job turnover, took unprecedented interest in hiring the right worker and keeping him contented on the job. Management turned to psychologists and other behavioral scientists for help, and the amount of psychological testing quickly increased. Surveys showed that in 1939 only 14 percent of businesses were using such tests; in 1947 the proportion rose to 50 percent, and in 1952, 75 percent.[76]

One of the areas of industrial psychology not touched upon by Napoli in that quotation is what is called human factors psychology or engineering psychology.

Human Factors Psychology

Human factors psychology emerged during World War II when the military experienced a number of costly accidents involving the loss of lives and very expensive equipment. Engineers had been successful in designing complicated weapon systems, tanks, and aircraft that were highly effective tools of war. Yet these million-dollar machines could be lost in an instant as a result of human error. Engineers often designed these devices with little thought of human capacity or human behavior. The problems of that oversight soon became apparent. After pilots crashed landed several airplanes by raising the landing gear when they were attempting to land, the Air Force asked for help from psychologists. The crashes occurred when the pilots thought they were adjusting the flaps on the wings, an action used to slow the plane in landing, and instead raised the landing gear. The errors occurred when pilots switched from one type of aircraft to another and were confused because the aircraft control layouts were different. In landing, their visual attention was directed at the airspeed, attitude, and altimeter gauges on the instrument panel and at the runway ahead, so they typically adjusted the flaps by feel, without looking at the controls. The fact that the knob shapes on the two sets of levers were similar only added to the problem. William Jenkins, a psychologist, was assigned the problem. He reasoned that because the task was one of touch, the aircraft should use one kind of knob on the flap levers and another on the landing gear levers. Jenkins conducted a series of psychophysical experiments in which he blindfolded subjects and had them make discriminations among various shaped knobs by tactile perception alone. His research identified eight knob shapes that yielded zero errors (see Figure 4-8). When the easily discriminated knobs were placed on the aircraft controls, that particular pilot error disappeared.[77]

Psychologists did considerable human factors work during the war, for example, helping to design altimeters that were easier to read, radar images that were easier to interpret, and bombsights that produced fewer visual errors of judgment. After the war, human factors psychologists continued to work for the military but also for private industry. It was a field that blended what psychologists knew about human behavior—for example, perception, learning, memory, fatigue, and motivation—with product design. Working with engineers, human factors psychologists would design everything from clothes irons, arc welders, telephones, candy machines, and computers to automobiles, nuclear power plants, and space shuttle control panels. Human factors psychologists were employed by IBM, General Mills, American Telephone and Telegraph, General Motors, and many other companies. They were present in all aspects of the military and in a large

Figure 4-8. *The eight knobs that William Jenkins found to be error free in his studies for aircraft controls.*

military contract organization established by the Army in 1951 and headed by psychologist Meredith P. Crawford (1910–2002), the Human Resources Research Organization (HumRRO), where hundreds of experimental and industrial psychologists would receive their introduction to the techniques of field studies of human performance.[78]

Human factors psychology remained an important part of industrial psychology into the 1970s but gradually separated from the field. Some human factors training programs can still be found in psychology departments today, but most have gone to departments of industrial engineering in colleges of engineering. These psychologists are more likely to identify with the Human Factors Society or APA's Division 21, Engineering Psychology, both of which were founded in the late 1950s. Today human factors psychologists can be found in most places where product design engineers need to know something about the behavior and cognitive abilities of the humans who will be operating their products, for example, in the computer hardware and software industries.[79]

Personnel Psychology After the War

In addition to the growth of human factors as a part of industrial psychology, the work in personnel psychology continued, partly stimulated by the success of psychologists during the war involving testing, selection, training, and performance appraisal. A new journal entitled *Personnel Psychology* began publication in 1948 to provide another outlet for the applied research. Recall Napoli's data on the use of psychological testing by businesses; only 14% of companies used such tests before the war, but that number rose to 50% by 1947 and to 75% in 1952. Such testing reflected the growth of personnel departments in industry, meaning the hiring of additional industrial psychologists, a fact evidenced in the growth of membership in Division 14. Of the approximately 750 members of Division 14 in 1960, 75% were employed outside of academia, and of those, 75% listed personnel selection as their chief activity.[80] For companies that could not afford personnel departments or those that might be interested in establishing such a department, there were new consulting firms of industrial psychologists ready to provide those services. One of the oldest was Rohrer, Hibler, & Replogle, founded in 1945 with offices in New York, Detroit, and Chicago. The firm billed itself as "Psychological Counsel to Management."[81] Today it is known as RHR International, with offices in 15 locations in North America and Europe.

The Evolution of Graduate Training

With the postwar boom in the economy, the effects of the GI Bill greatly increasing undergraduate and graduate enrollments at colleges and universities, the expanding international markets for US goods, and the technological advances in society (not the least of which was the advent of television), the demand on applied psychology was great. Psychology graduate programs expanded rapidly, particularly programs in clinical, counseling, and industrial psychology. Most of the new industrial psychology programs were doctoral programs but some offered only a master's degree with training directed particularly at personnel work in industry. And industry was eager to hire these master's-level practitioners. Psychology departments debated the nature of this training. Some academics argued for minimal coursework in industrial psychology (e.g., management, personnel psychology, human relations) and instead sought to emphasize research methods and data analysis. Others argued for more extensive training in industry-related coursework, including courses from business colleges, and especially for experience in internships in industrial settings. In 1957, Division 14 appointed Robert Guion (1924–2012) to chair a committee to develop guidelines for the professional education of industrial psychologists. That committee and a subsequent one eventually developed a training model including a recommended core curriculum.[82]

Organizational Psychology Comes of Age

Although Division 14 did not add the word "organizational" to its title until 1973, we have shown that the roots of organizational psychology—work on employee attitudes and morale, job satisfaction, leadership, group processes—can be found in the 1930s (and arguably earlier). We have stressed, in particular the interpretations of the Hawthorne studies pointing toward the importance of social and psychological factors in the workplace. As stated by Katzell and Austin, with the advent of organizational emphases, "I-O psychology was now equally concerned with fitting people to their work and fitting work to people."[83]

Lewin's Continuing Influence

Another significant force has also been mentioned earlier. Kurt Lewin, who conducted important research on leadership styles, level of aspiration, and group processes when he was at the University of Iowa, moved to the Massachusetts Institute of Technology (MIT) in 1944 where he established the Research Center for Group Dynamics. His work there was cut short when he died three years later in 1947; the center he had established moved to the University of Michigan to become part of what would later be called the Institute for Social Research, headed by Rensis Likert (1903–1981). Lewin's work at Iowa and MIT made a number of theoretical and experimental contributions that proved important, especially to social psychology and I/O psychology. Lewin was known for his advocacy of action research, research that was intended to solve problems, usually social problems. Action research required the researcher to be in the field, that is, in the setting where the research was to be applied. This emphasis on research in field settings would form the dominant model for much of I/O research. Lewin's work on group dynamics included the famous work on leadership styles, studies of prejudice, group decision making, communication within groups, and social comparisons. Principles of group facilitation learned from this research were later applied successfully in organizational and other group settings, including some industrial consulting work by Lewin and his students.[84] One of Lewin's final contributions was the establishment of the journal, *Human Relations*, in 1947. His ideas continue to have currency in I/O psychology today—for example, in theories of motivation in the workplace.[85]

Industrial Strife

When Morris Viteles decided in the 1950s to revise his 1932 textbook, *Industrial Psychology*, he felt that a new kind of book was needed. The title of his new book—*Motivation and Morale in Industry*—spoke volumes about the growth of organizational issues in industrial psychology. But it also spoke to Viteles's conversion as an I/O psychologist. His list of the three priority objectives in industry kept increased production at the top. The other two, however, were promoting employee satisfaction and adjustment, and reducing industrial strife. Viteles wrote:

> These objectives cannot be fully achieved in any plant, or in industry or business as a whole, unless accurate information is available as to the effectiveness of the various appeals or incentives which can be used to arouse the co-operation of individual workers. This involves an exact determination of basic motives in work, in the sense of evaluating the nature and strength of various wants and needs which require gratification through the work situation. Only with such knowledge can management arrive at a balanced and effective program of personnel policies and practices which will produce maximum results in the attainment of goals which simultaneously have significance for industry, the worker, and society at large.[86]

No doubt the hard core of the Taylorists would have found that medicine impossible to swallow. But for the new breed of I/O psychologists in the

1950s, the message was one they understood. Moreover, there is evidence that it was a message that a new breed of managers grasped as well.

Industrial strife was on Viteles's list and on the minds of some other I/O psychologists as well. Union-management conflicts were always the stuff of front-page news. In 1942, President Franklin Roosevelt had created the National War Labor Board to prevent strikes and control wages during the war. But at the end of the war there was a massive strike in 1946 across many industries. Ross Stagner (1909–1997), an I/O psychologist at Wayne State University in union-friendly Detroit, was one of several psychologists who called on his colleagues to study union-management relations. Stagner had been one of the founders of the Society for the Psychological Study of Social Issues (SPSSI) in 1937 and did little to hide his leftist leanings.[87] His dismay at the lack of research on industrial strife is evident in the following quotation written in 1956: "The physical sciences have now achieved such success that it is possible for all men to die together. Relatively little is being done to make it possible for us to live together."[88] Like Viteles, he believed that understanding how to reduce industrial conflict would contribute to an understanding of how to reduce international conflict, and he was frustrated that more psychologists did not take up the torch. But few did. I/O psychologists were still employed by management; that made it difficult to have a balanced view in labor-management disputes.

Part of industrial strife and part of the failure to live (and work) together was racial discrimination. In 1964 President Lyndon B. Johnson signed the Civil Rights Act which, among other provisions, banned discrimination based on race, color, religion, sex, or national origin by employers or unions. This act would have profound implications for industrial psychologists, especially in terms of the demonstrated validity of selection instruments.

Contemporary I/O Psychology

We stated earlier that in 1960, of the psychologists working in industry, 75% reported that their primary duties were in personnel issues. In that same survey, 38% reported primary involvement in organizational issues. The percentages are greater than 100 because individuals could report more than one principal duty. Another way to gauge I/O psychology of the 1960s is to examine the curriculum portion of the doctoral guidelines approved by Division 14 in 1965. One of the recommendations concerned whether students should have a concentration area within industrial psychology. The guidelines listed five concentration areas, three considered traditional and two as new. The Division 14 committee noted that some industrial psychologists felt that students should not concentrate but should have some familiarity with each of the five areas; where the other position held that students should chose a concentration. The committee did not take a stand on the issue but did predict that as I/O psychology grew as a science and profession, the pressures to specialize would accelerate.

The traditional concentrations were labeled personnel psychology, human factors psychology, and industrial-social psychology. The two newer concentrations were designated industrial-clinical psychology and marketing psychology.[89] Industrial-social psychology was said to have grown out of the human relations movement and was defined as the area of work in industry that includes "worker motivation, perception, morale, and job satisfaction, communication, leadership, organization theory, small group effects, union-management relations, and so forth."[90] In essence that was a reasonable definition of organizational psychology in 1965. The field would change dramatically in the next 30 years.

The last 50 years have seen enormous changes in American business. Family farms have largely disappeared as American agribusiness is now composed of large farming corporations with international connections. Mom and pop restaurants have been replaced by fast-food establishments and other franchised restaurants. Dime stores and small department stores have given way to ubiquitous big-box retailers. Much manufacturing has been replaced by what is principally a service industry. Information and information management are the new treasured commodities. Prisons have been privatized. Public schools have been privatized. New federal laws have been passed to eliminate job discrimination based on age or disability. Mandatory retirement ages have been eliminated in most job settings. Affirmative action laws sought to reverse the long-standing discrimination against ethnic minorities and women in the workplace. Sexual harassment laws have further dealt with issues faced principally by women. Deregulation of industries created many new companies, and corporate mergers and acquisitions reduced that number. The American stock market enjoyed a 20-year run of unprecedented gains, then several years of declines, and is enjoying several years of continued and steady growth as of this writing. The World Wide Web made economic globalization a reality. All of these changes, and more, would impact what I/O psychologists did and do in their jobs.

Contemporary Personnel Issues

The traditional personnel areas—job analysis, selection, and performance appraisal—are still an important focus for I/O psychologists. Testing, the hallmark of applied psychology since its inception, has been a concern for all three of those, although especially so for selection. Job analysis has been much improved by the use of several approaches that exhibit greater flexibility and better standardization.

With a society and a profession more attuned to the issues of discrimination, and with the force of federal laws and federal agency guidelines on personnel decisions, businesses have been forced to demonstrate the validity and fairness of their instruments for making critical decisions such as hiring, promoting, and downsizing. Those outcomes are based on selection and performance appraisal methods. In 1975, Division 14 published *Principles for Validation and Use of Personnel Selection Procedures*, a booklet intended to bring personnel selection procedures into line with federal laws/guidelines and with sound scientific practices. The importance of this booklet is evidenced by its having been cited by the courts in several significant legal decisions that changed the nature of employee selection by companies and altered the interpretation of Equal Employment Opportunity Commission guidelines. The *Principles* continue to be revised, with the most recent edition published in 2003.[91] Moreover, better evidence of the validity of predictors, better defined criterion measures for performance, use of test batteries as opposed to single tests, use of situational procedures such as assessment centers, better training of assessment personnel, and improvement of structured interview procedures have all contributed to improved procedures for selection and performance appraisal.

Training

Training, another of the mainstays of the industrial side of I/O psychology, also continues as part of contemporary practice. I/O psychologists have helped to develop better training methods, especially computer-based training, and better ways of evaluating the outcomes of training. Managerial training is especially popular today, as is career training. Moreover, much of contemporary training treats issues arising from personnel law, such as problems of sexual harassment in the workplace. With the financial scandals disclosed in recent years by giant corporations such as JP Morgan Chase, Enron, WorldCom, Arthur Anderson, and Xerox, ethics training for corporate officers and managers has been one of the quick-fix solutions proposed by members of Congress and leaders in the business community. Ethicists may have much to do with developing these training programs, but it is likely that the success or failure of them will be assessed by I/O psychologists.

Organizational Psychology

Changes in the field in the past 30 years have occurred on the organizational side as well. Older topics such as worker motivation, job satisfaction, and leadership have continued to receive attention, influenced especially by the rise of cognitive theories.[92] Furthermore, there has been increased interest in analyses and interventions at the organizational level. This interest began in the late 1950s as psychologists, influenced by theories on group behavior and on the organization as a behavioral entity, began to focus on the organization as a unit of behavioral analysis.[93] Many I/O psychologists came to believe that they could have greater impact in achieving their goals if they focused their efforts on changing organizations rather than on changing workers or managers directly. Indeed, it had become clear that interventions at the lower levels were often useless unless the overarching organizational environment could be changed. Psychologists studied "communication in organizations, conflict management, choice processes between individuals and organizations, organizational socialization, careers in organizations, and organizational influences on individual work behavior."[94] From this work came new areas such as organizational development, organizational climate, and organizational commitment.

Organizational Development. In studying organizational structures and processes, I/O psychologists often borrowed a model from their clinical and counseling colleagues. They studied an organization that was reporting problems and made an "organizational diagnosis," that is, a description of what was wrong in the way the organization functioned.[95] Based on those findings they developed a plan for treatment, a process known as "organiza-tional development" (also called OD), that would be used to try to change the organization in positive ways. Stagner and Smalley have described the critical importance of the procedures this way:

> [Organizations can be conceived of] as systems of interrelated parts and processes in dynamic interaction with their surrounding environments. The world is constantly changing and placing new demands, threats, and opportunities before its inhabitants. Organizations, like living crea-tures, often must first sense a change or a problem and then find ways of responding in order to continue to thrive, or perhaps, exist. Organi-zational diagnosis defines the problems and organizational development provides the solutions.[96]

Organizational development plans typically provide workers with a greater voice in company decision making and more choices about their work while simultaneously wresting some control and authority from manage-ment levels. The outcome is normally a better work environment, less stress for all, and greater production. Certainly organizational diagnosis and organizational development are not easy tasks. To be successful they require the best tools of a psychologist, both from a scientific and an interpersonal perspective. The proposed interventions often involve considerable risk, but the rewards can be considerable as well.[97]

Organizational Climate. Organizational climate is a construct closely related to the process of organizational diagnosis and development. Typi-cally it is defined as the psychological nature of the workplace with regard to such issues as the pleasantness or unpleasantness of the work environ-ment, the clarity of the rules for conduct and for expected production, and the openness of the lines of communication within and across levels. This concept is clearly related to job satisfaction, and work in this area has spawned several programs, such as the "quality of work life" movement designed to increase worker satisfaction. When the organizational climate is bad, good workers may leave the company. And if they do not leave, their health may be adversely affected by the stress of the work environ-ment. Given the rising costs of health care in the United States and the role companies have in paying for that care, as well as the lost dollars in production from ill employees, it makes a great deal of sense for companies to do what they can to improve organizational climate. One of the ways that companies try to deal with the psychological health of their employees has been through the establishment of employee assistance programs (EAPs). These centers within the company are typically staffed by mental health professionals who offer confidential services to employees. These EAPs bear some resemblance to the personnel counseling programs that came out of the Hawthorne studies. In recent years, programs have been established to provide psychological assistance to personnel in managerial and supervisory positions. Labeled "executive coaching," these services are offered by a wide range of providers.[98] Whereas many I/O psychologists have viewed executive coaching as an infringement on their territory, some critics might argue that it was territory lost through neglect. The results of the Hawthorne studies led Mayo and his colleagues to advocate the hiring of personnel counselors to work in industry. These counselors were to be part of the I/O field. But I/O psychology showed little interest in such a function, and so the personnel counselors disappeared, only to return in the 1980s and 1990s with the services often being provided by others than those trained in I/O psychology.[99]

Conclusion

According to Division 14, their membership is made up of some 8,000 members. Of that number, most are employed outside of universities.[100] Some of those now hold the PsyD or Doctor of Psychology degree, earned in programs that have greater emphases on practical experience than on research. Of those employed in universities, many are not in psychology departments but in departments of management, typically located in colleges of business. Some I/O psychologists can be found in marketing departments in universities and an even smaller number in engineering schools. Women make up a third of the membership of SIOP and they account for more than 50% of the enrollments in doctoral I/O programs. Were Scott and Münsterberg to appear today they would likely be astounded at what they had helped to create.

In this chapter we have traced the field of industrial/organizational psychology from the consulting work of a few university professors working with advertising agencies at the beginning of the 20th century to a field today that employs thousands in industry and other practice/research settings. We have described the transformation of the field from its early days as a tool of management, seeking to increase production and efficiency through job analysis and worker selection, to its modern expanse that continues the old roles but includes new foci on more molar concerns such as organizational development and organizational change. We began this chapter with a brief discussion of the salience of the workplace and its impact on the lives of individuals and, more broadly, on societies. The changes in our world in the past several decades promise to escalate in the near future. As certain as death and taxes is the statement that the workplace will continue to change. These changes will bring new stresses but also new opportunities, opportunities for companies and workers, including I/O psychologists. Industrial/organizational psychology will continue to be a field that can contribute much to economic prosperity and to the quality of individual lives.

Chapter 5
Counseling Psychology

When included alongside clinical psychology and school psychology, counseling psychology completes the trio of doctoral programs in professional psychology accredited by the American Psychological Association (APA).

According to APA's Division 17 (Counseling Psychology) most recent definition:

> Counseling Psychology is a specialty within professional psychology that maintains a focus on facilitating personal and interpersonal functioning across the life span. The specialty pays particular attention to emotional, social, vocational, educational, health-related, developmental, and organizational concerns. The practice of Counseling Psychology encompasses a broad range of culturally-sensitive practices that help people improve their well-being, alleviate distress and maladjustment, resolve crises, and increase their ability to function better in their lives. With its attention to both normal developmental issues and problems associated with physical, emotional, and mental disorders, the specialization holds a unique perspective in the broader practice-based areas of psychology. Counseling Psychologists serve persons of all ages and cultural backgrounds in both individual and group settings. They also consult regularly with organizations seeking to enhance their effectiveness or the well-being of their members. Interventions used by Counseling Psychologists may be either brief or long-term; they are often problem-specific and goal-directed. These activities are guided by a philosophy that values individual differences and diversity and a focus on prevention, development, and adjust-

ment across the life-span. Counseling Psychologists adhere to the standards and ethics established by the American Psychological Association.[1]

The statement reflects an ambitious specialty, one that offers a range of services to a range of populations in a variety of settings. Illumination of the unique nature of counseling psychology is not to be found in its modern manifestations, rather a true understanding is found with a backward glance, with a consideration of its inception and development.

A Context for Counseling Psychology

The formal development of counseling psychology can be conveniently located in the 20th century. As we have mentioned numerous times, historical development in psychology cannot be separated from the times in which they occur. In essence, to understand counseling psychology is to understand much of the transformation of American psychology at the start of the 20th century. Transformation in America was evident in almost every aspect of daily life. The shift from rural to urban was almost complete, cotton was yielding to steel. The industrial urban center was the embodiment of the modern. Technology thrived and modern conveniences amazed and seduced. Telephones, electricity, movies, radio, and automobiles offered the promise of the new, helping to create a culture of consumerism that kept hopes high and the economy moving. As expenditures for goods and services increased, so too did demand for human labor. The influx of immigrants from overseas and the migration of rural Americans to the major cities of the Northeast and Midwest provided industry with labor and individuals with hope for a better life. Changes in demographics, culture, and capital were believed to be signs of progress, progress that depended on human and mechanical machinery.

A More Perfect Union

Mass production appeared as a major achievement of human ingenuity and technological sophistication. However, mass production was useless unless it was efficient. Progress, precision, and efficiency quickly became the central tenants of the new social order. It was a vision of perfection, a union of person and machine, and where we find the beginnings of the counseling profession.[2]

The name most associated with the efficiency movement in industry is Frederick Taylor (1856–1915). As discussed in chapter 4, Taylor advocated scientific management, a system based on scientific methods that could be used to select and train workers, analyze job tasks, and improve relations between management and labor. According to Taylor, improved efficiency was a benefit to all. The better-trained worker was likely to be more productive, thus increasing the possibility of promotion and improved wages, greater profit for management, and a better product for the consumer.[3] Such an egalitarian ideal was just that, an ideal. In reality, improvement in efficiency largely benefited the captains of American industry, a small and elite group.

The efficiency movement and the search for perfection were not limited to scientific management; they were part and parcel of a system of political beliefs known as the progressive movement. Those identified as progressives sought a better social order through the application of scientific principles and Christian charity. A central tenant of the Progressive Party was that the government had an obligation to see to it that the institutions of society responded to the needs of all its members. On the national scene, political progressives would lobby on behalf of such issues as women's suffrage, government regulation of industry, child labor laws, and educational reform.[4]

The progressive movement expressed faith in science and technology, tempered by an equal measure of public concern for the well-being of the individual. At the turn of the century there was plenty to be worried about. Those who migrated to America's urban centers were often poor and uneducated. Immigrants from other nations did not know the language or the culture. Exploitation was always a concern, but immediate needs such as food and shelter were often all the new city inhabitants could be concerned with. The most vulnerable of this already vulnerable group were children. America, a young nation itself, took a significant interest in its youngest citizens. The result was the child saving movement, a national commitment to protect children from the ravages of poverty, exploitation, and neglect. It was a time when children's aid societies flourished and child labor laws were instituted.[5] The impulse toward child saving propelled the beginnings of the vocational guidance movement, a major precursor to the development of counseling psychology.

Newspaper Alley, Chicago. "Vocational misfits" waiting
to learn of a possible job

Figure 5.1. *Without vocational guidance many believed human potential was wasted.*

Seeking Guidance

Political progressives and child savers met at one particular intersection where the concerns and interests of both could easily be focused. The issue was school leaving, or what today we would call dropping out. Education, seemingly always considered the ticket out and the way up, did not function the way it could or should for poor children. Many left school early to work and contribute to the family income. For those destined to work in the factories or trades, the school curriculum did not teach skills needed for the world of work.

In the progressive scheme of things children leaving school to drift aimlessly was seen as a tremendous waste of human potential and an inefficient use of human resources (see Figures 5-1 & 5-2). The issue was of enough concern that a national debate began about the place of public education in American society. A variety of visions for the future of the nation and its youth were offered. The results were any number of reforms aimed at increas-

In contrast with the blind-alley job of the messenger boy is the dignified position of the postman

Figure 5.2. *Proper vocational guidance could prevent one from becoming a vocational misfit and assist in finding an adequate job.*

ing vocational education for both urban (industrial arts) and rural (agricultural education) children. During this time compulsory schooling became law.[6] Although many sought to aid children, such caring was not expressed equally for Native American and African American children. For them the system was and would remain limited, segregated, and largely indifferent.[7]

An answer to many of the social ills besetting poor children and families could be found in the establishment of settlement homes. A unique form of social science experiment, settlement homes first appeared in England in the 19th century. Through the joint efforts of charitable and religious groups, settlement homes were established in poor neighborhoods to aid workers and their families. Coming across the Atlantic, the movement was embraced by philanthropic social reformers such as Jane Addams (1860–1935), Lillian Wald (1867–1940), and Pauline Agassiz Shaw (1841–1917).

In America, the settlement home movement became a centerpiece of the progressive cause. Homes were established in working class neighborhoods in cities such as Boston, Chicago, New York, and Philadelphia. Staffed by artists, clergy, professors, and college students, these social progressives were committed to enhancing the efficiency of individual adjustment to the new industrial and social order. Staff members and volunteers would take up residence in the homes and become active in the social, economic, cultural, artistic, and intellectual interests and needs of the communities they served. The settlement home provided a place for neighborhood residents to complete high school, learn about the arts, and organize efforts to lobby local government for needed services. Of particular importance in the history of counseling psychology was Boston's Civic Service House. Opened in 1901 with the support of Pauline Agassiz Shaw, it is recognized by many as the birthplace of modern guidance.[8]

The Work of Frank Parsons

The Civic Service House was largely envisioned as an educational center, a place where immigrants could learn English, and engage in a wide range of educational activities. A frequent visitor to the house was Boston attorney Frank Parsons (1854–1908) (see Figure 5-3). Well educated and socially minded, he was an advocate for the rights and needs of those whom he believed were exploited by industrial monopolies.[9]

As a progressive, Parsons was interested in efficiency, believing (as many progressives did) that the proper balance of federal control, scientific reasoning, and thoughtful planning could improve the quality of life of individuals and of society.[10] Parsons described human efficiency as inextricably linked to the choice of a life's work:

> The wise selection of the business, profession, trade, or occupation to which one's life is to be devoted and the development of full efficiency in the chosen field are matters of the deepest moment to young men and to the public. These vital problems should be solved in a careful, scientific way, with due regard to each person's aptitudes, abilities, ambitions, resources, and limitations, and the relations of these elements to the conditions of success rather than if he drifts into an industry for which he is not fitted. An occupation out of harmony with the worker's aptitudes and capacities means inefficiency, unenthusiastic and perhaps distasteful labor, and low pay; while an occupation in harmony with the nature of the man means enthusiasm, love of work, and high economic values, superior product, efficient service, and good pay.[11]

Figure 5.3. *Frank Parsons.*

Speaking on occupational choice to the students at the Civic Service House brought numerous requests for personal meetings. Parsons soon found himself at the center of a need that was going unmet, the provision of guidance in helping students plan their vocational futures. Apparently the need was great enough that Pauline Agassiz Shaw saw fit to fund a new office at the Civic Service House. In January 1908, the Vocational Bureau was created under the motto, *Light, Information, Inspiration, and Cooperation.*[12]

Parsons' beliefs were actualized in a program of individual guidance that he developed based on the triadic formulation of: (a) knowledge of oneself, (b) knowledge of occupations, and (c) knowledge of the relationship between the two. Parsons had to develop many of the methods he used or borrow from questionable practices such as physiognomy and phrenology. The matching of self and job traits retained popular appeal, and Parsons earned a place of historical distinction in the history of guidance and counseling. His legacy, threatened by his premature death in 1908, lived on in the posthumous publication in 1909 of his treatise on vocational guidance, *Choosing a Vocation*.

The Expansion of Guidance

Very soon after Frank Parsons began his efforts at the Civic Service House, vocational guidance was on its way to a place of national visibility and support. While Parsons was busy with individual guidance, others such as educator Jesse Davis (1871–1955) were exploring methods of group guidance. Davis, a high school principal in Grand Rapids, Michigan, developed a guidance curriculum that extended into all subject areas. In his autobiography Davis recalled:

> The teachers of Latin had their pupils preparing lists of words derived from Latin that were of special interest to the lawyer, the doctor, the scientist, or writer. History teachers had their pupils looking up the origins or historical backgrounds of the vocations in which they were interested. The applications of science, mathematics, and the practical arts to engineering, manufacturing, and to business made most interesting reports. Periodically we held exhibits of charts, diagrams, and written materials that aroused much competition and inspired the use of the career motive throughout the school.[13]

Davis believed that vocational guidance was not simply a process of job choice. It involved a serious obligation to develop the moral fabric of the students as well. According to Davis, the purpose of guidance was:

> The pupil's better understanding of his own character: it means an awakening of the normal consciousness that will lead him to emulate the character of the good and the great who have gone on before; it means a conception of himself as a social being in some future occupation, and from this viewpoint the appreciation of his duty and obligation toward his business associates, toward his neighbors, and toward the law.[14]

The fusion of moral guidance with vocational guidance suggested by Davis was common throughout the period, reflecting the progressive emphasis on rational humanism. Thus, the beginnings of the guidance movement showed interest not only in vocational guidance, but guidance in living a good life. As we will see, humanism remained a constant throughout the evolution of guidance and counseling, becoming a central feature of counseling psychology.

Almost overnight, the work of people like Parsons and Davis were incorporated into school-based vocational guidance programs and vocational bureaus across America. The timing was right. There were plenty of jobs to fill, plenty of people to fill them, and a zeitgeist of efficiency that valued the individual as much as the swift completion of tasks. Interest in vocational guidance was significant and widespread. Recognizing the interest in vocational guidance, David Snedden, Massachusetts Commissioner of Education, convened the first national meeting on vocational guidance in Boston in 1910.

By any standard the meeting was a success. It was well attended and represented the state of the art in vocational guidance. The Vocational Bureau that Parsons had established at the Civic Service House was a source of much pride. By 1910, many of the bureau's board members were on the faculty of nearby Harvard University. Harvard President Charles W. Eliot, himself a staunch supporter of vocational guidance, addressed the conferees, as did Boston mayor, John Fitzgerald (also the maternal grandfather of American President John Fitzgerald Kennedy). Jesse Davis and others involved in school guidance programs were also active participants. The group met each year and in 1913 officially organized as the National Vocational Guidance Association (NVGA).[15]

The interest of Harvard University in the Vocational Bureau was substantial and in 1917 the bureau was transferred from the Civic Service House to Harvard University's Division of Education. It was here that educators and psychologists framed some of the earliest debates about the nature of guidance and counseling, debates that have echoed throughout the history of counseling psychology.

Education and Psychology

A polarity was developing between those who saw vocational guidance as an educational function and those who saw it as a province of the new applied psychology. This was embodied in Harvard faculty members like John Brewer (1877–1959) of education and Hugo Münsterberg (1863–1916) of psychology. Brewer, reflecting the progressive education espoused by John Dewey (1859–1952), argued that guidance was a part of the educational experience, a process by which the student is an active agent in seeking out experiences that help determine the appropriate choice of an occupation. Psychologists, such as Münsterberg, viewed guidance as an activity well suited to the new applied psychology, especially the measurement of individual differences. Psychology, Münsterberg wrote, could replace the impressionistic approach of counselors with the tools of science:

> We now realize that questions as to the mental capacities and functions and powers of an individual can no longer be trusted to impressionistic replies. If we are to have reliable answers, we must make use of the available resources of the psychological laboratory. These resources emancipate us from the illusions and emotions of the self-observer. The well-arranged experiment measures the mental states with the same exactness with which the chemical or physical examination of the physician studies the organism of the individual.[16]

Brewer (who must have had some personal acquaintance with Münsterberg) eschewed psychological tests, and was especially critical of the tendency to categorize people into types based on psychological tests, claiming:

> Vocational guidance has still another score to settle with a pseudo-psychology, and this is the belief in the "spread" or transfer of mental qualities. Can the attention of a boy be tested, so that the conclusion can be drawn that he is attentive or inattentive? Can a simple examination be devised to test the powers of observation? Can honesty in examinations qualify a girl for the label, "honest girl?" In short, are such activities as attending, observing, concentrating, persisting, using energy, being fair, being honest, remembering, analyzing, etc., if applied to one situation, likely to be applicable to all? We are of course, touching on the whole question of general training or formal discipline. It is the belief in the general nature and transferability of mental and moral qualities that is at the bottom of the beliefs that we have just been examining: the beliefs in types and in the efficacy of psychological types.[17]

Brewer emphasized process (education) over product (testing) and called for an experiential approach that would introduce students to a variety of ideas and experiences. Over time, interests and abilities emerged, leading eventually to occupational choice. It was a process that took time and required familiarity between counselors and those counseled.

Schools provided the perfect setting for vocational exploration. As Davis had demonstrated, vocational activities could be incorporated into the curriculum with teachers and administrators providing the needed guidance and counsel. Brewer had established himself as a key figure in the vocational guidance movement, bringing him many key national appointments. Of particular importance was his appointment to the Commission on the Reorganization of Secondary Education, a group that developed a national plan of vocational guidance. Vocational education already had a strong record of service and funding, now vocational guidance was poised to get its share of federal dollars and support. The report of the committee released in 1918, placed education in the center of guidance and counseling, and accorded psychology a back seat stating that:

> It will be some time before actual proof of the validity of psychological tests for vocational guidance can be established, meanwhile, young people must be guided. It is also to be noted that the psychologist "tests" and that there are many other factors in the problem of vocational guidance all of which the counselor must consider, for his problem is one demanding immediate solution. At the present time few tests have been given in such a way as to determine the ability of youth to improve with instruction and training. The province of the vocational counselor, however, is to see that education and training become prominent elements in guidance. Therefore the ideal vocational counselor will be something of a psychologist, but he will also be a sociologist, an economist, and most of all an educator in the best modern sense of the word. The committee believes that we should welcome continued experimentation in the field of vocational psychology, but that we should put the present emphasis upon education, training, and supervision. We are of the opinion that when false expectations are abandoned and unreasonable demands are withdrawn, psychology will be able to render worthy service in vocational guidance, and the psychologist may have a large share in making adjustments between individuals and society.[18]

The report accomplished what it had intended; after 1918, vocational guidance received substantial funding from the federal government and established a presence throughout America's public schools. Colleges of education could now offer training and guidance alongside teacher training. Psychology was not a presence, and some psychologists were listening to the complaints of educators. Münsterberg wrote in 1913:

> All taken together, we may, therefore, say that in the movement for vocational guidance practically nothing has been done to make modern experimental psychology serviceable to the new task. But on the other side, it has become evident that in the vocation bureaus appropriate social agencies are existing which are ready to take up the results of such work, and to apply them for the good of the American youth and of commerce and industry, as soon as the experimental psychologist has developed the significant methods.[19]

For his part, Münsterberg developed tests of selection for motormen, ship captains, and telephone operators. Other psychologists were very much concerned with the application of psychology to issues of vocational selection. Helen Woolley (1874–1947) directed the psychological laboratory at the Vocational Bureau of Cincinnati, and in a series of well-designed and executed studies was able to provide evidence of the deleterious effects on ability and achievement when children left school prematurely for menial work. From this work she went on to study the utility of ability tests for use in vocational guidance. Her test-based approach provided useful and practical information, as reported in the following case of a 15-year-old boy who came to the clinic in 1915:

> He ranked exceptionally high in the mental tests but relatively poorly in the manual tests. He was practically defective in the steadiness of his hand. The boy was taking the cooperative course in machine-shop work. When questioned about it, he said that he did not like the work and had no intention whatever of becoming a skilled mechanic, though he was keeping up with his classes. Literary and academic subjects appealed to him far more. A note to the high school procured a change of course for the boy.[20]

Vocational Psychology

Psychologists Harry Hollingworth (1880–1956) and Leta Hollingworth (1886–1939) were also important contributors to the new vocational psychology. You will recognize that both appear throughout this book, Harry Hollingworth associated with the beginnings of industrial psychology, and Leta Hollingworth with the development of clinical and school psychology. This demonstrates an important point, namely that the history of professional psychology is the study of related developments. We cannot forget that in the early 20th century there were few distinctions made among psychologists. At most, psychologists like Harry and Leta Hollingworth were labeled applied psychologists. Their interest was the application of psychological principles and methods to the study of a host of common problems and questions about everyday life. This included the burgeoning vocational guidance movement.

Harry Hollingworth held a healthy suspicion of pseudoscientific methods of assessing individual traits. In 1916 he published *Vocational Psychology*,[21] a book that promoted the benefits of the new psychology to the assessment of individual differences while debunking such character reading techniques as physiognomy. Leta Hollingworth, an early advocate for the psychological study of women and women's issues, added a chapter on the vocational aptitudes of women, a topic that had received limited attention heretofore. The purpose of the chapter, she wrote was:

> To inquire whether there are any innate and essential sex differences in tastes and abilities, which would afford a scientific basis for the apparently arbitrary and traditional assumption that the vocational future of all girls must naturally fall in the domestic sphere, and consequently presents no problem, while the future of boys is entirely problematical and may lie in any of a score of different callings, according to personal fitness.[22]

Reflective of much of her work on gender differences and mental abilities she concluded that, "so far as is at present known, women are as competent in mental capacity as men are, to undertake any and all human vocations."[23]

Even if some educators were resistant to the use of psychological tests and measures in the educational guidance process, such instruments were becoming increasingly necessary. Rising enrollments (due to immigration,

migration, and compulsory attendance laws) made the selection and classification of students a necessity. In the gulf between the psychology lab and the lab school, educational psychology grew and flourished. Its champion, Edward L. Thorndike (1874–1949) made significant contributions to education and learning. He sought to improve classroom instruction and worked to develop objective measures of learning. A highly productive and prolific researcher, he played a major role in the rise of educational testing in 20th century America.[24] The scientific study of individual difference using experimental methods and psychological tests to aid in adaptation to the world of work was soon to finds its way onto a much larger stage.

Testing and the Times

Throughout this book, we make frequent mention of the role psychological testing has played in the development of professional psychology. The advent of the First World War provided a unique opportunity for applied psychology to contribute to, and leave a mark on, American society. Soon after the United States entered World War I in 1917, American Psychological Association President Robert Yerkes (1876–1956) called on psychologists to assist in the war effort. The result was a program of testing that utilized psychology's existing knowledge and expertise as a basis for further development. Yerkes headed a group on intelligence testing, and appointed Walter Dill Scott (1869–1955) to direct the committee on the classification of personnel. Scott was not new to the classification business. Before the war, he was a member of a pioneering group of applied psychologists at the Carnegie Institute of Technology in Pittsburgh, Pennsylvania, active in the development of tests of selection and classification for use in business. During the war, tests of intelligence, abilities, aptitudes, and interests were combined with academic, social, and employment histories to yield information on finding the right soldier for the right job. As noted in chapter 2, the project was of huge proportions and a tremendous success, creating an industry and culture of testing in America that has shown no sign of slowing.

For all the possibilities there were also limitations. Group testing, still in its infancy, had problems, none more apparent than the questions of the reliability and validity of intelligence tests that failed to recognize cultural bias. The questionable use of questionable tests led to numerous claims of racial differences in intelligence and education that contributed to continued perpetuation of racial stereotyping and bias.[25]

Civilian Applications

Returning from the war, psychologists found that the measures they had used and developed had a wide range of applications. Clinical psychology benefited from developments in tests of intelligence and personality, industrial psychology found utility in tests measuring aptitudes and abilities, and counseling and guidance discovered that almost all of these developments could be applied to the scientific management of the student.

Concerned with issues of mass migration after the war, the National Research Council (NRC) appointed a committee to study problems of human migration, and the measurement of human traits and abilities. It was hoped that the findings would help delineate a sound immigration policy. One line of work concerned the measurement of mechanical ability and was carried out by Richard M. Elliott (1887–1969) and Donald G. Paterson (1892–1961), both faculty members in the department of psychology at the University of Minnesota (Elliott was chair, Paterson a professor). Both had served as psychological examiners during the war. Elliott, a Harvard PhD, studied with Münsterberg and was familiar with the work of Frank Parsons. Paterson had worked for Walter Dill Scott for two years after the war and was facile with the measurement of abilities and traits.

The Minnesota Mechanical Ability investigation lasted over four years and provided an in-depth examination of the characteristics of mechanical ability and its measurement. Beyond establishing the existence of mechanical ability and effective means for its measurement, the program did not answer many of the questions that the NRC had originally asked, such as the existence and inheritance of racial and national differences in mechanical ability. Still, in the introduction to the project published in 1930, Robert Yerkes revealed his enthusiasm for the undertaking, "It is difficult for me to write calmly and objectively of this report, so stirred am I by its contributions of fact, method, and insight, and its promise of developments which should significantly improve educational, vocational, and industrial procedures."[26]

Elliott and Paterson were convinced of the need for scientific vocational guidance using a measurement approach and instilled this as a core value at Minnesota in the postwar years. Such activity was not restricted to the University of Minnesota. In 1923, the American Council on Education formed the Committee on Cooperative Experiments in Student Personnel. It was a program that stimulated the growth of student personnel work in higher education by providing significant support for the development of the psychometrics of selection. Tests of interest, aptitude, ability, and achievement were further refined by such well-known psychologists as E. K. Strong, Jr. (1884–1963), L. L. Thurstone (1887–1955), and E. L. Thorndike.

Testing and the Great Depression

It would take another national emergency to put to use the gains made in applied psychology since World War I, and by extension, give formal definition to the emergence of counseling psychology. The stock market crash of 1929 ushered in the Great Depression of the 1930s. The size and magnitude of the depression is hard to comprehend. Roughly 25% of the population was out of work, industry stood idle, and a severe drought ruined agriculture production in the Midwest. The depression that brought so much hardship to so many, however, provided ample opportunities for measurement and classification work.

When Franklin D. Roosevelt was elected president, he instituted a series of reforms aimed at getting the economy back on its feet. Many of his initiatives involved programs to get people back to work, and resulted in the establishment of a host of large federal agencies and activities that had direct benefit to vocational education and guidance. Of this time, Richard Johnson and Walter Johnson wrote:

> The U. S. Employment Service was organized in 1933 and at first was preoccupied with placement but later included vocational counseling in its services. The depression years also saw the organization of the Occupational Information and Guidance Service under the Division of Vocational Education of the U. S. Office of Education, the publication of the Dictionary of Occupational Titles, the inauguration of the Occupational Outlook Service, and the expansion of civilian vocational rehabilitation services. The major effort of vocational guidance during the depression years was on placement.[27]

In 1931, Donald Paterson and the University of Minnesota took on a new role. The Minnesota Employment Stabilization Research Institute was established at the University of Minnesota to study occupations and employment scientifically, while simultaneously finding jobs for its unemployed clients. Under Paterson's direction, the program clearly demonstrated the efficacy of guidance and employment selection techniques. Paterson's work helped to solidify a set of principles of practice for vocational guidance that became the norm in industry and education. Paterson's commitment to scientific measurement of human traits and abilities never wavered. In 1930, adding to the chorus of voices that denounced pseudoscience, he authored *Physique and Intellect*. Drawing on data from a host of studies, Paterson showed the lack of relationship between physical traits and intellectual ability. Like many before him, he decried the use of physiognomy, phrenology, and related practices.[28]

By the 1930s, and largely influenced by decades of psychological testing, there was increasing specialization and localization of function in applied psychology. Not only were psychologists offering more services, more people were seeking services for a variety of concerns (see Figure 5-4). Psychologists in industry used testing and counseling procedures to increase productivity and to select and train workers for labor and management, others interested in applying testing and counseling to individuals with severe forms of maladjustment worked in hospital settings under the supervision of psychiatrists, some could be found working with children in schools and clinics, and those in vocational guidance found employment in government agencies, university testing and counseling bureaus, and the public schools. Today these psychologists would be identified by specialty (industrial/organizational, clinical, school, and counseling), but as we have pointed out, in the 1930s and 1940s, such labels were not in popular use nor were there organized and systematic training programs for professional psychologists. All was about to change.

The Emergence of Counseling Psychology

America's entrance into the Second World War greatly expanded the services that American psychologists offered the nation. Classification and other assessment activities remained an integral part of the work, and

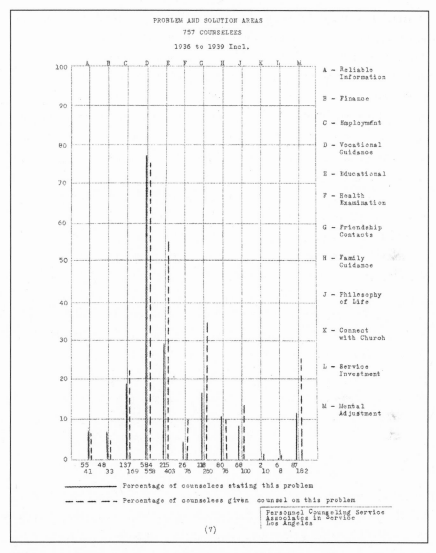

Figure 5.4. *Graph showing counseling usage at a YMCA counseling center.*

unlike the First World War, which stressed intellectual functioning, the concern shifted to issues of mental health.

Mental health problems were being discovered on each end of military service. Rates of psychiatric illness among new recruits were surprisingly high, averaging around 17%.[29] The majority of discharges from service were for psychiatric reasons, and psychiatric casualties occupied over half of all beds in Veteran's Administration (VA) hospitals.[30]

Not only was this cause for concern among the military, it also alerted federal authorities to the issue among the general population. As was discussed in chapter 2, the mental hygiene movement had created greater understanding of severe mental illness and its consequences, although the perception remained that it was a relatively rare occurrence. Thus, federal efforts and resources had not been sustained or sufficient.

It was one thing to estimate the incidence of mental illness in the general population and to anticipate the number of psychiatric casualties from a war, and quite another to have an established plan of treatment. Here was a problem; the available supply of trained personnel was a fraction of the need. With less than 3,000 trained psychiatrists and estimated shortages of psychologists at 92%, something needed to be done quickly to increase the ranks of mental health professionals.[31] In a response that was fast and sweeping, the federal government passed the National Mental Health Act of 1946, legislation that has been a major determinant in the growth of the mental health profession in America.[32]

The introduction to the act clearly identifies its purpose:

> The improvement of the mental health of the people of the United States through the conducting of researches, investigations, experiments, and demonstrations relating to the cause, diagnosis, and treatment of psychiatric disorders; assisting and fostering such research activities by public and private agencies, and promoting the coordination of all such researches and activities and the useful application of their results; training personnel in matters relating to mental health; and developing, and assisting States in the use of the most effective methods of prevention, diagnosis, and treatment of psychiatric disorders.[33]

The act provided for a massive program of federal assistance to address research, training, and service in the identification, treatment, and prevention of mental illness. It created the National Institute of Mental Health (NIMH), and provided broad support to psychiatry, psychiatric social work, psychiatric nursing, and psychology for the training of mental health professionals. For psychology it was a time of tremendous change.

Through the joint efforts of the USPHS and the VA, funds were made available to psychology departments willing to train professional psychologists. Never before had such large sums of money been available to academic psychology. The American Psychological Association (APA) supported the efforts and in coordination with the VA and the USPHS, convened the Boulder Conference on Graduate Education in Clinical Psychology in 1949.

Preludes to Boulder

The growth and political power of applied psychology had been rising for years prior to World War II. The war helped to accelerate the issue as many psychologists participated in the war effort and in doing so, demonstrated the diversity of psychology. Still, applied psychologists did not feel part of the mainstream of psychology, especially as it was represented by the membership of the APA. The American Association for Applied Psychology (AAAP) was the organization that best represented the interests of applied psychologists prior to World War II. When the nation went to war and recognized the need for applied psychology and professional psychologists, a unification of psychology was called for. The result was the reorganization of the APA in 1945. Joining together with the AAAP, a new APA emerged, one that included a divisional structure whereby the diverse interests of all the membership could be represented.[34] It was a major turning point for what was to become counseling psychology.

The reorganization of the APA in 1945 was accomplished in part by having psychologists self-identify the areas that best represented their interests and work. The result was the differentiation of the professional areas into the divisions we recognize today as clinical psychology (Division 12), industrial psychology (Division 14), school psychology (Division 16), and counseling psychology (Division 17).

First known as the Division of Personnel and Guidance Psychologists (quickly changed to the Division of Counseling and Guidance), Division 17 came into existence due in large part to many faculty members at the University of Minnesota, including Donald Paterson, E. G. Williamson (1900–1979), and John Darley (1910–1990). By the time of the Boulder Conference in 1949, counseling psychologists were clearly a presence in the push toward the establishment of professional psychology in America.

The Meaning of Boulder

The Boulder Conference was an ambitious undertaking. For 15 days, 73 representatives of academic and applied psychology, medicine, nursing, and education debated and discussed the establishment of the professional psychologist. Boulder tried to be many things to many people. The VA and the USPHS wanted well-trained mental health professionals, academic psychology wanted to maintain the standards of the science of psychology, and those in the applied areas wanted greater support for their work. Most got what they wanted. The federal authorities received a plan of action for the training of clinical psychologists, academic psychologists received reassurances through the recognition of the primacy of research embodied in the model of the scientist-practitioner, and clinical psychology was given the green light to grow and develop without undue interference from the federal government, but with plenty of financial support.[35]

According to the conference report, Boulder also brought with it a call of unity between the rapidly developing camps of applied psychology, especially in relation to clinical and counseling psychologists:

> The majority of the conference was clearly in favor of encouraging the broad development of clinical psychology along the lines that extend the field of practice from the frankly psychotic or mentally ill to the relatively normal clientele who need information, vocational counseling, and remedial work. Specialization in any of these less clearly defined branches has now become an open issue that must be faced sooner or later.[36]

The conferees went so far as to offer a vote of support for the recommendation that, "The APA and its appropriate division should study the common and diverse problems and concepts of clinical psychology and counseling and guidance with a view to immediate interfield enrichment of knowledge and methods. Consideration should also be given to the possibility of eventual amalgamation of these two fields."[37] Such an amalgamation never occurred and as we shall see later, the gulf only widened.

Constructing Counseling Psychology

The like-minded colleagues who formed Division 17 were of varying backgrounds and interests. They could be found in any number of applied and educational settings. However, the growing mental health movement brought them closer to clinical psychology.[38]

The move toward clinical psychology was largely a move toward new opportunities. Mental health counseling appealed to many in Division 17. It was new and exciting, offered opportunities in the postwar economy, and fit well with the emphasis on adjustment so common throughout the history of guidance and counseling. However, the difference between clinical and counseling psychology, and the competition for resources, would not bring the amalgamation that the delegates at Boulder had suggested.

Counseling psychology was no longer best represented by the National Vocational Guidance Association (NVGA), nor were its interests best represented by postwar clinical psychology. As the guidelines for APA accreditation of clinical psychology training programs were being formulated, Division 17 members were seeking to establish their own standards of training.

A Model of Training

With the support of the United States Public Health Service (USPHS), which was soon to be known as the National Institute of Mental Health (NIMH), a meeting on the training of counselors was held at the University of Michigan on July 27 and 28, 1949, and again on January 6 and 7, 1950. A joint project of the USPHS, Division 17, and the University of Michigan, its chief engineer was Michigan faculty member and counseling center director, Edward S. Bordin (1913–1992). A major figure in the evolution of counseling psychology, Bordin was close to developments in professional training. The deliberations at the Ann Arbor conference illustrated the divergence in counseling and clinical approaches to training and teaching of professional psychology. Psychological counselors and counseling were differentiated from clinical psychologists and psychotherapy. The attendees attempted to highlight commonalities but could not disguise some true differences. The psychological counselor was likely to be found in an educational setting, working with essentially normal individuals seeking information that would aid in adjustment to everyday life. This was in contrast to the clinical psychologist who was most likely to be in a hospital setting working with mentally ill populations whose treatment was aimed at personality reorganization.

The roads began to diverge more fully when subdoctoral training was discussed. Boulder affirmed the primacy of the doctoral degree as the entry-level degree in professional psychology, however, the Ann Arbor group was willing to consider a program of training for the masters-level psychological counselor.[39]

The deliberations at Ann Arbor were brought before the larger group of Division of 17 representatives meeting on the campus of Northwestern University just prior to the 1951 annual meeting of the APA in Chicago. Known as the Northwestern Conference, its purpose was to produce a formal statement on the training of counseling psychologists. Reviewing the recommendations of the Ann Arbor conference and the Boulder Conference, the group approved a statement on doctoral training of counseling psychologists. Among other things, it upheld the Boulder standard of the scientist-practitioner model of training, and defined the goal of counseling psychology as:

> fostering the psychological development of the individual. This included all people on the adjustment continuum from those who function at tolerable levels of adequacy to those suffering from more severe psychological disturbances. Counseling psychologists will spend the bulk of their time with individuals within the normal range, but their training should qualify them to work in some degree with individuals at any level of psychological adjustment. Counseling stresses the positive and the preventative. It focuses upon the stimulation of personal development in order to maximize personal and social effectiveness and to forestall psychologically crippling disabilities.[40]

In a further attempt to declare an independent identity, the conferees voted to change the name of the division from counseling and guidance to counseling psychology.

The adoption of recommended training standards at the doctoral level brought with it many new opportunities and brought counseling psychology closer to its current identity as a health service profession. Shortly after the Northwestern Conference, the APA began accrediting doctoral training programs in counseling psychology, and the Veterans Administration (VA) sought to incorporate counseling psychologists into its cadre of

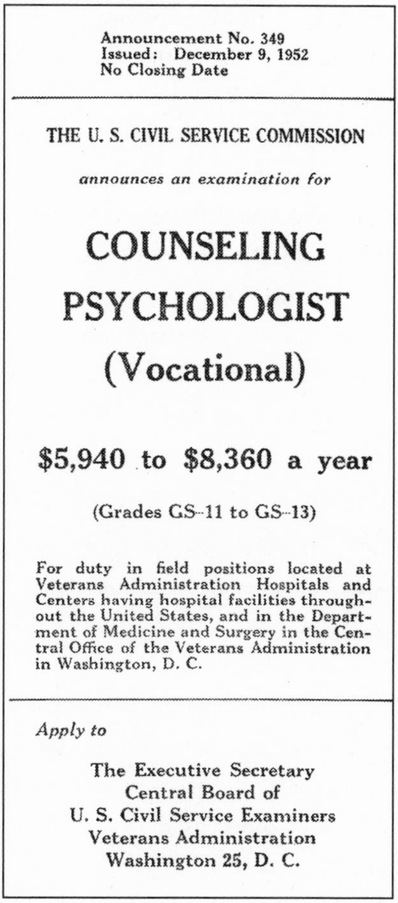

```
Announcement No. 349
Issued:  December 9, 1952
No Closing Date
```

THE U. S. CIVIL SERVICE COMMISSION

announces an examination for

COUNSELING
PSYCHOLOGIST
(Vocational)

$5,940 to $8,360 a year

(Grades GS-11 to GS-13)

For duty in field positions located at
Veterans Administration Hospitals and
Centers having hospital facilities throughout the United States, and in the Department of Medicine and Surgery in the Central Office of the Veterans Administration
in Washington, D. C.

Apply to

The Executive Secretary
Central Board of
U. S. Civil Service Examiners
Veterans Administration
Washington 25, D. C.

Figure 5.5. *Announcement of counseling psychology positions at the VA (1952).*

mental health service providers (see Figure 5-5). Years before, a provision of the GI Bill of Rights created the Vocational Rehabilitation and Education (VR&E) Service to help returning veterans find suitable employment, obtain needed rehabilitation (for both physical and emotional problems), and gain placement in training and educational programs for which they were determined to be eligible. VR&E services were provided through VA regional offices, with satellite clinics located on many university campuses. Personnel staffing these offices were usually teachers, counselors, and advisors from the public schools, including vocational and trade schools. The need, rather the overwhelming demand for mental health personnel, prompted the VA to establish a new counseling service that would serve its expansive hospital system. In 1952, counseling psychologist Robert Waldrop (1912–2012) became the first chief of the newly founded Vocational Counseling Service of the Department of Medicine and Surgery of the VA. Largely unrecognized for his efforts, Waldrop persuaded the VA to have counseling psychologists classified at the same rank as clinical psychologists. His insistence that counseling psychologists in the VA's medical service have doctoral-level training caused consternation among many in the VR&E service, who perceived his efforts as a threat to their employment. Insisting on the doctoral standard also meant that Waldrop would have to travel the country, coaxing, cajoling, and convincing academic department to establish doctoral training programs in counseling psychology:

> Support of the APA and the universities was essential, thus personal visits to department chairs, directors of clinical programs, and heads of counseling centers had to be made. It should be kept in mind that at this time most universities were still rebuilding following the decimation of staff by the war effort. I visited 44 university settings. Here again the response varied. There was suspicion of just another government program. There were more immediate concerns with the development of faculty and staff. There was concern expressed about the dilution of the science of psychology by another service-oriented program. However, others showed interest in the expanding role of psychology in a recuperating society and demonstrated an eagerness to meet the challenge.[41]

Influences on Identity

The counseling psychology of the 1950s was straying further from its historical roots in vocational guidance. Many in Division 17 held joint membership in the APA and the National Vocational Guidance Association (NVGA), which due to its own internal differences joined together with others interested in guidance and student personnel work to form the American Personnel and Guidance Association (APGA) in 1951 (now known as the American Counseling Association). However, over time there materialized a perception of two types of professionals: psychologists (represented by members of Division 17), and counselors (represented by APGA).

A number of factors influenced the direction that counseling psychology took in the 1950s. The flood of returning veterans required counseling of all types. The transition from war to civilian life could be difficult. Soldiers had to get reacquainted with friends and family who knew little of the experience of war. Many returned home to find themselves and their surroundings changed. Returning to work was an adjustment, as was the decision to return to school. The GI Bill of Rights afforded a college education to many who otherwise might not have been able to afford one. In many cases, the veteran had to deal with all of these issues at once. Clearly, counseling needed to be able to account for the adjustment of the whole person. Counseling methods and theories began to reflect this emphasis, especially the nondirective approach of Carl Rogers (1902–1987).

Rogers, with a background in theology and psychology, began his professional career in the 1930s working with children. He realized that the provision of a nurturing and supportive environment was an important determinant in adjustment. Based on his own experience and the influence of the neo-Freudian analyst Otto Rank (1884–1939), Rogers' first major statement on his approach to counseling appeared in his 1942 publication, *Counseling and Psychotherapy*.[42] It was a quite a shock to the guidance and counseling community. Rogers advocated that the counselor be nondirective, allowing the client to take the lead in the counseling session. Through active listening and reflection of feeling, the counselor helped the client explore concerns and seek possible solutions. There were no tests and no advice. In an early incarnation of the humanism of the 1960s, Rogers believed that each person had the capacity for emotional growth and adjustment. It was the counselor's role to provide a safe and supportive environment that allowed the client to safely explore thoughts and feelings. Rogers backed his words with action. He was among the first to record counseling sessions. He and his students meticulously coded transcripts of sessions in search of the data that would confirm or refute his claims of the benefits derived from the nondirective method (see Figure 5-6). To some, Rogers counseling methods were heresy. Since the time of Frank Parsons, counselors learned about clients through responses to interviews and tests, and after the data had been gathered, the counselor basically instructed clients what to do. Known as the trait and factor approach, its adherents

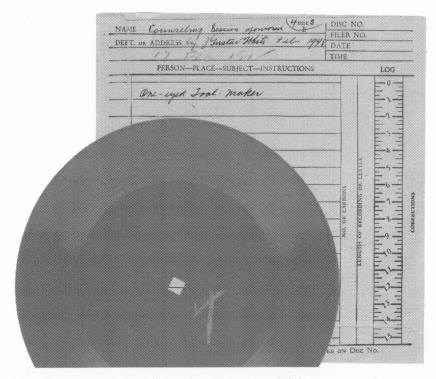

Figure 5.6. *The recording of counseling sessions provided the opportunity for training and research on the process of counseling. Here is a recording disk of a counseling session with a "one eyed toolmaker" conducted by psychologist Gustav White.*

were aghast at Rogers' seeming inaction and lack of direction. This was particularly true at the University of Minnesota, where the counseling faculty was considered among the most influential in the field. Addressing a group there in 1940, Rogers recalled, "I was totally unprepared for the furor the talk aroused. I was criticized, I was praised, I was attacked, I was looked on with puzzlement."[43]

Somewhere in-between the directive and nondirective approaches were a host of theories and practices advanced by other significant figures in the history of counseling psychology, including Leona Tyler (1906–1993) and C. Gilbert Wrenn (1902–2001).

Another major influence that shaped the direction of counseling psychology at midcentury was its association with psychology. The reorganization of the APA in 1945, the push for a national program of mental health, the establishment of doctoral training standards, the APA accreditation process, and the large-scale employment of professional psychology through the VA, all placed counseling psychology within the realm of psychology. The doctoral standard for professional psychology meant that students would be inculcated into the traditional academic values of theory, research, and publication. It also brought counseling psychologists into much closer contact with the issues that dominated psychology at the time, including learning, developmental and personality theories, and research methods and statistics. Vocational behavior and career development were popular topics among counseling psychologists, with advances in theory and research led by such people as Donald Super (1910–1994), David Tiedeman (1919–2004), and Anne Roe (1904–1991). Multivariate statistics and computer-assisted data analysis contributed to more elaborate and original uses of measurement tools such as the Strong Interest Inventory and the Kuder Preference Record Test.[44]

Toward the end of the 1950s yet another world event would impact counseling psychology. The launch of the Russian satellite Sputnik on October 4, 1957, brought attention back to the issue of school counseling and provided new opportunities for counseling psychology. Sputnik, no larger than a basketball, brought a single static-filled "beep" that instilled considerable panic in the American public. The thought of the Russians having a superior hand in science and technology brought fears of an invisible attack from space, not unlike the attack on Pearl Harbor more than a decade earlier. There was widespread concern that the public schools were not producing enough students interested in math and science, and the finger of blame was pointed directly at progressive education, which was faulted for failing to provide a demanding curriculum that would bring out the best in American youth. There was a rallying cry for a clear emphasis on ability and intellect, an area in which educational psychologists in the tradition of E. L. Thorndike had much to offer. President Eisenhower, under considerable pressure to act quickly, pushed for new legislation. Within months lawmakers were busy drafting the National Defense Education Act (NDEA).[45]

At the heart of the NDEA was the identification and guidance of students who showed promise in math and science at all levels of schooling.

In higher education, there were provisions for aid to students at both the undergraduate and graduate level. In elementary and secondary schools, the identification of students would require a significant increase in the number of school counselors.

In 1957, it was estimated that there were 11,000 full-time counselors in the public schools, with a need for 26,000. NDEA set aside a large portion of funds for a national program of testing (including aptitude, vocational, and scholastic) and guidance. Just as WWII had pointed out the dire need for mental health professionals, the Sputnik scare pointed out the dire need for school counselors.

In congressional hearings on NDEA there was substantial debate on the role of the federal government in educational testing, guidance, and counseling. Arizona Senator Barry Goldwater opposed a national program of testing and guidance and in debate on the Senate floor, declared:

> If the Federal Government is going to say to the families of America that we now have to guide and counsel the children of America as to what is the best course for them to take in college and what should be their best pursuit in life, I think we have really tossed in the sponge. I do not want the Federal Government counseling my children. I do not want my own state counseling my children. That is part of the job of American parents and American churches. Have we gone so far down the ladder on rubbery legs that we are frightened to death by Russia and must say to parents of the country, "Do not bother with your children. We are going to take them over. We will tell them what to study and what we want them to do, and how to do it. You keep on drinking your beer and watching television"? If so, this country is going to pot in a Cadillac, and not in a chariot, as happened in the days of Rome.[46]

The American Personnel and Guidance Association (APGA), whom you might imagine would have seen this as an opportunity, actually had severe misgivings. Releasing an official position statement, the APGA voiced concern about the potential of the federal government to place the needs of the nation above the freedom of individuals:

> This generation has been called upon to make a decision that will shape the destinies of many future generations. At the heart of this decision lies

one of this nation's basic freedoms—*freedom of choice*. Faced by a tragic shortage of scientists and technologists, we are strongly tempted to solve the manpower problem by channeling outstanding high school and college students into scientific and technical careers. Here lies the danger of tampering with freedom of choice. If the top academic potentiality of this nation were to be forced into a singular, selected career pattern, generations of youth would lose the privilege of freely choosing their life careers—a privilege cherished by youth throughout the history of this nation. Such a course of action might not solve even part of the problem, for a lack of educated talent persists in all areas of our national life. The solution, therefore, must be viewed from a broader perspective, and we must aim toward utilizing *every* available talent.[47]

Despite these misgivings, the NDEA was signed into law on September 2, 1958. Like other federal initiatives discussed in this chapter, the range and scope was sweeping. Of particular interest to counseling psychologists was Title V of the NDEA: Guidance, Counseling and Testing, Identification and Encouragement of Able Students. This section of the act made funding available to colleges and universities to conduct counseling and guidance institutes. Approximately 80 institutes were conducted a year. These could be summer institutes of 6–8 weeks or yearlong sequences. Participants were generally drawn from the ranks of high school guidance counselors, many of whom were attracted to the opportunities and the stipends the institutes offered.

Institute staffs were frequently counseling psychologists. Topics of study included tests and measurement, statistics, and individual and group counseling methods (see Figure 5-7). The use of group experiences was common, as was supervised practicum experience. A report by counseling psychologist Leona Tyler, evaluating the first 50 institutes, found that practicum experience was rated the most meaningful and most well-liked activity, statistics the least. Tyler commented, "perhaps some hostility toward things mathematical is dormant in many people ready to be aroused with a minimum of stimulation."[48]

The institutes were supported for eight years from 1958–1966, after which time they continued under a variety of educational acts serving

Figure 5.7. *NDEA participants in a statistics course.*

a broad array of needs. The institutes increased demand for professors of counselor education and also made training requirements for graduate degrees in counseling and guidance more concrete. In the eight years of the program some 44,000 counselors were trained.

The Question of Identity

Throughout the 1950s counseling psychology increased its range of services and activities. Its position somewhere between education and psychology remained a vexing one, bringing many to question just what it was that defined counseling psychology. In 1956, Division 17 issued a statement on definition:

> At the present time, the specialty of counseling psychology is approaching a state of balance among the emphases upon contributions to (a) the development of an individual's inner life through concern with his or her motivation and emotions, (b) the individual's achievement of harmony with his or her environment thorough helping him or her to develop the

resources that he or she must bring to this task (for example, by assisting him or her to make effective use of appropriate community resources), and (c) the influencing of society to recognize individual differences and to encourage the fullest development of all persons within it.[49]

From outside, the status of counseling psychology appeared good. There were doctoral training programs, strong job opportunities, an established division of APA, and a professional journal, the *Journal of Counseling Psychology* (established in 1954). However, there was a chorus of detractors and in 1959 they persuaded the Education and Training (E&T) Board of the APA to appoint a committee to investigate the status of counseling psychology. Made up of three counseling psychologists; Irwin Berg (1913–2001), Harold Pepinsky (1917–1998), and Joseph Shobin (1918–1996). They produced a report that was scathing. The tone of the opening paragraph provides some indication of what was to follow:

> The reasons for the Board's action was a general feeling that all was not well with counseling psychology. Although counseling as an activity in fields other than psychology appeared to be flourishing, as witness the provisions of the National Defense Education Act, *counseling psychology* appeared, in the opinion of some members of the Board, to have lagged being other specialty areas of psychology. Two or three decades ago, counseling psychology was immensely prestigious as a specialty, but now it appears to be in some ways on the wane.[50]

Admitting to much in the way of personal opinion, the committee cited any number of problems with counseling psychology, including the lack of a research emphasis, a continuing decline in the number and quality of students, few candidates holding or seeking certification by the American Board of Examiners in Professional Psychology (ABEPP), and a poor status ranking among psychologists.[51] In conclusion, it was the recommended that consideration be given to dissolving Division 17, and moving it under the auspices of Division 12, Clinical Psychology.

The report touched off a firestorm of controversy and was never released. The Executive Committee of Division 17 protested vigorously, claiming they were never asked to participate in the preparation of the report, and demanding that they appoint their own committee to prepare a status report on counseling psychology. The request was granted and a new report issued. Authored by Leona Tyler, C. Gilbert Wrenn, and David Teideman, it was offered not as a rebuttal to the Berg, et al. report, but as a statement based on conclusions drawn from documented evidence. In preparing the report the authors noted:

> Counseling psychology, particularly in its important components of vocational psychology and vocational counseling, is in need of careful reexamination and clarification at this time. The scientific and professional interests of the members of Division 17 are multiple and complex. Some pulling together of some of the main threads in the more recent development of the Division is desirable. The relatively new label, *Counseling Psychology*, has caused this well-established field of work to be frequently compared with *Clinical Psychology* and other areas of specialization. Evaluation of the overlapping and differentiating features of these various areas of specialization is desirable. If Counseling Psychology, or any other field of psychology, appears to be contributing to human welfare, this distinctive contribution should be defined from time to time and suggestions for strengthening it should be proposed.[52]

Data describing counseling psychology and psychologists was presented. Drawing from a variety of published sources, the report concluded that counseling psychology was indeed alive and well. It was noted that Division membership was growing, as was the number of graduates, and that the similarities and differences between counseling psychology and other areas of professional psychology made for a more rounded and balanced offering of mental health services to the public. According to the report, counseling psychology was unique in that it focused on helping people make plans to play productive roles in the social environment. This required special skills and training, and they noted:

> It does not seem to matter whether the curriculum is placed in an arts and science psychology department or under a psychology staff in a school of education. It matters a great deal whether the curriculum is psychologically sound and whether psychologists teach the courses. The practice in some institutions of adding courses in group measurement and occupa-

tional information to a clinical psychology program or of adding courses in personality dynamics and clinical psychology to an educational psychology program or a pupil personnel program does not provide a counseling psychology program. Nor does it develop respect for the program.[53]

The report closed with a series of recommendations aimed at educating others about the unique features of counseling psychology, and improving existing programs of study.

Counseling psychology ended the decade of the 1950s just as it had begun, focused on the question of identity. An emerging theme was that of social action. Counseling psychology was a specialty area that helped people find a place in the world, regardless of their condition, physical, emotional, or otherwise. It had special tools and techniques to guide people into thoughtful consideration of a plan of life: it was in essence an extension of the work of early pioneers like Parsons who sought to maximize human potential through the thoughtful choice of a life's work.

Consolidation

For a three-day period in January 1964, 60 participants representing a broad spectrum of the counseling psychology community gathered at the Greyston Mansion (a gift to Teachers College, Columbia University) to consider their specialty. Known as the Greyston Conference, it was three years in the planning, spanning the terms of office of Division 17 presidents Robert Waldrop, Albert Thompson (1909–2004), and surprisingly, Irwin Berg, the person who chaired the committee that issued the controversial E&T Board report of 1960. It is interesting to note that Berg approved the funds for the meeting, yet was not invited to attend. The conference deliberations were organized under four themes: (a) the roles of counseling psychologists, (b) the content of professional preparation, (c) organizational aspects of training, and (d) unity and diversity.

At the meeting, support was offered for the evolving role of counseling psychology in larger social issues such as poverty, equal rights, and education. It is an excellent example of the influence of contextual factors. The concern over social issues that counseling psychologists were beginning to address in the 1950s emerged in the larger culture in 1964 when President

Lyndon Johnson delivered his Great Society speech at the University of Michigan (the same place counseling psychologists had gathered 15 years earlier to discuss their identity and training). Johnson argued forcefully for a just society that cared about the well-being of all its members. Through his efforts, major programs of aid and assistance were offered to many, including the poor, the unemployed, and the mentally ill. In 1964, Johnson also signed the Civil Rights Act into law. The deliberations at Greyston occurred during these times.

Discussing the preparation of counseling psychologists renewed discussion of the place of subdoctoral training. The long-time association of counseling psychology and education meant that many were familiar and comfortable with the training of subdoctoral personnel. No doubt, federal programs such as the NDEA, which offered opportunities for counseling psychologists to train and supervise master's-level counselors, encouraged Division 17 to look more kindly upon the issue of subdoctoral training. However, to call oneself a counseling psychologist still required the doctoral degree. Greyston affirmed the scientist-practitioner model of training with the addition of coursework that reflected the core values and unique nature of counseling psychology. Thus it was recommended that attention be given to coursework in sociology, the world of work, and education. A great deal of emphasis was placed on what might be thought of as impression management. Many at Greyston believed that counseling psychology needed to be much more proactive, explaining the specialty area to others and educating them about it (much in the spirit of the Tyler, Wrenn, and Teideman report). This included dispensing more and better information to students and faculty, public service agencies and training centers, and the APA.

In looking back over the meeting, Albert S. Thompson, who along with Donald Super, coauthored the report of the Greyston Conference[54] reported:

> At the end of the conference we came up with 32 recommendations. Some were for Division 17, some for APA, some for universities, some for practicum and internship settings, and some for employers. Most were designed to be practical. I would like to go on record to say that the recommendations did stimulate further developments such as American

Board of Examiners of Professional Psychologists (ABEPP) certification, a brochure put out by Division 17 on what counseling psychology is, and criteria for internship. There was general agreement that counseling psychology had a special substance and emphasis in training, which were not necessarily included in the current preparation.[55]

Greyston, if nothing else helped to unite counseling psychologists in a spirit of shared mission. After Greyston there was less talk about disbanding and more talk of identity. The brochure that Thompson referred to appeared in 1968.[56] The document, offered to the public, synthesized much of the data, both internal and external, about the scope and function of counseling psychology.

Recent Developments

The history of counseling psychology over the last four decades points to continued growth and expansion of the specialty as a health service profession. The social upheavals of the 1960s greatly accelerated the humanistic perspective in counseling and psychotherapy. Carl Rogers' client-centered perspective was humanistic at its core, but in the early years it was utilized in the service of adaptation and adjustment. In the 1960s, the humanistic philosophy of Abraham Maslow (1908–1970) replaced adjustment with self-fulfillment. Counseling and psychotherapy were often seen as tools of self-discovery and a variety of alternative approaches to achieving self-knowledge grew in popularity. The interest in personal growth, declining federal support of training and research, and retrenchment in academia all contributed to the growth of independent practice in the 1970s and 1980s. Licensure and third party (insurance) reimbursement for psychological services has continued the development of counseling psychology as a health service specialty.

Since the days of Carl Rogers, research has been conducted on the psychotherapy process. The rise of research and theory in psychotherapy is by no means unique to counseling psychology (see chapter 2). As psychotherapy became increasingly popular in American culture and psychology, many offered ideas, gathered data, and worked to understand a process that still remains largely a mystery.

Counseling psychology has retained a record of advances in theory, research, and practice in the area of vocational psychology. It is the one area where counseling psychology has a clear link to its past. The template of vocational psychology can be applied to any of the topical areas of interest to counseling psychologists, such as gender, ethnicity, sexual orientation, and life-span development.

Organizational Structure

Counseling psychology has grown in size and strength. Division 17, with over 2,000 members,[57] remains the largest representative body of counseling psychologists There are 65 active APA accredited doctoral programs,[58] and two major journals, *The Journal of Counseling Psychology* and *The Counseling Psychologist*.

Division 17, like the whole of psychology, continues to expand into areas of special interest and activity, often tied to issues in the larger culture. In Division 17 this is accomplished through the mechanism of sections and special interest groups (SIGS). Sections are formal organizations within Division 17 that actively seek to promote their special interests. Current sections include: Independent Practice; International; Positive Psychology; Racial and Ethnic Diversity; LGBT Issues; Psychotherapy Science Promotion; Supervision and Training; University Counseling Centers; Health Psychology; Advancement of Women; Vocational Psychology; Human/Animal Interaction; and Prevention. SIGs are more informal groups composed of individuals who share a common interest. As of this writing there are nine SIGs in operation: Older Adults & Aging; Couples and Families; Hypnosis; Organizational Counseling Psychology; Rural Practice and Scholarship; Adoption Research and Practice; PsyD Programs; Military Issues in Counseling Psychology; and Religion and Spiritual Issues in Counseling Psychology.[59]

The division works closely with other groups whose work impacts counseling psychologists directly. In the 1970s, directors of training programs in counseling psychology sought to increase their presence in professional psychology through the establishment of the Council of Counseling Psychology Training Programs (CCPTP). The group, which now has representation on the APA's Committee on Accreditation (CoA), provides a common meeting ground for training directors across the country to discuss training issues. CCPTP also serves an advocacy function, representing the interests of counseling psychologists in an ever more competitive market-place.[60] Likewise, the Association of Counseling Center Training Agencies (ACCTA) exists to represent the needs and interests of those working in one of counseling psychology's primary settings.[61]

Division 17 is not the only organization to represent the interests of counseling psychologists. The American Counseling Association (ACA), with its 17 divisions, represents a wide range of counseling organizations and activities.[62] The relationship between Division 17 and the ACA has been marked by growing distance, due in large measure to issues of accreditation, certification, and professional practice. Commenting on this Heppner, Casas, Carter, and Stone observed:

> In essence, the APA began to focus on credentialing *psychologists*, while the ACA (American Counseling Association) then concentrated on credentialing *counselors*. Accreditation of doctoral programs in counseling psychology was housed in the APA in the late 1970s, and licensure was tied to accredited programs in various states. Partly as a means of protecting its membership, in the early 1980s the APGA created an independent Council for Accreditation of Counseling and Related Educational Programs (CACREP).[63]

Social Action

Issues of training and accreditation remain constant. What changes is the content and context in which these issues unfold. In 1988, counseling psychologists convened for what was termed the Third National Conference for Counseling Psychology: Planning the Future.[64] Lawrence Brammer, who proposed the conference during his 1987 term as Division 17 president, described the meeting as follows:

> About three hundred participants heard eleven position papers; working groups discussed thirteen basic issues that were identified by the planning group under George Gaza the year before. Twenty recommendations covering a range of issues including relationships to APA, management problems in Division 17, underrepresentation of various ethnic, gender,

disability, and interest groups in Division 17 governance, encouragement of ethnic and cultural diversity, need for strategic planning, need for regional conferences, need for more contacts with related professional groups, and unresolved licensing matters.[65]

Of these recommendations, the ones most closely embraced were those involving diversity and inclusivity. Counseling psychology has taken considerable initiative in forwarding an inclusive agenda. Counseling psychology and psychologists played a major role in the Multicultural Summit of 1999. Women and ethnic minorities commonly serve in leadership roles in Division 17, and consideration of individual and group differences on factors such as age, gender, ethnicity, sexual orientation, disability, and socioeconomic status are now commonplace in counseling psychology theory, research, and practice. The Houston 2001 Counseling Psychology Conference had as its theme, Counseling Psychologists, Making a Difference.[66]

These issues have become a part of our larger national dialogues and are certainly not unique to professional psychology. However, a case can be made that counseling psychology has a long history of social action and justice. We have traced the roots of counseling psychology to the beginning of the 20th century and the social progressives and reformers who shared a concern for the well-being of those who were disenfranchised and at the mercy of the new industrial order. In the span of 100 years that mission has expanded to include many more who are excluded from the ideals of a democratic society. Long in coming, and with much still to be done, counseling psychology has made social action a central feature of its current mission.

Conclusion

We have painted a picture of the history of counseling psychology using broad strokes. In many ways the history of counseling psychology is the history of the 20th century. It is a story of the melding of the progressive ideal of a chance for a better and more satisfying life for all people of all ages with the psychology of individual differences that offered a scientific basis for the measurement of human abilities, aptitudes, and interests. It found application in all corners of society, especially in those areas concerned with education and rehabilitation. Under the force and weight of two world wars, a cold war, and a war of generations, counseling psychology showed an ability to adapt and change with the times.

In the late 20th century, counseling psychologists were most often found on college campuses, involved in training counselors and providing counseling services to students. Those numbers have steadily declined. Today the majority of counseling psychologists work outside of the academy. Counseling psychology is recognized as a health service profession, aligned with a training model for professional psychology. Counseling psychologists, like other professional psychologists, can be found in most any setting that deals with mental health and behavior. Thus, the future of counseling psychology is linked to the future of professional psychology. This joint future is the topic of our next and final chapter.

Chapter 6
The Psychological Profession in the 21st Century

In the preceding chapters we have told the story of the evolution of the modern profession of psychology, focusing on the four specialty areas that have long been identified as the core applied specialties in psychology. In this concluding chapter we want to continue this story and offer some predictions—always a risky enterprise—about the future of the profession. The material that follows primarily concerns issues affecting those professional psychologists who work as mental health service providers, principally counseling and clinical psychologists, and to a lesser extent school psychologists. Overall industrial/organizational psychologists have not taken this route, although many make a living or supplement their income through consultation, a role that has presented and will continue to present opportunities for psychological practice.

We have three chief objectives for this chapter. First, we review two modern issues that continue to be debated in the practice of psychology, namely managed care and prescription privileges. Second, we describe several of the newer specialties of professional psychology to illustrate the growth of the profession beyond the four traditional specialties already covered.

Finally, we discuss the continuing debate about the scientific underpinnings of the contemporary practice of psychology. We close that section and this book with a discussion of the opportunities for professional psychologists in a 21st-century America that is arguably changing more rapidly and more dramatically than at any time in its history.

Managed Care

In the 1970s, the long-held public stereotype of the psychologist as clinician with a patient on the couch finally became a reality. Well, it was not really a couch, but the prototypical psychologist at that time was a clinical or counseling psychologist delivering psychotherapy to clients in a private practice. And after many years of battling psychiatry and insurance companies, the psychologist was able to see those clients without having to have them referred by a psychiatrist or other physician and could be paid directly by the insurance companies for the delivery of psychological services. Licensing laws had finally been passed in all 50 states, protecting the use of the label "psychologist" and defining the practices of the profession. Such regulation certainly helped to protect the public, but it also protected the profession, to some degree, from encroachment by others with lesser or different training. The profession of psychology had indeed come a long way. Yet the 1980s would bring dramatic changes to the nature of psychological practice, and disillusionment and dismay to many practitioners. The agent of change was known as "managed care." For many psychologists, managed care was seen as anathema to the proper practice of psychotherapy. It was viewed by some psychologists as patently unethical because it compromised high-quality mental health care in the name of cutting health care costs. Some psychologists fought against it, predicting that when its ethical shortcomings were recognized, the restrictions of managed care would disappear. They were wrong.

Managed care actually began in the 1950s as a way to provide more uniform medical care to employees, as a means to increase preventive medicine, and, many would emphasize, as a way to control the ever rising costs of health care. Indeed, if there is a mantra to managed care it is "cost containment." Managed care began in the form of prepaid health care plans from health maintenance organizations known as HMOs, organizations that provided medical services for the employees of companies for a fixed price. However, these plans did not include benefits for mental health care because such care was considered too expensive. Some HMOs began to offer limited mental health coverage in the late 1960s and that coverage escalated in the 1970s after the Health Maintenance Organization Act of

1973 was passed. This act required HMOs that were funded, even partially, by federal monies to offer outpatient mental health services, specifically, at least 20 outpatient psychotherapy sessions per year.[1]

Cost and Service Containment

Mental health care costs have long been a significant percentage of health care costs in the United States, exceeding 25% of the annual dollars spent on health care. But most of that cost is for hospitalization of people with mental illness, including long-term hospitalization for those with serious persistent mental illness. As research demonstrated that outpatient psychotherapy could greatly reduce the overall costs of mental health care by reducing the need for hospitalization, HMOs and insurance companies were more willing to expand outpatient benefits.[2] Indeed, companies and workers demanded such benefits, and in order to remain competitive, HMOs and insurance companies were forced to provide them. Still, there was concern about the expense of such benefits and companies used a number of strategies including behavioral health carve-outs to hold down costs.

Carve-outs were designed to separate out medical from mental health care, in essence creating two silos for health care delivery. The impact was significant, "Carve-outs have emphasized cost cutting measures like: reducing reimbursement rates; use of subdoctoral providers; gatekeeping (i.e., requiring primary care physician referral); dumping of patients with severe mental disorders into the public sector; high copayments and deductibles; preauthorization of treatment; and other paper utilization review procedures."[3]

Managed care has also changed the practice of psychological assessment. Critics, mostly within the managed care industry, have argued that psychological testing is too time-consuming and too expensive, and that the information learned from such assessments is not all that useful. Yet research on the validity of psychological tests, including a large study of more than 125 meta-analyses, has demonstrated their importance. This study found that "(a) psychological test validity is strong and compelling, (b) psychological test validity is comparable to medical test validity, (c) distinct assessment methods provide unique sources of information, and (d) clinicians who rely exclusively on interviews are prone to incomplete understanding."[4] In a system that emphasizes cost containment, it should not be surprising that clinical assessment would be reduced. In spite of the evidence in support of psychological assessment, clinicians are often forced to obtain preauthorization for assessment protocols and are reimbursed for brief, symptom-oriented measures and diagnostic interviews. Such outcomes have consequences not only for the quality of patient care, but also for the way professional psychologists are trained today.[5]

Ethics

Ethical concerns are central in much of the dissatisfaction expressed about psychotherapy within a managed care system. Psychologists worry about informed consent issues, that is, that managed care systems are not forthcoming with employees about the lack of control that employees have over their care and the limitations that may be imposed on psychological services. Individuals often learn about these limitations in periods of crisis, when such knowledge can compound the psychological problems and undermine trust in the psychologist. Psychologists also worry, with good cause, about confidentiality of sensitive and private information. Information that the patient would normally share only with the psychologist is shared with individuals outside of the therapeutic relationship, namely, personnel in the managed care system who interview the employee and arrange for the psychotherapy. Among the ethical concerns that have most plagued psychologists working in a managed care system is what is called abandonment, a premature termination of psychological services to an individual because additional psychological sessions will not be covered by the company. The code of ethics that governs the practice of psychology does not permit abandonment, at least not in crisis situations. Psychologists must find ways to continue services for those in crisis, regardless of financial issues. Yet many patients will cease participation in therapy once payments are cut off.[6]

Impacts

Managed care has had a significant impact on lowering the annual income of psychological practitioners while at the same time increasing the administrative load associated with communication and documentation required for reimbursement. Some psychologists have declined to work in a managed care structure and instead treat patients who can pay the full costs of therapy without insurance reimbursement (in much the same way that some physicians refuse to treat Medicare and Medicaid patients). Yet for most practitioners, earnings for psychotherapy have dropped because of the reduction in the number of sessions patients receive and because of negotiated decreases in the hourly rates charged by therapists. The economic impact is perhaps clearest when one realizes that the insurance reimbursement for mental health services today is about one half of what it was 10 years ago. Reimbursements for medical costs for physical illnesses have shown reductions as well, but nothing that approximates the cuts for mental health. So severe has been the decline that psychologists are now the lowest paid members of the doctoral health profession.[7]

Still, most clinical and counseling psychologists have accepted the reality of managed care and have adapted their practices to fit the new rules. Brief, evidenced-based treatments (EBTs) are the gold standard in managed care and many practitioners have altered the way they do psychotherapy to make sessions more focused and to increase the therapeutic pace.[8]

Responses to Managed Care

So, what is the answer for the delivery of psychological services in mental health care? Those who are older or at least familiar with mid-20th-century American history may long for the time of the family doctor making a house call, a doctor who knew everything about you (not just what could be gleaned from a 10-second read of your medical chart) and who would spend 30 minutes talking with you and listening to you (as opposed to the six minutes more typical today). Clearly those days are long gone.

> Healthcare today is a business, a big business. It commands one-seventh of the nation's resources, provides one-eleventh of all jobs, and has central importance to all labor-management negotiations by being the most prized benefit for seven-eighths of all employed persons...healthcare has become a commercialized and competitive industry. It is no longer prudent for mental health practitioners to see themselves as being outside the competitive fray that characterizes the consumer marketplace. They need to understand the implications of "peddling their wares" in a venue teeming with quality-conscious consumers and value-conscious purchasers.[9]

Older practitioners, those who fought the turf battles with psychiatry and for freedom-of-choice laws with the insurance companies, who thrived in the 1970s practicing psychotherapy independently in a fee-for-services arrangement, can be excused for their reluctance to embrace managed care. They helped to create the golden age of psychotherapy for psychologists and it proved all too short-lived. Their frustration is captured well by Cummings who wrote, "It has not been easy for psychology, which struggled many years to attain autonomy only to see the rules of the game change just as it became the preeminent psychotherapy profession."[10] But the golden age is gone; managed care has forced psychological practitioners to reinvent themselves. The pressures for that are certainly economic. As we have noted, insurance coverage for mental health has been substantially reduced and fees for services have also been reduced in the arrangements between managed care systems and psychologists in their network of practitioners. Furthermore, there is greater competitive pressure from other practitioner groups, including marriage and family counselors, licensed professional counselors, social workers, and master's-level psychologists (who, when they are licensed, rarely can practice under the title "psychologist"), all of whom can practice in many states with a master's degree and all of whom typically are willing to provide services at lower rates than doctoral-level psychologists.

Managed care is here to stay. Professional psychologists, if they are to continue to be successful, have to evolve in their thinking about the delivery of psychological services. Many have adapted well to this new system. They have undergone what Nicholas Cummings has labeled the "resocialization of psychology."[11]

Cummings, one of the pioneers in the development of the modern profession of psychology, described several aspects of this resocialization. First, he lauded the fact that some psychologists have recognized the value of group practices and joined together, combining their diverse specialties (e.g., pediatric psychology, group psychotherapy, eating disorders treatments, pain management, couples therapy) in order to appeal to managed care systems looking for providers of multiple psychological services. While there will be a larger market for such groups, some providers are concerned about losing their autonomy.[12]

Second, the new practitioners have sought retraining in what are called "time-effective" or brief therapies, therapies that often last no more than six to eight sessions. Research on brief therapies shows that they often produce the same success rates as longer therapies and that they can be effective with serious psychological disorders and not just less severe problems. Part of the success of brief therapies has been an adjustment of the expectations of the therapist and client so that change is anticipated in a short period of time. Psychologists Mary Koss and Julia Shiang have written:

> It is now generally recognized that when patients enter psychological treatment, they do not anticipate that their therapy will be prolonged but believe that their problems will require a few sessions at most. Indeed, patients typically come to psychological treatment seeking specific and focal problem resolution, rather than general personality "overhauls" as assumed in the past.[13]

Acknowledging this change in attitude, there are still many practicing psychologists who believe that longer-term therapies are the only effective means by which some people are able to make the major changes that are required in their lives for therapy to be considered a success. Such practitioners will find a small clientele who will be able to afford such treatment, but it will no longer be the dominant course of treatment for most clients.

Third, Cummings has argued that under managed care, psychologists will have to demonstrate their effectiveness, not just their efficiency. Outcome research is expected to be a part of what managed care systems will use to assess the relative effectiveness of therapists. Confidentiality will be an issue in such research, but as Cummings has noted, "Confidentiality is for the protection of the client and must be zealously guarded. It was never intended to protect the practitioner from inefficiency or ineptitude."[14]

The limitations of managed care have been many and obvious. Challenges and demands for reform have come from many quarters and promising changes are occurring. It is interesting to note that these changes have resulted largely from the efforts of those outside of professional psychology. The Mental Health Parity and Addiction Equity Act of 2008, authored by two US senators, the late Paul Wellstone and Pete Domenici, requires health plans to provide the same financial requirements (co-pays, deductibles, out of pocket minimums, etc.) and treatment benefits (such as number of visits) for mental health services as for medical and surgical services. It is a shift in the direction of consumers and service providers and should help to alleviate some of the shortcomings of the managed care system.[15] Likewise, the landmark Patient Protection and Affordable Care Act signed into law by President Barack Obama in 2010 extends health insurance to Americans who have been previously uninsured. It is too early to tell what the impact will be on service providers, but it is clear that millions of American will now have access to mental health services and benefits in parity with medical benefits.

Prescription Privileges for Psychologists

As providers of mental health services, psychologists have long distinguished themselves from psychiatrists, largely on the basis of their adoption of a behavioral model for psychological problems, as opposed to the medical model that represents the training of psychiatrists, and by an emphasis on psychological assessment as key to the process of treatment. For psychologists, psychotherapy is used to bring about behavior and cognitive changes. Such changes not only eliminate or lessen the problems, but they typically reduce the likelihood of future occurrences. Psychiatry, as a medical specialty, has always had the option of prescribing drugs, a practice denied to psychologists by legislation. As psychotropic medications have increased in number and effectiveness in recent years, the use of drugs as a first line of treatment in psychiatry has greatly increased. Given psychology's quest for parity with psychiatry in the mental health field, as indicated by the struggle to be able to provide psychotherapy, to be a provider of choice in mental health insurance plans, and to be granted hospital privileges, it was only a matter of time before psychologists would attack this one very visible boundary—that of prescription authority.

Psychological practitioners began to explore this issue in the 1980s and by the 1990s had solicited the backing of the American Psychological Association (APA).[16] By no means have psychologists been unanimous in their support of prescription privileges. In fact, when the idea was first introduced it seemed clear that most practitioners were against it. Today though, the majority of professional psychologists clearly support gaining prescription privileges. In truth, practicing psychologists have long been involved in the medication issues of their clients. A survey of nearly 600 practitioners showed that almost all (94%) "were involved in at least one activity that directly or indirectly affected whether a patient received medication." The most frequent activity was making a patient referral for medical evaluation, something that 99% of the psychologists had done. They recommended medications based on clinical interviews, consulted with their client's physician about changing the client's medication, were involved in the decision with the client's physician to prescribe medication, discussed medication issues as part of the psychotherapy, and so forth.[17] Thus many practicing psychologists have a long-standing familiarity with psychotropic medications. Certainly such knowledge is not sufficient background for prescription privileges, but it demonstrates the importance and relevance of such information for the practice of psychology. Recognizing that practicing psychologists are involved in a range of medication issues, a task force of the American Society for the Advancement of Pharmacotherapy (Division 55 of the American Psychological Association) drafted *Guidelines Regarding Psychologists' Involvement in Pharmacological Issues*. Adopted by the APA Council of Representatives in 2009, the document provides guidance practice issues and identifies three roles of psychologists in pharmacological treatment: (1) as prescriber; (2) collaborator; or, (3) when providing information on medication.[18]

Opposition to Prescription Privileges

Clearly psychiatrists and other physicians have been adamantly opposed to psychologists gaining prescription privileges. Yet opponents within psychology have been quite vocal as well.[19] They have argued that the job of the psychologist is to improve human functioning and the way to do that is with therapies that give individuals insights about their behaviors and thoughts and provide strategies to change them. Garland DeNelsky has described it this way:

> There is a powerful seductiveness about medications. When a patient presents with a condition such as depression, anxiety, panic, or sleep disorder, it is both easier and faster to turn to a prescription pad than

to those behavioral and psychotherapeutic techniques that have been shown to be effective and more lasting, but which require more time and effort. The prescribing practitioner feels that he or she is doing something now, and the patient may gain some immediate relief.[20]

Some practitioners have argued that a combination of drugs and psycho-therapy may be best for most disorders but DeNelsky has argued against this view:

> [T]here is mounting evidence...that, frequently, medication may interfere with the patient acquiring more adaptive thinking and behavioral pat-terns. Patients tend to attribute help as coming from outside of themselves, rather than seeing improvement as the product of their own efforts.[21]

DeNelsky, and others who oppose prescription privileges, believe that psy-chologists will eventually rely more and more on prescribing medications and less on psychotherapy and other psychological interventions. He wor-ries that:

> In a society whose members have been criticized as turning too readily to pills or chemicals to try to solve their problems, this could hardly be considered a positive development. It would be particularly regrettable because increasing evidence indicates that appropriate psychological interventions have been shown to be at least as effective as medications for treating depression, panic, and a variety of other disorders, and psy-chological interventions are more likely to prevent relapse than medica-tions in each of these instances.[22]

DeNelsky's worries seem well founded. According to a 2004 consumer poll more Americans are being treated for mental health issues with medication alone. Among the findings:

> For those with a treatment history, 81%, or an estimated 48 million people, report taking or having taken a prescription medication for a personal, emotional or mental health problem in the past two years. In contrast, only 53% report undergoing psychotherapy.
>
> 25% of American adults who have taken prescription drugs for a men-tal health problem did not report the level of distress typically associated with those in need of treatment.

One-quarter of those taking only medication have received a recommendation from a doctor that they receive talk therapy as well, but have not done so.

Older Americans (ages 50+) are significantly more likely to receive medication alone than are those between the ages of 18 and 49.[23]

Such findings have increased calls for making psychological evaluation and psychotherapy the first line of treatment for mental health issues.[24]

Opponents to prescription privileges have also voiced concerns about graduate professional training. The APA has endorsed a model psychopharmacology curriculum that would be part of professional psychology training programs or, alternatively, as part of postdoctoral training.[25] Critics view these courses as an added burden on an already overly crowded graduate school curriculum. They wonder what kinds of psychological training will be eliminated so that the psychopharmacological material can be added.[26]

Clinical Trials for Psychologists

The psychologists who are opponents of prescription privileges are very likely to see whether their dire predictions come true because many state psychological associations are working to get bills passed in their legislatures. The first state to give psychologists prescription authority was New Mexico, which did so in 2002, followed by Louisiana in 2004. However, the first US territory to take this step was Guam, which voted to give psychologists prescription privileges in 2000. Bills in Hawaii and Oregon were passed by their state legislatures, but later vetoed by their governors.

Prescription privileges are not the sole domain of medical doctors, that is, MDs. The authority to prescribe has previously been granted to podiatrists, optometrists, and dentists. Other groups can also prescribe, such as pharmacists, nurse practitioners, and physician assistants, but they can do so only under the supervisory authority of a physician. Psychologists are seeking to join the first group, which enjoys autonomy, at least for a limited class of drugs.

Part of the impetus for prescription privileges for psychologists was a series of trials conducted by the Department of Defense (DoD). In the same way that psychologists were judged to be effective providers of psychotherapy in government testing at the end of World War II, the DoD began trials in 1991 using Army and Navy psychologists who were given training in psychopharmacology and experience with psychiatric cases in preparation for the clinical trials. Subsequent evaluations of their performance (in terms of the accuracy of diagnosis and appropriateness of drug recommendations), compared with medically trained psychiatrists, showed no differences in competency.[27]

Today, there are more prescribing psychologists and there does not appear to be any issues in competency. According to Morgan Sammons (a prescribing psychologist):

> At this point, however, approximately 100 prescribing psychologists are utilizing those skills within the Department of Defense, other federal agencies, and the two states in which psychologists have been granted legislative authority to prescribe (New Mexico and Louisiana). To date, there has been no evidence of any of these providers harming patients by deviating from the standard of care in the utilization of psychotropics, although these psychologists practice in a number of jurisdictions and healthcare systems, so there is no central database that accrues data to determine whether their practice as a group differs from that of other healthcare providers.[28]

Proponents for Prescription Privileges

Those in favor of prescription privileges have made the following arguments. They have expressed concern about the overuse of medications at the hands of psychiatrists and other physicians (it is nonpsychiatrist physicians who prescribe the bulk of psychotropic medications for their patients). They argue that psychologists, because of their better behavioral training, would do a better job in seeing that medications are used appropriately. They point especially to problems in prescribing psychotropic medications for women, children, and persons in nursing homes. They note the inefficiency and added expense of therapy (plus some additional compromised confidentiality) when a psychologist sees a patient who would benefit from medication and has to ask the patient to see a physician to gain access to the prescription.[29]

Proponents argue that prescription privileges will allow psychologists to treat individuals with more serious mental illnesses, for example, patients with schizophrenia. New antipsychotic medications not only reduce or eliminate some of the disabling symptoms of the disease but enhance patient compliance and improve cognitive functioning. "[P]atients treated with these agents may be more amenable to psychological and psychosocial interventions, suggesting that psychologists may encounter increased opportunities to render services to this population."[30]

It is clear that the issue of prescription privileges is a complex one in terms of both training issues and practice issues. There are many important questions yet to be answered, for example, related to generic licensing and malpractice insurance. Despite resistance by forces inside and outside psychology, the push for prescriptive authority for psychologists remains. How that will change the profession of psychology remains to be seen, but change it will.[31]

New Practice Specialties

In the previous four chapters we focused on what are the largest of the practitioner specialties today: clinical, school, industrial/organizational, and counseling psychology. Each of those practice specialties has been in existence for a long time; thus it is not surprising that today there are many subspecialties, such as clinical child psychology, consumer psychology, clinical neuropsychology, geropsychology, and family psychology. In addition to these subspecialties, there are new specialties as well. We have selected three of these specialties for coverage here: forensic psychology, sport psychology, and health psychology. Although each of these emerged as an area of specialized practice in the late 20th century, all have roots that go much farther back. These areas represent interesting psychological challenges, they fill unmet needs, and they represent good career opportunities.

Forensic Psychology

Forensic psychology is a broad field and thus not easily defined. The word "forensic" refers to judicial issues, and forensic psychology is the interface of psychology and the legal system. Psychologists can be found working today in all areas of the judicial system, in police departments, courts, juvenile detention centers, jails, and especially in prisons. In that context they might work with police officers and their families, judges, attorneys,

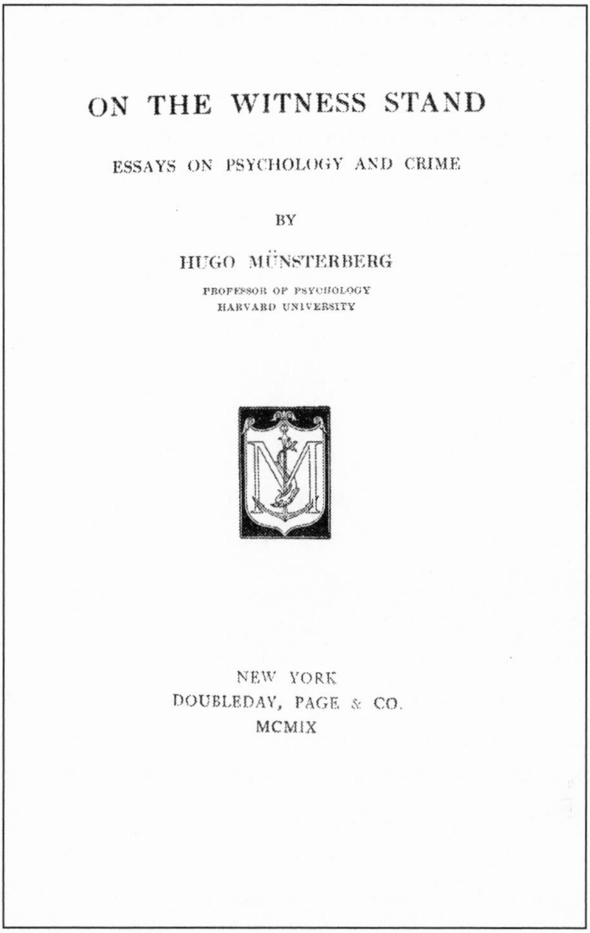

ON THE WITNESS STAND

ESSAYS ON PSYCHOLOGY AND CRIME

BY

HUGO MÜNSTERBERG

PROFESSOR OF PSYCHOLOGY
HARVARD UNIVERSITY

NEW YORK
DOUBLEDAY, PAGE & CO.
MCMIX

Figure 6-1. *Title page of Hugo Münsterberg's 1908 book.*

accused persons, prisoners, guards, hospital administrators, corporate executives, and victims of crime. Most of the individuals who work in this field today are trained principally as clinical and counseling psychologists, but other kinds of psychologists—for example, social and experimental psychologists—have also found work in forensics, and there are new graduate programs that train psychologists specifically for forensics work.

Münsterberg and the Psychology of the Courtroom. Perhaps the earliest work in this field was done by Hugo Münsterberg, whose contributions to industrial psychology were described in chapter 4. Münsterberg began his work in forensic psychology in 1906, when he was asked by a defense attorney to review the records of his client who had been convicted of murder. The convicted man had confessed but later withdrew his confession. In studying the records of the investigation and trial, Münsterberg concluded that the confession had been obtained under suspicious circumstances and that the accused murderer, who was mentally disabled, was very likely innocent. Münsterberg's letter was released to the press and its publication infuriated the judge in the case who expressed his outrage that Münsterberg, who had no involvement with the trial, would see himself as an expert on the question of the man's guilt or innocence. The conviction stood and the man was hanged. Münsterberg was upset with the court's reaction. He considered the decision to be not only a rebuff of his own expertise but an attack on the validity of scientific psychology.

This case and several others led to the publication of one of Münsterberg's most famous books, *On the Witness Stand*, published in 1908 (see Figure 6-1). In the introduction to that book he wrote: "The lawyer and the judge and the juryman are sure that they do not need the experimental psychologist.... They go on thinking that their legal instinct and their common sense supplies them with all that is needed."[32] He argued that the science of psychology was critical in evaluating evidence, detecting false confessions, and determining the accuracy of eyewitness testimony. His book debunked the idea that crimes could be caused by posthypnotic suggestion while illustrating how suggestion could create false memories and beliefs. One of the chapters dealt with the fallibility of recall in witnesses, anticipating much contemporary work on memory problems in eyewitness testimony.[33]

A chapter entitled "The Detection of Crime" discussed the work on word-association methods and how the technique could be used to detect lying.[34] In his own work, Münsterberg used a chronoscope to measure response latencies in thousandths of a second. That is, he measured the time from the reading of the stimulus word to the subject's supplying the association word. He believed that individuals took longer to speak in response to words that were emotionally laden. Münsterberg waxed and waned in his certainty about the validity of his word-association method as a lie-detection procedure. Eventually he began to investigate other measures, including physiological measures such as respiration, blood pressure, and the resistance to electrical conductance in the skin (the Galvanic Skin Response or GSR).[35] Münsterberg recognized that his methods in lie detection had no legal standing in court, but he believed that one day they would. He wrote, "Justice demands that truth and lies be disentangled. The time will come when the methods of experimental psychology cannot longer be excluded from the court of law."[36] Although the modern polygraph, a machine that measures many of the autonomic nervous system responses that Münsterberg measured, is still not admissible in court today, there are many other ways that psychologists have become involved in the judicial system.

Münsterberg was not the only psychologist involved in the courtroom. Psychologists, including Münsterberg, were often commissioned by attorneys to provide expert testimony in the courtroom. Recall from chapter 4 the testimony that Harry Hollingworth gave in 1911 on his caffeine research in support of the legal defense of the Coca Cola Company.

Contemporary Forensic Psychology. Contemporary forensic psychologists are often called upon to render their expertise in an attorney's office, in a jail or prison, or in the courtroom. Assessment of the behavior and mental capacity of individuals is a common function and includes addressing "questions of law such as the insanity defense, competency to stand trial, civil competency, risk to self or others, and child custody."[37] Forensic psychologists often work with courts and parole boards to make assessments of the readiness of individuals for probation or parole. Such assessments use clinical instruments, family history data, and other psychological and statistical (actuarial) measures to make predictions about future behavior of convicted or incarcerated individuals. For example, in parole cases a psychologist might be asked to evaluate a criminal convicted of a violent offense and to predict the likelihood of that person's engaging in future violence if released. Such evaluations are far from perfect; psychologists continue to work to improve their measures of assessment.

Clients for Forensic Psychology. Forensic psychologists work with corporations that are being sued (for example, for negligence leading to an employee's death) to help them decide their chances of winning the case. By studying the decisions of mock juries and by comparing differing argumentative strategies, psychologists can better gauge the chances of a favorable or unfavorable verdict. In a similar vein, psychologists often work with attorneys to advise in the selection of jurors, listening to the questioning of potential jurors (perhaps, suggesting questions to ask), watching for facial expressions or other body language that may give insights into a person's biases, and reading what potential jurors write on their standard information forms. More commonly, psychologists in this work are employed by defense attorneys. In essence their job is to help the attorney select jurors who are more likely to be sympathetic to that attorney's client. Yet forensic psychologists also work on the other side, in cases in which employees are alleging employment discrimination or have suffered personal injury in the workplace.

Forensic psychologists work as behavioral profilers for the FBI, Secret Service, and some police departments. In the case of the Secret Service, their job includes identifying the potential risk of individuals who have made threats, for example, against the president of the United States; they also might maintain a list and keep track of other individuals whose conduct and comments have made them suspect as someone who might be a danger to federal institutions and federal workers. Forensic psychologists are often the subject of television shows and movies as profilers, typically portrayed in a search for a serial killer. Forensic psychologists develop and lead treatment programs for various kinds of offenders, such as violent youth, drug addicts, sex offenders, and individuals arrested for domestic violence. They offer clinical and counseling psychological services to police officers and their spouses. They are sometimes involved in hostage negotiations.

The Psychological Autopsy. One of the more unusual services provided by some forensic and clinical psychologists is what is called a psychological autopsy—a clinical evaluation of a deceased individual, in which the psychologist seeks to describe the mental state of the individual at a particular point prior to death. In one example, because of several disputed wills written at different times, a clinical psychologist, Raymond Fowler, was asked by the attorneys for deceased billionaire Howard Hughes to render a psychological autopsy on Hughes' state of mind at the times of the several wills. And in another example, when an explosion aboard the USS Iowa in 1989 killed 47

Navy sailors, the FBI and a Naval Review Board concluded that the explosion was the suicidal act of a single sailor who was killed in the explosion. The US House of Representatives Armed Services Committee, however, was not accepting of the verdict and commissioned a panel of psychologists to evaluate the evidence gathered in the case and the interpretation of that evidence. Part of the analysis by the psychologists was to include a psychological autopsy on the accused sailor. Ten of the 14 panelists disagreed with the judgment against the sailor and the other panelists also expressed some reservations with the decision. Eventually the decision was reversed and the explosion was ruled an accident. The psychological autopsy, although one of the possible services in forensic psychology, is somewhat rare and, not surprisingly, controversial given that a clinical evaluation is being performed on a subject who is incapable of responding to any questions the psychologist might ask. Despite its flaws, this technique is about the only procedure available to make the kinds of clinical decisions required.[38]

Growth of Forensic Psychology. Many of these forensic practitioners are clinical and counseling psychologists who have gained much of their forensics training through continuing education workshops or by being mentored by other psychologists who have worked in the legal system. Yet, as the field has grown, more specialized university training programs have emerged, including forensic psychology programs that are specialty programs within more traditional fields, such as clinical psychology, and joint psychology and law programs that offer a doctorate in psychology and a law degree (JD).[39] As of 2010, there are over 20 doctoral programs that offer some form of training in forensic psychology.[40] Most recently, the APA Council of Representatives approved guidelines for forensic psychology.[41] Within the APA, forensic psychologists often belong to Division 41, also known as the American Psychology-Law Society. In 2012, this group numbered approximately 2,200.[42] Interest in forensic psychology continues to grow. There are hundreds of books and more than 20 journals that cover research and practice in this field. At this point it is difficult to predict the future of the field. However, given the litigious nature of American society, the power of the legal profession based on its dominance in state and federal legislative bodies, and the growing number of prisons in America (virtually all of whom employ one or more psychologists to provide clinical and counseling services), it seems safe to say that a principal role for psychologists in legal and judicial matters seems assured.[43]

Sport Psychology

Professional sports are big business today. A golfer can win more than a million dollars in a single tournament; professional baseball players earn average annual salaries of more than $2 million and at least one player receives more than $30 million per year; boxers can earn $20 to $50 million a year; and most professional basketball, hockey, and football players are millionaires as well. Even in sports where the cash prizes for winning are not at those levels, such as cycling or track and field, winning may lead to commercial endorsements that earn the athlete millions of dollars.

Athletes, and those who study athletic competition, have long realized that although much of an athlete's success comes from physical talents, mental factors also play a hugely important role. Indeed, in so many instances when physical talents seem evenly matched, it is the mental factors that will make the difference in winning or losing. This desire for gaining every possible competitive edge has led many athletes to seek the services of psychologists as part of their training and coaching team. Today psychologists work as sport psychologists for Olympic teams, professional teams, and individual athletes.[44]

The modern profession of sport psychology has its roots in the 1960s when the first international sport psychology organization, the International Society of Sport Psychology (ISSP), was formed in Italy in 1965, followed by national organizations in the United States in 1966 and Canada in 1969. These organizations provided a forum where these early sport psychologists could discuss their work and plan for the future of the profession. By the mid-1980s the field had come of age with additional organizations better aimed at promoting professional interests, such as the Association for the Advancement of Applied Sport Psychology (AAASP) [now known as the Association for Applied Sport Psychology (AASP)] in 1986 and Division 47 of the APA, the Division of Exercise and Sport Psychology; the latter organization was also begun in 1986 and today has about 700 members.[45] Several journals have appeared as well to publish the work in this new field, such as the *Sport Psychologist*, the *Journal of Applied Sport Psychology*, and the *Journal of Sport and Exercise Psychology*.

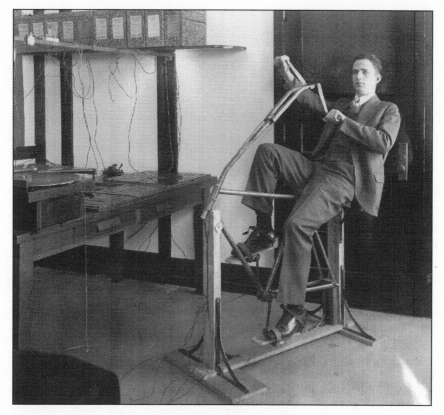

Figure 6-2. *Coleman Griffith, pioneering sport psychologist.* Courtesy of the University of Illinois Archives

Although the roots of the modern profession can be found in the 1960s, the story of sport psychology is much older and dates at least to the beginnings of the science of psychology in America.[46] Beginning in the 1890s several psychologists published work on athletics. Norman Triplett (1861–1934) studied cycling in 1898, showing that cyclists recorded faster times when racing in the presence of others than when racing alone, a demonstration of what social psychologists would later name social facilitation.[47] At about the same time, Edward W. Scripture (1864–1945) of Yale University studied reaction times in runners. There would be other investigations, such as studies by Walter Miles (1885–1978) in the late 1920s on the psychology of football, but all of these represented only a brief foray into the psychology of sport.[48] None of these individuals would have been labeled a sport psychologist. That label, however, could be accurately applied to Coleman R. Griffith (1893–1966).

Coleman Griffith: Pioneer in Sport Psychology. Griffith's work was largely forgotten in the history of American psychology until the emergence of interest in sport psychology in the last third of the 20th century caused it to be rediscovered (see Figure 6-2). Griffith received his doctorate in psychology from the University of Illinois in 1920 and remained on the faculty there until his retirement in 1953. His studies of sport psychology began in 1918 when he was a graduate student, studying vision and attention in the laboratory as factors predicting performance in basketball and football. In 1920 he offered a special section of the introductory psychology class for athletes, using examples of athletic competition in his teaching of psychology. By 1923 this course had evolved into a separate course entitled, "Psychology and Athletics." Griffith's well-equipped research laboratory to study athletic performance opened in 1925. In the next five years he conducted research on

a) the relation between physical exercise and learning, b) the effects of extreme physical exercise on longevity and disease resistance, c) the nature of sleep in athletes, d) methods of teaching psychological skills in football, e) measurement of physical fitness, f) the effects of emotion on learning of habits, g) muscular coordination, h) persistence of errors, i) the effects of fatigue on performance, j) measures of motor aptitude, and k) mental variables associated with excellent athletic performance.[49]

In the 1920s Griffith published two books on sport psychology, *Psychology of Coaching* (1926) and *Psychology and Athletics* (1928).[50] He planned a book on the psychology of football with Robert Zuppke, Illinois's head football coach, but the book was never published.

Griffith's work at Illinois had been supported by the athletic department from the early 1920s. He was allowed access to the athletic teams and even performed some of his psychological testing during athletic events—for example, testing football players on the sidelines. But by 1932 the athletic department, whose budget was reduced in the Great Depression, decided the benefits from the research were not evident and thus withdrew financial support for Griffith's lab. He would publish a few more articles on sport psychology, but his days as a sport psychologist were largely ended. He did, however, venture into the field once more as a consultant with the professional baseball team the Chicago Cubs from 1938 to 1940, perhaps the first instance of a psychologist being hired by a professional sports team. He was hired by the team's owner, Philip K. Wrigley, the chewing gum magnate. Although Griffith made many suggestions—for example, about how practices could be made better so as to enhance performance—the team's manager, Charlie Grimm, was resistant to what he saw as the meddling of a college professor, thus most of Griffith's recommendations were ignored.[51]

Griffith trained no students in sport psychology nor did his work spark the sport psychology movement of the 1960s. Thus there is no intellectual linkage between him and modern sport psychology. Still, his goals for his psychology are wholly consistent with what sport psychologists do today. Whereas earlier psychologists such as Triplett and Miles dabbled in the field, Griffith truly functioned as a sport psychologist in both his research and his attempts to apply that work in field settings.[52]

Modern Practice of Sport Psychology. Modern sport psychology has roots not only in psychology but also in the field of physical education, especially in the areas of motor learning and exercise physiology. Indeed, the physical education branch can claim priority. This multiple parentage has caused some problems in reaching agreement on just who is a sport psychologist and what qualifications that person should have. Individuals from a physical education background argue that psychologists do not have sufficient background in sport and exercise physiology to practice as a sport psychologist. Psychologists in the field have argued that they are the only ones qualified to be called sport psychologists and that those practicing without a doctoral degree in psychology should have to practice under some other label, such as mental trainer.[53] In fact, psychology licensing laws prevent anyone except licensed psychologists from using the label, whether it is clinical psychologist, counseling psychologist, or sport psychologist. Both AASP and Division 47 of the APA recognize the need to work together to establish some agreements on training and certification for the label sport psychologist.[54] In the meantime, numerous psychologists, most of them from clinical and counseling backgrounds, have found and continue to find employment in the field of sport and exercise.[55]

The Work of Sport Psychologists. So what is it that sport psychologists do? Some of them work in research, typically in academic settings, and many of those do some consulting work in the field. Others work full time in applying psychological principles and methods to the enhancement of performance in sports. In doing so they often work with some of sport's most elite athletes. It is these full-time practitioners that we want to describe briefly.

Sport psychologists work on both behavioral and mental problems. An athlete may have a motor habit that causes problems—for example, in a golf swing, in the running approach to a high jump bar, or in the mechanics of throwing a baseball. Habits are often difficult to break, partly because people are often unaware of what they are doing. Calling attention to the problem behavior, getting the athlete to recognize it when it happens, and altering or eliminating the behavior is how these bad habits are treated. One strategy is to practice the behavioral sequence in slow motion, making sure the problem behavior does not occur, and then speeding up the practice until it occurs at normal speed. Perhaps the problem behavior is some slight movement when the athlete needs to be as still as possible, as in target shooting pistols or rifles. One sport psychologist taught sharpshooters to be cognizant of their heartbeats (by using a biofeedback device) and to learn to fire the gun between heartbeats, thus giving them a slight advantage in steadiness.[56]

For many athletes the problem is anxiety that confronts them as they are preparing for a competition or perhaps just as they are about to perform. Psychologists have a long history in treating anxiety. Some of the methods used by sport psychologists include progressive relaxation in which the individual learns to relax various muscle groups by learning to monitor the cues from those muscles when the person is tense versus relaxed. Biofeedback devices—machines that measure muscle tonus, respiration, heart rate, or skin temperature—may be used to provide cues about these bodily changes. If the anxiety seems caused by a specific situation, then systematic desensitization might be used; this method reduces anxiety by having the subject imagine the event while in a state of relaxation. The relaxation is maintained at a stronger level than the anxiety so that through repeated pairings the anxiety is desensitized. Teaching athletes how to use meditation is another procedure that may be used in dealing with anxiety.[57]

For some athletes, the problem may be screening out distractions, such as crowd noise, or a strike out in the previous at bat, or a foot fault in the previous discus throw. Athletes talk about the importance of being able to concentrate, to stay focused, and to maintain attention while blocking out other sounds and thoughts. Cognitive behavioral techniques can be particularly effective at eliminating such unwanted thoughts.

Emotion is an issue for many athletes. Too much emotion can hinder performance, particularly when it interferes with the athlete's ability to think. Too little emotion can produce lackluster performance. Psychologists have long understood that emotion and anxiety affect performance both positively and negatively. They refer to the optimum level of arousal to indicate that point at which performance is maximized by just the right amount of emotion. Techniques like meditation, stress inoculation, and anger management can help athletes deal with problem emotions so that they can stay focused on the task at hand.

Imagery training, sometimes called mental rehearsal, is one of several techniques that sport psychologists teach athletes to use as a means of practice. Jack Nicklaus is said to have practiced every golf shot in his head before he actually made the shot. Olympic champion diver Greg Louganis mentally rehearsed each of his dives before making them. He won a gold medal for platform diving in the 1988 Olympics in Seoul, South Korea, (one of four gold medals he won in two Olympics) after hitting his head on the platform on one of his earlier dives. He would not look at the videotapes of that errant dive because he did not want that imagery in his mind, interfering with the perfect dives that he visualized. These imagery techniques, in which the athlete is taught to visualize every component of the event, be it the components of a platform dive, or a tennis serve, or a pole vault, work well for some athletes and not for others. Not surprisingly, they work best for those individuals who have good visual imagery skills. Apparently they are better able to see these mental pictures quite vividly and to translate those mental pictures into appropriate actions.

Archeologists tell us that sport and exercise have been a part of human life for approximately the last 5,000 years. Certainly they appear to be a part of contemporary life in all countries today. They continue to be a huge enterprise in the United States, from professional stadiums to hotel fitness centers to physical education classes in the schools. As a form of behavior, exercise and sports invite the experts on behavior. A continued role for sport psychologists in the near future seems assured.[58]

Health Psychology

One of the oldest topics in the philosophy that gave birth to modern psychology is the mind-body problem. For hundreds of years philosophers considered the two as separate entities, a position known as dualism. During the Renaissance that view changed because of the writings of philosophers such as Rene Descartes (1596–1650) who described the influences of one upon the other—that is how the body affects mental states and how mental states affect the body. He still viewed mind and body as separate forces, but he changed the landscape by illustrating the nature and site of their interaction. This interactive dualism, as it has been called, would be an important precursor to psychology, and nowhere is that more evident than in the field of health psychology. Whereas most forensic psychologists and many sport psychologists have come from the ranks of clinical and counseling psychologists, this parentage is especially salient for the field of health psychology. Today most health psychology training programs are housed within programs of clinical psychology, although some are part of counseling psychology and social psychology programs.

Health psychologists have largely adopted a model of health and illness known as the biopsychosocial model, reflecting a belief in the impact of biological, psychological, and sociocultural factors on health and illness. The traditional medical model focuses on biological factors, such as genetics, hormones, and neurotransmitters. The biopsychosocial model does not deny the role of those factors but expands the list of causes to include such psychological and social factors as diet, exercise, stress, social support network, family relationships, and cultural practices.[59]

The health psychology specialty has its roots in the 1960s in the interdisciplinary field of behavioral medicine, a field that combined information from medicine, the neurosciences, and the behavioral sciences in seeking to improve health, both physical and mental, and prevent disease. Health psychology emerged from that field as a psychological specialty in the 1970s, coming of age at the end of that decade as signified by the formation of APA's Division 38, the Division of Health Psychology. Today that division has approximately 2,800 members.[60]

Whereas it can be readily understood that psychology can be used to heal the mind, it has been assumed by many that it had little role in affecting health of the body. This dualistic view has certainly been challenged in recent years. One of the ways to understand the importance of psychology in affecting physical well-being is to compare causes of death over the last 100 years. At the beginning of the 20th century the leading causes of death in the United States were influenza, pneumonia, and tuberculosis. The first of those is caused by a virus, the second and third by bacterial infections. Today none of those is among the top five. Instead, the three leading causes of death at the beginning of the 21st century are heart disease, cancer, and stroke. How are these killers different from those of 1900? The answer, in one word, is *behavior*. The modern ones all have a significant behavioral component. Indeed, the Centers for Disease Control and Prevention's (CDC) recognition that lifestyle is a key component in the leading causes of death in the United States has led that agency to add more psychologists and other behavioral scientists to its staff and to allocate significantly more of its research and prevention budget to behavioral factors in health and illness.[61] Another sign of the recognition of the behavioral role in health and illness is that beginning in 2015, the Medical Colleges Admissions Test (MCAT) will add a new section that tests individuals on their knowledge of psychology and sociology.

Consider deaths from cancer. The leading cause of cancer deaths is lung cancer, which kills about 350,000 Americans each year. The majority of those deaths are due to cigarette smoking, which means those deaths are preventable if people can be prevented from starting smoking or helped to stop smoking. Deaths due to heart disease, cancer, and stroke can be greatly reduced by changing people's behavior. Indeed, these reductions could be considerable. Bernard Levin, a distinguished oncologist at Houston's famed M. D. Anderson Hospital, one of the leading cancer research and treatment centers in the United States, has written that lifestyle changes could prevent between 65% and 85% of all cancers. He cites such behavioral changes as eliminating tobacco use; reducing exposure to sun; exercising more; eating more fruits, vegetables, and whole grains; reducing fat consumption; limiting alcohol consumption; and being aware of one's family disease history and seeking proper medical screenings.[62] None of those are medical issues per se; instead they are behavioral issues. They require that people change their behavior. Such changes are in the domain of the psychologist. Of course those behaviors and others are related to heart disease and stroke as well. For example, stress is extremely important as a causative agent in heart disease and stroke, and more recent research has demonstrated its role in cancer as well. Stress reduction is one of the foci of the health psychologist.

The Practice of Health Psychologists. The practices of the health psychologist are similar to what is done in many of the other psychological specialty areas. Health psychologists do assessment work, both cognitive and behavioral. They may do psychophysiological assessments in which they measure autonomic nervous system functions such as heart rate and blood pressure, often as part of a broader assessment of the patient's stress. Personality assessments are also made. The principal goal of assessment in health psychology is to increase the accuracy of clinical judgments. Such assessments help health psychologists to distinguish the symptoms that are due to physical illness from the symptoms that are due to the person's psychological reaction to that illness. Sometimes those are not easily separated. For example, a person suffering from chronic pain might be diagnosed as depressed based on observations of the person's inability to concentrate. Yet the concentration problems may stem from the presence of the pain and have nothing to do with depression. Such differentiations can be aided significantly by good assessment instruments, many developed between 1980 and 1990, such as the Millon Behavioral Health Inventory (MBHI), the Symptom Checklist-90 (SCL-90), and the Psychosocial Adjustment to Illness Scale (PAIS), Refinements of these assessment instruments and newer ones continue to enhance this part of the health psychologist's job.[63]

Interventions. Interventions are also a significant part of the health psychologist's job and include a number of stress management techniques, such as relaxation therapies, biofeedback, and cognitive restructuring. One particularly successful approach that has been used effectively with groups, and not just individuals, is stress inoculation. In stress inoculation programs, individuals are taught to anticipate stressors and to recognize them, to acknowledge that some stressors are inevitable, and by such acceptance learn to live with those things that cannot be changed. For example, job-related stress is a problem for many occupations, such as firefighters, police officers, prison guards, hospital emergency room workers, miners, and stock exchange brokers. Stressors are an inherent part of these jobs and cannot be eliminated. However, individuals who work in these and other stressful jobs can be taught coping strategies that can reduce the impact of the stressors. In addition to the stress reduction techniques mentioned earlier, individuals in high stress jobs might be taught how to manage their anger or how to make better use of social support networks in ways that reduce stress levels. Thus health psychologists may not be able to reduce the stressors in a job but they can change the way people react to those stressors.[64]

One of the most troubling of medical problems has been individuals who suffer with chronic pain, pain that can sometimes be debilitating. It may be in the form of frequent migraine headaches, lower back pain, joint pain, and so forth. Drugs are often helpful but sometimes they prove ineffective or sometimes they produce such terrible side effects that the person is unable to take them. An alternative or supplement to drug therapy is pain management, a set of psychological techniques used to help people cope with pain. The subjective experience of pain can often be reduced with hypnosis, relaxation techniques, biofeedback, and cognitive techniques that provide the person with a sense of control over the situation.[65]

Health Psychology in Hospitals. The recognized impact of health psychology in the 21st century is evidenced by the fact that the fastest growing place of employment for psychologists in the past decade has been hospitals. Psychologists have long worked in hospitals, dating to the beginning of the 20th century. Yet those numbers were not large until after World War II when the VA hospitals employed hundreds of psychologists. The 1960s and 1970s witnessed a dramatic increase in the number of psychologists on medical school faculties and by 1997 that number had reached nearly 5,000.[66] In addition to placements in medical schools and hospitals, health psychologists began to consult with numerous medical specialties, such as "pediatrics, geriatrics, surgery, obstetrics and gynecology, rehabilitation, cardiology, and neurology, as physicians became increasingly aware of the broader needs of their patients and the capabilities of their psychologist colleagues to respond to those needs."[67] Further evidence of psychology's place at the health care table was the substantial increase in behavioral science and practice research in the budgets of the National Institutes for Health (NIH) for more than three decades. In the 1980s there was less than a half percent in the NIH budget for behavioral research; by 2000 that figure was more than 10%.[68] The economic recession of 2008, along with bitter partisan politics, have led to reductions in funding for behavioral science research.

Health care will continue to be a significant topic in the decades to come. The reforms brought about by the Patient Protection and Affordable Care Act impact state and federal legislatures, insurance companies, hospital corporations, pharmaceutical companies, special interest lobbies, and the health care professions, including medicine, nursing, and psychology. Under the provisions of the act many more Americans will have access to health care and given the importance of behavioral variables in health and illness, health psychologists will certainly have an important and expanding role to play.

Science and the Practice of Psychology

We began this book with a history of the 18th and 19th century practices of phrenology, physiognomy, mesmerism, spiritualism, and other subjects we labeled as pseudoscientific. That is, although they made scientific claims, they were found to be without scientific basis. When the modern profession of psychology emerged in the 20th century, it did so on the claim that it was translating the new scientific psychology into practical application. The title of this book, *From Séance to Science*, was chosen to emphasize that metamorphosis. Since the beginnings of applied psychology at the end of the 19th century, there have been naysayers in the universities and elsewhere, psychologists who doubted or openly disputed the scientific validity of psychological applications to businesses, schools, vocational counseling, or clinical assessments. That science and practice have been viewed differently is evidenced in numerous ways, including the history of the APA, whose leaders rebuffed the practitioners at every turn in the first half of the 20th century and resisted for more than 50 years any revision of the APA bylaws that would acknowledge the role of the association in working on behalf of psychological practitioners.

Still, these early practitioners went through the same doctoral training as the scientists who stayed in the universities. They took the same classes in research methods and statistics, and they conducted research for their dissertations, presumably judged by the same standards of scientific rigor. In truth, in the first half of the 20th century the training of the practitioners differed little from that of the academics, with the exception of, perhaps, an applied course or two and, more rarely, a year's internship that was added to the load and not substituted for other academic work. Specialized training programs for the practice specialties began to emerge mostly after World War II. When the conferees ended their two weeks of intense meetings in Boulder, Colorado, in the summer of 1949, they had agreed to the first national standards for doctoral students who would be trained in clinical psychology. The Boulder model, also known as the scientist-practitioner model, was to produce psychologists who were knowledgeable about and competent to do psychological research as well as accomplished in the assessment techniques and intervention methods that were part of the practice of clinical psychology. For many it seemed a huge task. Some doubted that it could be done in the time allotted for graduate training. Time would tell if it was a workable model.

Contemporary Concerns About Professional Schools of Psychology

Now more than 60 years later the Boulder model has more than a few detractors, mostly from the professional side of psychology. Critics have argued that academic departments, populated mostly by nonclinical faculty, structured the requirements of the graduate programs in professional psychology so that the scientist side of the model got considerably more attention than the practitioner side. This dissatisfaction eventually led to other training models, such as the PsyD degree that shifted the emphasis to the practice side, and to alternative training programs, such as free-standing professional schools, that shifted the emphasis even more. As we indicated in chapter 2, today more than two thirds of the doctorates awarded in professional psychology are awarded by professional schools.

These professional school programs range considerably in their quality, as do programs in universities. The professional school programs, however, have come under attack by academic and research psychologists, as well as some professional psychologists, who are concerned that the scientific training in those programs has been reduced to such an extent that the professional psychologists they train do not have the background or mindset to employ a scientific approach to the conduct of their practice or to an evaluation of its results. Donald Peterson, a pioneer in the professional school movement in psychology who founded the first PsyD program in psychology at the University of Illinois, summarized data comparing the performance of PhD and PsyD graduates from professional programs on the national licensing exam, the Examination for Professional Practice in Psychology (EPPP), a multiple-choice exam that measures psychological knowledge across the many subfields that make up the discipline (Peterson reminds us that this test measures knowledge of psychology and does not necessarily tell us anything about how people would function as a psychologist). His analysis showed that of the 45 programs in the top quartile, all 45 awarded the PhD degree. There were a total of 39 PsyD programs in the total sample and 27 of those were in the bottom quartile (making up 60% of the programs in that bottom fourth). In 1973, the year of the Vail Conference that explored professional training alternatives to the Boulder model, there was 1 PsyD program in the United States. By 2001 there were 56 such programs (45 of them in clinical), and as we have noted earlier, these PsyD programs, most of them at free-standing professional schools, are graduating most of the students turned out in professional psychology today. Peterson notes that the weakest programs (as measured by EPPP performance of its graduates) are graduating far more students than the stronger programs. For example, between 1988 and 1995, the 45 programs in the bottom quartile produced 6,996 graduates, compared to 2,024 from the 45 programs in the top quartile (a ratio of 3.5 to 1). Regarding the criticisms that professional psychologists "ignore scientific research and engage in practices that are demonstrably useless or harmful," Peterson writes that these "data show ample cause for concern." He continues, "If psychology is to maintain its stature as a profession, exclusionary controls as well as hortatory requirements for the practice of psychology and the education of practitioners must be established and enforced."[69]

Debates over the proper balance of science and practice and the best models for training professional psychologists continue unabated. In 1990,

Richard McFall delivered his "Manifesto for a Science of Clinical Psychology," calling for clinical training and practice to be anchored in science.[70] The model has been advanced by the Academy of Psychological Clinical Science (APCS), which has also developed a system of accreditation to promote science-centered education and training in clinical psychology.[71]

Nicholas Cummings, continuing his long record of innovation in the training and delivery of mental health services, has established a Doctor of Behavioral Health program at Arizona State University. The program prepares mental health providers who can provide integrated behavioral care in primary care and other medical settings.[72]

The "Myth" of Professional Psychology

An outspoken (some would say strident) critic of professional psychology was Robyn Dawes (1936–2010), a distinguished cognitive psychologist and holder of an endowed chair at Carnegie Mellon University. His reputation as a scientist and his position in a prestigious university gave his voice considerable weight in the science-practice debates. His exceptionally critical indictment of the practice of psychology was laid out in his 1994 book, *House of Cards: Psychology and Psychotherapy Built on Myth*. Dawes accused professional psychology of abandoning the commitment it made as the new profession was launched.

> That commitment was to establish a mental health profession that would be based on research findings, employing insofar as possible well-validated techniques and principles. At least, professional practitioners in psychology were to make clear to their clients and to society at large that they were proceeding in the absence of relevant scientific knowledge when none existed. What was never envisioned was that a body of research and established principles would be available to inform practice, but that practice would ignore that research and those principles. Worse yet, far too much professional practice in psychology has grown and achieved status by espousing principles that are known to be untrue and by employing techniques known to be invalid. Instead of relying on research-based knowledge in their practice, too many mental health professionals rely on "trained clinical intuition." But there is ample evidence that such intuition does not work well in the mental health profession.[73]

Dawes' critical review has drawn plenty of attention over the years. Indeed, his views have found support from some of America's most distinguished scientist-practitioners, who have expressed grave concerns about the growing chasm between the science and practice of psychology.

Doing and Applying Research

We noted earlier that critics of the practice of psychology are not a recent phenomenon. Recall our discussion from chapter 2 of Hans Eysenck's 1952 article questioning the efficacy of psychotherapy, an analysis that incensed many clinical psychologists and psychiatrists.[74] Yet as the profession has undergone explosive growth in the last half century, so have the criticisms multiplied. In 1981, David Barlow, a clinical psychologist well known for his research on anxiety disorders, acknowledged what perhaps every psychologist knew, that most professional psychologists, even though trained in research at that time, did not engage in any research of their own. He argued that this failure to be involved in research was not the result of inadequacies in training but was a manifestation of the difficulties of conducting clinical research in the midst of a clinical practice. Perhaps of greater concern, Barlow noted that "clinicians are not even influenced by clinical research findings, resorting instead to a trial-and-error eclecticism in their clinical practice."[75] Herein lies a key reason for the science-practice split in modern psychology: Psychological scientists complain that practitioners are largely ignorant of psychological science and make use of a multitude of questionable "therapeutic" techniques, whereas professional psychologists complain that they find little in the science of psychology that is directly applicable to their needs as practitioners. Practitioners argue that scientists need to leave the isolation of their ivy-covered walls and become better informed about the nature of practice and patient/therapist needs. Scientists counter that practitioners need to be part of the research process, that their clinical work should be used to inform scientific work. Hans Strupp (1921–2006), who served many years as a clinical psychologist at Vanderbilt University and long-time trainer of clinical psychologists, has written eloquently about the potential contributions from practitioners who understand the methods of science and recognize that good science begins with astute observation. Writing about the unique position of the psychotherapist, he noted:

The human observer in this as in other areas of scientific work reigns supreme. As participants in and observers of immensely intricate human interactions, we have the opportunity—if we are sufficiently ingenious, perceptive, and sensitive—to make observations, discern connections, form hypotheses, and, within limits, test them.... [E]ach therapeutic dyad constitutes an experiment, albeit an experiment with built-in limitations. The therapeutic situation can be...a unique laboratory situation. Because of their specialized training, therapists are in the unique position of being aware of their own stimulus value and their influence on their data in a manner comparable to scientists peering through a high-powered microscope. They can arrive at generalizable principles from these observations even though, in the final analysis, these principles must be tailored to the exigencies of the individual case.[76]

Recognizing that it is not likely that practitioners will (or can, given the ethics and time demands of practice) conduct experimental research,[77] other means have been suggested to encourage their contributions to a science-practice enterprise—for example, contributing detailed case studies that provide internally valid conclusions, or using multiple case studies in what are called time series experiments.[78] Despite the calls to involve practitioners in the research enterprise, such activity has rarely occurred. It seems likely that the muses that draw individuals to careers as researchers or as practitioners too rarely reside in the same individuals.[79]

Practice Guidelines

The utility of science for practice and practice for science are not part of that separation. Indeed, the relationship between psychological science and psychological practice has been a hot topic in recent years with the advent of managed care and the greater attention paid to concerns about demonstrated therapeutic effectiveness and lower costs. From the managed care perspective it is a question of accountability, a question that has been talked about within psychology in the framework of practice guidelines, that is, procedures that prescribe specific interventions for specific disorders.

The development of practice guidelines began in the late 1980s when the US government established the Agency for Healthcare Policy and

Research (AHCPR), an agency whose mission was to reduce health care costs and provide higher quality services to patients (now known as the *Agency for Healthcare Research and Quality* [AHRQ]). A guiding principle for the agency is that clinical and medical practice be informed by science, and that for various disorders, from arthritis to depression, guidelines should describe treatments in terms of their effectiveness and their costs. In 1993, both the AHCPR and the American Psychiatric Association published guidelines on the treatment of depression. The psychiatric association followed in the next few years with guidelines on bipolar disorder, substance abuse (alcohol, cocaine, and opioids), nicotine dependence, and schizophrenia. Reacting to the fact that entities other than psychology were defining practice guidelines for psychological disorders, Division 12, the Clinical Psychology division of the American Psychological Association, issued its own practice guidelines in 1995, and added supplements in 1996 and 1998. These guidelines identified treatments judged to be effective for a number of different psychological disorders specified in the fourth edition of the *Diagnostic and Statistical Manual of Mental Disorders* (*DSM-IV*).[80]

At the start of the 21st century, practice guidelines proliferated. The AHRQ now contains over 2,500 guidelines. The APA continues to offer practice guidelines and as of 2013 there are 16 guidelines that cover a wide range of practice issues. Reflecting the interplay between society and psychology, the most recent guidelines deal with the practice of telepsychology.[81]

Conflict Over Guidelines

Professional psychologists have been divided on the subject of practice guidelines. Peter Nathan, a distinguished clinical psychologist and researcher, has described the conflict as follows: "Advocates for practice guidelines assert that they promote therapeutic accountability and motivate adoption of the best current practices; critics question their empirical bases, diverse standards of proof, and potential to constrain clinical decision making."[82] Practitioners argue that such guidelines are too inflexible in dealing with the realities of diversity and ambiguity in psychological cases. They point out that practice guidelines often assume that the psychologist is dealing with a client with a single diagnosis, whereas the reality in many cases is some number of comorbid conditions, each of which might require different practice guidelines, some of which could be contradictory. Some critics see such guidelines as a hindrance to the ethical practice of psychology because of their prescriptive and restrictive nature. The criticisms notwithstanding, there is evidence of growing awareness in the practitioner community of the importance of psychologists' involvement in developing such guidelines.[83]

Practice guidelines are still a work in progress and work that must continue. Peter Nathan has summarized the argument well: "Although practice guidelines are not yet ideal, they have the potential to enhance both the effectiveness and the accountability of the interventions. Achievement of this potential depends on the continuing maturation of the research base that underlies practice guidelines."[84] Furthermore, the importance of practice guidelines is not only critical for the practice of psychology but also for the reputation of the profession. Nathan has identified the goal of this pursuit while reminding us of the dangers should we continue to ignore their critical need: "When the potential for psychosocial treatment guidelines is reached, psychologists will no longer be at risk of having to cede responsibility for their standards of practice to other professional groups."[85]

The Future of the Profession

We have no crystal ball that will allow us to see where the profession of psychology is headed in the next 20 or 50 or 100 years. Still, we believe that we should end this historical account with at least some informed (we hope) speculation about what may be ahead in psychology's immediate future in the professional arena. In recent years, some psychologists have been writing eulogies for the field, especially for the practice of psychotherapy. This crisis of confidence is certainly owed to the effects of managed care, an event that, as we have shown, has dramatically affected the practice of psychology. For those psychologists who saw themselves practicing long-term psychotherapy, the current realities are no doubt devastating. Yet whereas managed care has discouraged some, it has encouraged others, either to practice in new ways or to reinvent themselves as practitioners by moving into related fields or expanding their practices in novel ways.

When one door closes another typically opens, and that metaphor is clearly descriptive of what is happening in professional psychology.

Growth in Health Psychology

The field of health psychology, which we described earlier in this chapter, is one area where doors have opened and likely will continue to do so. Assuming that better interventions can be developed in psychology to deal with behaviors such as smoking cessation; compliance with safety procedures, such as wearing seat belts and using child-restraint seats appropriately; compliance with medical and psychosocial treatments; alcohol and other substance abuse; promoting prevention of sexually transmitted diseases; seeking appropriate medical screenings; control of appetite and choice of foods; and exercising, the opportunities will continue to expand.[86] One area that is particularly promising is geropsychology, providing psychologists with the opportunity to work with the fastest growing segment of the American population in terms of age.

As mentioned earlier the provisions of the Patient Protection and Affordable Care Act are moving professional psychology rapidly towards a central identity as a health care profession. With things moving as quickly as they are, there is much that psychology and psychologists need to do.[87] There is increased recognition that psychologists need to work alongside medical professionals in the health care setting. It is quite common for medical problems to have a psychological basis. A patient's stomachaches may actually be symptoms of anxiety, just as lethargy and poor appetite could be the result of depression and not a physical condition.

Moving psychologists from private practice to the physician's office will be an adjustment, but it is the new reality. Anticipating this, the American Psychological Association created the Center for Psychology and Health in 2013. Its core mission is to:

> Expand psychology's role in the nation's evolving health care system, including advocacy and educational efforts that promote psychological expertise on integrated, interprofessional health care teams, involvement in interdisciplinary health research and policy formation. One of the center's initial priorities is to emphasize psychology's contributions to health promotion and disease prevention.[88]

Given the enormous size of the health care field in terms of the number of jobs it offers and the growing awareness of the role played by behavioral factors in physical health, behavioral health care looks like a growth industry.

One really does not need a crystal ball to see that the opportunities for professional psychologists in health and mental health are great.[89] But there are many other problems facing our society that call for help from the scientists and practitioners of psychology. We will list only a few of these; we will not propose programs for the solution of these problems. In some cases psychology already has much to offer; in others we have much work yet to do. What should be obvious from this listing is that the problems have serious consequences for society at large and that the problems are behavioral ones that likely will require behavioral solutions. Our list would include many forms of violence such as domestic abuse, child abuse, rape, gang conflicts, school shootings by classmates; reducing accidents at work and in the home; improving marital therapies and reducing divorce; reducing energy consumption and pollution; improving learning outcomes in schools and ensuring that children who are "different" get the extra help they need; and parent training programs. Others can be added, but we hope it is obvious that psychologists face no shortage of problems to solve.

Growth in Psychological Services to Minorities

Another professional area that holds great promise is in the delivery of psychological services to ethnic minorities. The projected demographics are clear for the United States over the next 50 years. Ethnic minority populations are increasing at much faster rates than Anglo American populations. At present it is estimated that 33% of the US population are people of color, and that figure is expected to rise to 50% by 2050. In some states, ethnic minorities have collectively become the majority and they will soon do so in some more populous states, such as Texas and California. At the moment, American psychology is poorly prepared to be of service to these individuals. Psychology doctoral programs are traditionally weak in providing students with information about multicultural issues. As a science, American psychological research is still based largely on white populations. There is a growing literature on psychological science and practice on issues of culture and ethnicity, but many issues remain.[90] There are too few faculty members and doctoral students in psychology who are ethnic minorities and too few cultural and ethnic sites being used for practicum and internship opportunities for doctoral students in psychology.[91] Both the science and profession of psychology must sustain an investment in these topics or risk becoming irrelevant as a science and as a profession. Christine Iijima Hall, a social psychologist and expert on minority issues, has warned of the "growing obsolescence of psychology." She has written, "[P]sychology must make substantive revisions in its curriculum, training, research, and practice. Without these revisions, psychology will risk professional, ethical, and economic problems because psychology will no longer be a viable professional resource to the majority of the U. S. population." To continue in the same path without making these changes, Hall warns, would be "cultural malpractice."[92]

Slow as they may be, there are signs of progress. The Society for the Psychological Study of Culture, Ethnicity and Race (Division 45 of the APA) remains a leader in the field in advancing research and practice around ethnic minority issues and concerns.[93] Recognition of the need for the development of multicultural competencies is reflected in updates to the APA code of ethics in 2002 and the introduction in 2003 of the Guidelines on Multicultural Education, Training, Research, Practice, and Organizational Change for Psychologists.[94] Professional psychologists will either prepare to deliver their services in this changing marketplace or, as history has shown us, other professional groups will.

Changing Roles for Psychologists

We have indicated that psychology's role in psychotherapy is changing.[95] Managed care has had a hand in that, but so has competition from other service providers, largely individuals with master's degree training. This reality, driven by issues of cost containment, has been acknowledged by many in professional psychology's leadership. Keith Humphreys has written that "clinical psychologists will be increasingly supplanted in the role of psychotherapist by lower cost providers such as social workers, marriage and family counselors, and master's-level psychologists."[96] Nicholas Cummings predicts that this trend will continue:

The future professional psychologist will be primarily a health psychologist...The most likely role will be that of a supervisor to master's-level therapists who are performing from empirically derived protocols of focused, targeted interventions, from which there will be as many as 70% of the patients not covered by the intended protocol who will require the benefit of doctoral-level skills. Furthermore, the future doctoral-level psychologist is in an excellent position to conduct outcomes research and to plan and implement effective and efficient delivery systems in an expanded clinical management role. In summary, the future doctoral practitioner will be an innovative clinician, a creative researcher, an inspired supervisor, a knowledgeable health psychologist, a caring skilled manager, and an astute business person.[97]

This expanded role of services is echoed by Keith Humphreys who argues that part of the problem in contemporary psychology is that the profession foreclosed prematurely on other realms of practice at the end of World War II. He believes that there was an ill-advised rush to psychotherapy—an activity that was seductive because of its prestige and long-term association with the medical profession—while other professional possibilities were ignored. He argues that the doctoral-level training of psychologists prepares them to do so many things other than deliver one-on-one psychotherapy. And while he does not demean the value of that activity[98] he points out the potential of using such skills as research design, program development, and program evaluation for providing help to hundreds or thousands or tens of thousands of people at a time through services to governments, communities, organizations, businesses, schools, and families, as well as to individuals.[99] It is clear that there are so many ways that psychologists can contribute.

A Final Comment

Our purpose in writing this book was to provide a historical account of the development of the profession of psychology in America, to trace its evolution from the pseudopsychologies of the 19th century to the changes in the current professional specialties brought about by managed care and those promised in the near future as professional psychologists add prescription privileges to their tool box. Not surprisingly, we are more confident in our recounting the past than we are in predicting the future.

Among the historical lessons that we have sought to convey in this book is the flexibility, adaptability, and innovativeness of psychology as a discipline. Psychologists have long been trained as problem solvers, whether it was predicting which advertisements would be most effective or discovering why a child had difficulty reading; whether it was selecting individuals for various military jobs, developing paper-and-pencil tests to assess brain damage, or designing aircraft control knobs to prevent crashes; whether it was helping people choose vocations, eliminating phobias, or increasing worker satisfaction; whether it was helping a troubled couple to fix their marriage or working with a city council to increase seat belt compliance in a community. The training does not necessarily provide the answers to those problems, but it does provide the knowledge of how to approach problems and how to ask the right questions and arrange conditions so that the solutions may be forthcoming. The secret to the future of the profession of psychology is really no secret at all. It resides in the doctoral training programs that have produced psychologists for more than 100 years. The profession will continue to thrive as long as what is learned in those programs has applicability to the world's behavioral problems. And of those, there is no shortage.

Notes

Preface

1. Simpson, J. A., & Weiner, E. S. C. (1989). *The Oxford English dictionary* (2nd ed., Vol. 12). New York: Oxford University Press, p. 572.

2. *The American heritage dictionary of the English language* (3rd ed). (1992). Boston: Houghton Mifflin, p. 1446.

3. Gove, P. B. (Ed.). (1961). *Webster's new third international dictionary of the English language unabridged.* Springfield, MA: G. & C. Merriam Co., p. 1811.

4. For an excellent treatment of this question, see: Peterson, D. R. (1976). Is psychology a profession? *American Psychologist, 31,* 572–581.

5. See: APA Committee on Professional Standards (1981). Specialty guidelines for the delivery of services. *American Psychologist, 36,* 639–681. This is a sequence of four separate reports detailing the "specialty guidelines for the delivery of services" in clinical psychology (pp. 640–651), counseling psychology (pp. 652-663), industrial/organizational psychology (pp. 664–669), and school psychology (pp. 670–681)

6. Data from Cattell, J. M. (1937). Retrospect: Psychology as a profession. *Journal of Consulting Psychology, 1,* 1–3.

7. These data are based on figures from several sources, including the Bureau of Labor Statistics and the Research Office of the American Psychological Association.

Chapter 1

1. The case of the young thief is from B. J. G. (1845). Phrenological facts. *American Phrenological Journal and Miscellany, 7,* 19–20. The case of Harriet Martineau is from her letter (1845) published in the *American Phrenological Journal and Miscellany, 7,* 167–172. The description of Charles Dickens is from Wells, S. (1866). *New physiognomy or signs of character as manifested through temperament and external forms and especially in the human face divine.* New York: Fowler & Wells, p. 721.

2. Combe, G. (1835). *The constitution of man considered in relation to external objects.* Boston: Marsh, Capen, & Lyon, pp. 54–56.

3. Leahey, T. H., & Leahey, G. E. (1983). *Psychology's occult doubles: Psychology and the problem of pseudoscience.* Chicago: Nelson-Hall, p. 64.

4. For an excellent treatment of phrenologists as psychological practitioners, see Sokal, M. M. (2001). Practical phrenology as psychological counseling in the 19th-century United States. In C. D. Green, M. Shore, & T. Teo (Eds.), *The transformation of psychology: Influences of 19th-century philosophy, technology, and natural science* (pp. 21–44). Washington, DC: American Psychological Association. For an example of phrenology in vocational counseling, see Sizer, N. (1889). *Choices of pursuits or what to do, and why, describing seventy-five trades and professions and the talents and temperaments required for each.* New York: Fowler and Wells. And for a later look at phrenology and vocational guidance, see Risse, G. B. (1976). Vocational guidance during the Depression: Phrenology versus applied psychology. *Journal of the History of the Behavioral Sciences, 12,* 130–140.

5. Fowler, O. S., & Fowler, L. N. (1859). *Illustrated self instructor in phrenology and physiology.* New York: Fowler and Wells, p. 97. Sales estimate is from Sizer, N., & Drayton, H. S. (1890). *Heads and faces and how to study them: A manual of phrenology and physiognomy.* New York: Fowler and Wells. See also Fowler, O. S. (1855). *Fowler's practical phrenology.* New York: Fowler and Wells.

6. Brown, R. T. (1996, August). *"Lake Wobegon Effect": Alive and well in 1800s practical phrenology.* Paper presented at the annual meeting of the American Psychological Association, Toronto.

7. Sokal, M. M. (2001), pp. 38–39.

8. For other sources on the history of phrenology see the following. For a history of phrenology in Great Britain, Cooter, R. (1984). *The cultural meaning of popular science: Phrenology and the organization of consent in nineteenth-century Britain.* New York: Cambridge University Press. For coverage of the scientific discrediting of phrenology see Fancher, R. E. (1996). *Pioneers of psychology* (3rd ed.). New York: W. W. Norton. And for an excellent historical overview, see Leahey & Leahey (1983), chapters 3 and 4.

9. Lavater, J. (1775). Essays on physiognomy. As cited in Wells (1866), p. 36. The shape of his nose almost cost Charles Darwin (1809–1882) his chance at fame. Darwin was being interviewed for the position of ship's naturalist by Robert FitzRoy, captain of H. M. S. Beagle. FitzRoy was a believer in physiognomy and judged the shape of Darwin's nose to indicate that he lacked energy and determination. Likely his nose would have disqualified Darwin but his congeniality proved more important and in the end, FitzRoy gave him the job. And the rest, as they say, is history. Darwin accompanied FitzRoy on that historic five-year scientific voyage where his discoveries and the theory of species change they spawned would transform the world forever. For an account of Darwin and FitzRoy, see Fancher, R. E. (1996).

10. Wells, S. R. (1866). Quotation regarding the Jewish nose and the sub-Saharan African nose are from p. 196. The quotation on characteristics of Jews is from p. 445.

11. Redfield, J. W. (1849). *Outlines of a new system of physiognomy*. New York: Redfield.

12. Lombroso, C. (1911). *Criminal man*. New York: G. P. Putnam's Sons. Lombroso, C., & Ferrero, W. (1899). *The female offender*. New York: D. Appleton.

13. Wolf, L. (Ed.) (1975). *The annotated Dracula*. New York: Clarkson N. Potter, Inc, p. 300.

14. Parsons, F. (1909). *Choosing a vocation*. Boston: Houghton Mifflin. See also Brewer, J. M. (1942). *History of vocational guidance: Origins and early development*. New York: Harper.

15. Blackford, K. M. H., & Newcomb, A. (1914). *The job, the man, the boss*. New York: Doubleday & Page, p. vii. See also Blackford, K. M. H., & Newcomb, A. (1916). *Analyzing character: The new science of judging men, misfits in business, the home, and social life* (2nd ed.). New York: Review of Reviews Co.

16. Ibid., pp. 154–155.

17. Ibid., p. 156.

18. Ibid., pp. 140–141.

19. John Gottman earned his doctorate in psychology at the University of Wisconsin and is a distinguished research psychologist at the University of Washington. He is recognized in psychology as the preeminent authority on the subject of marriage and relationships. In his research, he has seen hundreds of couples. He has published more than 100 scientific articles on the subject of relationships and several important books, including two for the lay public, *Why marriages succeed or fail* (1994) and *The seven principles for making marriages work* (1999). John Gray has a 'doctoral degree' from a correspondence course from an unaccredited institution, has never done research on couples, has never published a scientific article, but has written several books on relationships, including the best seller, *Men are from Mars, women are from Venus* (1992). It is estimated that John Gray's book on marriage and relationships has sold more than 8 million copies, whereas John Gottman's 1994 book has sold approximately 55,000 copies. Clearly the public doesn't always look to science for answers. Source for much of this information is from Marano, H. E. (1997, Nov/Dec). Gottman and Gray: The two Johns. *Psychology Today, 30*, 28.

20. Cushman, P. (1995). *Constructing the self, constructing America: A cultural history of psychotherapy*. Reading, MA: Addison-Wesley, p. 119.

21. See, for example, Dumont, T. Q. (1913). *The art and science of personal magnetism*. London: L. N. Fowler & Co.; Dumont, T. Q. (1914). *The advanced course in personal magnetism*. London: L. N. Fowler & Co.

22. For histories of mesmerism see Crabtree, A. (1993). *From Mesmer to Freud: Magnetic sleep and the roots of psychological healing.* New Haven, CT: Yale University Press; Leahey & Leahey (1983), chapter 5; Fancher (1996), chapter 10; Bloch, G. J. (Trans.) (1980). *Mesmerism: A translation of the original medical and scientific writings of F. A. Mesmer, M.D.* Los Altos, CA: William Kaufmann; Cushman (1995), chapter 5. And for biographical material on Mesmer see Buranelli, V. (1975). *The wizard from Vienna: Franz Anton Mesmer.* New York: Coward, McCann, & Geoghegen.

23. Cushman (1995), p. 119.

24. James, W. (1890). *Principles of psychology* (2 vols.). New York: Henry Holt.

25. For a description of the conflicts between James and his colleagues in the science of psychology, see Coon, D. J. (1992). Testing the limits of sense and science: American experimental psychologists combat spiritualism, 1880–1920. *American Psychologist, 47,* 143–151.

26. Murphy, G., & Ballou, R. O. (Eds.) (1961). *William James on psychical research.* London: Chatto and Windus.

27. Leahey & Leahey (1983), p. 162.

28. Ibid., p. 166.

29. For historical treatments of spiritualism see Leahey & Leahey (1983), chapter 6; Murphy & Ballou (1961); Crabtree (1993), chapters 10 and 11; Moore, R. L. (1977). *In search of white crows: Spiritualism, parapsychology, and American culture.* New York: Oxford University Press. For a history of the conflicts between spiritualism and the new psychology, see Coon, D. J. (1992).

30. Anderson, C. A. (1993). *Healing hypotheses: Horatio W. Dresser and the philosophy of new thought.* New York: Garland Publishing, p. 40.

31. Caplan, E. (1998). *Mind games: American culture and the birth of psychotherapy.* Berkeley: University of California Press.

32. Ibid., p. 69.

33. Murphy & Ballou (1961), p. 8.

34. Ibid., p. 11.

35. For histories of mental healing, mind cure, and new thought movement, see Caplan (1998), chapter 4; Parker, G. T. (1973). *Mind cure in New England: From the Civil War to World War I.* Hanover, NH: University Press of New England.

36. For historical treatments of Wundt and his psychology see Blumenthal, A. L. (1975). A reappraisal of Wilhelm Wundt. *American Psychologist, 30,* 1081–1088; Danziger, K. (1980). The history of introspection reconsidered. *Journal of the History of the Behavioral Sciences, 16,* 241–262. Bringmann, W., & Tweney, R. D. (Eds.) (1980). *Wundt studies.* Toronto: C. J. Hogrefe.

37. For information on Wundt's American students, see Benjamin, L. T., Jr., Durkin, M., Link, M., Vestal, M., & Acord, J. (1992). Wundt's American doctoral students. *American Psychologist, 47,* 123–131. For a brief history of the founding of the American psychology laboratories from 1883 to 1900, see Benjamin, L. T., Jr. (2000). The psychology laboratory at the turn of the 20th century. *American Psychologist, 55,* 318–321.

38. For an excellent biography of G. Stanley Hall, see Ross, D. (1972). *Granville Stanley Hall: The psychologist as prophet.* Chicago: University of Chicago Press.

39. For information on the early American psychologists who wrote articles for popular magazines, see Viney, W., Michaels, T., & Alan, G. (1980). An annotated bibliography of psychological articles in selected cultural magazines. *Journal Supplement Abstract Service,* Ms. # 2096.

40. See Napoli, D. S. (1981). *Architects of adjustment: The history of the psychological profession in the United States.* Port Washington, NY: Kennikat Press, and Sokal, M. M. (1982). The Committee on the Certification of Consulting Psychologists: A failure of applied psychology in the 1920s. In C. J. Adkins, Jr., & B. A. Winstead (Eds.), *History of applied psychology: Department of Psychology colloquium series II* (pp. 12–42). Norfolk, VA: Old Dominion University.

41. Hall, G. S. (1883). The contents of children's minds. *Princeton Review, 2,* 249–272.

42. Hall, G. S. (1894). The new psychology as a basis of education. *Forum, 17,* 710–720. Quotation is from p. 718.

43. See Ross (1972), chapter 15; Davidson, E. S., & Benjamin, L. T., Jr. (1987). A history of the child study movement in America. In J. A. Glover & R. R. Ronning (Eds.), *Historical foundations of educational psychology* (pp. 41–60). New York: Plenum Press.

44. Witmer, L. (1897). The organization of practical work in psychology (Abstract of a paper presented at the meeting of the American Psychological Association, Boston). *Psychological Review, 4,* 116–117. Quotation is from p. 116.

45. Witmer, L. (1907). Clinical psychology. *The Psychological Clinic, 1,* 1–9. Reprinted in the *American Psychologist, 1996, 51,* 248–251.

46. For additional information on Witmer see McReynolds, P. (1997). *Lightner Witmer: His life and times.* Washington, DC: American Psychological Association; O'Donnell, J. M. (1979). The clinical psychology of Lightner Witmer: A case study of institutional innovation and intellectual change. *Journal of the History of the Behavioral Sciences, 15,* 3–17; and Baker, D. B. (1988). The psychology of Lightner Witmer. *Professional School Psychology, 3,* 109–121.

47. Scott's two books on advertising are Scott, W. D. (1903). *The theory of advertising.* Boston: Small, Maynard, & Co. and Scott, W. D. (1908). *The psychology of advertising.* Boston: Small, Maynard, & Co. For a discussion of Scott's

contributions to the psychology of advertising, see Kuna, D. P. (1976). The concept of suggestion in the early history of advertising psychology. *Journal of the History of the Behavioral Sciences, 12*, 347–353.

Chapter 2

1. Dworkin, R. W. (2010). The rise of the caring industry. *Policy Review, 116.* Accessed July 7, 2013.

2. Figure constructed using data from the American Psychological Association.

3. Shorter, E. (1997). *A history of psychiatry: From the era of the asylum to the age of Prozac.* New York: John Wiley, p. 33.

4. Grob, G. N. (1994). *The mad among us: A history of the care of America's mentally ill.* Cambridge, MA: Harvard University Press, pp. 23–24.

5. From Benjamin Franklin (1754) as cited in Grob (1994), p. 19.

6. For a description of Pinel's views on insanity and its treatment, see Pinel, P. (1962). *A treatise on insanity.* New York: Hafner (originally published in 1801).

7. Shorter (1997), pp. 46–48.

8. Most Americans learned of the sad conditions of the state hospitals in a series of exposés after World War II. Particularly important were a series of newspaper articles by Albert Deutsch and a novel, *The snake pit* (1946), written by Mary Jane Ward and made into a movie in 1948. Both the novel and the movie were exceptionally popular and served to arouse public indignation regarding state hospitals. Ward's novel was published by Random House. Deutsch's articles were collected in his book, *Shame of the states*, published in 1948 by Harcourt, Brace.

9. Sidis, B. (1898). *The psychology of suggestion: A research into the subconscious nature of man and society.* New York: D. Appleton; Sidis, B. (1911–1912). Fear, anxiety, and psychopathic maladies. *Journal of Abnormal Psychology, 6*, 107–125.

10. Krohn's article was entitled "Laboratory psychology as applied to the study of insanity" and was likely published in an 1898 issue of *The Psychiater*, a quarterly publication edited by the superintendent of the Kankakee hospital. As cited in Popplestone, J. A., & McPherson, M. W. (1984). Pioneer psychology laboratories in clinical settings. In J. Brozek (Ed.), *Explorations in the history of psychology in the United States* (pp. 196–272). Lewisburg, PA: Bucknell University Press. See this article for a discussion of the early 20th century clinical laboratories.

11. Galton, a first cousin of Charles Darwin, made several important contributions to psychology, including his intelligence tests (anthropometric tests), the word-association technique, the twin-study method, and the correlation coefficient. He is perhaps best known today as the originator of eugenics, a program intended to improve the human race through selective breeding, essentially through what he called judicious marriages. Galton proposed that governments offer incentives for

marriages among the most gifted individuals, leading, Galton believed, to the birth of individuals who would have the capacity to make great contributions to the betterment of the world. Sadly, there would be others in society who would envision a different form of eugenics (often labeled negative eugenics), for example the Nazis, who established a program of genocide in their quest to create a master race. The horrors of the Nazi atrocities caused the world to see the subject of eugenics in a different light after World War II.

12. Sokal, M. M. (1987). James McKeen Cattell and mental anthropometry: Nineteenth-century science and reform and the origins of psychological testing. In M. M. Sokal (Ed.), *Psychological testing and American society, 1890–1930* (pp. 21–45). New Brunswick, NJ: Rutgers University Press.

13. Cattell, J. M. (1893). Tests of the senses and faculties. *Educational Review, 5*, 257–265. Quotation is from pp. 265–266.

14. Witmer, L. (1897). The organization of practical work in psychology. *Psychological Review, 4*, 116–117.

15. Witmer, L. (1907). Clinical psychology. *The Psychological Clinic, 1*, 1–9.

16. Anthropometry refers to measurements of the human body. Initially these measurements were of physical characteristics of the body—for example, circumference of the head, length of the middle finger, breathing capacity, and arm span. Yet anthropometry also came to include mental anthropometry, which added psychological measurements such as reaction time, memory, color discrimination, and pain sensitivity. In psychology, anthropometric testing has been chiefly associated with the work of Galton and Cattell. See Sokal, M. M. (1982). James McKeen Cattell and the failure of anthropometric mental testing, 1890–1901. In W. R. Woodward & M. G. Ash (Eds.), *The problematic science: Psychology in nineteenth-century thought* (pp. 322–345). New York: Praeger.

17. In the beginnings of the science of psychology one of the key methods of study was introspection. Doctoral psychology students were trained to introspect, that is to report on their own psychological experiences (e.g., perceptual, emotional, cognitive), typically in very systematic ways. In Witmer's clinic, children, even though untrained as introspectionists, were asked to give these self-reports, and such reports were regarded as important observations taken in conjunction with other measures. For discussions of how introspection was used in the early years of psychological science, see Danziger, K. (1980). A history of introspection reconsidered. *Journal of the History of the Behavioral Sciences, 16*, 241–262. Also see Danziger, K. (1990). *Constructing the subject: Historical origins of psychological research.* New York: Cambridge University Press.

18. O'Donnell, J. M. (1979). The clinical psychology of Lightner Witmer: A case study of institutional innovation and intellectual change. *Journal of the History of the Behavioral Sciences, 15*, 3–17. Quotation is from pp. 6–7.

19. Witmer (1897), p. 116.

20. O'Donnell (1979), p. 14.

21. For more information about Lightner Witmer see the excellent biography: McReynolds, P. (1997). *Lightner Witmer: His life and times.* Washington, DC: American Psychological Association. See also the special section on Witmer in the March 1996 issue of the *American Psychologist, 51*, 235–251.

22. See Sokal (1982). The failure of Cattell's psychological tests to predict school performance is reported in Wissler, C. (1901). The correlation of mental and physical tests. *Psychological Review Monograph Supplements, 3* (No. 6).

23. For a history of intellectual disability in the United States, see: Trent, J. W., Jr. (1994). *Inventing the feeble mind: A history of mental retardation in the United States.* Berkeley: University of California Press.

24. The first research by a psychologist at an institution for individuals with intellectual disability was conducted by George F. Johnson at the Massachusetts School for the Feeble-Minded at Waltham. Johnson, G. F. (1894). Contribution to the psychology and pedagogy of feeble-minded children. A. R. T. Wylie (1871–1941) began work in 1896 at the Minnesota School for Idiots and Imbeciles in Fairbault, Minnesota. As cited in Hilgard, E. R. (1987). *Psychology in America: A historical survey.* San Diego: Harcourt Brace Jovanovich.

25. See Wolf, T. H. (1970). *Alfred Binet.* Chicago: University of Chicago Press.

26. Goddard was one of the strongest supporters of the view that mental deficiencies and criminal tendencies were inherited, views expressed in his 1912 book, *The Kallikak family: A study in the heredity of feeble-mindedness* (New York: Macmillan). Goddard was concerned about increases in the population of persons with intellectual disability and argued that steps needed to be taken to prevent them from bearing children. He recommended early institutionalization, but noted that from an economic view, a better long-term solution was sterilization. For a time he belonged to an American organization that lobbied state legislatures for laws that permitted what has been referred to as 'eugenic sterilization' for persons with intellectual disability (The Committee for the Sterilization of the Feebleminded). About 15 states did pass such laws in the 1920s and 1930s and as many as 30,000 sterilization operations, mostly on young females, were carried out, largely in institutions for individuals with intellectual disability. Although there were other psychologists of his time who shared Goddard's views on the heritability of intelligence, there were many who did not. One of the most visible, and one who attacked Goddard's ideas in print, was Lightner Witmer. For some of Goddard's correspondence on his work at Vineland, see Benjamin, L. T., Jr. (1993). Psychology and "feeblemindedness." In *A history of psychology in letters.* New York: McGraw-Hill. See also the outstanding biography on Goddard and an excellent treatment of the history of intelligence testing in America: Zenderland, L. (1998). *Measuring minds: Henry Herbert Goddard and the origins of American intelligence testing.* New York: Cambridge University Press.

27. See Samelson, F. (1977). World War I intelligence testing and the development of psychology. *Journal of the History of the Behavioral Sciences, 13*, 274–282.

28. See Levine, M., & Levine, A. (1992). *Helping children: A social history.* New York: Oxford University Press, p. 104. For a description of the work of Healy and Bronner see Healy, W. (1915). *The individual delinquent.* Boston: Little Brown; Healy, W., & Bronner, A. F. (1936). *New light on delinquency and its treatment.* New Haven: Yale University Press; Healy, W., Bronner, A. F., Baylor, E. M. H., & Murphy, J. Prentice. (1938). *Reconstructing behavior in youth: A study of problem children in foster families.* New York: Alfred A. Knopf.

29. Freud, S. (1910). The origin and development of psychoanalysis. *American Journal of Psychology, 21*, 181–218.

30. Hornstein, G. A. (1992). The return of the repressed: Psychology's problematic relations with psychoanalysis, 1909–1960. *American Psychologist, 47*, 254–263.

31. For the definitive history of Freud's American visit, see Rosenzweig, S. (1992). *Freud, Jung, and Hall the kingmaker: The historic expedition to America.* St Louis: RANA House. This book also contains English translations of Freud's five lectures. For a history of psychoanalysis in the United States, see Hale, N. G., Jr. (1995). *The rise and crisis of psychoanalysis in the United States: Freud and the Americans, 1917–1985.* New York: Oxford University Press. There are many biographies of Sigmund Freud. Two particularly good ones are Gay, P. (1988). *Freud: A life for our time.* New York: Norton; and Sulloway, F. J. (1979). *Freud: Biologist of the mind.* New York: Basic Books.

32. Beers, C. W. (1908). *A mind that found itself: An autobiography.* New York: Longmans, Green.

33. Grob (1994), p. 155.

34. For a brief overview of Prince's contributions, see White, R. W. (1992). Who was Morton Prince? *Journal of Abnormal Psychology, 101*, 604–606.

35. This quote is by one of Worcester's disciples from a 1909 magazine article. It is cited in Caplan, E. (1998). *Mind games: American culture and the birth of psychotherapy.* Berkeley: University of California Press, p. 123.

36. For information on Marshall see Benjamin, L. T., Jr., & Wallers, K. (1985). Henry Rutgers Marshall: The forgotten American Psychological Association president. In H. Carpintero, & J. M. Piero (Eds.), *Psychology in its historical context* (pp. 63–67). Valencia, Spain: University of Valencia.

37. Caplan (1998), p. 148.

38. Münsterberg, H. (1909). *Psychotherapy.* New York: Moffat, Yard and Co., p. 9.

39. Münsterberg (1909), p. x.

40. See chapter 6, Embracing psychotherapy: The Emmanuel Movement and the American medical profession in Caplan (1998) for an excellent brief history of the

Emmanuel Movement. Worcester's autobiography is fascinating reading and a story of real tragedy (all five of his sisters died violent deaths): Worcester, E. E. (1932). *Life's adventure: The story of a varied career.* New York: Scribner.

41. Hollingworth, L. S. (1918). Tentative suggestions for the certification of practicing psychologists. *Journal of Applied Psychology, 2,* 280–284. Quotation is from p. 281.

42. Ibid., p. 281.

43. See: Geissler, L. R. (1918). A plan for the technical training of consulting psychologists. *Journal of Applied Psychology, 2,* 77–83. Baird, J. W., Hall, G. S., & Geissler, L. R. (1918). Communications regarding "A plan for the technical training of consulting psychologists." *Journal of Applied Psychology, 2,* 174–178. Doll, E. A. (1919). The degree of PH.D. and clinical psychology. *Journal of Applied Psychology, 3,* 88–90.

44. Hollingworth, L. S. (1918), pp. 282–283.

45. Activities of clinical psychologists. (1917). *Psychological Bulletin, 14,* 224–225. Quotation is from p. 224.

46. Ibid., p. 225.

47. See, for example, Franz, S. I. (1917). Psychology and psychiatry. *Psychological Bulletin, 14,* 226–229.

48. For an excellent treatment of clinical psychology organizations from 1917 to the 1990s, see Routh, D. K. (1994). *Clinical psychology since 1917: Science, practice, and organization.* New York: Plenum Press.

49. Napoli, D. S. (1981). *Architects of adjustment: The history of the psychological profession in the United States.* Port Washington, NY: Kennikat Press, p. 26.

50. For coverage of the 1920s APA certification effort, see Sokal, M. M. (1982). The Committee on the Certification of Consulting Psychologists: A failure of applied psychology in the 1920s. In C. J. Adkins, Jr., & B. A. Winstead (Eds.), *History of applied psychology: Department of Psychology colloquium series, II* (pp. 71–90). Norfolk, VA: Old Dominion University.

51. The title for this section comes from an article written by Canadian humorist Stephen Leacock lamenting what he felt was America's absurd love affair with psychology. See Leacock, S. (1924, March). A manual for the new mentality. *Harpers,* pp. 471–480.

52. Wiggam, A. E. (1928). *Exploring your own mind with the psychologists.* New York: Bobbs Merrill, p. 13.

53. Benjamin, L. T., Jr., & Bryant, W. H. M. (1997). A history of popular psychology magazines in America. In W. Bringmann, et al. (Eds.), *A pictorial history of psychology* (pp. 585–593). Carol Stream, IL: Quintessence Publishers.

54. Watson, J. B. (1925). *Behaviorism*. New York: The People's Institute Publishing Co., p. 82.

55. For histories of the Child Guidance Movement, see Horn, M. (1989). *Before it's too late: The child guidance movement in the United States, 1922–1945*. Philadelphia: Temple University Press. See also Levine & Levine (1992), chapter 9: The child guidance clinic: A product of the 1920s.

56. See Benjamin, L. T., Jr. (1997). The origin of psychological species: A history of the beginnings of the divisions of the American Psychological Association. *American Psychologist, 52*, 725–732.

57. For more information on Scott and this program, see Von Mayrhauser, R. T. (1989). Making intelligence functional: Walter Dill Scott and applied psychological testing in World War I. *Journal of the History of the Behavioral Sciences, 25*, 60–72.

58. Hollingworth, H. L. (1920). *The psychology of functional neuroses*. New York: D. Appleton, p. ix.

59. For a history of PTSD, see Holden, W. (1998). *Shell shock*. London: Channel 4 Books.

60. Jones, E., & Wessely, S. (2005). War syndromes: the impact of culture on medically unexplained symptoms. *Medical History, 49*, 55–78; Myers, C. S. (1915, Feb. 13). A contribution to the study of shell shock. *Lancet*, 316–320.

61. Hollingworth, H. L. (1920), pp. 255–256.

62. Cattell played another important role in psychological testing as founder in 1921 of the Psychological Corporation, which eventually became the major publisher of important psychological tests. It is still in business today with its headquarters located in San Antonio, Texas. For a history of the founding and early years of this organization, see Sokal, M. M. (1981). The origins of the Psychological Corporation. *Journal of the History of the Behavioral Sciences, 17*, 54–67.

63. Jung, C. G. (1907). On psychophysical relations of the association experiment. *Journal of Abnormal Psychology, 1*, 249–257. Jung, C. G. (1910). The association method. *American Journal of Psychology, 31*, 219–269. Note: Galton, Wundt, psychiatrist Emil Kraepelin (1856–1926), and Gestalt psychology founder Max Wertheimer (1880–1943) independently worked on word association. It was Jung's work, however, that precipitated the use of it as a clinical technique in America.

64. See Kent, G. H., & Rosanoff, A. (1910). A study of association in insanity. *American Journal of Insanity, 67*, 317–390. See also Shakow, D. (1974). Grace Helen Kent. *Journal of the History of the Behavioral Sciences, 10*, 275–280.

65. Hilgard (1987), pp. 516–517.

66. For a critical analysis of the scientific status of the Rorschach and other projective techniques, see Lilienfeld, S. O., Wood, J. M., & Garb, H. N. (2000). The scientific status of projective techniques. *Psychological Science in the Public Interest, 1*, 27–66.

67. Klopfer, W. G. (1973). The short history of projective techniques. *Journal of the History of the Behavioral Sciences, 9*, 60–65.

68. Buchanan, R. D. (1994). The development of the Minnesota Multiphasic Personality Inventory. *Journal of the History of the Behavioral Sciences, 30*, 148–161. Dahlstrom, W. G. (1992). The growth in acceptance of the MMPI. *Professional Psychology: Research & Practice, 23*, 345–348.

69. A manual from the Walter Reed General Hospital in Washington, DC (no date, but circa 1950), listed 27 psychological tests "at the disposal of the clinical psychologist." The manual also described ways in which the tests could be "of aid in evaluating and understanding the patient." The list included Army Alpha and Beta (revised), Wechsler-Bellevue, Rorschach, TAT, MMPI, Bernreuter Personality Inventory, Bender Visual-Motor Gestalt Test, Kuder Preference Record, Minnesota Paper Form Board, and Gray Oral Reading Test. Manual is in the Saul Sells Papers, Archives of the History of American Psychology, University of Akron, Akron, OH.

70. Buchanan (1994), p. 149.

71. See Langer, W. C. (1972). *The mind of Adolf Hitler: The secret wartime report.* New York: Basic Books.

72. See Capshew, J. H. (1999). *Psychologists on the march: Science, practice, and professional identity in America, 1929–1969.* New York: Cambridge University Press.

73. For information on the founding of the VA psychology training program, see Moore, D. L. (1992). The Veterans Administration and the training program in psychology. In D. K. Freedheim (Ed.), *History of psychotherapy: A century of change* (pp. 776–800). Washington, DC: American Psychological Association.

74. Miller, J. G. (1946). Clinical psychology in the Veterans Administration. *American Psychologist, 1*, 181–189.

75. Baker, D. B., & Benjamin, L. T., Jr. (2000). The affirmation of the scientist-practitioner: A look back at Boulder. *American Psychologist, 55*, 241–247.

76. American Psychological Association, Committee on Training in Clinical Psychology. (1947). Recommended graduate training program in clinical psychology. *American Psychologist, 2*, 539–558.

77. Benjamin, L. T., Jr., & Baker, D. B. (2000). Boulder at 50: Introduction to the section. *American Psychologist, 55*, 233–236. Quotation is from p. 233.

78. The report of the Boulder Conference was published as Raimy, V. C. (Ed.) (1950). *Training in clinical psychology.* Englewood Cliffs, NJ: Prentice Hall. See Baker & Benjamin (2000) and Benjamin & Baker (2000) for a history of the Boulder Conference.

79. See, for example, O'Sullivan, J. J., & Quevillon, R. P. (1992). 40 years later: Is the Boulder model still alive? *American Psychologist, 47*, 67–70. Albee, G. W. (2000). The Boulder model's fatal flaw. *American Psychologist, 55*, 247–248. Belar,

C. D. (2000). Scientist-practitioner does not equal science plus practice: Boulder is bolder. *American Psychologist, 55*, 249–250. Nathan, P. E. (2000). The Boulder model: A dream deferred—or lost? *American Psychologist, 55*, 250–252. Peterson, D. R. (2000). Scientist-practitioner or scientific practitioner? *American Psychologist, 55*, 252–253. Stricker, G. (2000). The scientist-practitioner model: Ghandi was right again. *American Psychologist, 55*, 253–254.

80. Hunt, W. A. (1975). Clinical psychology in 1944–45. *Journal of Clinical Psychology, 31*, 173–178. Quotation is from p. 174.

81. For a history of clinical psychologists in one branch of the military, see McGuire, F. L. (1990). *Psychology aweigh! A history of clinical psychology in the United States Navy, 1900–1988*. Washington, DC: American Psychological Association.

82. See VandenBos, G. R., Cummings, N. A., & DeLeon, P. H. (1992). A century of psychotherapy: Economic and environmental influences. In D. K. Freedheim (Ed.), *History of psychotherapy: A century of change* (pp. 65–102). Washington, DC: American Psychological Association.

83. For a historical treatment of lobotomies and other forms of psychosurgery, see Valenstein, E. S. (1986). *Great and desperate cures: The rise and decline of psychosurgery and other radical treatments for mental illness*. New York: Basic Books.

84. Eysenck, H. J. (1952). The effects of psychotherapy: An evaluation. *Journal of Consulting Psychology, 16*, 319–324.

85. Wolpe, J. (1958). *Psychotherapy by reciprocal inhibition*. Stanford, CA: Stanford University Press.

86. Jones, M. C. (1924). A laboratory study of fear: The case of Peter. *Pedagogical Seminary, 31*, 308–315. Jones, M. C. (1924). The elimination of children's fears. *Journal of Experimental Psychology, 7*, 382–390.

87. Skinner, B. F. (1938). *The behavior of organisms: An experimental analysis*. New York: Appleton Century; Kazdin, A. E. (1978). *History of behavior modification: Experimental foundations of contemporary research*. Baltimore: University Park Press.

88. See Ellis, A. & Harper, R. A. (1961). *A guide to rational living*. Englewood Cliffs, NJ: Prentice-Hall; Ellis, A. (1962). *Reason and emotion in psychotherapy*. New York: Lyle Stuart; Ellis, A. (1993). Reflections on rational-emotive therapy. *Journal of Consulting and Clinical Psychology, 61*, 199–201.

89. Beck, A. T. (1976). *Cognitive therapy and the emotional disorders*. New York: International Universities Press; Beck, A. T. (1993). Cognitive therapy: Past, present, and future. *Journal of Consulting and Clinical Psychology, 61*, 194–198.

90. Arnkoff, D. B., & Glass, C. R. (1992). Cognitive therapy and psychotherapy integration. In D. K. Freedheim (Ed.). *History of psychotherapy: A century of change* (pp. 657–694). Washington, DC: American Psychological Association.

91. See DeCarvalho, R. J. (1991). *The founders of humanistic psychology*. New York: Praeger; Bugental, J. F. T. (1967). *Challenges of humanistic psychology*. New

York: McGraw-Hill; Giorgi, A. (1987). The crisis of humanistic psychology. *The Humanistic Psychologist, 15,* 5–20.

92. Licensure requirements are still being debated both in terms of the need for a national standard and a need to reevaluate the nature of the requirements. See Vaney Olvey, C. D., Hogg, A., & Counts, W. (2002). Licensure requirements: Have we raised the bar too far? *Professional Psychology: Research & Practice, 33,* 323–329.

93. Benjamin, L. T., Jr. (1996). The founding of the *American Psychologist*: The professional journal that wasn't. *American Psychologist, 51,* 8–12.

94. Wolfle, D. (1946). The reorganized American Psychological Association. *American Psychologist, 1,* 3–6. Quotation is from p. 3.

95. American Psychological Association. (n.d.). About APA. Retrieved October 18, 2013 from http://www.apa.org/about/index.aspx.

96. *Guidelines and Principles for Accreditation of Programs in Professional Psychology.* Available free of charge from the APA.

97. For an excellent collection of essays on the history of education and training for professional psychologists, see Peterson, D. R. (1997). *Educating professional psychologists: History and guiding conception.* Washington, DC: American Psychological Association.

98. For a firsthand account of the founding of professional schools in psychology, see Stricker, G., & Cummings, N. A. (1992). The professional school movement. In D. K. Freedheim (Ed.), *History of psychotherapy: A century of change* (pp. 801–828). Washington, DC: American Psychological Association.

99. See Bourg, E. F., Bent, R. J., McHolland, J., & Stricker, G. (1989). Standards and evaluation in the education and training of professional psychologists: The National Council of Schools of Professional Psychology Mission Bay Conference. *American Psychologist, 44,* 66–72.

100. The Vail Conference report was published as Korman, M. (Ed.) (1973). *Levels and patterns of professional training in psychology.* Washington, DC: American Psychological Association.

101. American Psychological Association. (2012). *Commission on Accreditation: 2012 annual report.* Retrieved October 18, 2013 from http://www.apa.org/ed/accreditation/about/research/index.aspx.

102. Kohout, J., & Wicherski, M. (2010). *Data brief: Psychology PhD and PsyD Degrees in Health Service Provider (HSP) fields: 1987–2008.* Retrieved October 23, 2013 from http://www.apa.org/workforce/publications/08-hsp/psychology-degrees.aspx.

103. Capshew (1999), p. 241.

104. Ellis, A. (1991). My life in clinical psychology. In C. E. Walker (Ed.), *The history of clinical psychology in autobiography* (Vol. 1, pp. 1–37). Pacific Grove, CA: Brooks/Cole.

105. Hill, E. F. (1999). A history of Division 42 (Independent Practice). In D. A. Dewsbury (Ed.), *Unification through division: Histories of the divisions of the American Psychological Association* (Vol. 3, pp. 143–174). Washington, DC: American Psychological Association.

106. VandenBos, Cummings, & DeLeon (1992), p. 97.

107. See Humphreys, K. (1996). Clinical psychologists as psychotherapists: History, future, and alternatives. *American Psychologist, 51*, 190–197. We discuss this subject in more detail in chapter 6.

Chapter 3

1. Dewey, J. (1916). *Democracy and education: An introduction to the philosophy of education.* New York: Macmillan.

2. For more on Dewey and his writing see, Campbell, J. (1995). *Understanding John Dewey.* Chicago: Open Court.

3. To learn more about American education during these years see Cremin, L. A. (1988). *American education: The metropolitan experience 1876–1980.* New York: Harper and Row.

4. For a biography of Hall see, Ross, D. (1972). *G. Stanley Hall: The psychologist as prophet.* Chicago: University of Chicago Press.

5. White, S. (1992). G. Stanley Hall: From philosophy to developmental psychology. *Developmental Psychology, 28*, 25–34. Quotation is from p. 32.

6. Hall, G. S. (1904). *Adolescence: Its psychology and its relation to physiology, anthropology, sociology, sex, crime, religion and education* (2 vols.). New York: D. Appleton.

7. Ibid., Vol. II, p. 676.

8. For more information about Frances Ceil Sumner see, Guthrie, R. V. (1998). *Even the rat was white: A historical view of psychology* (2nd ed.). Boston: Allyn and Bacon. For more on Hall's view on women see, Diehl, L. A. (1986). The paradox of G. Stanley Hall: Foe of coeducation and educator of women. *American Psychologist, 41*, 868–878.

9. Minton, H. L. (1987). Lewis M. Terman and mental testing: In search of the democratic Ideal. In M. M. Sokal (Ed.), *Psychological testing and American society, 1890–1930* (pp. 95–112). New Brunswick, NJ: Rutgers University Press, p. 97.

10. Fancher, R. E. (1985). *The intelligence men.* New York: W. W. Norton, p. 142.

11. Leslie, M. (2000, July/August). The vexing legacy of Lewis Terman. *Stanford Magazine.* Available on-line at http://www.stanfordalumni.org/news/magazine/2000/julaug/articles/terman.html.

12. Fagan, T. K. (1987). Gesell: The first school psychologist. Part II: Practice and significance. *School Psychology Review*, *16*, 399–409.

13. For more about Witmer see, Baker, D. B. (1988). The psychology of Lightner Witmer. *Professional School Psychology*, *3*, 109–121; McReynolds, P. J. (1997). *Lightner Witmer: His life and times*. Washington, DC: American Psychological Association.

14. Witmer, L. (1907). Clinical psychology. *The Psychological Clinic*, *1*, 1–9.

15. Witmer, L. (1922). The analytical diagnosis. *The Psychological Clinic*, *14*, 129–135. Quotation is from p. 134.

16. Witmer, L. (1915). On the relation of intelligence to efficiency. *The Psychological Clinic*, *9*, 61–86.

17. Witmer, L. (1909). The study and treatment of retardation: A field of applied psychology. *Psychological Bulletin*, *6*, 121–127. Quotation is from p. 122.

18. The field experiences offered by Witmer also earned him credit as the founder of the internship in psychology. See, Morrow, W. R. (1946). The development of psychological internship training. *Journal of Counseling Psychology*, *10*, 165–173.

19. Witmer (1907), p. 5.

20. Ibid., p. 3.

21. Witmer, L. (1919). The training of very bright children. *The Psychological Clinic*, *13*, 88–96. Quotation is from p. 66.

22. Witmer, L. (1911). Criminals in the making. *The Psychological Clinic*, *4*, 221–239. Quotation is from p. 232.

23. Van Sickle, J. H., Witmer, L., & Ayres, L. P. (1911). *Provisions for exceptional children in public schools* (Report no. 461). Washington, DC: United States Bureau of Education.

24. Ibid., p. 21.

25. Ibid, p. 8.

26. Wallin, J. E. W., & Ferguson, D. G. (1967). The development of school psychological services. In J. F. Magary (Ed.) *School psychological services*. Englewood Cliffs, NJ: Prentice-Hall.

27. For an autobiographical account see, Wallin, J. E. W. (1955). *The odyssey of a psychologist: Pioneering experiences in special education, clinical psychology, and mental hygiene with a comprehensive bibliography of the author's publications*. Wilmington, DE: Author.

28. Wallin, J. E. W. (1914). *The mental health of the school child*. New Haven, CT: Yale University Press.

29. Fagan, T. K., & Wise, P. S. (2007). *School psychology: Past, present, and future.* Bethesda, MD: National Association of School Psychologists, p. 35.

30. Leta Hollingworth made important contributions to the study of sex differences, shattering many myths about the abilities of women. Throughout her career she worked with children, including the intellectually disabled and the gifted. Her research and writing on exceptional children was an important part of the early school psychology literature. For more about her see, Shields, S. A. (1991). Leta Stetter Hollingworth: "Literature of opinion" and the study of individual differences. In G. A. Kimble, M. Wertheimer, and C. L. White (Eds.), *Portraits of pioneers in psychology* (pp. 243–255). Hillsdale, NJ: Erlbaum; Fagan, T. K. (1990). Contributions of Leta Hollingworth to school psychology. *Roeper Review, 12,* 157–161.

31. Routh, D. K. (1994). *Clinical psychology since 1917: Science, practice, and organization.* New York: Plenum Press.

32. The papers of Gertrude Hildreth are housed at the Educational Testing Service (ETS) Archives. The test collection at the ETS library contains all the versions of the Metropolitan Tests.

33. Fagan, T. K. (1993). Separate but equal: School psychology's search for organizational identity. *Journal of School Psychology, 31,* 3–90.

34. See Benjamin, L. T., Jr. (1997). The origin of psychological species: A history of the beginnings of the divisions of the American Psychological Association. *American Psychologist, 52,* 725–732.

35. Fagan, T. K. (1996). A history of Division 16 (school psychology): Running twice as fast. In D. A. Dewsbury (Ed.), *Unification through division: Histories of the divisions of the American Psychological Association* (Vol. 1, pp. 101–135). Washington, DC: American Psychological Association. Quotation is from p. 103.

36. Fagan, T. K., & Jacks, S. (2012). A history of the founding and early development of the *Journal of School Psychology. Journal of School Psychology, 50,* 701–735.

37. American Psychological Association (2012). 2012 APA member profiles. Retrieved October 17, 2013 from http://www.apa.org/workforce/publications/12-member/index.aspx.

38. Fagan (1993).

39. Wallin (1914), p. 395.

40. Both the PhD and PsyD programs in school psychology at NYU are being phased out.

41. Fagan, T. K. (1986). The historical origins and growth of programs to prepare school psychologists in the United States. *Journal of School Psychology, 24,* 9–22.

42. Hildreth, G. (1930). *Psychological service for school problems.* Yonkers-on-Hastings, NY: World Book, p. 21.

43. Symonds, P. M. (1942). The school psychologist—1942. *Journal of Consulting Psychology*, 6, 173–176. Quotation is from p. 173.

44. Meeting of Subcommittee on Mental Hygiene Personnel in School Programs. (1949, November 5–6). (Shakow Papers, M1360). Archives of the History of American Psychology, University of Akron. Akron, OH.

45. For information on the development at the Pennsylvania State University see, French, J. L. (1984). On the conception, birth, and early development of school psychology: With special reference to Pennsylvania. *American Psychologist*, 39, 976–987. For more information about the Illinois program and its founder see Newland, T. E. (1981). School psychology-observation and reminiscence. *Journal of School Psychology*, 19, 4–20.

46. Cutts, N. E. (Ed.) (1955). *School psychologists at mid-century: A report on the Thayer conference on the functions, qualifications, and training of school psychologists.* Washington, DC: American Psychological Association.

47. Ibid., p. viii.

48. American Psychological Association, Division 16, Committee on Training Standards and Certification. (1963). Proposals for state departments of education certification of school psychologists. *American Psychologist*, 18, 711–714.

49. Ibid., p. 712.

50. Fagan, T. (1996).

51. Eiserer, P. E. (1965). *Training Programs in School Psychology: Growth through Improvement of Communication.* Unpublished manuscript. (Tindall Papers, M2006). Archives of the History of American Psychology, University of Akron. Akron, OH.

52. Driscoll, G. P. (1957). The School Psychologist Looks to the Future. Presidential address delivered at the 1957 meeting of the American Psychological Association. (Tindall Papers, M2006). Archives of the History of American Psychology, University of Akron. Akron, OH.

53. Presenting the school psychologist as child mental health specialist created issues in professional identity and roles. According to historian of school psychology Tom Fagan, the Thayer conference endorsed two levels of training, titles and practice, with credentialing to be done by state education agencies for school practice and state boards of psychology for nonschool practice. See Fagan, T. K. (2005). The 50th anniversary of the Thayer Conference: Historical perspectives and accomplishments. *School Psychology Quarterly*, 20(3), 224–251.

54. For an example see, Lambert, N. M. (Ed.) (1964). The protection and promotion of mental health in schools. *Mental Health Monograph 5.* Bethesda, MD: U. S. Department of Health Education and Welfare.

55. Gray, S. W. (Ed.) (1963). *The internship in school psychology: Proceedings of the Peabody Conference, March 21–22, 1963.* Nashville, TN: George Peabody College for Teachers.

56. Bardon, J. I. (Ed.) (1964–1965). Problems and issues in school psychology—1964: Proceedings of a Conference on New Directions in School Psychology. *Journal of School Psychology 3*, 1–44.

57. Newland, T. E. (1981), p. 7.

58. For an in-depth discussion of these developments and their aftermath see Fagan, T. (1993).

59. Farling, W. H. (1970). *School psychology in the 70's—A profession looks at itself and its responsibilities*. Proceedings of the second national NASP convention. National Association of School Psychologists, p. 1–3.

60. The NASP web site, http://www.nasponline.org/index2.html, contains an abundance of information about the organization and its activities.

61. Taken from http://www.nasponline.org/certification/message.html.

62. For more about these meetings see, Ysseldyke, J., & Weinberg, R. (1981). The future of psychology in the schools: Proceedings of the Spring Hill symposium. *School Psychology Review 10*, 116–318, Brown, D. T., Cardon, B. W., Coulter, W. A., & Meyers, J. (1982). The Olympia proceedings. *School Psychology Review, 11*, 107–214, and Fagan, T. (2013). School psychology. In D. K. Freedheim (Ed.) & I. B. Weiner (Editor-in-Chief), *Handbook of psychology: Vol. 1. History of psychology* (2nd ed., pp. 448–467). New York: Wiley.

63. Fagan, T. (1993), pp. 59–60.

64. Information on school psychology programs is available on the NASP website: http://www.nasponline.org/graduate-education/grad-edu.aspx.

Chapter 4

1. The opening to this chapter is adapted from Arthur, W. A., Jr., & Benjamin, L. T., Jr. (1999). Psychology applied to business. In A. Stec & D. Bernstein (Eds.), *Psychology: Fields of application* (pp. 98–115). Boston: Houghton Mifflin. It is reprinted by permission from Houghton Mifflin Publishers. Hollingworth's caffeine studies were published as Hollingworth, H. L. (1912). The influence of caffein on mental and motor efficiency. *Archives of Psychology, 3*, 1–166. For a more detailed historical account of the caffeine studies for Coca-Cola, see Benjamin, L. T., Jr., Rogers, A., & Rosenbaum, A. (1991). Coca-Cola, caffeine, and mental deficiency: Harry Hollingworth and the Chattanooga trial of 1911. *Journal of the History of the Behavioral Sciences, 27*, 42–55.

2. Bryant, K. L., Jr., & Dethloff, H. C. (1990). *A history of American business* (2nd ed.). Englewood Cliffs, NJ: Prentice Hall.

3. Gale, H. (1900). On the psychology of advertising. *Psychological Studies, 1*, 39–69. Quotation is from p. 39.

4. Bryant & Dethloff (1990), p. 190.

5. Gibson, D. (1908). The common sense of psychology. *Profitable Advertising*, *17*, 955.

6. Hollingworth, H. L. (1938). Memories of the early development of the psychology of advertising suggested by Burtt's Psychology of Advertising. *Psychological Bulletin*, 35, 307–311. Quotation is from p. 308.

7. Kuna, D. P. (1976). The concept of suggestion in the early history of advertising psychology. *Journal of the History of the Behavioral Sciences, 12*, 347–353. Quotation is from p. 353.

8. Scott, W. D. (1903). *The theory of advertising*. Boston: Small, Maynard, and Co., p. 59.

9. For further information on Scott's ideas about advertising, see: Scott, W. D. (1908). *The psychology of advertising*. Boston: Small, Maynard, and Co. and Scott, W. D. (1904). The psychology of advertising. *Atlantic Monthly*, 93(1), 29–36.

10. See Hollingworth, H. L. (1913). *Advertising and selling: Principles of appeal and response*. New York: D. Appleton. See also Kuna, D. P. (1979). Early advertising applications of the Gale-Cattell order-of-merit method. *Journal of the History of the Behavioral Sciences, 15*, 38–46.

11. Benjamin, L. T., Jr. (2004). Science for sale: Psychology's earliest adventures in American advertising. In J. Williams, W. N. Lee, & C. Haugtvedt (Eds.). *Diversity in advertising* (pp. 21–42). Mahwah, NJ: Erlbaum.

12. For an excellent account of the life and work of John Watson, including his work in the field of advertising, see Buckley, K. W. (1989). *Mechanical man: John Broadus Watson and the beginnings of behaviorism*. New York: Guilford Press. See also Coon, D. J. (1994). "Not a creature of reason": The alleged impact of Watsonian behaviorism on advertising in the 1920s. In J. T. Todd & E. K. Morris (Eds.), *Modern perspectives on John B. Watson and classical behaviorism* (pp. 37–63). Westport, CT: Greenwood Press.

13. Münsterberg, H. (1909, November). Psychology and the market. *McClure's Magazine, 34*, 87–93.

14. Münsterberg, H. (1913). *Psychology and industrial efficiency*. Boston: Houghton Mifflin; Münsterberg, H. (1915). *Business psychology*. Chicago: Lasalle Extension Service.

15. Münsterberg, H. (1908). *On the witness stand: Essays on psychology and crime*. New York: Doubleday, Page; Münsterberg, H. (1909). *Psychotherapy*. New York: Moffat, Yard; Münsterberg, H. (1909). *Psychology and the teacher*. New York: D. Appleton.

16. Hale, M., Jr. (1980). *Human science and social order: Hugo Münsterberg and the origins of applied psychology*. Philadelphia: Temple University Press, p. 148.

17. Münsterberg (1909, November).

18. For a brief treatment of Münsterberg's life and work, see Benjamin, L. T., Jr. (2000). Hugo Münsterberg: Portrait of an applied psychologist. In G. A. Kimble & M. Wertheimer (Eds.), *Portraits of pioneers in psychology* (Vol. 4, pp. 113–129). Washington, DC: American Psychological Association.

19. Strong, E. K., Jr. (1943). *Vocational interests of men and women*. Palo Alto, CA: Stanford University Press.

20. In addition to the two advertising books cited in Notes 8 and 9, Scott published the following two books in 1911: *Influencing men in business*. New York: Ronald Press, and *Increasing human efficiency in business*. New York: Macmillan.

21. Ferguson, L. W. (1963). First students and their careers: Bureau of Salesmanship Research. *The heritage of industrial psychology* (ch. 4). Privately printed booklet in the Ferguson Papers in the Carnegie Mellon University Archives, Hunt Library, Pittsburgh, PA.

22. Benjamin, L. T., Jr., & Baker, D. B. (2003). Walter Van Dyke Bingham: Portrait of an industrial psychologist. In G. A. Kimble & M. Wertheimer (Eds.), *Portraits of pioneers in psychology* (Vol. 5, pp. 141–157) Washington, DC: American Psychological Association, p. 146.

23. Bingham, W. V. D. (1952). Walter Van Dyke Bingham. In E. G. Boring, H. S. Langfeld, H. Werner, & R. M. Yerkes (Eds.), *A history of psychology in autobiography* (Vol. 4, pp. 1–26). Worcester, MA: Clark University Press.

24. See Benjamin & Baker (2003) for a discussion of the reasons for the elimination of Bingham's applied psychology division. See also Prien, E. P. (1991). The Division of Applied Psychology at Carnegie Institute of Technology. *The Industrial-Organizational Psychologist, 29*(2), 41–45.

25. For additional information on Bingham and the CIT applied psychology division, see: Ferguson, L. W. (1963). Walter Van Dyke Bingham: Dean of industrial psychologists (ch. 2) and Division of Applied Psychology, Carnegie Institute of Technology (ch. 3) in *The heritage of industrial psychology*. Privately printed chapters located in the Leonard Ferguson Papers, Carnegie Mellon University Archives, Hunt Library, Pittsburgh, PA. See also Kraus, M. P. (1986). *Personnel research, history and policy issues: Walter Van Dyke Bingham and the Bureau of Personnel Research*. New York: Garland Publishing.

26. Taylor's system evolved in a series of articles and pamphlets beginning in 1895 but is most fully described in his book: Taylor, F. W. (1911). *Scientific management*. New York: Harper & Row. For biographical information on Taylor and a discussion of the history of Taylorism, see Nelson, D. A. (1980). *Frederick W. Taylor and the rise of scientific management*. Madison: University of Wisconsin Press; and Kakar, S. (1970). *Frederick Taylor: A study in personality and innovation*. Cambridge, MA: MIT Press.

27. Taylor (1911), pp. 142–143.

28. For a discussion of the difficulties faced by scientific management, see Van De Water, T. J. (1997). Psychology's entrepreneurs and the marketing of industrial psychology. *Journal of Applied Psychology, 82,* 486–499.

29. Lillian M. Gilbreth was a remarkable person, the subject of the movie, "Cheaper by the Dozen." The mother of 12 children, she carved out a distinguished career in engineering, first working with her husband Frank Gilbreth, and then running their consulting firm on her own after his death. There are several biographical accounts of the Gilbreths written by some of their children. See Gilbreth, F. B., Jr., & Carey, E. G. (1948). *Cheaper by the dozen.* New York: Thomas Y. Crowell; and Gilbreth, F. B., Jr., & Carey, E. G. (1950). *Belles on their toes.* New York: Thomas Y. Crowell. In 1984 she was honored by the issuance of a United States postage stamp (40 cents) featuring her portrait. The campaign to recognize her contributions was originated by the women's division of the American Society of Mechanical Engineers. She is the only American psychologist to appear on a US stamp, although some would argue that philosopher John Dewey (1859–1952), who received a stamp in 1968, could be considered a psychologist.

30. As quoted in Gies, J. (1991, Winter). Automating the worker. *Invention & Technology,* pp. 56–63. Quotation is from p. 62.

31. For an excellent discussion of Scott's work in WWI, see von Mayrhauser, R. T. (1989). Walter Dill Scott and applied psychological testing in World War I. *Journal of the History of the Behavioral Sciences, 25,* 60–72.

32. See, for example Samelson, F. (1977). World War I intelligence testing and the development of psychology. *Journal of the History of the Behavioral Sciences, 13,* 274–282.

33. Van de Water (1997), p. 492.

34. Van de Water (1997).

35. Hall, G. S., Baird, J. W., & Geissler, L. R. (1917). Foreword. *Journal of Applied Psychology, 1,* 5–7. Quotation is from pp. 5–6.

36. Witmer, L. (1897). The organization of practical work in psychology (Abstract of a paper presented at the meeting of the American Psychological Association, Boston). *Psychological Review, 4,* 116–117.

37. Hall, Baird, & Geissler (1917), p. 6.

38. Van de Water (1997).

39. Ferguson, L. W. (1976). The Scott Company. *JSAS Catalog of Selected Documents in Psychology, 6,* 128. Ms. 1397, 73 pp.

40. Sokal, M. M. (1981). The origins of The Psychological Corporation. *Journal of the History of the Behavioral Sciences, 17,* 54–67.

41. Hollingworth, H. L. (1916). *Vocational psychology: Its problems and methods.* New York: D. Appleton; Link, H. C. (1919). *Employment psychology: The application of scientific methods to the selection, training and rating of employees.* New York: Macmillan; Kornhauser, A. W., & Kingsbury, F. A. (1924). *Psychological tests in business.* Chicago: University of Chicago Press; Griffiths, C. H. (1924). *Fundamentals of vocational psychology.* New York: Macmillan; Laird, D. A. (1925). *The psychology of selecting men.* New York: McGraw-Hill.

42. Link (1919), p. ix.

43. Kornhauser & Kingsbury (1924), p. vii.

44. Gilmer, B. von H. (Ed.) (1962). *Walter Van Dyke Bingham, memorial program.* Pittsburgh, PA: Carnegie Institute of Technology, p. 59.

45. Benjamin, L. T., Jr., & Bryant, William H. M. (1997). A history of popular psychology magazines in America. In W. G. Bringmann, H. E. Lück, R. Miller, & C. E. Early (Eds.), *A pictorial history of psychology* (pp. 585–593). Carol Stream, IL: Quintessence.

46. Koppes, L. L. (1997). American female pioneers of industrial and organizational psychology during the early years. *Journal of Applied Psychology, 82,* 500–515.

47. Katzell, R. A., & Austin, J. T. (1992). From then to now: The development of industrial-organizational psychology in the United States. *Journal of Applied Psychology, 77,* 803–835.

48. For an excellent account of the European psychologist émigrés in the 1930s, see Mandler, J., & Mandler, G. (1969). The diaspora of experimental psychology: The Gestaltists and others. In D. Fleming & B. Bailyn (Eds.), *The intellectual migration: Europe and America, 1930–1960* (pp. 371–419). Cambridge, MA: Harvard University Press.

49. Morris Viteles lived nearly 99 years. His career as an industrial psychologist was quite a remarkable one. His obituary, written by Albert S. Thompson, appeared in the *American Psychologist,* 1998, 53, 1153–1154. Viteles wrote two autobiographical chapters that appeared in Boring, E. G., & Lindzey, G. (Eds.) (1967). *A history of psychology in autobiography* (Vol. 5, pp. 415–449). New York: Irvington, and Krawiec, T. S. (Ed.) (1974). *The psychologists* (Vol. 2, pp. 441–500). New York: Oxford University Press.

50. Viteles, M. S. (1932). *Industrial psychology.* New York: W. W. Norton.

51. Viteles (1932), p. 8.

52. Viteles (1932), p. 17.

53. Baritz, L. (1960). *The servants of power: A history of the use of social science in American industry.* Middletown, CT: Wesleyan University Press.

54. Gillespie, R. (1988). The Hawthorne experiments and the politics of experimentation. In Jill G. Morawski (Ed.), *The rise of experimentation in American psychology* (pp. 114–137). New Haven: Yale University Press. Quotation is from p. 117.

55. Baritz (1960), pp. 92–93.

56. Baritz (1960), p. 95.

57. Baritz (1960), p. 77. In describing the impact of the Hawthorne studies, Baritz wrote that they "modified permanently the nature and direction of industrial personnel work" (p. 77).

58. Regarding the reinterpretations of the data from the Hawthorne studies, psychologist Ernest Hilgard has written that the social and interpersonal explanations for improvement, offered by Mayo, proved not to be supported by later statistical analyses. Hilgard wrote: "By this time, however, other studies on human relations had been done in other ways, and the fact that the Hawthorne studies were faulty and their generalizations overblown could not alter the fact that the interest they aroused in human relations in the factory was a lasting one; sometimes a provocative idea is more important than the data which support it." Hilgard, E. R. (1987). *Psychology in America: A historical survey*. San Diego: Harcourt Brace Jovanovich, p. 718.

59. For a description of the interviewing methods developed by Mayo, which would become the basis for advocating the position of "personnel counselor" in industry, see Mahoney, K. T., & Baker, D. B. (2002). Elton Mayo and Carl Rogers: A tale of two techniques. *Journal of Vocational Behavior, 60*, 437–450.

60. For a history of the personnel counseling that Mayo's ideas initiated, see Highhouse, S. (1999). The brief history of personnel counseling in industrial-organizational psychology. *Journal of Vocational Behavior, 55*, 318–336. See also Dickson, W. J., & Roethlisberger, F. J. (1964). *Counseling in an organization: A sequel to the Hawthorne researches*. Cambridge: Harvard Graduate School of Business Administration.

61. For first-hand descriptions of the Hawthorne studies by the researcher involved, see Mayo, E. (1933). *The human problems of industrial civilization*. New York: Macmillan; and Roethlisberger, F. J., & Dickson, W. J. (1939). *Management and the worker: An account of a research program conducted by the Western Electric Company, Hawthorne Works, Chicago*. Cambridge, MA: Harvard University Press.

62. See Katzell & Austin (1992).

63. For the Procter & Gamble study, see Uhrbrock, R. S. (1934). Attitudes of 4430 employees. *Journal of Social Psychology, 5*, 365–377. And for the Kimberly Clark study, see Kornhauser, A. S., & Sharp, A. A. (1932). Employee attitudes: Suggestions from a study in a factory. *Personnel Journal, 10*, 393–404.

64. Lewin, K., Lippitt, R., & White, R. K. (1939). Patterns of aggressive behavior in experimentally created "social climates." *Journal of Social Psychology, 10*, 271–299.

65. Hoppock, R. M. (1935). *Job satisfaction*. New York: Harper & Brothers.

66. Report of the Committee on Psychology in Industry. (1936, May 9). Unpublished report in the American Psychological Association Archives, Library

of Congress Manuscript Division, Washington, DC. The committee was chaired by Richard Uhrbrock (Procter & Gamble) and included Marion Bills (Aetna Life Insurance), Rensis Likert (Life Insurance Sales Research Bureau), Henry Link (the Psychological Corporation), Millicent Pond (Scovill Manufacturing Co.), Sadie Shellow (Police Department, Milwaukee, WI), and Morris Viteles (University of Pennsylvania). The committee makeup is interesting in that it is dominated by psychologists in work settings outside of universities and includes several women.

67. Uhrbrock, R. S. (1938). Industrial psychology as a career: Report of the A. C. P. Committee on Psychology in Industry. *Journal of Social Psychology, 9*, 251–286.

68. Reports of the AAAP. (1938). *Journal of Consulting Psychology, 2*, 77–82. Table is from p. 80.

69. Benjamin, L. T., Jr. (1997). Organized industrial psychology before Division 14: The ACP and the AAAP (1930–1945). *Journal of Applied Psychology, 82*, 459–466.

70. Benjamin, L. T., Jr. (1997). The origin of psychological species: A history of the beginnings of the divisions of the American Psychological Association. *American Psychologist, 52*, 725–732.

71. Benjamin, L. T., Jr. (1997). A history of Division 14 (The Society for Industrial and Organizational Psychology). In D. A. Dewsbury (Ed.), *Unification through division: Histories of the divisions of the American Psychological Association* (Vol. 2, pp. 101–126). Washington, DC: American Psychological Association. For a description of the backgrounds and activities of the first 10 presidents of Division 14, see Benjamin, L. T., Jr. (1997). The early presidents of Division 14: 1945–1954. *The Industrial-Organizational Psychologist, 35*(2), 29–34.

72. Meyer, H. (1997). An early stimulus to psychology in industry: A history of the Dearborn Conference Group. *The Industrial-Organizational Psychologist, 34*(3), 24–27.

73. Carlson, H. C. (1991, August 13). *The No-Name Group: History treading on the heels of the future.* Paper presented at the annual meeting of the Academy of Management, Miami Beach, FL; Crissey, O. L. (1980). The No-Name Group. In the Orlo Crissey Papers, Archives of the History of American Psychology, University of Akron, Akron, OH.

74. Harrell, T. W. (1992). Some history of the Army General Classification Test. *Journal of Applied Psychology, 77*, 875–878.

75. Benjamin, L. T., Jr. (1997), A history of Division 14, p. 114.

76. Napoli, D. S. (1981). *Architects of adjustment: The history of the psychological profession in the United States.* Port Washington, NY: Kennikat Press, p. 138.

77. Jenkins, William O. (1947). The tactual discrimination of shapes for coding aircraft-type controls. In P. M. Fitts (Ed.), *Psychological research on equipment design*, Report No. 19 (pp. 199–205). Washington, DC: U. S. Government Printing Office.

For a comprehensive account of work in human factors psychology in the decade after World War II, see McCormick, E. J. (1957). *Human engineering*. New York: McGraw-Hill.

78. Whereas many of the psychologists employed at HumRRO worked on human factors problems, the majority of their work was directed at training problems, one of the mainstays of industrial psychology. For a description of the founding and work of HumRRO, see Crawford, M. P. (1984). Highlights in the development of the Human Resources Research Organization (HumRRO). *American Psychologist*, 39, 1267–1271. Meredith Crawford (1910–2002) was the founding director of HumRRO and served as director and president for its first 25 years. His career in psychology, and particularly at HumRRO, is described in his obituary by L. T. Benjamin, Jr., C. L. MacKay, W. C. Osborn, & W. W. Prophet in the *American Psychologist*, 2002, 57, 980–982.

79. For a history of human factors psychology, see Meister, D. (1999). *The history of human factors and ergonomics*. Mahwah, NJ: Erlbaum.

80. Katzell & Austin (1992), p. 813.

81. Janney, J. E. (1947). Qualifications for Staff Psychologists of Rohrer, Hibler, & Replogle: Psychological Counsel to Management. Document in American Psychological Association Archives, Library of Congress Manuscript Division, Washington, DC.

82. For some of the arguments over training models, see Uhrbrock, R. S. (1955). Internships vs. field training for industrial psychologists. *American Psychologist*, 10, 535–538; Wilson, R. F. (1956). Internships in industrial psychology. *American Psychologist*, 11, 243–246; Division 14 Committee on Professional Education Policy. (1959). Professional education in industrial psychology: A statement of policy. *American Psychologist*, 14, 233–235; and Division of Industrial Psychology Education and Training Committee. (1965). Guidelines for doctoral education in industrial psychology. *American Psychologist*, 20, 822–831. Today, SIOP has developed a document entitled *Guidelines for Training and Education of I/O Psychologists*. Separate guidelines exist for master's-level and doctoral training. These documents can be found at the SIOP web site: http://siop.org/PhDGuidelines98.html.

83. Katzell & Austin (1992), p. 811.

84. For a description of Lewin's action research in industry, see chapter 14 of Marrow, A. J. (1969). *The practical theorist: The life and work of Kurt Lewin*. New York: Basic Books. One of the unsuccessful applications of Lewin's ideas was the use of what were called training groups, or T-groups (predecessors of the sensitivity groups popular in the 1960s and 1970s). In industry these sensitivity training groups proved to be good at helping people identify the strengths and weaknesses of themselves and their fellow group members, but they too often produced disastrous results by creating psychological problems in group members. After many demonstrated failures, T-groups have mostly disappeared from business.

85. I/O psychologist Paul Levy has written that goal setting and expectancy theory are current motivational theories that derive from Lewin's work. See Levy, P. E. (2013). *Industrial/organizational psychology: Understanding the workplace* (4th ed.). New York: Worth Publishers.

86. Viteles, M. S. (1953). *Motivation and morale in industry.* New York: W. W. Norton, p. ix.

87. For an account of the founding of SPSSI, see Stagner, R. (1986). Reminiscences about the founding of SPSSI. *Journal of Social Issues, 42*(1), 35–42.

88. Stagner, R. (1956). *Psychology of industrial conflict.* New York: Wiley, p. v.

89. Psychologists involved in marketing research today are often called consumer psychologists. Many belong to the APA Division 23, the Society of Consumer Psychology. I/O psychologists are part of this group, but so are social psychologists and experimental psychologists. In universities they are often found in marketing departments, and in industry they are frequently employed by advertising agencies, polling entities, and consumer research divisions.

90. Division of Industrial Psychology Education and Training Committee (1965), p. 828.

91. The most recent edition of this publication is Society for Industrial and Organizational Psychology. (2003). *Principles for the validation and use of personnel selection procedures.* See the SIOP Web site: http://www.siop.org.

92. See, for example, how cognitive psychology has affected views of leadership: Lord, R. G., & Maher, K. J. (1991). *Leadership and information processing: Linking perceptions and performance.* New York: HarperCollins.

93. See March, J. G., & Simon, H. A. (1958). *Organizations.* New York: Wiley; and Bass, B. M. (1965). *Organizational psychology.* Boston: Allyn & Bacon.

94. Katzell & Austin (1992), p. 815.

95. Psychologist Harry Levinson (1922–2012) was a pioneer in applying psychoanalytic principles to organizations. See Levinson, H. L., Molinari, J., & Spohn, A. G. (1972). *Organizational Diagnosis.* Cambridge, MA: Harvard University Press.

96. Stagner, R. & Smalley, M. D. (1990). Industrial-organizational psychology. In L. T. Benjamin, Jr., J. R. Hopkins, & J. R. Nation. *Psychology* (pp. 635–648). New York: Macmillan. Quotation is from p. 646.

97. For more information on organizational development, see Cummings, T. G., & Worley, C. G. (2008). *Organization development and change* (9th ed.). Mason, OH: South-Western Cengage Learning.

98. Kilburg, R. R. (2000). *Executive coaching: Developing managerial wisdom in a world of chaos.* Washington, DC: American Psychological Association.

99. See Highhouse (1999).

100. Data available from the SIOP website: http://www.siop.org/media/What.aspx.

Chapter 5

1. Society of Counseling Psychology. *What is Counseling Psychology?*. Retrieved December 29, 2013 from http://www.div17.org/about/what-is-counseling -psychology/.

2. Mann, A. (Ed.) (1975). *The progressive era* (2nd ed.). Hinsdale, IL: Dryden Press.

3. Taylor, F. W. (1911, May). The gospel of efficiency: III. The principles of scientific management. *American Magazine*, 101–113.

4. Mann (1975).

5. See Davidson, E. & Benjamin, L. T., Jr. (1987). A history of the child study movement in America. In J. A. Glover & R. R. Ronning (Eds.), *Historical foundations of educational psychology* (pp. 187–208). New York: Plenum Press. See also: Levine, Murray, & Levine, Adeline (1992). *Helping children: A social history.* New York: Oxford University Press.

6. For an extended discussion of this period, see Cremin, L. (1968). *The transformation of the school: Progressivism in American education 1876–1957.* New York: Alfred A. Knopf. For a broad history of compulsory schooling and child saving see, Fagan, T. K. (1992). Compulsory schooling, child study, clinical psychology, and special education: Origins of school psychology. *American Psychologist, 47,* 236–243.

7. For some examples see, Guthrie, R. V. (1998). *Even the rat was white: A historical view of psychology* (2nd ed.). Boston: Allyn and Bacon.

8. For a more detailed history of the settlement home movement, see Carson, M. (1990). *Settlement folk: Social thought and the American settlement movement, 1885–1930.* Chicago: University of Chicago Press. For information on the role of the settlement home in the establishment of vocational guidance, see Brewer, J. M. (1932). *Education as guidance; An examination of the possibilities of a curriculum in terms of life activities in elementary and secondary school and college.* New York: The Macmillan Company.

9. For more information about Frank Parsons see McDaniels, C. & Watts, G. A. (Eds.) (1994). A thematic issue on the life and work of Frank Parsons. *Journal of Career Development, 20,* 259–332. For a biography about Parsons, see Davis, H. V. (1969). *Frank Parsons: Prophet, innovator, and counselor.* Carbondale, Ill.: Southern Illinois University Press.

10. For an excellent account of these themes see, Stevens, W. R. (1970). *Social reforms and the origins of vocational guidance.* Washington, DC: National Vocational Guidance Association.

11. Parsons, F. (1909). *Choosing a vocation.* Boston: Houghton Mifflin.

12. For details about the founding see, Watts, G. A. (1994). Frank Parsons: Promoter of a progressive era. *Journal of Career Development, 20,* 265–286. See also, Brewer (1932), pp. 53–75.

13. Davis, J. B. (1956). *The saga of a schoolmaster: An important, personal account of American secondary education 1886–1950.* Boston: Boston University Press, pp. 179–180.

14. Davis, J. B. (1914). *Vocational and moral guidance.* Boston: Ginn, p. 17.

15. For histories of the National Vocational Guidance Association see Brewer (1932). See also Norris, W. (1954). *The history and development of the National Vocational Guidance Association.* Unpublished doctoral dissertation, George Washington University.

16. Münsterberg, H. (1910). Finding a life work. *McClures,* 34, 398–403. Quotation is from p. 401.

17. Brewer, J. M. (1918). *The vocational guidance movement: Its problems and possibilities.* New York: Macmillan, pp. 161–162.

18. Department of the Interior Bureau of Education (1918). *Vocational guidance in secondary education.* Bulletin no. 19, Washington, DC: Government Printing Office.

19. Münsterberg, H. (1913). *Psychology and industrial efficiency.* New York: Macmillan.

20. Woolley, H. T. (1916). The mind of a boy: The future of experimental psychology in vocational guidance. *The Survey,* 37(5). Quotation is from p. 125.

21. Hollingworth, H. L. (1916). *Vocational psychology: Its problems and methods.* New York: Appleton and Company.

22. Ibid., p. 223.

23. Ibid., p. 244.

24. For more information about E. L. Thorndike see, Joncich, G. M. (1968). *The sane positivist: A biography of Edward L. Thorndike.* Middletown, Conn.: Wesleyan University Press.

25. For more information about the interpretation and meaning of the WWI data on intelligence, see Fancher, R. E. (1985). *The intelligence men.* New York: W. W. Norton. See also, Guthrie (1998).

26. Yerkes, R. M. (1930). Foreword. In D. G. Paterson, R. M. Elliott, L. D. Anderson, H. A. Toops, & E. Heidbreder, *Minnesota Mechanical Ability Tests: The report of a research investigation subsidized by the Committee on Human Migrations of the National Research Council and conducted in the Department of Psychology at the University of Minnesota* (p. i). Minneapolis: The University of Minnesota Press.

27. Johnson, R. G., & Johnson, W. F. (1958). The vocational guidance movement. *National Business Education Quarterly,* 12, 13–21. Quotation is from p. 15.

28. Paterson, D. G. (1930). *Physique and intellect.* New York: Century Co.

29. Deutsch, A. (1949). *The mentally ill in America: A history of their care and treatment from colonial times* (2nd ed.). New York: Columbia University Press.

30. Vandenbos, G. R., Cummings, N. A., & DeLeon, P. H. (1992). A century of psychotherapy: Economic and environmental influences. In D. K. Freedheim (Ed.), *History of psychotherapy: A century of change* (pp. 65–102). Washington, DC: American Psychological Association. See also Miller, J. G. (1946). Clinical psychology in the Veterans Administration. *American Psychologist, 1,* 181–189.

31. Brand, J. L., & Sapir, P. (Eds.) (1964). *An historical perspective on the National Institute of Mental Health.* Washington, DC: National Institute of Mental Health.

32. For an extended discussion see, Baker, D. B., & Benjamin, Ludy T., Jr. (2004). Creating a profession: NIMH and the training of psychologists, 1946–1954. In W. Pickren (Ed.), *Psychology and the National Institute of Mental Health* (pp. 181–207) Washington, DC: American Psychological Association.

33. Public Law 487, 1946, p. 421.

34. For details on the reorganization see, Hilgard, E. R. (1945). Psychologist's preferences for divisions under the proposed APA by-laws. *Psychological Bulletin, 42,* 20–26. See also, Benjamin, L. T., Jr. (1997). The origin of psychological species: A history of the beginnings of the divisions of the American Psychological Association. *American Psychologist, 52,* 725–732.

35. For a historical review of the Boulder Conference see, Baker, D. B., & Benjamin, L. T., Jr. (2000). The affirmation of the scientist-practitioner: A look back at Boulder. *American Psychologist, 55,* 233–236.

36. Raimy, V. C. (Ed.) (1950). *Training in clinical psychology.* Englewood Cliffs, NJ: Prentice Hall, pp. 112–113.

37. Ibid., p. 148.

38. Pepinsky, H. B., Hill-Frederick, K. & Epperson, D. L. (1978). The Journal of Counseling Psychology as a matter of policies. *Journal of Counseling Psychology, 25,* 483–498.

39. Bordin, E. (1950). *Training of psychological counselors: Report of a conference held at Ann Arbor, Michigan, July 27 and 28, 1949, and January 6 and 7, 1950.* Ann Arbor, MI: University of Michigan Press.

40. American Psychological Association, Division of Counseling and Guidance, Committee on Counselor Training. (1952). Recommended standards for training counselors at the doctoral level. *American Psychologist, 7,* 175–181.

41. Waldrop, R. S. (2000). *History of professional psychology in the Veterans Administration: The development of counseling psychology.* Paper presented at the annual meeting of the American Psychological Association.

42. Rogers, C. R. (1942). *Counseling and psychotherapy: Newer concepts in practice.* Boston: Houghton Mifflin.

43. Rogers, C. R. (1961). *On becoming a person.* Boston: Houghton Mifflin, p. 13.

44. For an overview of these developments see, See Holland, J. L. (1964). Major programs of research on vocational behavior. In H. Borow (Ed.) *Man in a world of work* (pp. 259–284). Boston: Houghton Mifflin.

45. Public Law 85-864, 1958.

46. Congressional Record-Senate, August 13, 1958, p. 17324.

47. American Personnel and Guidance Association (1958). A statement of policy concerning the Nation's human resources problems. *Personnel and Guidance Journal, 36,* 454–455.

48. Tyler, L. E. (1963). *The national defense counseling and guidance training institutes program; A report of the first 50 institutes sponsored during the summer of 1959 by 50 colleges and universities under contract with the U. S. Office of Education authorized by the National Defense Education Act of 1958.* Washington, DC: U. S. Dept. of Health, Education, and Welfare, Office of Education, p. 65.

49. American Psychological Association. Division of Counseling Psychology, Committee on Definition (1956). Counseling psychology as a specialty. *American Psychologist, 11,* 282–285. Quotation is from p. 283.

50. Berg, I., Pepinsky, H. B., & Shoben, E. J., Jr. (1980). The status of counseling psychology: 1960. In J. M. Whitely (Ed.), *The history of counseling psychology* (pp. 105–113). Monterey, CA: Brooks/Cole. Quotation is from p. 105.

51. This was based on a study that rated counseling psychology as having the lowest rated status of occupations at the doctoral level. For the complete study see, Granger, S. G. (1959). Psychologists' prestige rankings of 20 psychological occupations. *Journal of Counseling Psychology, 6,* 183–188.

52. Tyler, L., Tiedeman, D., & Wrenn, C. G. (1980). The current status of counseling psychology: 1961. In J. M. Whitely (Ed.), *The history of counseling psychology* (pp. 114–124). Monterey, CA: Brooks/Cole. Quotation is from p. 115.

53. Ibid., p. 122.

54. Thompson, A. S., & Super, D. E. (Eds.) (1964). *The professional preparation of counseling psychologists: Report of the 1964 Greyston Conference.* New York: Teachers College Press.

55. Baker, D. B., & Myers, R. A. (2001). Albert S. Thompson: A man of the world of work. *The Counseling Psychologist, 29,* 308–323. Quotation is from p. 318.

56. Jordaan, J. P., Myers, R. A., Layton, W. L., & Morgan, H. H. (1968). *The Counseling Psychologist.* New York: Teachers College Press.

57. American Psychological Association. Division 17:2012. Retrieved December 29, 2013 from http://www.apa.org/about/division/div17-2012.aspx.

58. Society of Counseling Psychology. List of APA-accredited Counseling Psychology PhD and PsyD programs. Retrieved December, 29, 2013 from http://www.div17.org/about/what-is-counseling-psychology/.

59. See the Division 17 website for descriptions of special interest groups and sections: http://www.div17.org/.

60. For more detailed information on the CCPTP and its history see, http://www.lehigh.edu/ccptp/.

61. Heppner, P. P., Casas, J. M., Carter, J., & Stone, G. L. (2000). The maturation of counseling psychology: Multifaceted perspectives, 1978–1998. In S. D. Brown and R. W. Lent (Eds.). *Handbook of counseling psychology* (3rd ed., pp. 3–49). New York: J. Wiley.

62. For information about ACS and its divisions see, http://www.counseling.org/.

63. Heppner, Casas, Carter, & Stone (2000), p. 23.

64. For more about the context of these times see, Blocher, D. H. (2000). *The evolution of counseling psychology*. New York: Springer Publishing Company.

65. Heppner, Casas, Carter, & Stone (2000), p. 11.

66. For a copy of the conference program see, http://www. div17.org/conference/.

Chapter 6

1. For a more detailed history of the beginnings of managed mental health care, see DeLeon, P. H., VandenBos, G. R., & Bulatao, E. Q. (1991). Managed mental healthcare: A history of the federal policy initiative. *Professional Psychology: Research and Practice, 22*, 15–25.

2. Alperin, R. M., & Phillips, D. G. (Eds.) (1997). *The impact of managed care on the practice of psychotherapy*. New York: Brunner/Mazel.

3. Gasquoine, P. G. (2010). Comparison of public/private healthcare insurance parameters for independent psychological practice. *Professional Psychology: Research and Practice, 41*, 319–324. Quotation is from page 320.

4. Meyer, G. J., Finn, S. E., Eyde, L. D., Kay, G. G., Moreland, K. L., Dies, R. R., Eisman, E. J., Kubiszyn, T. W., & Reed, G. M. (2001). Psychological testing and psychological assessment: A review of evidence and issues. *American Psychologist, 56*, 128–165. Quotation is from p. 128. For several articles dealing with the impact of managed care on the use of psychological assessment, see the April 2000 issue of the journal, *Professional Psychology: Research and Practice, 31*(2).

5. For more on the impact of managed care on assessment and other practice issues, see Gasquoine, P. G. (2010). Comparison of public/private healthcare insurance parameters for independent psychological practice. *Professional Psychology: Research and Practice, 41*, 319–324; and Cantor, D. W., & Fuentes, M. A. (2008). Psychology's response to managed care, *Professional Psychology: Research and Practice, 39*, 638–645.

6. Acuff, C., Bennett, B. E., Bricklin, P. M., Canter, M. B., Knapp, S. J., Moldawsky, S., & Phelps, R. (1999). Considerations for ethical practice in managed care.

Professional Psychology: Research and Practice, 30, 563–575. See also Small, R. F., & Barnhill, L. R. (Eds.) (1998). *Practicing in the new mental health marketplace: Ethical, legal, and moral issues*. Washington, DC: American Psychological Association.

7. Cummings, N. A., O'Donohue, W. T., & Cummings, J. A. (2011). The financial dimension of integrated behavioral/primary care. In N. A. Cummings & W. T. O'Donohue (Eds.), *Understanding the behavioral healthcare crisis* (pp. 33–57). New York: Routledge.

8. For a discussion of the issues around EBT, see Duncan, B. L., & Reese, R. J. (2013). Empirically supported treatments, evidenced-based treatments, and evidenced based practice. In I. B. Weiner (Ed.), *Handbook of psychology* (Vol. 8, pp. 489–513). Hoboken, NJ: John Wiley & Sons.

9. Goodman, M., Brown, J. A., & Deitz, P. M. (1996). *Managing managed care II: A handbook for mental health professionals* (2nd ed.). Washington, DC: American Psychiatric Press.

10. Cummings, N. A. (1995). Impact of managed care on employment and training: A primer for survival. *Professional Psychology: Research and Practice*, 26, 10–15. Quotation is from p. 12. For an account by a psychologist critical of managed care, see Karon, B. P. (1995). Provision of psychotherapy under managed healthcare: A growing crisis and national nightmare. *Professional Psychology: Research and Practice*, 26, 5–9.

11. Cummings (1995), 10–15.

12. Kaiser Health News (2013). Health law brings changes in how therapists do business. Retrieved January 2, 2014 from http://www.kaiserhealthnews.org/stories/2013/october/24/health-law-changes-therapy-business.aspx?.

13. Koss, M. P., & Shiang, J. (1994). Research on brief psychotherapy. In A. E. Bergin & S. L. Garfield (Eds.), *Handbook of psychotherapy and behavior change* (4th ed., pp. 664–700). New York: Wiley.

14. Cummings (1995), p. 11.

15. For more on the issue, see Drum, D. J., & Sekel, A. C. (2013). The U.S. health-care marketplace: Future tense. In I. B. Weiner (Ed.), *Handbook of psychology* (Vol. 8, pp. 558–584). Hoboken, NJ: John Wiley & Sons; The American Psychological Association also offers a FAQ page on the Mental Health Parity and Addiction Equity Act for practitioners available at http://www.apa.org/helpcenter/parity-law.aspx?item=2.

16. In 1995, the Council of Representatives of the American Psychological Association, the policy-making body of the association, voted unanimously to seek prescription privileges for psychologists.

17. VandenBos, G. R., & Williams, S. (2000). Is psychologists' involvement in the prescribing of psychotropic medication really a new activity? *Professional Psychology: Research and Practice*, 31, 615–618. Quotation is from p. 616.

18. The Guidelines can be accessed from the APA website at http://www.apa.org/practice/guidelines/pharmacological-issues.aspx?item=5.

19. See, for example Hayes, S. C., & Heiby, E. (1996). Psychology's drug problem: Do we need a fix or should we just say no? *American Psychologist, 51*, 198–206; and Robiner, W. N., Bearman, D. L., Berman, M., Grove, W. M., Colon, E., Armstrong, J., & Mareck, S. (2002). Prescriptive authority for psychologists: A looming health hazard? *Clinical Psychology: Science and Practice, 9*, 231–248.

20. DeNelsky, G. Y. (1996). The case against prescription privileges for psychologists. *American Psychologist, 51*, 207–212. Quotation is from p. 207.

21. Ibid., p. 207.

22. Ibid., pp. 207–208.

23. PR Newswire (n.d.). *Therapy in America 2004*. Retrieved January 4, 2014 from http://www.napabipolardepression.org/images/therapy in America.pdf.

24. The National Alliance of Professional Psychology Providers (NAPPP) provides advocacy on these and other issues impacting practicing psychologists. Position papers are available on their website, http://nappp.org/.

25. American Psychological Association Board of Educational Affairs. (1995, December). *Final report of the BEA working group to develop a Level 1 curriculum for psychopharmacology education and training: Curriculum for Level 1 training in psychopharmacology*. Washington, DC: APA. In 1996, the document *Recommended Postdoctoral Training in Psychopharmacology for Prescription Privileges* was approved and set forth as a standard for education and training programs for psychologists seeking prescription authority. The document was revised in 2009 and is available as a PDF from the APA website.

26. See, for example Fox, R. E., Schwelitz, F. D., & Barclay, A. G. (1992). A proposed curriculum for psychopharmacology training for professional psychologists. *Professional Psychology: Research and Practice, 23*, 216–219; Chafetz, M. D., & Buelow, G. (1994). A training model for psychologists with prescription privileges: Clinical pharmacopsychologists. *Professional Psychology: Research and Practice, 25*, 149–153; Evans, G. D., & Murphy, M. J. (1997). The practicality of predoctoral prescription training for psychologists: A survey of directors of clinical training. *Professional Psychology: Research and Practice, 28*, 113–117; and Dunivin, D. L., & Southwell, G. D. (2000). Psychopharmacology training in psychology internships: A brief curriculum. *Professional Psychology: Research and Practice, 31*, 610–614.

27. Newman, R., Phelps, R., Sammons, M. T., Dunivin, D. L., & Cullen, E. A. (2000). Evaluation of the psychopharmacology demonstration project: A retrospective analysis. *Professional Psychology: Research and Practice, 31*, 598–603. See also DeLeon, P. H., Sammons, M. T., & Sexton, J. L. (1995). Focusing on society's real needs: Responsibility and prescription privileges? *American Psychologist, 50*, 1022–1032.

28. Sammons, M. T. (2011). Can prescribing psychologists assist in providing more cost-effective, quality mental healthcare? In N. A. Cummings & W. T. O'Donohue (Eds.), *Understanding the behavioral healthcare crisis* (pp. 129–148). Quotation is from pp. 137.

29. See, for example, Resnick, R. J., & Norcross, J. C. (2002). Prescription privileges for psychologists: Scared to death? *Clinical Psychology: Science and Practice*, 9, 270–274.

30. Rivas-Vazquez, R. A., Blais, M. A., Rey, G. J., & Rivas-Vazquez, A. A. (2000). Atypical antipsychotic medications: Pharmacological profiles and psychological implications. *Professional Psychology: Research and Practice*, 31, 628–640.

31. The Fall 2002 issue (Vol. 9, No. 3, pp. 231–274) of the journal, *Clinical Psychology: Science and Practice*, contains six articles debating the pros and cons of prescription privileges for psychologists.

32. Münsterberg, H. (1908). *On the witness stand: Essays on psychology and crime.* New York: Doubleday and Page, pp. 10–11.

33. See Wells, G. L., & Loftus, E. F. (2013). Eyewitness memory for people and events. In I. B. Weiner (Editor-in-Chief), *Handbook of psychology* (Vol. 11, pp. 617–629). Hoboken, NJ: John Wiley & Sons.

34. The word association technique was developed independently by Wilhelm Wundt, Francis Galton, Max Wertheimer, and Carl Jung. It was Jung's work that was principally influential in America.

35. One of Münsterberg's graduate students who worked on the blood pressure correlates of lying was William Moulton Marston, who later claimed credit for inventing the lie detector (which he did not); he would gain fame as the creator of the comic book super hero Wonder Woman who used her lasso with magical powers to force people to tell the truth. For information on Marston and his work on lie detection, see Bunn, G. C. (1997). The lie detector, Wonder Woman, and liberty: The life and work of William Moulton Marston. *History of the Human Sciences*, 10, 91–119.

36. Münsterberg (1908), pp. 108–109.

37. Roesch, R. (2000). Forensic psychology. In A. Kazdin (Ed.), *Encyclopedia of psychology* (Vol. 3, pp. 383–386). Washington, DC and New York: American Psychological Association and Oxford University Press. Quotation is from p. 383.

38. For a description of the psychological autopsy of Howard Hughes, see Fowler, R. (1986, May). Howard Hughes: A psychological autopsy. *Psychology Today*, pp. 22–33. For a description of psychologists' involvement in the USS Iowa investigation, see Poythress, N. G., Otto, R. K., Darkes, J., & Starr, L. (1993). APA's expert panel in the Congressional review of the USS Iowa incident. *American Psychologist*, 48, 8–15. For articles expressing reservations about the use and/or validity of the clinical autopsy, see Selkin, J. (1994). Psychological autopsy: Scientific psychohistory or

clinical intuition? *American Psychologist, 49*, 74–75, and Shneidman, E. S. (1994). The psychological autopsy. *American Psychologist, 49*, 75–76.

39. A conference was held at the Villanova Law School in Philadelphia in 1995 to reach agreement on models for training in forensic psychology. See Bersoff, D. N., Goodman-Delahunty, J., Grisso, J. T., Hans, V. P., Poythress, N. G., & Roesch, R. G. (1997). Training in law and psychology: Models from the Villanova Conference. *American Psychologist, 52*, 1301–1310.

40. Data is taken from Packer, I. K., & Borum, R. (2013). Forensic training and practice. In I. B. Weiner (Editor-in-Chief), *Handbook of psychology* (Vol. 11, pp. 16–36). Hoboken, NJ: John Wiley & Sons.

41. A copy of the guidelines are available at http://www.apa.org/practice/guidelines/forensic-psychology.aspx.

42. American Psychological Association. Division 41:2012. Retrieved January 8, 2014 from http://www.apa.org/about/division/div41-2012.aspx.

43. For a thorough discussion of professional issues facing the field, see Otto, R. K. (2013) (Ed.). Forensic psychology. In I. B. Weiner (Editor-in-Chief), *Handbook of psychology* (2nd ed.) (Vol. 11, pp. 16–36). Hoboken, NJ: John Wiley & Sons.

44. See Gardner, F. L. (2001). Applied sport psychology in professional sports: The team psychologist. *Professional Psychology: Research and Practice, 32*, 34–39.

45. American Psychological Association. Division 47:2012. Retrieved January 8, 2014 from http://www.apa.org/about/division/div47-2012.aspx.

46. For an overview of the history of sport psychology, see Green, C. D., & Benjamin, L. T., Jr. (2009). *Psychology gets in the game: Sport, mind, and behavior, 1880–1960*. Lincoln, NE: University of Nebraska Press.

47. Triplett, N. (1897–1898). The dynamogenic factors in pacemaking and competition. *American Journal of Psychology, 9*, 507–533. See also Davis, S. F., Huss, M. T., & Becker, A. H. (1995). Normal Triplett and the dawning of sport psychology. *Sport Psychologist, 9*, 366–375.

48. For Scripture's work, see Scripture, E. W. (1896). Researches on reaction time. *Studies from the Yale Psychology Laboratory, 4*, 12–26. For Miles's work, see Miles, W. R. (1928). Studies of physical exertion: I. A multiple chronograph for measuring groups of men. *American Physical Education Review, 33*, 379–387; Miles, W. R. (1931). Studies of physical exertion: II. Individual and group reaction time in football charging. *Research Quarterly, 2*(3), 5–13; Miles, W. R. & Graves, B. C. (1931). Studies of physical exertion: III. Effect of signal variation on football charging. *Research Quarterly, 2*(3), 14–31.

49. Benjamin, L. T., Jr. (1993). *A history of psychology in letters*. New York: McGraw-Hill, p. 145.

50. Both published by Scribner's Sons, New York.

51. Green, C. D. (2003). Psychology strikes out: Coleman Griffith and the Chicago Cubs. *History of Psychology, 6,* 267–283.

52. For information on Griffith, see Benjamin (1993), pp. 143–152. See also LeUnes, A. (1986). A sport psychologist and a football legend discuss the psychology of coaching: Coleman Griffith and Knute Rockne. *Journal of Applied Research in Coaching and Athletics, 1,* 127–134.

53. APA recognizes sport psychology as a proficiency area in psychology. For a description of the proficiency that was updated in 2011, see http://www.apa.org/ed/graduate/specialize/sports.aspx.

54. Fletcher, D., & Maher, J. (2013). Toward a competency-based understanding of the training and development of applied sport psychologists. *Sport, Exercise, and Performance Psychology, 4,* 265–280.

55. For a description of how counseling and clinical psychologists have been urged to get into the field of sport psychology, see Hays, K. F. (1995). Putting sport psychology into (your) practice. *Professional Psychology: Research and Practice, 26,* 33–40. See also Anderson, M. B., Van Raalte, J. L., & Brewer, B. W. (2001). Sport psychology service delivery: Staying ethical while keeping loose. *Professional Psychology: Research and Practice, 32,* 12–18.

56. Landers, D. M. (1985). Psychophysiological assessment and biofeedback: Application for athletes in a closed skill sport. In J. Sandweiss & S. Wolf (Eds.), *Biofeedback and Sport Science* (pp. 65–105). New York: Plenum.

57. Sometimes the psychological problems plaguing athletes are more than anxiety. Eating disorders, such as anorexia nervosa and bulimia nervosa, are particularly problematic in athletes such as gymnasts and jockeys, but also in other sports where maintaining a specific weight is a job requirement. See Sherman, R. T., & Thompson, R. A. (2001). Athletes and disordered eating: Four major issues for the professional psychologist. *Professional Psychology: Research and Practice, 32,* 27–33; Petrie, T. A., Greenleaf, C, Reel, J., & Carter, J. (2008). Prevalence of eating disorders and disordered behaviors among male collegiate athletes. *Psychology of Men and Masculinity, 9,* 267–277.

58. For a comprehensive and excellent treatment of the field of sport psychology, see LeUnes, A. (2008). *Sport psychology: An introduction* (4th ed.). New York: Psychology Press. This book was an important source for our treatment of contemporary sport psychology.

59. For a contemporary review of health psychology, see Marks, D. F (2013). Health psychology: Overview. In I. B. Weiner (Editor-in-Chief), *Handbook of psychology* (2nd ed., Vol. 9, pp. 3–25). Hoboken, NJ: John Wiley & Sons.

60. For information on the emergence of health psychology in the 1960s and 1970s, see the following three seminal articles: Schofield, W. (1969). The role of psychology in the delivery of health services. *American Psychologist, 24,* 893–896;

Matarazzo, J. (1980). Behavioral health and behavioral medicine: Frontiers for a new health psychology. *American Psychologist*, 35, 807–817; Weiss, S. M. (1982). Health psychology: The time is now. *Health Psychology*, 1, 4–13. For a history of APA's Division of Health Psychology, see Wallston, K. (1997). A history of Division 38 (Health Psychology): Healthy, wealthy, and Weiss. In D. A. Dewsbury (Ed.), *Unification through division: Histories of the divisions of the American Psychological Association* (Vol. 2, pp. 239–267). Washington, DC: American Psychological Association.

61. The relationship between the Centers for Disease Control and the American Psychological Association continues to grow. See Anderson, N. B. (2011). APA and CDC: A common purpose. *Monitor on Psychology*, 42(3), p. 9; Dingfelder, S. F. (2011). The intersection of psychology and public health, *Monitor on Psychology*, 42(3), p. 28.

62. Barth, L. (1998, August). Leading the charge. *Continental Magazine*, pp. 35–38.

63. Thacher, I., & Haynes, S. N. (2000). Health psychology: Assessments and interventions. In A. Kazdin (Ed.), *Encyclopedia of psychology* (Vol. 4, pp. 89–97). Washington, DC: American Psychological Association.

64. For a description of stress inoculation and other stress reduction strategies, see Dobson, K. S. (2009). *Handbook of cognitive-behavioral therapies* (3rd ed.). New York: Guilford Press.

65. For a review of managing chronic pain, see Turk, D. C., & Wilson (2013). Chronic pain. In I. B. Weiner (Editor-in-Chief), *Handbook of psychology* (2nd ed., Vol. 9, pp. 292–317). Hoboken, NJ: John Wiley & Sons.

66. Williams, S., & Kohout, J. L. (1999). Psychologists in medical schools in 1997: Research brief. *American Psychologist*, 54, 272–276. See also Sheridan, E. P. (1999). Psychology's future in medical schools and academic healthcare centers. *American Psychologist*, 54, 267–271.

67. Weiss, S. M. (2000). Health psychology: History of the field. In A. Kazdin (Ed.), *Encyclopedia of psychology* (Vol. 4, pp. 85–89). Washington, DC: American Psychological Association.

68. Ibid., p. 86.

69. Peterson, D. R. (2003). Unintended consequences: Ventures and misadventures in the education of professional psychologists. *American Psychologist*, 58, 791–800. Quotation is from p. 791. For an updated and expanded study comparing outcomes between PhD and PsyD programs, see Graham, J. M. and Kim, Y.-H. (2011). Predictors of doctoral student success in professional psychology: characteristics of students, programs, and universities. *Journal of Clinical Psychology*, 67, pp. 340–354.

70. McFall, R. M. (1991). Manifesto for a science of clinical psychology. *Clinical Psychologist*, 44, 75–88.

71. For detailed information about the efforts and activities, see http://www.psychologicalscience.org/PCSAS_new/history.cfm.

72. For more about the DBH program, see http://asuonline.asu.edu/dbh.

73. Dawes, R. M. (1994). *House of cards: Psychology and psychotherapy built on myth.* New York: The Free Press, p. vii.

74. Eysenck, H. J. (1952). The effects of psychotherapy: An evaluation. *Journal of Consulting Psychology, 16,* 319–324. For contemporary accounts on the effectiveness of psychotherapy, see Nathan, P. E., Stuart, S. P., & Dolan, S. L. (2000). Research on psychotherapy efficacy and effectiveness: Between Scylla and Charybdis? *Psychological Bulletin, 126,* 964–981; and Wampold, B. E. (2001). *The great psychotherapy debate: Models, methods, and findings.* Mahwah, NJ: Lawrence Erlbaum.

75. Barlow, D. H. (1981). On the relation of clinical research to clinical practice: Current issues, new directions. *Journal of Consulting and Clinical Psychology, 49,* 147–155. Quotation is from p. 147.

76. Strupp, H. H. (1981). Clinical research, practice, and the crisis of confidence. *Journal of Consulting and Clinical Psychology, 49,* 216–219. Quotation is from p. 216.

77. Although many psychologists have questioned whether scientific research on the effectiveness of psychotherapy is possible, there are plenty of voices on the other side who argue that it can and must be done. See Jacobson, N. S., & Christensen, A. (1996). Studying the effectiveness of psychotherapy: How well can clinical trials do the job? *American Psychologist, 51,* 1031–1039; Erwin, E. (2000). Is a science of psychotherapy possible? Subjectivity problems. *American Psychologist, 55,* 1133–1138.

78. See, for example Hersen, M., & Barlow, D. H. (1976). *Single case experimental designs: Strategies for studying behavior change.* New York: Pergamon; Hayes, S. C. (1981). Single case experimental design and empirical clinical practice. *Journal of Consulting and Clinical Psychology, 49,* 193–211; and Barlow, D. H. (1996). Healthcare policy, psychotherapy research, and the future of psychotherapy. *American Psychologist, 51,* 1050–1058.

79. For another view on this issue, see Stricker, G. (1997). Are science and practice commensurable? *American Psychologist, 52,* 442–448.

80. American Psychiatric Association. (1994). *Diagnostic and statistical manual of mental disorders* (4th ed.). Washington, DC: American Psychiatric Association.

81. For more information and copies of all the APA practice guidelines, see http://www.apa.org/practice/guidelines/.

82. Nathan, P. E. (1998). Practice guidelines: Not yet ideal. *American Psychologist, 53,* 290–299. Quotation is from p. 290.

83. Bennett-Johnson, S. (2012). In support of APA's treatment guidelines efforts. *Monitor on Psychology, 43*(7), p. 5.

84. Nathan (1998), p. 298.

85. Ibid., p. 298. See also Nathan, P. E. (2000). The Boulder model: A dream deferred—or lost? *American Psychologist, 55,* 250–252.

86. The APA established a task force to identify new professional roles for psychologists. Their report was published in 2001 as Levant, R. F., Reed, G. M., Ragusea, S. A., DiCowden, M., Murphy, M. J., Sullivan, F., Craig, P. L., & Stout, C. E. (2001). Envisioning and accessing new roles for professional psychology. *Professional Psychology: Research and Practice, 32,* 79–87. See also Reed, G. M., Levant, R. F., Stout, C. E., Murphy, M. J., & Phelps, R. (2001). Psychology in the current mental health marketplace. *Professional Psychology: Research and Practice, 32,* 65–70.

87. For some examples, see Cummings, N. A. & O'Donohue, W. T. (Eds.) (2011). *Understanding the behavioral healthcare crisis.* New York: Routledge.

88. APA Access (2014). APA Center for Psychology and Health works to expand psychology's role in health care. Retrieved January 14, 2014 from http://www.apa.org/pubs/newsletters/access/2014/01-14/psychology-health.aspx.

89. See Kiesler, C. A. (2000). The next wave of change for psychology and mental health services in the healthcare revolution. *American Psychologist, 55,* 481–487.

90. For a good review, see Bernal, G., Trimble, J. E., Burlew, A. K., & Leong, F. T. L. (Eds.) (2003). *Handbook of racial & ethnic minority psychology.* Thousand Oaks, CA.: Sage Publications.

91. Bernal, M. E., & Castro, F. G. (1994). Are clinical psychologists prepared for service and research with ethnic minorities? Report of a decade of progress. *American Psychologist, 49,* 797–805.

92. Hall, C. C. I. (1997). Cultural malpractice: The growing obsolescence of psychology with the changing U.S. population. *American Psychologist, 52,* 642–651.

93. For more on Division 45, see http://division45.org.

94. For a more complete description, see Manese, J., Saito, G., & Rodolfa, E. (2004). Diversity based psychology. *California Department of Consumer Affairs Board of Psychology Update, 11,* 16–20.

95. For a forecast of changes in the future practice of psychotherapy, see Norcross, J. C., Hedges, M., & Prochaska, J. O. (2002). The face of 2010: A Delphi poll on the future of psychotherapy. *Professional Psychology: Research and Practice, 33,* 316–322.

96. Humphreys, K. (1996). Clinical psychologists as psychotherapists: History, future, and alternatives. *American Psychologist, 51,* 190–197. Quotation is from p. 190.

97. Cummings (1995), pp. 14–15.

98. One of the attractions to psychotherapy is the intellectual challenge it brings and the pleasure experienced when a great mystery is solved. Clinical psychologist

Clifford L. Fawl (1930–2002) has described it this way: "There is another kind of gain to be derived from conducting psychotherapy, one not often discussed in the textbooks … and one which at times provides … immense satisfaction. I refer to the joy, the beauty, of seeing a puzzle fall into place. Too often the intellectual and emotional are considered as opposites, but for me those infrequent moments of intellectual insight are emotionally exciting moments that are intrinsically rewarding. And they apply to the insight gained in conducting therapy no less than insights elsewhere experienced. In fact, for me the most intellectually stimulating work I do is that of doing therapy. Each case is a new puzzle to be solved. … The intellectual exercise can truly be exhilarating!" From Fawl, C. L. (1977). *Thoughts on psychotherapy*. Unpublished paper. pp. 36–37.

99. For Sarason's ideas, see Sarason, S. B. (1981). An asocial psychology and a misdirected clinical psychology. *American Psychologist*, 36, 827–836; Sarason, S. B. (1983). Psychology and public policy: Missed opportunities. In R. D. Felner, L. A. Jason, J. N. Moritsugu, & S. S. Farber (Eds.), *Preventive psychology: Theory, research, and practice* (pp. 245–250). New York: Pergamon Press.

Image Credits

This page constitutes an extension of the copyright page. We have made every effort to trace the ownership of all copyrighted material and to secure permission from copyright holders. In the event of any question arising as to the use of any material, we will be pleased to make the necessary corrections in future printings. Thanks are due to the following authors, publishers, and agents for permission to use the material indicated.

Chapter 1 1-1: Image courtesy of the Center for the History of Psychology (CHP). 1-2: From O. S. Fowler (1869). *The practical phrenologist; and recorder and delineator of the character and talents*. Boston: O. S. Fowler. Courtesy of the CHP Book Collection. 1-3: From O. S. Fowler (1851). *Fowler's practical phrenology*. Boston: O. S. Fowler. Courtesy of CHP Book Collection. 1-4: Courtesy of the National Library of Medicine, Bethesda, Maryland. 1-5: From W. E. Robinson (1898). *Spirit slate writing and kindred phenomena*. New York City: Munn and Company. 1-6: Courtesy of the CHP Still Images Collection, Anna Berliner papers, box V35, folder 2. 1-7: Photo Courtesy of Harvard University Archives, HUPSF Psychological Laboratories (3). 1-8: H. L. Hollingworth, (1912). *The influence of caffeine on mental and motor efficiency*. Courtesy of the CHP Manuscripts Collection, Harry and Leta Stetter Hollingworth papers, box M4, folder 22.

Chapter 2 2-1: From T. S. Kirkbride (1845). *Report of the Pennsylvania Hospital for the Insane for the Year 1844*. Courtesy of the CHP Asylum Report Collection. 2-2: Courtesy of the Wynelle Deese Asylum Postcard collection, CHP Special Interest Collection. 2-3: From K. Pearson (1924). *The life, letters and labours of Francis Galton* Vol. II. Courtesy of the CHP Book

Collection. **2-4:** Photo courtesy of the CHP Test Collection. **2-5:** From S. Freud (1910). The origin and development of psychoanalysis, *American Journal of Psychology, 2*, 181–218. **2-6:** From E. Worcester, S. McComb, & I. Coriat (1908). *Religion and medicine: The moral control of nervous disorders.* New York: Moffat, Yard and Company. Courtesy of the CHP Book Collection. **2-7:** Image courtesy of the CHP Still Images Collection, V34, folder 8. **2-8:** Photo courtesy of the CHP Still Images Collection, Box V71, folder 6. Photographer: Thomas Joy, National Institute of Health Photography Section. **2-9:** Photo courtesy of the CHP Manuscripts Collection, Harry and Leta Stetter Hollingworth papers, Box M9, folder 2.

Chapter 3 **3-1:** Photo courtesy of the CHP Still Images Collection, Box V4, folder 3. **3-2:** Photo courtesy of the CHP Still Images Collection, Henry H. Goddard papers, box V37, folder 3. **3-3:** Photo courtesy of the CHP Still Images Collection, David Boder papers, box V44, folder 5. Credit: Crosby Studio, New Haven, CT. **3-4:** Courtesy of the CHP Special Interest Collection. **3-5:** Photo courtesy of the CHP Still Images Collection, J. E. Wallace Wallin papers, box V35, folder 1. **3-6:** Courtesy of the CHP, Division 16 records.

Chapter 4 **4-1:** Courtesy of the CHP Manuscripts Collection; Harry and Leta Stetter Hollingworth papers. **4-2:** Carnegie Institute of Technology, Psychological Examination Reading Test. CHP Test Collection. **4-3:** From System Company (1911). *How scientific management is applied.* Chicago: A. W. Shaw, p. 27. Courtesy of the CHP Still Images collection, box V34, folder 8. **4-4:** Courtesy of the CHP Special Interest Collection. **4-5:** Ibid. **4-6:** Ibid. **4-7:** F. J. Roethlisberger, & W. J. Dickson (1939). *Management and the worker: An account of a research program conducted by the Western Electric Company, Hawthorne Works, Chicago.* Cambridge, MA: Harvard University Press. **4-8:** W. O. Jenkins (1947). The tactual discrimination of shapes for coding aircraft-type controls. In P. M. Fitts (Ed.), *Psychological research on equipment design*, Report No. 19 (pp. 199–205). Washington, DC: U. S. Government Printing Office.

Chapter 5 **5-1:** From J. A. Puffer (1913). *Vocational guidance: The teacher as a counselor.* New York: Rand McNally and Company. **5-2:** Ibid. **5-3:** From the *Arena*, Volume 11 (1895). Boston, MA: Arena Publishing Company. **5-4:** Courtesy of CHP Special Interest Collection. **5-5:** Ibid. **5-6:**

Image courtesy of CHP Audio Collection. Photographer: Jamie Newhall. **5-7:** From L. E. Tyler (1963). *National Defense Counseling and Guidance Training Institutes Program; a report of the first 50 institutes.* Washington, DC: Office of Education.

    Chapter 6   **6-1:** From H. Münsterberg (1908). *On the witness stand: Essays on psychology and crime.* New York: Doubleday, Page and Company. Courtesy of the CHP Book Collection. **6-2:** Photo Courtesy of the University of Illinois Archives, Coleman R. Griffith Papers, RS 5/1/21.

Index

A

Abandonment, 225
Academy of Management, 166
Academy of Psychological Clinical
    Science (APCS), 253
Accreditation (APA), 81, 88, 131,
    203, 204, 209, 218, 219
Action research, 173–74
Adams, H. R, 141
Addams, J., 186
Adelphi University
    Professional School of Psychol-
    ogy, 91
Adler, A., 83
Adolescence, 98, 100
Advertising, 34–35, 137–142
African Americans, 99, 186
Agency for Health Care Policy and
    Research (AHCPR), 255–256
Agency for Healthcare Research and
    Quality (AHRQ), 256
Aging, 232, 233, 258
American Association for Applied
    Psychology (AAAP), 67–68, 76,
    78, 114, 115, 166–167, 201
American Association of Clinical
    Psychologists (AACP), 62–64,
    112, 131
American Board of Professional
    Examiners in Psychology (now
    ABPP), 88, 125, 213, 217
American Council on Education,
    197

American Counseling Association,
    206, 219
American Journal of Insanity, 43
American Journal of Psychiatry, 43
American Journal of Psychology,
    55–56, 72
American Medico-Psychological
    Association, 43
American Personnel and Guidance
    Association (APGA), 206, 210
American Phrenological Journal, 5, 16
American Psychiatric Association,
    43, 256
American Psychoanalytic Associa-
    tion, 57
American Psychological Association
    (APA), 31, 34, 38, 64, 65, 66,
    67, 69, 76–78, 89–90, 91, 94–95,
    98, 113–116, 121, 130–131, 157,
    167–168, 202, 206, 213, 216,
    218–219, 229–230, 258, 260
American Psychological Society
    (APS), 90
American Psychologist, 89
American Society of Psychologists in
    Private Practice (ASPPP), 94
Angell, F., 28
Animal magnetism. See mesmerism
Anna O (Bertha Pappenheim), 55
Anxiety disorders, 86, 254
Army Alpha, 52, 69, 102, 152
Army Beta, 52, 69, 102, 152
Army General Classification Test
    (AGCT), 168

Association for the Advancement
of Applied Sport Psychology
(AAASP). *See* Association for
Applied Sport Psychology
Association for Applied Sport Psy-
chology (AASP), 240, 243
Association of Consulting Psycholo-
gists (ACP), 31, 67, 114, 131, 166
Association of Counseling Center
Training Agencies, 219
Association of Medical Superinten-
dents of American Institutions for
the Insane (AMSAII), 42–43
Attitudes, 164

B
Baird, J. W., 154
Barlow, D., 254
Beck, A., 86
Beck, S., 73
Beers, C. W., 57–58
Behavioral health carve-outs, 224
Behavior therapy, 84–85
Behaviorism, 65, 84–85, 87
Benson, C. E., 141
Berg, I., 213, 214, 215
Best practices, 85, 255–257
Bicêtre Asylum, 41
Bills, M., 159
Binet, A., 52, 101
Bingham, W. V. D., 67, 144–147,
152, 154, 157, 158, 168, 169
Biofeedback, 244, 248, 249
Biopsychosocial model, 246
Blackford, K., 14–15, 157
Bordin, E. S., 203
Boulder Conference, 87, 121,
201–202, 204
Boulder model. *See* scientist-practi-
tioner model
Brammer, L., 219
Bregman, E., 159
Breitweiser, J. V., 141
Brewer, J., 190, 191, 192
Brief therapies, 87, 228
British empiricism, 28
Bronner, A., 54
Brotemarkle, R., 107

Brown, R., 9
Bryan, W. J., 103
Business psychology. *See* industrial/
organizational psychology

C
Caffeine, 36, 134–135, 237
California School of Professional
Psychology, 91
Carr, H., 58
Cattell, J. M., 28, 47, 50, 71, 76, 155,
157
Center for Psychology and Health,
258
Certification. *See* licensure
Characterology. *See* physiognomy
Chicago Cubs, 243
Child development, 98–100
Child Guidance Movement, 66, 81
Child saving, 98, 184
Child Study Movement, 31–32, 98,
100, 108
Christian Science, 20, 24, 25, 61
Civic Service House (Boston), 187,
188, 189
Civil Rights Act, 175, 216
Civil War, 4, 21
Clark Conference, 55, 72
Clark University, 27, 32, 46, 55
Client-centered therapy. *See* person-
centered therapy
Clinical psychology, 33–34, 38–95,
106, 107, 108, 112, 120, 131, 133,
196, 202, 203, 214–215
Coca-Cola Company, 35–36,
134–135
Coeducation, 100
Cognitive therapy, 86, 249
Combe, G., 4–5
Commission of the Reorganization of
Secondary Education, 192
Committee on Accreditation
(APA), 90, 218
Committee on the Certification of
Consulting Psychologists, 31
Committee on the Classification
of Personnel in the Army, 69,
152–153, 195

Commonwealth Fund, 66
Community mental health centers (CMHCs), 93, 128
Community Mental Health Centers Act, 45
Confidentiality, 228
Consulting firms, 155–157, 172
Consulting psychology, 31, 64
Correlation coefficient, 50
Council for the Accreditation of Educator Preparation (CAEP), 130
Council of Counseling Center Training Agencies, 219
Council of Counseling Psychology Training Programs (CCPTP), 218
Counseling Psychologist, The, 218
Counseling psychology, 32–33, 83, 132–133, 182–221
Cox, C., 102
Criminality, 13, 15
Cummings, N. A., 91, 227–228, 253

D
Darley, J., 201
Darwin, C., 264
Davis, J., 189–190, 192
Dawes, R., 253–254
Dearborn Conference (of industrial psychologists), 168
Death, causes of, 247
Deinstitutionalization, 45
Democracy, 96–97
DeNelsky, G., 230–231
Department of Scientific Pedagogy and Child Study, 111
Depression, 58, 75, 82, 86, 230, 231, 256, 258
Derner, G., 91
Descartes, R., 246
Developmental norms, 105, 111
Dewey, J., 97, 111, 152, 191
Dickens, C., 2
Dictionary of Occupational Titles, 197
Division 12 (Clinical Psychology) of APA, 69, 89–90, 201, 213, 256
Division 14 (Society of Industrial and Organizational Psychology)
of APA, 167, 168, 169, 172, 173, 201
Division 16 (School Psychology) of APA, 110, 114–116, 118, 121, 125, 130–132, 201
Division 17 (Counseling Psychology) of APA, 156, 201, 202, 203, 206, 212–217, 218, 219–220
Division 21 (Engineering Psychology) of APA, 171
Division 29 (Psychotherapy) of APA, 90
Division 38 (Health Psychology) of APA, 247
Division 41 (American Psychology-Law Society) of APA, 239
Division 42 (Independent Practice) of APA, 94
Division 45 (The Society for the Psychological Study of Culture, Ethnicity and Race) of APA, 260
Division 47 (Exercise and Sport Psychology) of APA, 240, 243
Division 55 (American Society for the Advancement of Pharmacotherapy) of APA, 230
Division of Applied Psychology (Carnegie Institute of Technology), 143–144, 147
Doctor of Behavioral Health (DBH), 253
Doctor of Psychology (PsyD), 62, 91, 180, 251–252
Doctoral standard for practice, 116, 125, 206, 209
Driscoll, G., 125–126
Drugs, antipsychotic, 82, 234
DSM-IV, 256
Dunlap, K., 58

E
Eddy, M. B., 24
Edison, T., 144
Education, 96–97, 190–195, 215
Educational psychology, 195, 209
Efficiency, 142, 147, 148, 184
Efficiency experts, 148, 161
Eisenhower, D., 209

Electroshock therapy, 82
Eliot, C. W., 190
Elliott, R. M., 196–197
Ellis, A., 86, 94
Emmanuel Movement, 58–61
Empirically supported treatments
    (ESTs), 85
Employee assistance programs
    (EAPs), 180
Engineering psychology. *See* human
    factors psychology
Ethics, 88–89, 225
Ethnic minority issues, 11–13,
    219–220, 259–260
Eugenics, 103, 108
Examination for Professional Prac-
    tice in Psychology (EPPP), 252
Exceptional children, 110
Executive coaching, 180
Evidenced-based treatments, 226
Evolution, 98
Eysenck, H. J., 84, 254

F
Fagan, T., 105, 111, 114,
Farling, W., 129
Feeble-Minded Club, 101
Felix, R., 121
Fernald, G., 54
Fitzgerald, J., 190
Forensic psychology, 234, 237, 239
Fox sisters, 21
Fowler, L., 5–8, 11, 16
Fowler, O., 5–8, 11, 16
Fowler, R. D., 238
Franklin, B., 18, 40
French Revolution, 18, 41
Freud, S., 46, 55, 56, 59, 83, 98
Fryer, D., 67

G
Gale, H., 137–138
Gall, F. J., 4, 10
Galton, F., 47, 50, 71, 102
Gaza, G., 219
Geissler, L. R., 154
Gender differences, 194
Gesell, A., 103–105

GI Bill, 77, 172, 205, 207
Giftedness, 103
Gilbreth, F., 151
Gilbreth, L. M., 151, 152
Goddard, H. H., 151
Goldwater, B., 210
Great Depression, 141, 160–162,
    197–198
Greyston Conference, 215–217
Griffith, C., 241–243
Griffiths, C., 156
Grimm, C., 243
Group testing, 195
Group work, 174, 218
Guidelines on Multicultural Educa-
    tion, Training, Research, Practice,
    and Organizational Change for
    Psychologists, 260
Guidelines Regarding Psychologists'
    Involvement in Pharmacological
    Issues, 230
Guillotin, J., 18
Guion, R., 173

H
Haeckel, E., 99
Hall, C. I., 260
Hall, G. S., 27, 31, 55, 98–100, 103,
    105, 154
Hamerschlag, A., 143–144
Harvard psychology clinic, 58, 74
Harvard University, 46, 190
Hathaway, S., 74
Hawthorne studies, 162–163, 180
Health Maintenance Organization
    (HMO), 223–224
Health psychology, 234, 246–249,
    258
Healy, W., 54
Hildreth, G., 114, 117, 118, 119
Hitler, A., 77
Hollingworth, H. L., 35, 36, 70–71,
    72–73, 134–135, 138, 139–140,
    141, 144, 155, 194
Hollingworth, L. S., 62, 78, 91, 112,
    135, 194
Hoopingarner, D. L., 146

Hoppock, R., 165
Hospitals, psychologists in, 249–250
Hughes, H., 238
Hughes, R. M., 94
Human factors psychology, 169–172
Human Factors Society, 171
Humanistic psychology, 86
Humanistic therapy, 86–87
Human Relations, 174
Human Resources Research Organization (HumRRO), 171
Hume, D., 28
Humphreys, K., 260–261
Hunt, W. A., 81
Hypnosis, 18, 59, 218, 249

I
Imagery training, 245
Immigration, 196
Independent practice, 93–95, 217, 218
Individual differences, 191, 194, 220
Individuals with Disabilities Education Act (IDEA), 128
Industrial/organizational psychology, 34–35, 133, 134–181
Industrial Psychologists Employed in Private Industry, 168
Industrial Psychology Monthly, 158–159
Industrial strife, 174–175
Institute for Social Research (University of Michigan), 173
Instruction cards, 149
Insulin coma therapy, 82
Intelligence quotient, 102
Intelligence testing, 50–52, 53, 70–71, 100–103, 195–196
International Society of Sport Psychology (ISSP), 240
Internship training, 77, 126, 216
IQ estimation, 102

J
J. Walter Thompson Advertising Agency, 140
James, W., 20, 24–25, 27, 57
Jastrow, J., 29, 47, 58

Jenkins, W., 170–171
Job satisfaction, 165, 173, 176, 178–179
Johns Hopkins University, 27
Johnson, L. B., 175, 216
Johnstone, E., 51
Jones, M. C., 84
Journal of Abnormal Psychology, 58, 72
Journal of Applied Psychology, 154, 158
Journal of Consulting Psychology, 31, 67, 87, 89, 117, 118
Journal of Counseling Psychology, 213, 218
Journal of Personnel Research, 157
Journal of School Psychology, 115
Judd, C., 28
Jung, C. G., 55, 72, 83
Juvenile delinquency, 54, 66
Juvenile Psychopathic Institute (Chicago), 54

K
Keillor, G., 9
Kelly, E. L., 121
Kennedy, J. F., 45, 92, 190
Kennedy, R., 92
Kent, G., 72–73
Kent-Rosanoff Association Test, 72
King, Jr., M. L., 92
Kingsbury, F., 156
Kitson, H. D., 141
Klopfer, B., 73
Kornhauser, A., 156
Krohn, W. O., 46
Kuder Preference Record Test, 209

L
Lab school, 195
Labor unions, 148, 165
Laboratories in psychology, 27–29
Laird, D., 156, 158
Lake Wobegon effect, 9
Lavater, J., 10–11
Lavoisier, A., 18
Leadership, 164–165
Learning, 195

Leipzig laboratory, 27
Levin, B., 247
Levy, D., 73
Lewin, K., 165, 173–174
Licensure, 31, 65, 87, 88, 112, 130, 157, 217, 219
Lie detection, 236–237
Life insurance salesmanship, 147
Likert, R., 173
Link, H., 155–156
Lippman, W., 103
Locke, J., 28, 58
Lombroso, C., 13
Louis XVI (King), 18
Luckey, B., 114
Lunatic asylums. See mental asylums

M

Magazines, popular psychology, 65, 158
Managed care, 223–229, 257
Marshall, H. R., 59
Maslow, A., 87, 217
Masters-level practitioners, 115–116, 124, 172, 227, 260–261
Mayo, E., 162–163, 180
McFall, R., 253
McKinley, J. C., 75
Mechanical ability, 196
Medical Colleges Admissions Test (MCAT), 247
Medicine, 58–61, 63, 106–108, 246
Meditation, 244–245
Mental asylums, 38–45, 93
Mental healing, 23–25
Mental Health Parity and Addiction Equity Act, 228
Mental Hygiene Movement, 57–58, 61, 200
Mental rehearsal. See imagery training
Mental retardation, 50–52, 106–109, 110
Mental tests. See also, testing, psychological
Mesmer, F. A., 17–19
Mesmerism, 2, 17–20

Metropolitan Readiness Tests, 114
Meyer, A., 57
Miles, W., 241, 243
Mill, J. S., 28
Miller, J. G., 82
Mind-body problem, 246
Mind cure. See mental healing
Miner, J. B., 144, 147
Minnesota Employment Stabilization Research Institute, 198
Minnesota Mechanical Ability, 196
Minnesota Multiphasic Personality Inventory (MMPI), 74
Moniz, E., 82
Montessori Cylinders, 106
Moral therapy, 41
Morale, 164
Moreno, J. L., 83
Morgan, C., 74
Motivation, 174
Multiple personality, 58
Münsterberg, H., 29, 58, 60–61, 142–143, 144, 147, 190–191, 193, 235–237
Murray, H. A., 74

N

NASP-APA Task Force, 131
Nathan, P., 256–257
National Association of School Psychologists (NASP), 129–132
National Council for Accreditation of Teacher Education (NCATE), 130
National Council of Schools of Professional Psychology (NCSPP), 91
National Defense Education Act (NDEA), 128, 209–212, 216
National Institute of Mental Health (NIMH), 78, 120–121, 126–127, 200, 203
National Institutes of Health (NIH), 250
National Mental Health Act, 120, 200
National Research Council (NRC), 196

National Vocational Education Act, 14

National Vocational Guidance Association (NVGA), 190, 203, 206

Native Americans, 186

Nature-nurture debate, 108–109

Newland, T. E., 126

New Jersey School for Feebleminded Boys and Girls (Vineland), 51–52, 101

New Thought Movement, 20

New York State Association of Consulting Psychologists, 31, 67

No-Name Group (industrial psychologists), 168

Northwestern Conference, 204

O

Operant learning, 85

Organizational climate, 179–180

Organizational development, 178–179

Organizational diagnosis, 179

Organizational psychology, 160–165, 173–175, 178–180

Orthogenics, 107, 108

P

Pace, E. A., 28

Pain management, 249

Parsons, F., 14, 15, 33, 144, 187–189, 190, 215

Paterson, D. G., 196, 197, 198

Patient Protection and Affordable Care Act, 229, 250, 258

Pavlov, I. P., 84

Pedagogical Seminary, 32

Pepinsky, H., 213

Person-centered therapy, 83, 217

Personal Data Sheet, 72

Personality testing, 72–76, 196

Personnel psychology, 154–155, 172, 176

Personnel Psychology, 172

Personnel Research Federation, 157–158

Peterson, D., 252

Phobia, 84

Phrenology, 4–10, 16–17, 188, 198

Physiognomy, 2, 10–17, 157, 188, 194, 198

Pinel, P., 41

Piper, L., 20–21

Poffenberger, A. T., 140, 141

Post-traumatic stress disorder (PTSD). *See* shell shock

Poyen, C., 19

Practice guidelines, 255–257

Practitioner research, 254–255

Prefrontal lobotomy, 82

Prescription privileges, 229–234

Prevention of mental illness, 57, 125–126, 200, 218

Prince, M., 58, 61, 72

Private practice. *See* independent practice

Professional School Psychology, 115

Professional schools, 90–91, 251–252

Profiling, 238

Progressive Movement, 184

Projective testing, 73–74

Psychiatry, 38–45, 63–64, 80–82, 198–201, 229

Psychoanalysis, 55–57, 83

Psychological autopsy, 238–239

Psychological Clinic (University of Pennsylvania), 33–34, 48–49, 103–110

Psychological Clinic, The, 34, 49

Psychological Corporation, the, 155, 156, 157, 160

Psychology Today, 93

Psychotherapy, 19–20, 55, 58–61, 76, 80–84, 93, 203, 207, 217, 223–227, 229, 230, 231–232, 254–255, 257, 260, 261

PsyD degree. *See* Doctor of Psychology

Public Law 94–142, 128

Pure Food and Drug Act, 35, 134

Q

Quimby, P. P., 23–24

R

Race. *See* ethnic minority issues

Rank, O., 207
Rating Scale for Selecting Salesmen, 69
Rational-emotive therapy, 86
Recapitulation theory, 99–100
Redfield, J., 11
Relaxation training, 59
Religion, 20, 22, 25, 59–60
Research Center for Group Dynamics (Massachusetts Institute of Technology), 173
Robinson, E. S., 146
Roe, A., 209
Rogers, C., 67, 83, 87, 114, 207–208, 217
Rohrer, Hibler, and Replogle (now RHR International), 172
Roosevelt, E., 168–169
Roosevelt, F. D., 146, 175, 197
Rorschach, H., 73–75
Rorschach Test, 73–74
Rosanoff, A., 72
Rosebrook, W. M., 114

S

Salesmanship, 146–147
Salpêtrière Asylum, 41
Sammons, M., 233
Sanford, E. C., 27
Schizophrenia, 75, 234, 256
School counselors, 210–212
School psychology, 33–34, 50, 96–133
Scientific management, 147–151, 153, 161, 184, 196
Scientist-practitioner conflict, 63–64, 89, 206, 250–257
Scientist-practitioner model, 78, 80, 202, 216, 251
Scott, W. D., 34–35, 58, 69, 71, 137, 138–139, 141–142, 144, 146–147, 152, 154–155, 180, 195, 196
Scott Company, 35, 155–156
Scripture, E. W., 28, 241
Seashore, C. E., 141
Seguin Form Board, 106
Selection (personnel), 142, 146, 155, 168, 193, 198

Self-actualization, 87
Settlement house movement, 186–187
Shakow, D., 78–79
Shaw, P. A., 186, 187–188
Shell shock, 69–70, 72
Shobin, J., 213
Sidis, B., 46, 58
Skinner, B. F., 84–85
Snedden, D., 190
Social action, 219–220
Social work, 49, 66, 73, 79, 106–107, 120
Society for the Psychological Study of Social Issues (SPSSI), 175
Society of Industrial and Organizational Psychology. See Division 14
Sociology, 192, 216
Special education, 110–112
Spiritualism, 20–22,
Sport psychology, 234, 240–246
Spurzheim, J., 4–5
Sputnik, 128, 209, 210
Stagner, R., 175, 179
Stanford-Binet intelligence test, 101, 102
Starch, D., 140, 141
Stern, W., 102
Stoker, B., 13
Stratton, G. M., 28
Stress, 248–249
Stress inoculation, 248–249
Strong, E. K., Jr., 140, 141, 144, 197
Strong Vocational Interest Blank, 144, 209
Strupp, H., 254
Substance abuse, 256, 258
Suggestion, 46, 59, 138–139
Sumner, F. C., 100
Super, D., 209, 216
Symonds, P., 117
Symptom substitution, 85
Systematic desensitization, 84–85, 244

T

Taylor, F. W., 143, 148–151, 161–162, 184

Taylorism. *See* scientific management
Terman, L. M., 52, 71, 100–103, 105, 108
Testing, psychological, 47, 63, 69–76, 77, 155–157, 168, 191–197, 224, 248
Thayer Conference, 120–125, 126
Thematic Apperception Test (TAT), 74
Therapeutic alliance, 25, 225
Thompson, A. S., 215, 216, 217
Thorndike, E. L., 195, 197, 209
Thurstone, L. L., 144, 147, 197
Tiedeman, D., 209
Time and motion studies, 148
Training in professional psychology, 62, 78–80, 81–82, 90–91, 124–125, 166, 172, 175–176, 202, 203–204, 218–219, 232, 251–253
Training in the workplace, 174, 177–178
Transfer, 191
Triplett, N., 241, 243
Twitmyer, E. B., 107
Tyler, L., 208, 211, 214, 216

U
United States Public Health Service (USPHS), 77, 82, 203
University of Michigan, 173, 203, 216
University of Minnesota, 197, 198, 201
University of Pennsylvania, 33

V
Vail Conference on clinical training, 91, 252
Veterans Administration (VA), 77, 78, 81–82, 120, 200, 201, 202, 204, 205, 206, 209
Vineland School. *See* New Jersey School for Feebleminded Boys and Girls
Viteles, M., 107, 160–161, 174–175
Vocational Bureau of Cincinnati, 193
Vocational guidance, 14–15, 32–33, 107, 147, 185–198, 218
Vocational Rehabilitation and Education Service, 205

W
Wald, L., 186
Waldrop, R., 206, 215
Wallin, J. E. W., 62, 111–112, 113, 114, 116
Watson, J. B., 65, 139, 140–141
Wechsler Scales of Intelligence, 155
Wells, S., 11–12
Whipple, G. M., 144
White, G., 208
Willard State Hospital (New York), 43
Williamson, E. G., 144
Wilson, W., 76
Witmer, L., 33–34, 38, 48–50, 53–54, 55, 60, 71, 103, 105–111, 118, 154–155, 160
Wolfe, H. K., 28
Wolpe, J., 84
Women in psychology, 28, 158–159, 194, 220
Woodworth, R. S., 70, 72
Woolley, H. B. T., 193
Worcester, E., 58–60
World War I, 21, 52, 61, 64, 66, 69, 70–71, 151–153, 154, 195, 199
World War II, 38, 52, 66, 76–77, 81, 114, 119–120, 125, 142, 168–171, 178, 195, 198, 201, 207, 210, 232, 261
World's Columbian Exposition (Chicago), 29, 32, 47, 58
Wrenn, C. G., 208, 214, 216
Wrigley, P. K., 243
Wundt, W., 25–28, 47, 55

Y
Yerkes, R. M., 58, 69, 71, 151, 152, 195, 196

Z
Zuppke, R., 242